KT-571-978

ABOUT THE AUTHORS

LES FREED is a recognized industry expert in wireless networking, home networking, personal productivity, and photography. Les has been a contributing editor at *PC Magazine* since 1994 and a frequent contributor since 1990. Before joining *PC Magazine*, Les was founder and CEO of Crosstalk Communications, developers of the popular Crosstalk data communications program for PCs—back in the days before the Internet made communications software obsolete. Prior to founding Crosstalk, Les was a senior technician and videotape editor at CBS News from 1976 to 1981 and a cameraman and news editor at WTVJ-TV in Miami from 1972 to 1976. He graduated from the University of Miami in 1974 with B.A. in electronic journalism. Les is the author or co-author of 14 books on networking, computing, and digital photography. Les's latest book is *PC Magazine's Guide to Home Networking*, published by Wiley Books. You can reach Les at les_freed@ziffdavis.com.

FRANK DERFLER has had multiple careers in telecommunications and computer system operation and management, government procurement, education, and publishing. Frank was one of the earliest columnists and reviewers in computer publishing and in 1986, he founded the *PC Magazine* LAN Labs. The LAN Labs developed the first widely distributed LAN benchmark tests and included both testing and editorial activities. Today, Frank continues to use his skill to explain what is important about products and technology. His understanding of both the technological and the human sides of the equation allows him to express the important ideas in technology without getting lost in technobabble. He regularly helps companies design, develop, and market products, and he has great insight into what will work. He conducts several online eSeminar tutorials a month and addresses many industry groups. He lives in the Florida Keys, where he spends a lot of time flying above, boating on, swimming in, and diving under the water. See his Web sites at www.derfler.net or www.flyinflorida.com.

We dedicate this book to our friend Steve Rigney. Together, we unraveled a million small technical mysteries, spent years huddled at cold lab benches, packed and unpacked thousands of boxes, walked hundreds of miles across trade show floors, and helped each other every step of the way. When it was good, it was very, very good.

How Networks Work

Seventh Edition

Frank J. Derfler, Jr. and Les Freed

Illustrated by Michael Troller

800 East 96th Street
Indianapolis, IN 46240

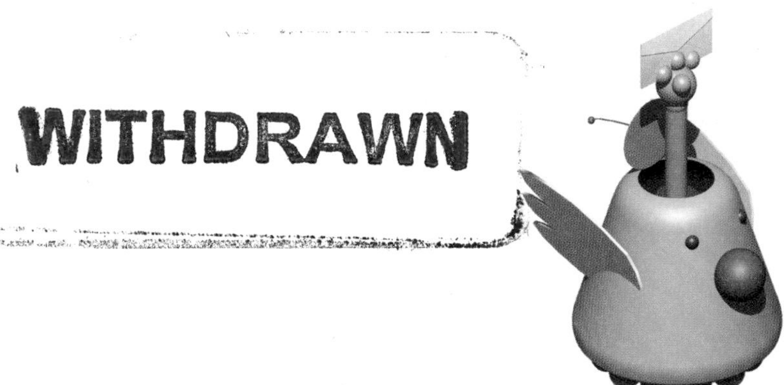

How Networks Work, Seventh Edition

International Standard Book Number: 0-7897-3232-7

Library of Congress Catalog Card Number: 2004107052

Printed in the United States of America

First Printing: August 2004

07 06 05 04 4 3 2 1

Trademarks

Warning and Disclaimer

Bulk Sales

Que Publishing offers excellent discounts on this book when ordered in quantity for bulk purchases or special sales. For more information, please contact

U.S. Corporate and Government Sales
1-800-382-3419
corpsales@pearsontechgroup.com

For sales outside the U.S., please contact

International Sales
international@pearsoned.com

Associate Publisher
Greg Wiegand

Acquisitions Editor
Stephanie J. McComb

Development Editor
Kevin Howard

Managing Editor
Charlotte Clapp

Project Editor
Tonya Simpson

Production Editor
Benjamin Berg

Indexer
Mandie Frank

Proofreader
Seth Kerney

Technical Editor
Jim Grey

Publishing Coordinator
Sharry Lee Gregory

Interior Designer
Trina Wurst

Cover Designer
Anne Jones

Part 4 Links Between LANs

Part 5 The Internet

Part 6 Networks for Online Business

Part 7 Intertainment

AS the reader of this book, *you* are our most important critic and commentator. We value your opinion and want to know what we're doing right, what we could do better, what areas you'd like to see us publish in, and any other words of wisdom you're willing to pass our way.

As an associate publisher for Que Publishing, I welcome your comments. You can email or write me directly to let me know what you did or didn't like about this book—as well as what we can do to make our books better.

Please note that I cannot help you with technical problems related to the topic of this book. We do have a User Services group, however, where I will forward specific technical questions related to the book.

When you write, please be sure to include this book's title and author as well as your name, email address, and phone number. I will carefully review your comments and share them with the author and editors who worked on the book.

Email: feedback@quepublishing.com

Mail: Greg Wiegand
Associate Publisher
Que Publishing
800 East 96th Street
Indianapolis, IN 46240 USA

For more information about this book or another Que Publishing title, visit our Web site at www.quepublishing.com. Type the ISBN (excluding hyphens) or the title of a book in the Search field to find the page you're looking for.

PUBLISHING giant Bill Ziff created practically all of the models for successful technical publishing. We've heard him say many times, "You have to make the information easily available to the readers!" Bill, we've tried as hard as we can to give the readers of *How Networks Work* technical insights that are "easily available" without a lot study. Readers, if you have this book in your hands, please turn the pages and look at the diagrams. We've used illustrations, historical perspective, tips, and a lot of insight to make this book useful to anyone who wants to know something about computer networking. This is our seventh edition and it's both current and understandable.

This is primarily a reference book, not a tutorial. You do not have to start at page 1 and "build a body of knowledge" before you can understand page 161. We've tried to make it easy for you to look up something in the index and to get an idea of the technology and practical functionality by scanning a few high quality illustrations and explanations. This is a practical book, not a textbook or a coffee table book.

We believe the historical perspective is important because it coats the technical information. Technical stuff goes down more easily, tastes better, and is more memorable if it has a coating of background material. Besides, the two of us actually lived a lot of this stuff. (Okay, not the Pony Express, but starting with the Teletype!) There is no false pride when we say that the two of us helped in many ways to make a lot of network evolutions happen. We created product ideas, wrote code, created advertising, designed packages, found money, addressed audiences of thousands, and spent years of our lives testing and reporting. We hope that our experiences polish the insight we provide.

Networking is now ubiquitous, affordable, and necessary for modern commerce. Our goal is to help you understand everything from cables to routers and from servers to enterprise management software. We think you'll find the information highly accessible and the book quite enjoyable.

COMMUNICATING BY WIRE

WE—being the modern, up-to-the-minute kind of people computer users tend to be—like to think of networking as something new. Although the art and science of connecting computers using network cable are fairly new, the essential concepts used in computer networks are relatively old—19th-century old, as a matter of fact. The modern-day computer industry owes its existence to three Victorian-era inventions: the telegraph, telephone, and printing telegraph.

Samuel F.B. Morse (father of the telegraph and Morse code) wouldn't recognize a computer if you dropped one on his big toe, but he would recognize the logic and simplicity of ASCII, the essential modern-day computer alphabet and a descendant of Morse's telegraph code. Morse's original telegraph sent data (in the form of letters and numbers) from one place to another by using a series of timed on-and-off pulses of electricity. Unlike today's electronic communications systems, Morse's telegraph required skilled operators who could send and receive data using the Morse Code. Modern-day data communication systems still use on-and-off pulses of electricity to convey information—they just do it much faster and more efficiently than Morse ever imagined possible. In many ways, the telegraph was the first digital data communications system.

Alexander Graham Bell also wouldn't know what a modem is, but he would recognize the Victorian-era telephone-line interface that still connects most telephones and modems to the phone company's central office. The worldwide telephone system has changed rapidly over the years (largely because of the use of computers), but the subscriber loop—the pair of wires between your home or office and the telephone company's equipment—hasn't changed much since Bell's day. The subscriber loop is an old-fashioned analog audio line. As we'll see, inventors over the years have gone to great lengths to connect digital computer systems to analog telephone lines.

Emile Baudot's invention didn't make his name a household word like Bell's and Morse's, but his multiplex printing telegraph (called a *teletypewriter*) was the forerunner of the computer printer and computer terminal. Other inventors improved and expanded on Baudot's ideas, and the teletypewriter was born. Before the invention of the computer, teletypewriters formed the basis of the Associated Press (AP) and United Press International (UPI) news services. These services (both are still in business today) used a network of teletype machines to deliver news articles to thousands of newspapers worldwide.

You might never have seen a teletypewriter, but you've probably heard its familiar *chunk-chunk-chunk* rhythm as the background noise on a radio or television newscast. Teletypewriters also formed the basis of the worldwide TELEX network—a loosely bound network of machines that enabled users to send printed messages to one another. (Although it was one of the most reliable of Teletype Corporation's machines, an ASR-33 Teletype machine played the part of the bad guy in the movie *Fail Safe*. The short version of the otherwise very complicated plot is that the United States and the former Soviet Union engage in nuclear warfare due to the failure of an ASR-33 at the American command headquarters. New York and Moscow are pulverized—all thanks to an errant scrap of paper stuck inside the machine.)

Although most of the equipment we'll describe in the next few chapters has been obsolete for many years, the underlying technology behind the telegraph, telephone, and teletypewriter is still with us today. In the following chapters, we'll show you how these three essential technologies converged to spark the beginning of the computer age.

But first we need to explain the basic underlying technology common to all digital communications systems. If you think we're about to launch off into some deep technical stuff, relax. Everything you need to know about digital electronics (at least, in the context of this book) can be described using an unlikely tool: the common flashlight.

CHAPTER

1 How Telegraphs Work

ON May 24, 1844, American artist and inventor Samuel Morse sat at a desk in the Supreme Court chamber of the U.S. Capitol building in Washington, D.C., and sent his famous telegraph message—"What hath God wrought?"—to a receiver 37 miles away in Baltimore. Morse had spent 12 years and every penny he owned to develop the telegraph.

To give credit where it is due, several other inventors in the United States and Europe also contributed to the development of the telegraph. Two English electrical pioneers, William Cooke and Charles Wheatstone, patented a telegraph in 1845. The Cooke-Wheatstone system was widely used by the British railroad system to relay traffic information between train stations.

The Cooke-Wheatstone telegraph used six wires and a delicate receiver mechanism with five magnetic needles. It was costly to build and cantankerous to operate. Morse's simpler telegraph used only one wire and a less complex, relatively rugged mechanism.

Fortunately for Morse, his telegraph was just what the young United States needed. America was expanding to the West, and Morse's telegraph followed the train tracks westward. Morse assigned his patents to the Magnetic Telegraph Company, and Magnetic signed up licensees to use the Morse patents. By 1851, there were 50 telegraph companies operating hundreds of telegraph offices—most of them located at railroad stations. You can still see old telegraph lines along the rail beds in many parts of the United States. In 1851, the Western Union Company was formed by the merger of 12 smaller telegraph companies. By 1866, Western Union boasted more than 4,000 offices nationwide, making it the world's first communications giant. By the turn of the century, Western Union operated more than one million miles of telegraph lines, including two transatlantic cables.

The telegraph seems incredibly simple by today's standards, but it provided a much-needed link between the established business world of the Eastern United States and the sprawling frontier of the West. In one of those pleasant coincidences of history, it was just the right thing at just the right time.

By today's standards, the telegraph seems decidedly low-tech. But it was a stunning technical accomplishment in its day—an era when electricity was still a technical curiosity, not a part of everyday life.

Like many great inventions, the genius of the Morse Telegraph lies in its simplicity. The telegraph is basically an electromagnet connected to a battery through a switch. When the switch (in this case, the Morse key, or telegraph key) is pressed down, current flows from the battery (located at the sending end of the line) through the key, down the wire, and into the electromagnetic sounder at the distant end of the line.

By itself, the telegraph can express only two states, on or off. But by varying the timing and spaces of the on-and-off pulses, telegraph operators can send all the letters of the alphabet, as well as numbers and punctuation marks. The Morse code defines the timing and spacing of each character in terms of long and short "on" states called *dashes* and *dots*. For example, the letter "A" is dot-dash; the letter "B" is dash-dot-dot-dot; and so on.

Improving on the Telegraph

Morse's telegraph opened up the frontiers of electronic communications, but it had several shortcomings.

First and foremost, the original Morse design allowed for only one conversation on the line at one time. Wire was handmade then, brittle, and very expensive. Installing the wire along the railroad tracks was time-consuming and often dangerous work. Because of the relatively weak signals used, the signal on the wire would deteriorate as it traveled over the wire—a problem that still plagues network designers today. Several inventors, including Thomas Edison, put themselves to the task of inventing a multiplex telegraph—one that would allow several telegraph operators to use the same line at the same time. (At the same point in time, inventors Alexander Bell and Elisha Gray were independently attempting to invent the harmonic telegraph—a form of multiplex telegraph. They accidentally invented the telephone instead. Had they succeeded in their original mission, the development of the telephone would likely have been delayed by many years.)

Multiplexing made telegraph service more efficient and cost-effective, but a larger obstacle still remained: Morse's code itself. Sending messages via Morse code required a trained operator at each end of the wire. Western Union and its competitors were keen to develop a system that did not require constant human intervention.

As early as 1846 (only two years after Morse's first successful telegraph demonstration), a man with the unlikely name of Royal House invented a printing telegraph. Unfortunately, House's machine had its own set of problems. Although House claimed his machine was "twice as fast as Morse," it required two operators at each end of the line. In 1873, Thomas Edison—still several years away from his breakthrough invention of the incandescent light bulb—designed a printing telegraph that was widely used to distribute stock prices to investors. Edison sold the rights to his printing telegraph to finance research in other areas. Edison's printing telegraph revolutionized the world of stock trading. The machine itself—in its bell-shaped glass case—became a stock-market icon.

Several other inventors worked on improved printing telegraph machines, but French inventor Emile Baudot made many of the breakthroughs. Baudot's printing telegraph was the first to use a typewriter-like keyboard, and it allowed eight machines to share a single wire. More importantly, Baudot's machines did not use Morse code.

Baudot's five-level code sent five pulses down the wire for each character transmitted. The machines themselves did the encoding and decoding, eliminating the need for operators to become proficient at Morse code. For the first time, electronic messages could be sent by anyone who could operate a typewriter.

English inventor Donald Murray expanded and improved on Baudot's work, and Murray sold the American rights to his inventions to Western Union and Western Electric. The Murray patents became the basis for the teletypewriter, also known by AT&T's brand name Teletype and by its generic nickname, TTY. At the dawn of the computer era, the teletypewriter was pressed into service as a combination computer terminal and printer.

Western Union applied the new technology on its own network. Over time, the teletypewriter replaced the Morse key and sounder in most of Western Union's offices. Western Union also used the teletypewriter technology to provide a service called *telex*. Telex service allows subscribers to exchange typed messages with one another.

Until the advent of the fax machine in the 1980s, telex service was widely used in international business. AT&T operated a similar service called the *Teletypewriter Exchange (TWX)*. Like telex, TWX service consisted of a teletypewriter connected to a dedicated phone line. TWX had the advantage of access to AT&T's wide-reaching telephone network. Like telex, TWX usage peaked in the 1960s and 1970s. In 1972, AT&T sold the TWX service to its old nemesis, Western Union.

In the 1930s and 1940s, several schemes were developed to allow the transmission of Teletype signals via shortwave radio. Radio Teletype, or RTTY, uses a technique called *frequency shift keying (FSK)* to simulate the on and off voltage used by conventional teletypes. In FSK, a signal on one frequency indicates ON, and a signal on the other indicates OFF. Because radio signals can be keyed on and off very quickly, RTTY signals run at speeds similar to land-line teletypewriters. The FSK signal modulation technique would later be used as the basis for the modem.

RTTY signals, broadcast via shortwave radio, allow many stations to receive the same signal. RTTY was widely used by United Press International (UPI) and the Associated Press (AP) wire services before cheaper, more reliable satellite links became available in the 1980s. RTTY in various forms is still used today for ship-to-shore telex service and for marine and aeronautical weather information.

How Basic Electricity Works

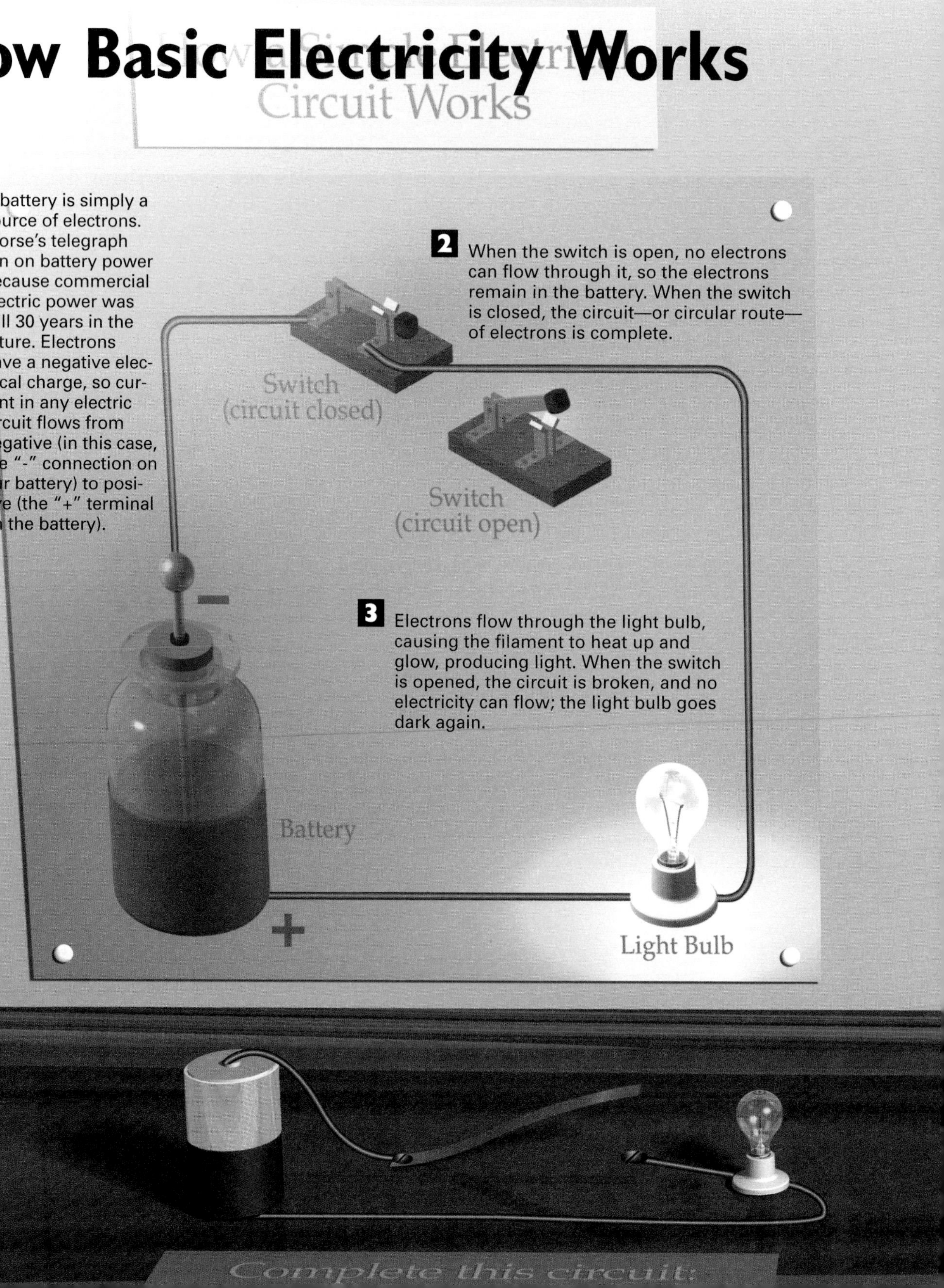

1. A battery is simply a source of electrons. Morse's telegraph ran on battery power because commercial electric power was still 30 years in the future. Electrons have a negative electrical charge, so current in any electric circuit flows from negative (in this case, the "-" connection on our battery) to positive (the "+" terminal on the battery).

2. When the switch is open, no electrons can flow through it, so the electrons remain in the battery. When the switch is closed, the circuit—or circular route—of electrons is complete.

Switch (circuit closed)

Switch (circuit open)

3. Electrons flow through the light bulb, causing the filament to heat up and glow, producing light. When the switch is opened, the circuit is broken, and no electricity can flow; the light bulb goes dark again.

Battery

Light Bulb

Complete this circuit:

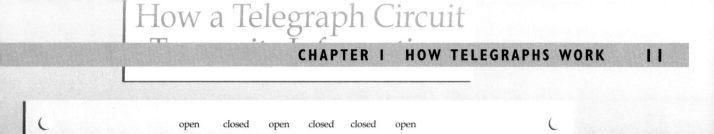

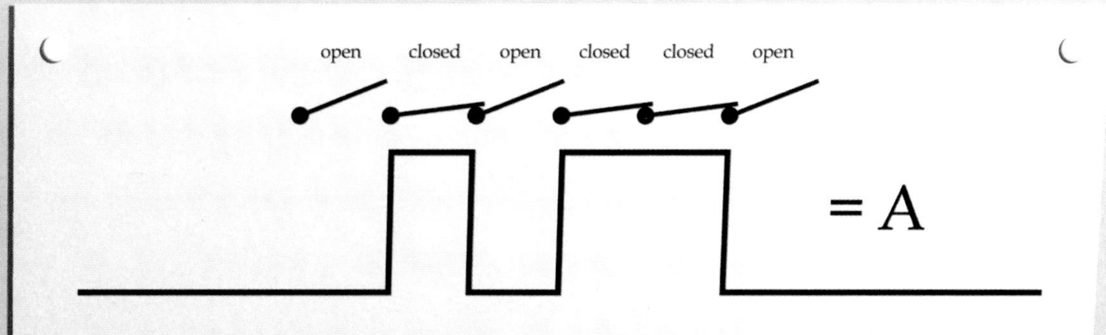
open
closed
open
closed
closed
open
= A

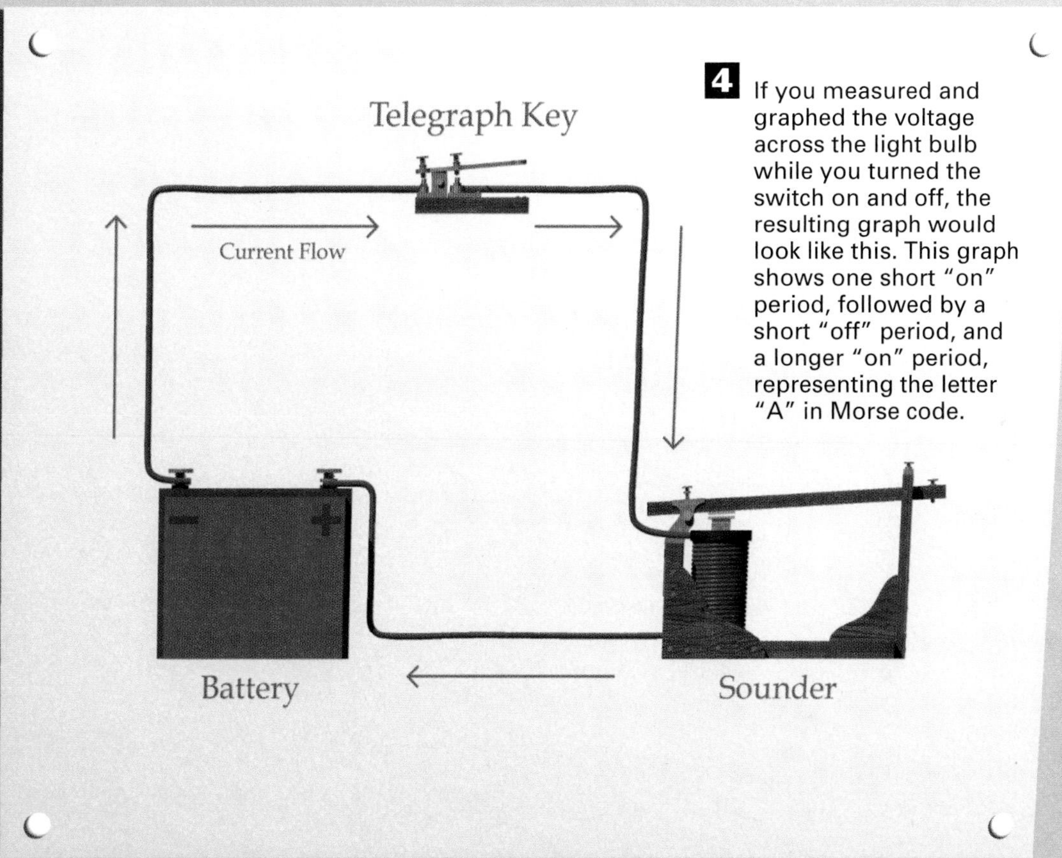
Telegraph Key
Current Flow
Battery
Sounder

4 If you measured and graphed the voltage across the light bulb while you turned the switch on and off, the resulting graph would look like this. This graph shows one short "on" period, followed by a short "off" period, and a longer "on" period, representing the letter "A" in Morse code.

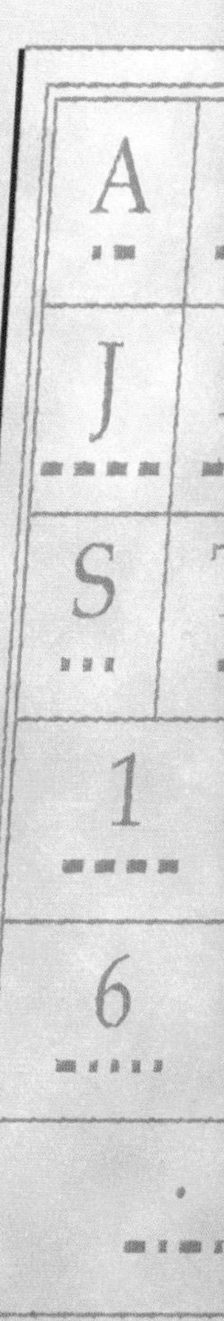
A
J
S
1
6

Press the red button to hear a telegraph sounder

How a Telegraph Works

1 Like a flashlight, Morse's telegraph drew power from a battery.

2 The battery, key, and sounder were connected into a circuit so that current could flow only when the key was pressed. When the telegraph operator pressed down on the key, the circuit was completed and current could flow.

Battery

Morse Key

3 The current traveled down the telegraph line to the sounder device at the receiving telegraph station. An electromagnet in the sounder made a clicking sound each time the sending key was pressed.

4 Operators sent messages using a standardized series of long and short clicks called the Morse Code.

Sounder
3

How a Printing Telegraph Works

1 Edison's printing telegraph could print messages in plain text on a narrow strip of paper, so users didn't need to know the Morse code to receive messages.

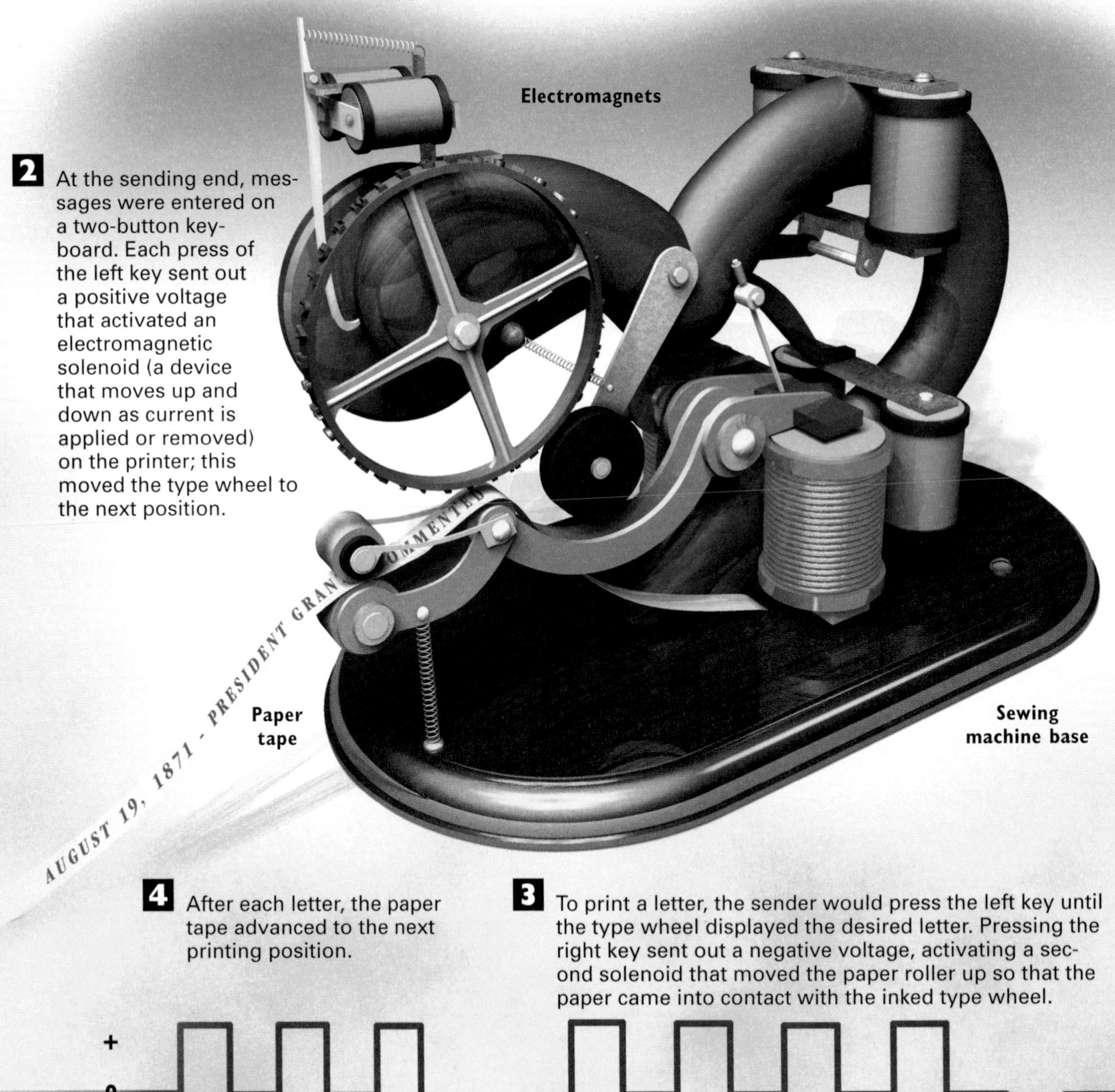
Electromagnets
AUGUST 19, 1871 - PRESIDENT GRANT COMMENTED
Paper tape
Sewing machine base

2 At the sending end, messages were entered on a two-button keyboard. Each press of the left key sent out a positive voltage that activated an electromagnetic solenoid (a device that moves up and down as current is applied or removed) on the printer; this moved the type wheel to the next position.

3 To print a letter, the sender would press the left key until the type wheel displayed the desired letter. Pressing the right key sent out a negative voltage, activating a second solenoid that moved the paper roller up so that the paper came into contact with the inked type wheel.

4 After each letter, the paper tape advanced to the next printing position.

+
0
-
"C"
"D"

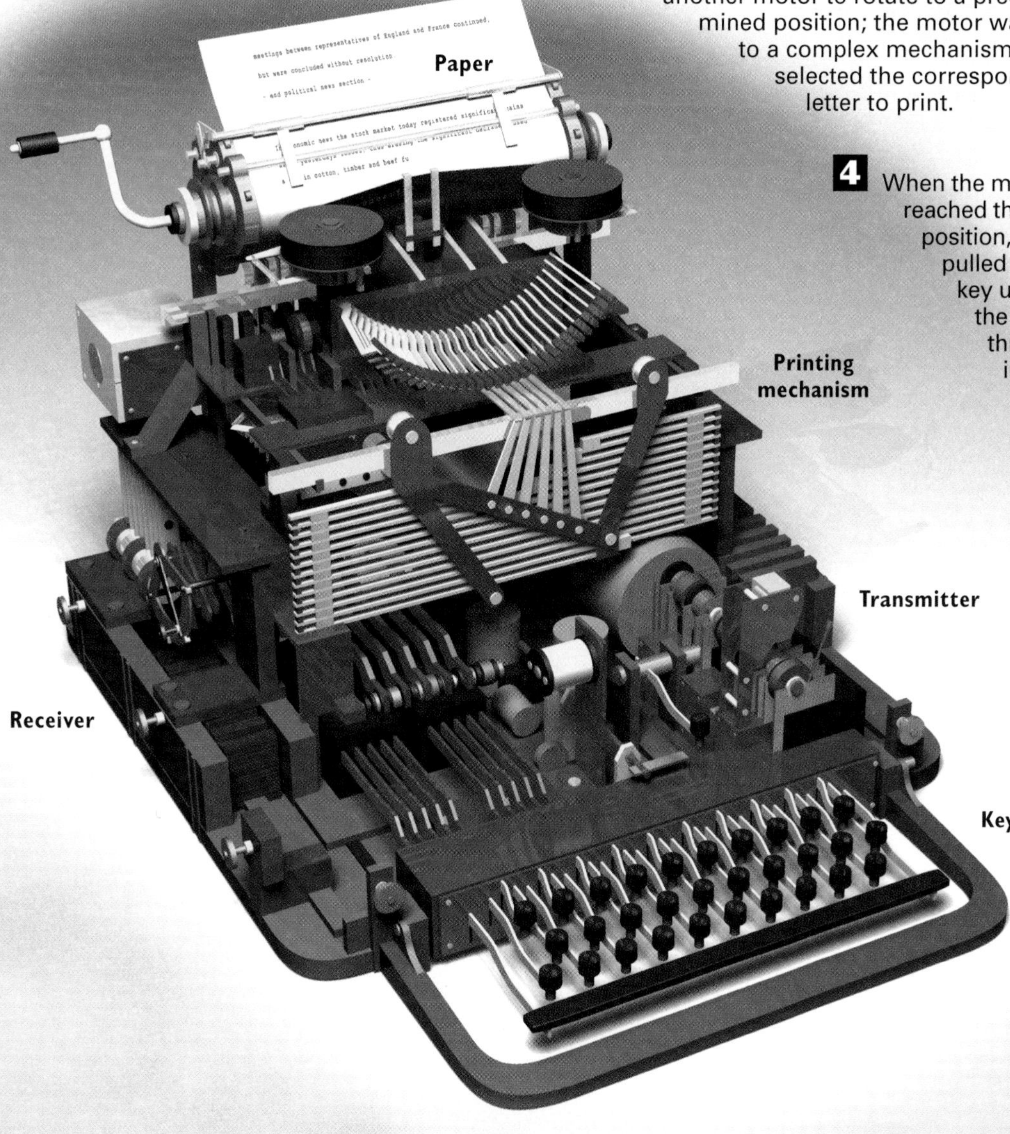

3 At the receiving end, the pulses caused another motor to rotate to a predetermined position; the motor was linked to a complex mechanism that selected the corresponding letter to print.

4 When the motor reached the proper position, a solenoid pulled the correct key up to strike the paper through an inked cloth ribbon.

Paper

Printing mechanism

Transmitter

Receiver

Keyboard

1 The Teletype Model 15 had a typewriter-style keyboard. To send a message, users would simply type the message on the keyboard.

2 Each keypress moved a motor shaft to a predefined position, where the shaft made contact with a set of electrical contacts. Each position of the motor shaft generated a unique combination of electrical pulses (we'd call them *bits* today) that were sent over the telegraph line. Early teletype systems used the five-level Baudot code.

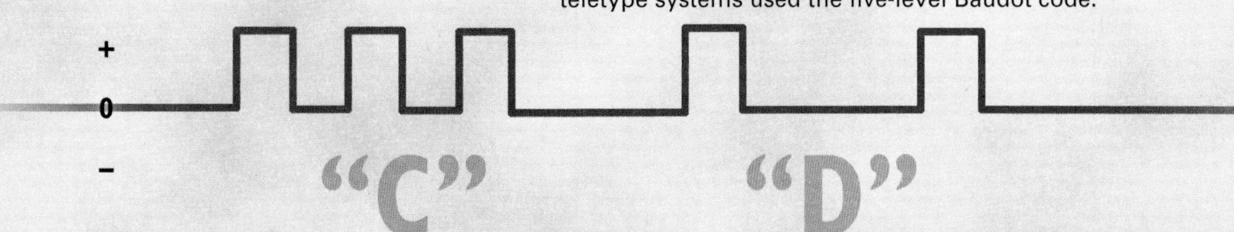
+
0
–
"C"
"D"

CHAPTER 2 How Early Telephones Worked

ALEXANDER Graham Bell invented the telephone, right? Well, right and wrong. Although Bell has received the lion's share of the credit, several other inventors also played major roles in the development of the telephone.

In 1861, German schoolteacher Phillip Reis created a device he called a telephone. Reis's device could transmit musical tones; had Reis spent more time refining the equipment, he might have succeeded in producing a viable voice telephone.

The two men who actually did invent the telephone did so under strikingly similar circumstances.

Some 15 years later, Alexander Graham Bell of Boston and Elisha Gray of Chicago were both attempting to invent the harmonic telegraph, a device that would improve on Morse's design by allowing several telegraph signals to share one telegraph line (a problem later solved by no less an inventor than Thomas Edison). Neither inventor ever produced a working harmonic telegraph and both men made the jump from telegraph to telephone at about the same time. Both men filed their patent papers with the U.S. Patent Office on the same day—February 14, 1876—but Bell arrived at the patent office a few hours ahead of Gray.

The patent issued to Bell, U.S. Patent Number 174,465, is likely the most valuable patent ever issued. Bell and his backers immediately turned their attention from inventing the telephone itself to perfecting and selling their invention.

The early years were not kind to Bell and company, and in early 1877 the Bell organization offered Western Union all rights to the Bell patents for $100,000. Western Union declined, setting off a series of encounters between the two companies that would finally culminate in AT&T's purchase of the remains of Western Union more than 100 years later.

Unimpressed with Bell's telephone, Western Union enlisted the services of Elisha Gray and Thomas Edison to design and market a technically superior telephone. Western Union was a giant corporation and had vast resources to spend on a legal battle. All the Bell Company had were its patents.

Western Union began to set up a telephone system to compete with Bell's. The Bell company filed suit. After two years of legal combat, Western Union's lawyers recommended that the company reach a settlement with Bell. The essential fact was that Bell had, indeed, beaten Gray to the patent office, and it was Bell, and not Gray, who held the basic telephone patents.

Under the terms of the agreement, Western Union surrendered its rights and patents in the telephone business to Bell. In addition, Western Union turned over its network of telephones to the Bell company in return for 20% of rental receipts for the life of the Bell patents.

The legal victory gave Bell a monopoly on the telephone business in the United States. One hundred years later, Bell's company (later known as AT&T) was the largest company in the world. Before the court-ordered dismantling of the AT&T empire in 1984, the company employed more than one million people and operated more than 100 million telephones.

Early Developments in Telephone Technology

All telephones consist of a transmitter (the mouthpiece) and a receiver (the earpiece). To create a working telephone, Bell and the other inventors had to invent those two critical pieces. Of these, the transmitter—the device that turns sound into electrical energy—was more difficult.

Bell Liquid Telephone Transmitter

Bell pursued two separate designs for the telephone transmitter. His first design used a membrane attached to a metal rod. The metal rod reached down into a cup of mild acid. As the user spoke downward into the microphone, the sound caused the membrane to move, which in turn moved the rod up and down in the cup of acid. As the rod moved up and down, the electrical resistance between the rod and the base of the cup varied.

There were several drawbacks to this variable-resistance, or liquid telephone, transmitter, not the least of which was requiring the user to keep a supply of acid on hand. It was the acid, in fact, that caused Bell to utter the famous phrase, "Mr. Watson, come here!"—Bell had spilled the acid on his trousers.

Bell Induction Telephone Transmitter

Bell's second (and acid-free) telephone transmitter used the principle of magnetic induction to change sound into electricity. Instead of a cup of acid, the induction transmitter used a membrane attached to a rod surrounded by a coil of wire. Sound striking the membrane moved the rod; as the rod moved back and forth inside the coil, it produced a weak electric current. The advantage of this device was that, theoretically, it could be used as both a transmitter and a receiver. But because the current it produced was very weak, it wasn't successful as a transmitter.

Despite its failure as a transmitter, the induction telephone worked very well as a receiver—so well, in fact, that most modern-day telephones and audio speakers still use a variation of Bell's original design.

Edison's Carbon Transmitter

The first truly practical telephone transmitter was designed by Thomas Edison, working under contract for Western Union. Edison had discovered that certain carbon compounds change their electrical resistance when subjected to varying pressure. Edison sandwiched a carbon button between a metal membrane and a metal support. When sound struck the membrane, it exerted pressure on the carbon button, varying the flow of electricity through the microphone.

Despite the hostilities between Bell and Western Union, the Bell people were quick to realize the superiority of Edison's design. When the Bell v. Western Union lawsuit was settled in 1879, Bell took over rights to Edison's transmitter. It became the standard telephone transmitter and is still in use today.

Strowger's Dial Telephone

The early Bell system used human operators to route calls. To place a call, users would pick up the phone and turn a crank, which generated an electrical impulse that let the operator know you wanted to make a call. When the operator answered, the user told her (all operators were women) the name or number of the party to call. The operator would then connect the call by connecting a cable from the caller's line to the called line using a device called a *switchboard.*

As the telephone grew in popularity, the operator-and-switchboard approach became woefully inadequate. In 1889, a Kansas City undertaker named Almon Brown Strowger took the first step toward automating the phone system. His inventions, the Strowger switch and the telephone dial, allowed a caller to dial the desired number, eliminating the need for an operator. How did an undertaker invent the dial telephone? Strowger was sure that unscrupulous operators were taking bribes to divert calls to his competitors. His invention allowed users to dial numbers directly, bypassing the operator. At the same time, AT&T estimated that if the telephone kept growing at its current pace, they would need to hire and train hundreds of thousands of operators. Strowger's technology was the right thing at exactly the right time.

Early Advances in Telephone Technology

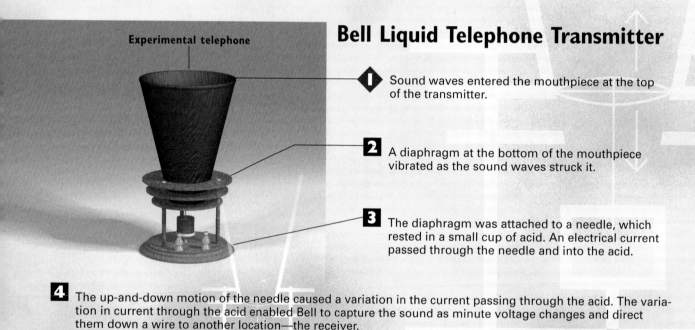

Bell Liquid Telephone Transmitter

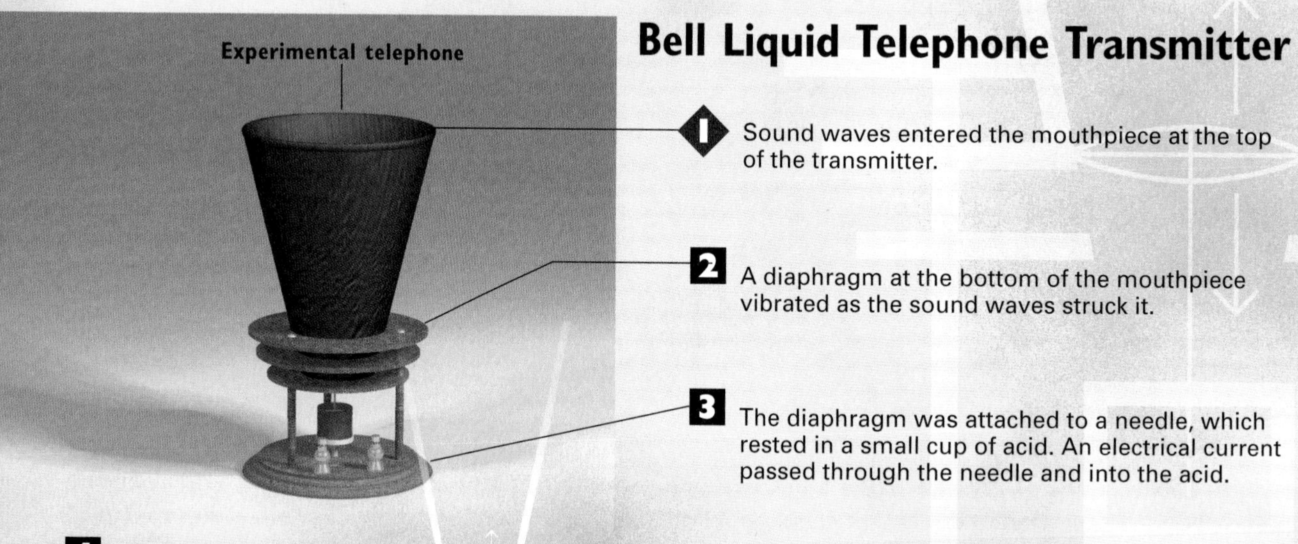
Experimental telephone

1. Sound waves entered the mouthpiece at the top of the transmitter.
2. A diaphragm at the bottom of the mouthpiece vibrated as the sound waves struck it.
3. The diaphragm was attached to a needle, which rested in a small cup of acid. An electrical current passed through the needle and into the acid.
4. The up-and-down motion of the needle caused a variation in the current passing through the acid. The variation in current through the acid enabled Bell to capture the sound as minute voltage changes and direct them down a wire to another location—the receiver.

Bell Induction Telephone Transmitter

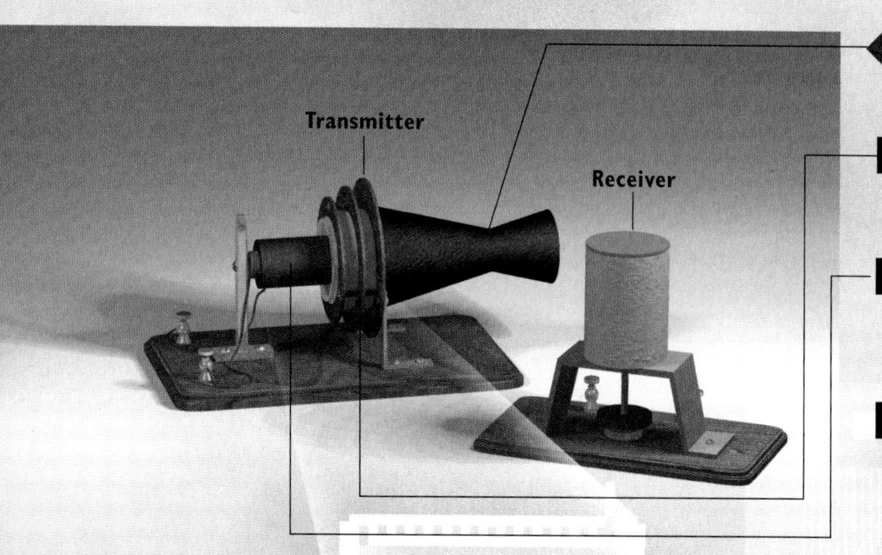
Transmitter
Receiver

1. Sound from the user's voice enters the mouthpiece.
2. The sound waves strike a diaphragm, causing the diaphragm to vibrate.
3. A magnetic rod is attached to the diaphragm and is surrounded by a coil of wire.
4. As the rod moves back and forth inside the coil, it generates a small electric current.

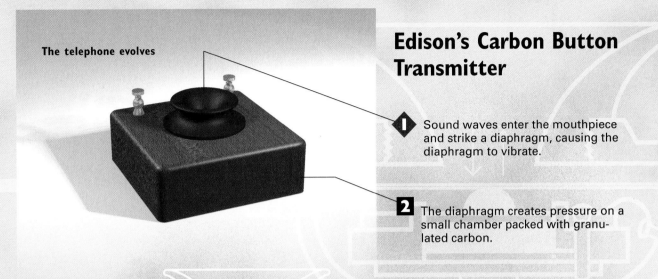

The telephone evolves

Edison's Carbon Button Transmitter

1. Sound waves enter the mouthpiece and strike a diaphragm, causing the diaphragm to vibrate.

2. The diaphragm creates pressure on a small chamber packed with granulated carbon.

3. The varying pressure created by the diaphragm causes a variation in the electrical current flowing through the carbon granules.

Strowger's Dial Telephone

1. The Strowger telephone allowed users to call another phone without an operator. To place a call, the user placed a finger in the appropriate numbered hole and rotated the dial clockwise. This motion wound a spring inside the telephone dial.

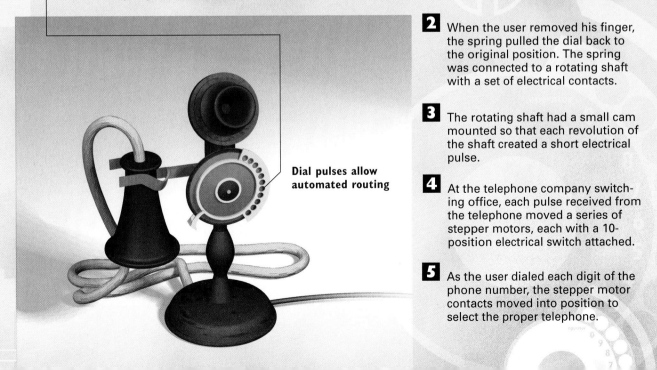

Dial pulses allow automated routing

2. When the user removed his finger, the spring pulled the dial back to the original position. The spring was connected to a rotating shaft with a set of electrical contacts.

3. The rotating shaft had a small cam mounted so that each revolution of the shaft created a short electrical pulse.

4. At the telephone company switching office, each pulse received from the telephone moved a series of stepper motors, each with a 10-position electrical switch attached.

5. As the user dialed each digit of the phone number, the stepper motor contacts moved into position to select the proper telephone.

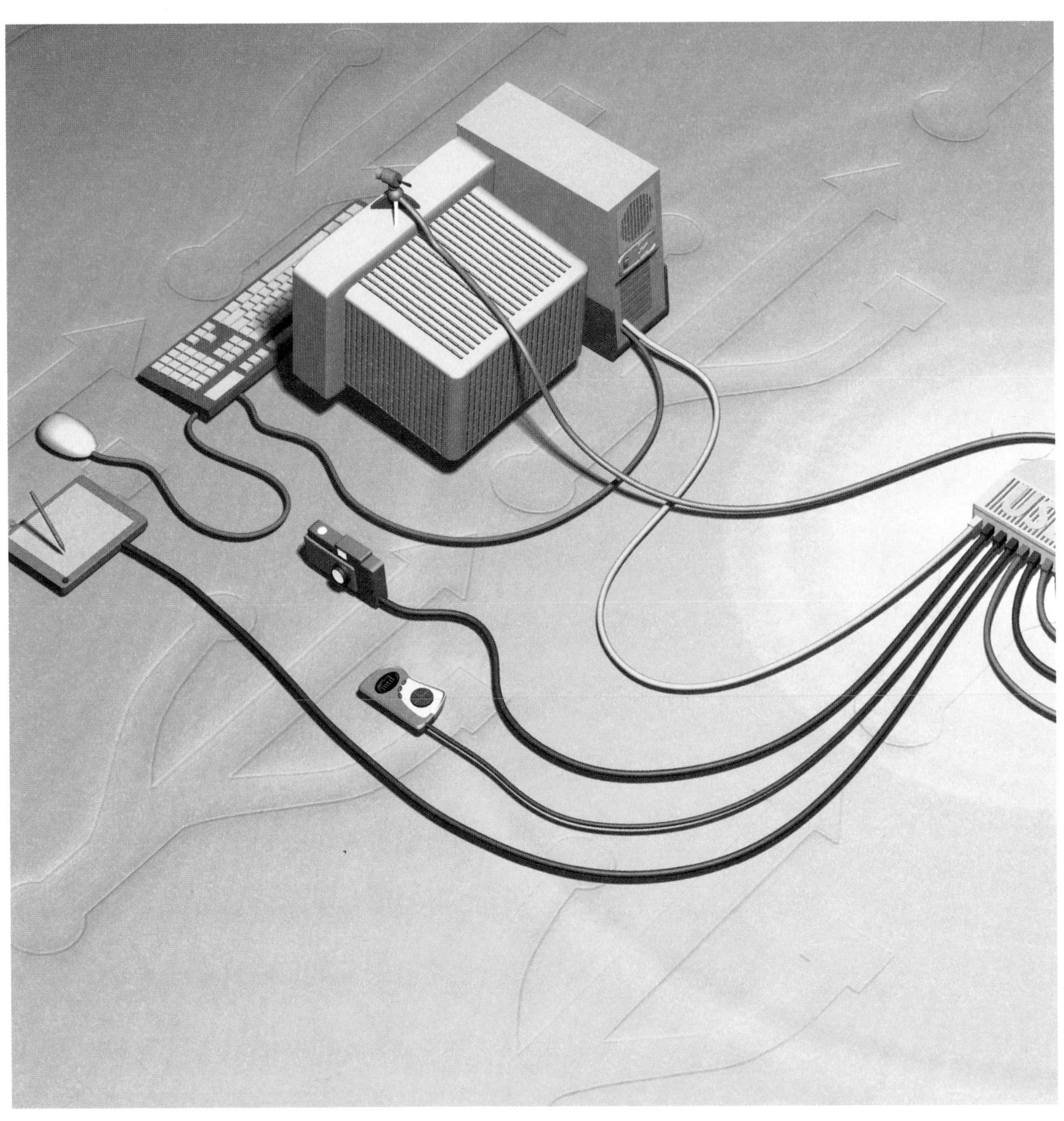

MIXING COMPUTERS AND TELEPHONES

ALTHOUGH they are products of different eras and different technologies, the computer and the telephone seem to have been made for each other. Today's telephone network could not exist without vast computing resources to process calls, route traffic, and print telephone bills. Conversely, the existence of a worldwide telephone network allows computers to connect to one another so that the machines (and their users) can exchange information.

Even though the computer and the telephone have been forced into a marriage of convenience, they are worlds apart. The computer's universe is digital: Everything that passes through the computer's CPU is either a 1 or a 0. The worldwide telephone network is largely digital, too—except for the last few miles of wire between the customer's home or office and the telephone company's switching equipment. To maintain compatibility with the millions of existing telephones, the local loop from the telephone company central office to the phone jack on your wall is the same two-wire circuit used by the Bell system since the 1890s. At some point in the future, we'll likely discard our analog phones and move to an all-digital telephone network; this has already happened in some smaller European and Asian countries. But such a move will require replacement or modification of every single telephone in North America!

AT&T was one of the first companies to adopt computers on a very large scale, and AT&T, through its Bell Labs subsidiary, funded some of the earliest computer research. The invention of the transistor at Bell Labs in 1948 made large-scale computers practical. AT&T also invented the first practical telephone modem—a device that allows digital data to travel via the analog world of the telephone network.

The phenomenal growth of the personal computer began in the late 1970s and continues today. In the early days of personal computing, relatively few computers were able to communicate with one another. But a few of those early computer users learned that although a standalone PC was a powerful tool, a networked PC was even more powerful. Several subscription information services—The Source, CompuServe, and America Online, among

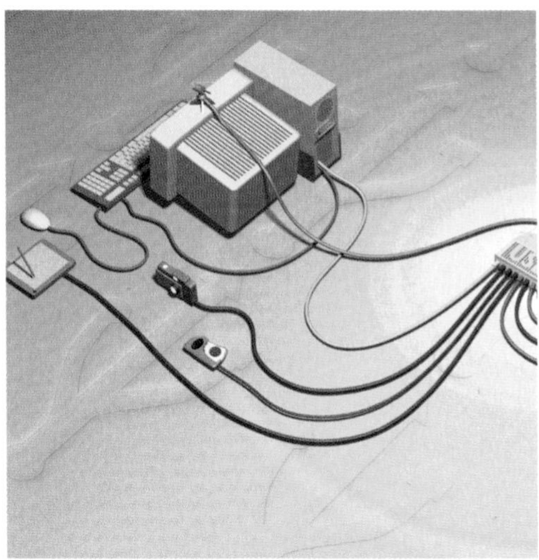

others—were created to allow computer users to exchange messages, share files, and access information stored in online databases. Of those early services, only AOL is still with us today, having swallowed up most of its competitors (along with Time-Warner and CompuServe) over the years.

Users connected to these early networks via a modem connected to a standard phone line. The terms "log on" and "go online" became part of the computing vernacular. Modem speeds became a standard cocktail-party discussion topic. But the early online services were islands unto themselves. Users on one service couldn't exchange messages with users on another. Each service used its own, often awkward, user interface.

In the early 1990s, an online revolution took place. The Internet—once a closed, obscure network linking military and research institutions—became open to the public. The Internet offered an amazing array of information published by governments, businesses, and individuals. Users flocked to the Internet by the millions, spurred on by the availability of inexpensive (and often free), easy-to-use software. Today, the Internet reaches hundreds of millions of users around the globe. The modem—once the domain of the few true geeks in the computing universe—became standard equipment on virtually all new PCs. Cocktail-party chatter shifted from modem speeds to busy signals as many Internet service providers became overloaded with demand.

As the Internet grew in size, it also grew in importance. Today's Internet is an important part of business and daily life for millions of users, and those users want faster, more reliable Internet connections. New developments in modem technology allow faster and faster modem speeds, to the point where current dial-up modem technology is limited only by the laws of physics.

Today's Internet users can choose from a variety of high-speed Internet connection technologies, including ISDN, DSL, and cable modem service. ISDN and DSL operate over standard copper telephone lines, whereas cable modem service is delivered using the cable television infrastructure.

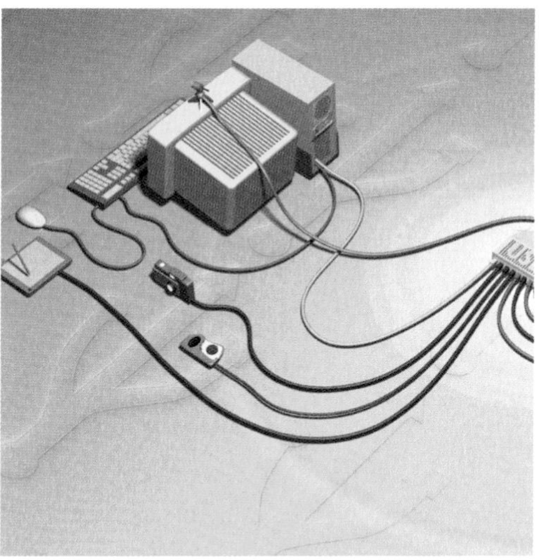

CHAPTER 3

How Early Networks Worked

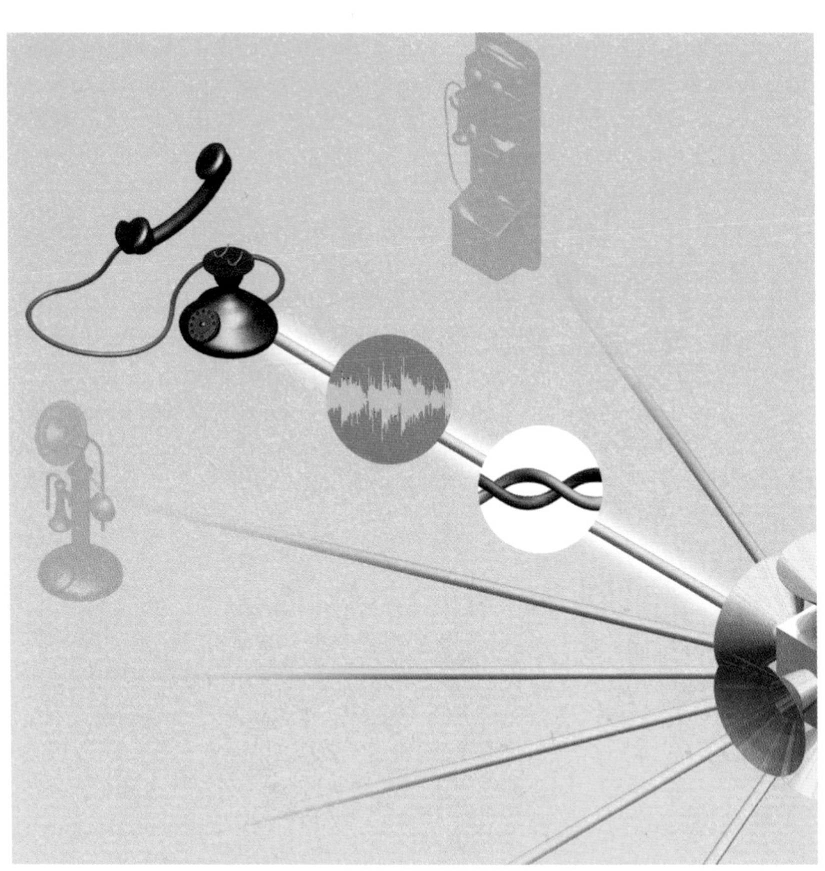

WHEN you hear the word *network* today, you probably think of computer networks, television networks, cable television networks, or local area networks. All of those networks owe their existence to two earlier networks: Western Union's network and the Bell system.

Western Union holds a special place in history: It was the world's first telecommunications giant. The completion of its first overland telegraph line ended the brief, exciting history—1860 to 1861—of the colorful pony express.

Western Union was formed by the merger of 12 smaller companies. By the time of the Civil War, Western Union's lines stretched across the United States, from New York to California.

Western Union's network was the first to span the North American continent. Following the railroad westward, Western Union struck deals with most of the railroads of the day. In exchange for access to the railroad right-of-way, Western Union provided a telegraph station and an operator at each train station. The operator handled schedule and load information for the railroad at no charge.

Western Union's service was point to point. To send a telegram to someone, you would go to the Western Union office and dictate the message to the telegraph operator. The operator would then send the message out in Morse code over the telegraph line to the appropriate station.

When Bell Telephone began operations in the late 1890s, it had no telephone lines. As subscribers signed up for service, Bell ran new lines to the subscribers' locations. Initially, telephone service was also point to point, meaning that each phone could connect to only one other phone. Many of the early telephone subscribers were doctors; they would connect one phone in an office to another at home. As telephone service grew, subscribers wanted to be able to talk to one another—so the telephone network, as we know it today, was born.

Today's public telephone network is a complex maze of telephone lines and central switching offices. The central offices connect to an even more complicated web of cables, microwave towers, fiber-optic cables, and communications satellites.

At one time, more than 90% of these facilities belonged to the Bell system. Since the court-ordered AT&T breakup in 1984, the facilities belong to dozens of companies, including AT&T, the regional Bell operating companies, Sprint, Verizon, and others. Despite all the behind-the-scenes complexity, the system remains easy to use. To make a call, you simply pick up the phone and dial the number.

Today's telephone network is a hybrid of analog and digital technologies. Although most of the home and small business telephone service in North America is analog, the switching network and long distance networks are all digital. AT&T pioneered the use of analog-to-digital conversion techniques as a way to combine hundreds of voice conversations into a single digital signal. This allowed AT&T (and other companies) to carry more conversations without building new (and very expensive) long distance circuits.

How a Telephone Network Works

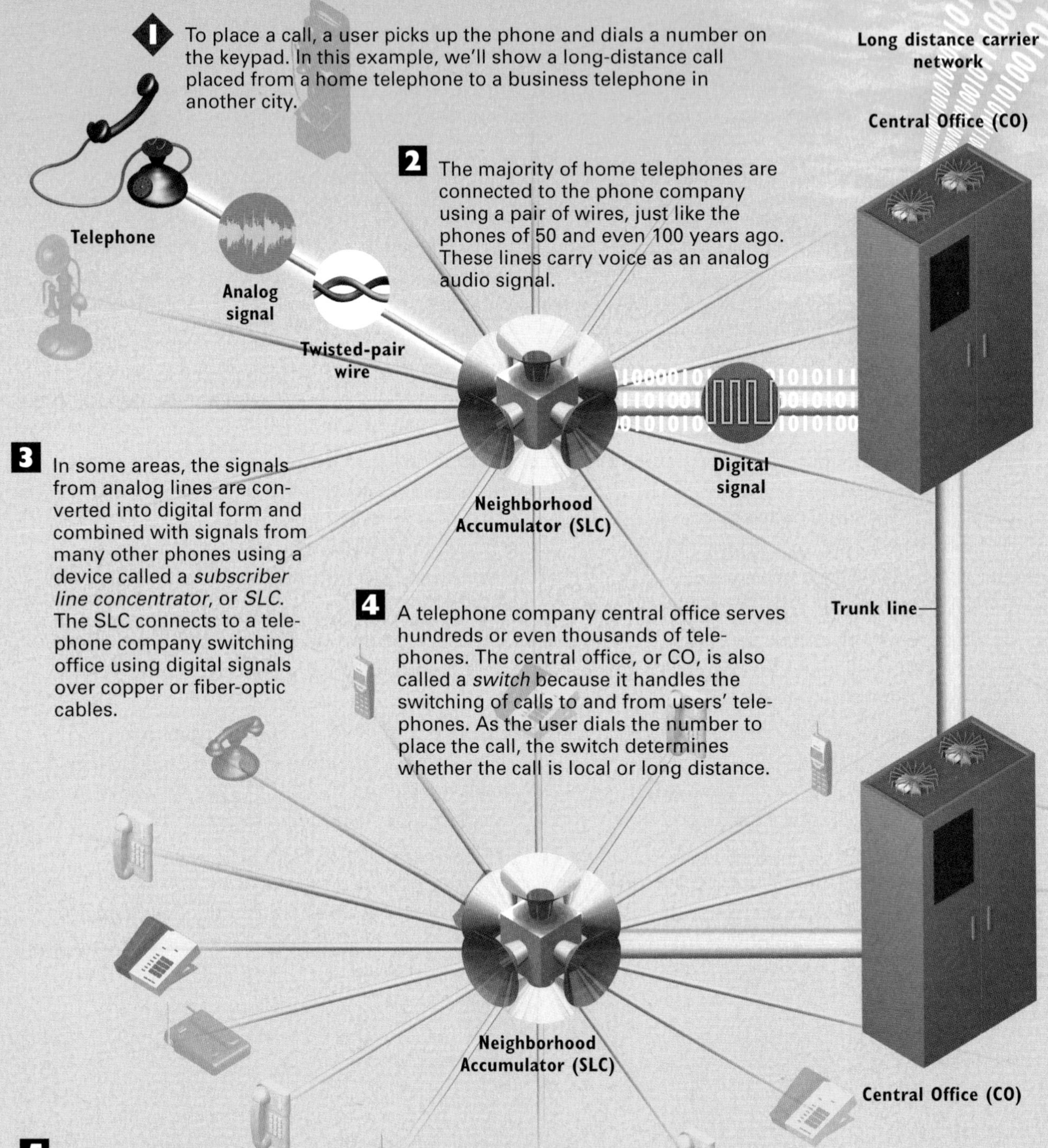

1 To place a call, a user picks up the phone and dials a number on the keypad. In this example, we'll show a long-distance call placed from a home telephone to a business telephone in another city.
Long distance carrier network
Central Office (CO)
2 The majority of home telephones are connected to the phone company using a pair of wires, just like the phones of 50 and even 100 years ago. These lines carry voice as an analog audio signal.
Telephone
Analog signal
Twisted-pair wire
Digital signal
Neighborhood Accumulator (SLC)
3 In some areas, the signals from analog lines are converted into digital form and combined with signals from many other phones using a device called a *subscriber line concentrator*, or *SLC*. The SLC connects to a telephone company switching office using digital signals over copper or fiber-optic cables.
4 A telephone company central office serves hundreds or even thousands of telephones. The central office, or CO, is also called a *switch* because it handles the switching of calls to and from users' telephones. As the user dials the number to place the call, the switch determines whether the call is local or long distance.
Trunk line
Neighborhood Accumulator (SLC)
Central Office (CO)
5 If the call is local but the called phone is connected to a different CO, the call is routed to a trunk line that connects to the two COs. If the call is long distance, the CO routes the call to the caller's long-distance phone company.

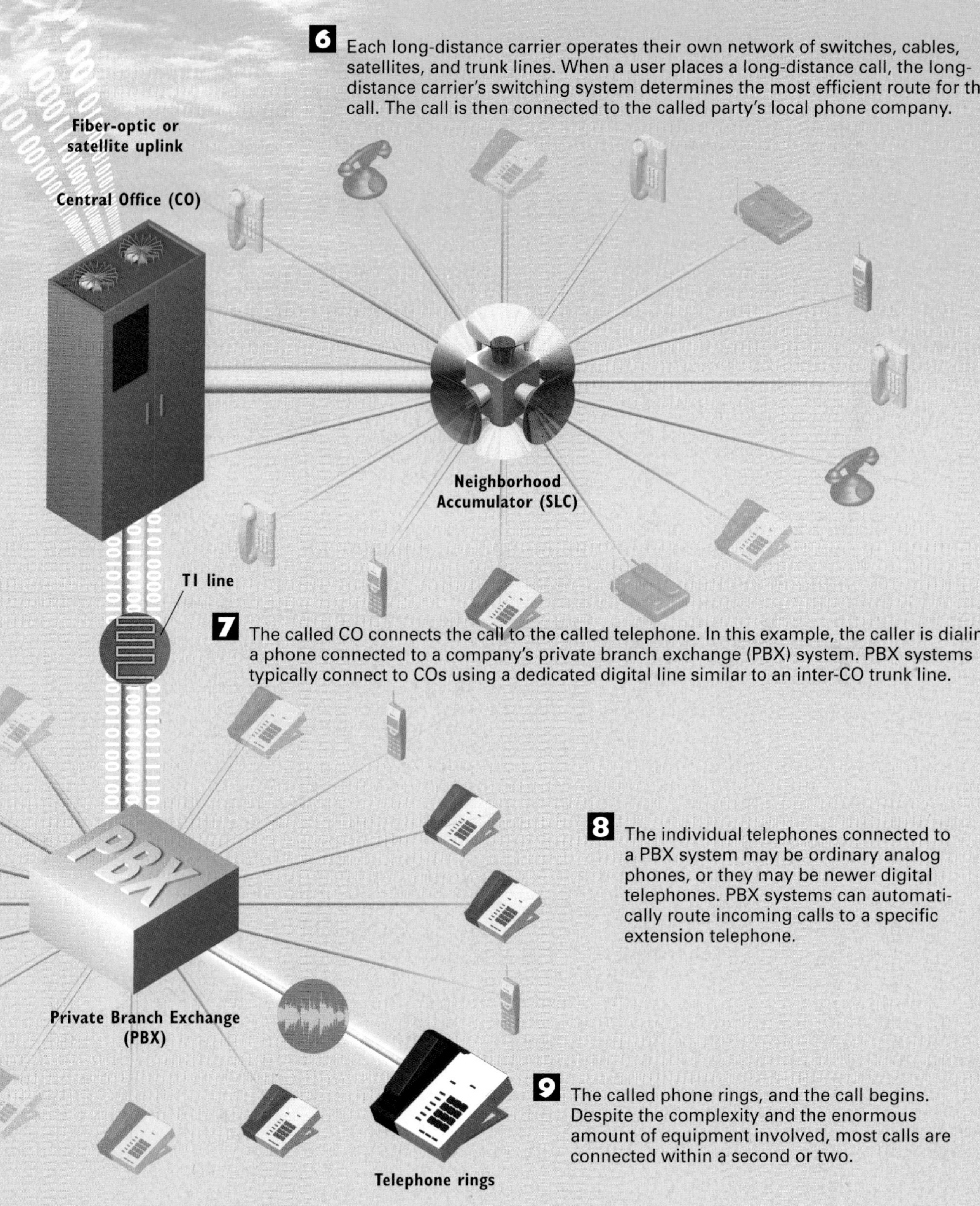
Fiber-optic or satellite uplink
Central Office (CO)
Neighborhood Accumulator (SLC)
T1 line
PBX
Private Branch Exchange (PBX)
Telephone rings

6 Each long-distance carrier operates their own network of switches, cables, satellites, and trunk lines. When a user places a long-distance call, the long-distance carrier's switching system determines the most efficient route for the call. The call is then connected to the called party's local phone company.

7 The called CO connects the call to the called telephone. In this example, the caller is dialing a phone connected to a company's private branch exchange (PBX) system. PBX systems typically connect to COs using a dedicated digital line similar to an inter-CO trunk line.

8 The individual telephones connected to a PBX system may be ordinary analog phones, or they may be newer digital telephones. PBX systems can automatically route incoming calls to a specific extension telephone.

9 The called phone rings, and the call begins. Despite the complexity and the enormous amount of equipment involved, most calls are connected within a second or two.

CHAPTER 4

How Early Communications Terminals Worked

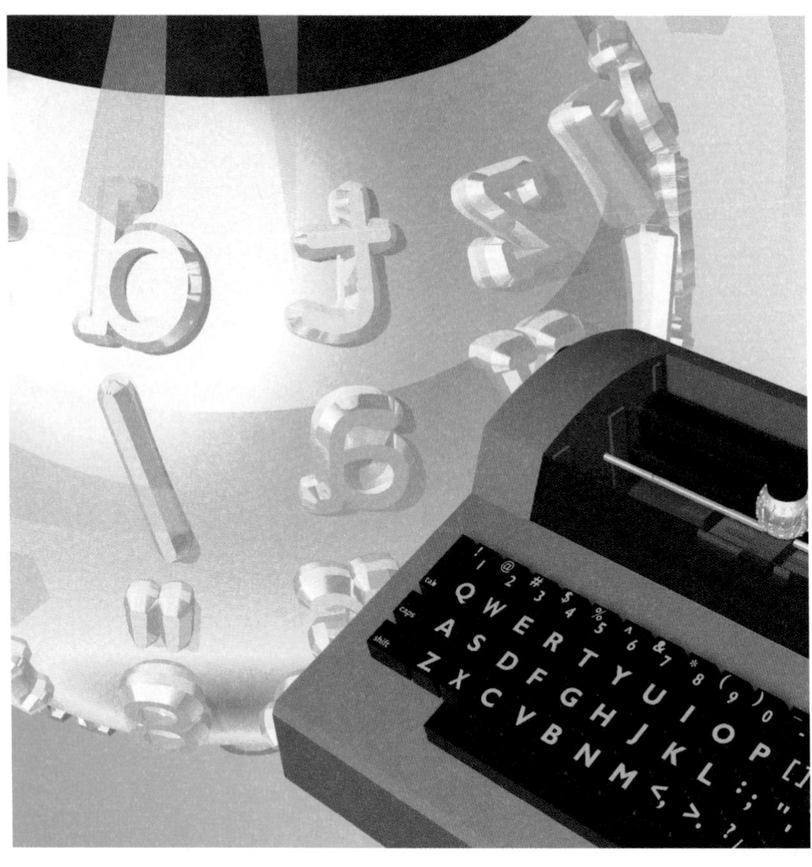
Q W E R T Y U I O P
A S D F G H J K L
Z X C V B N M

AS we write this chapter, we're sitting in front of an 18-inch color LCD screen with 1,280-by-1,024-pixel resolution. The screen can display text, graphics, photos, and full-motion video with millions of colors. The keyboard has 103 keys, many of them reserved for special functions such as moving paragraphs or underlining a passage of text. As we type, our keystrokes instantly appear on the color screen, the text formatted and displayed exactly as it will appear when this page is printed. The printer can faithfully reproduce hundreds of different typefaces with 1,200-dot-per-inch accuracy. When we're finished with this chapter, we'll click the "Send to..." button at the top of the screen and email this chapter to our editor halfway across the country.

The earliest computers didn't have any of these features—in fact, they didn't even have a keyboard and screen. The very first computers used a variety of input and output devices, including switches, lights, teletypewriters, and paper-tape readers.

Because early computers were used primarily by scientists for one specific task, there was no pressing need to make data input and output faster or easier. But when computers became available and affordable for general business use, efficiency and accessibility became important concerns.

Keypunch and Card Readers

The first input/output device to find widespread acceptance was the keypunch and card-reader combination. Data to be input to the computer was typed into a keypunch machine. The machine translated the operator's keystrokes into a series of holes punched in a card. The cards were then carried to the computer room, where they were placed into a card reader. The card reader "sensed" the holes in the cards, re-created the operator's keystrokes, and sent them off to the computer.

The punched-card system had many drawbacks: It was cumbersome, the cards could easily get out of order, and the input/output cycle took time—sometimes days or weeks. The punched-card system also had advantages: The keypunch machines could be located anywhere, even in locations that didn't actually have a computer. Card decks from multiple locations could be sent to one central location for processing. Keypunch operators didn't require extensive training because the keypunch keyboard resembled a standard typewriter keyboard. But the biggest disadvantage of the punched-card system was that it allowed only one program to run on the computer at a time.

Interactive Printing Terminals

The next step forward in the human-machine interface was the interactive printing terminal. Instead of punching holes in a card, the terminal sent keystrokes directly to the computer. The computer responded by sending characters to the terminal's printer. The early interactive terminals were usually teletypewriters or specially modified electric typewriters. The best known of these was IBM's Selectric terminal, a modified version of IBM's popular typewriter. The original IBM PC introduced in 1981 featured a keyboard that looked and felt just like a Selectric.

With the advent of the time-sharing operating system, several operators could run jobs on the same computer at the same time. These machines were cantankerous and noisy, but they provided an immediate response from the computer—something the punched-card system could never do. The capability to get immediate answers from the computer led to a host of new applications for computer technology.

Perhaps the most significant of these new applications was the online processing system such as those used in airline reservation systems. Using special leased telephone lines, airlines could place terminals in every city they served. Ticket agents across the country could use the central computer system to check fares and book flights. The online processing concept was and still is used in many other industries, including the computer industry itself.

Before the interactive terminal, programmers had to develop computer programs using punched cards. The delays and additional errors introduced by the punched-card system made an already difficult job even more difficult. The interactive terminal allowed programmers to see the results of their work immediately, thus reducing the amount of time required to develop a program.

Although the interactive printing terminal added a lot to the world of computing, it also left a great deal to be desired. Printing terminals are, by nature, mechanical devices. Although they're faster than punched cards, they're still relatively slow, noisy, and require a great deal of maintenance.

In the mid-1960s, several manufacturers began to replace the terminal's printing mechanism with a picture tube, and the video display terminal (VDT) was born. VDTs work much like printing terminals do, but they are faster, quieter, and more efficient. The earliest microcomputer systems—the immediate predecessors to today's personal computers—also used VDTs for input and output.

The Carterfone

In 1966, a small Texas company called Carterfone invented a simple device that allowed mobile two-way radios to connect to a telephone line. The Carterfone allowed construction workers, field service personnel, and traveling executives to make and receive telephone calls using their company's existing two-way radio system.

The Carterfone did not physically connect to the phone line. Nevertheless, AT&T maintained that the Carterfone posed a threat to the integrity of the telephone system. After a two-year legal battle, the FCC

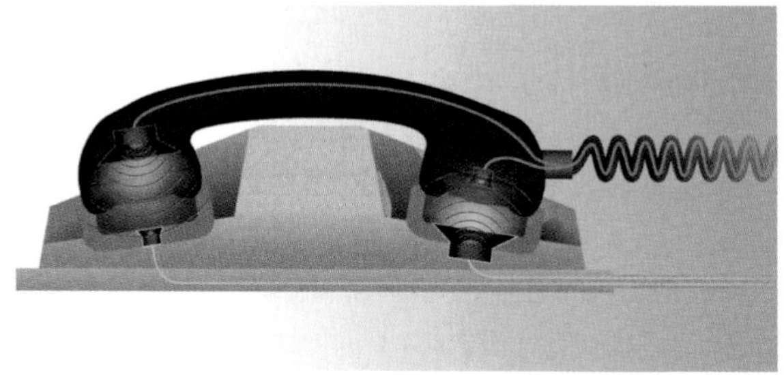

ruled that third-party equipment could indeed be connected to the telephone network as long as the connected device contained protective measures to ensure that no harm could come to the telephone network. The Carterfone decision was the beginning of the end of AT&T's near-monopoly on telephones and telephone-related equipment.

In 1975, the FCC went a step further. The FCC ruled that any piece of equipment could be attached to the telephone company's lines as long as the device met certain technical specifications. In 1977, the FCC published these technical specifications, known as Rules and Regulations of the Federal Communications Commission, Part 68: Connection of Terminal Equipment to the Telephone Network. The rules, commonly known as Part 68, describe how third-party equipment should connect to the telephone network. If you look on the bottom of almost any telephone or modem sold in the United States today, you'll see a sticker stating that the device conforms to Part 68 of the FCC rules.

The FCC's Part 68 rule opened a floodgate of new equipment. Dozens of manufacturers jumped into the telephone business. Instead of paying a few dollars every month to the local phone company, you could buy a phone of your own. Telephones became available in every imaginable shape, size, and color. Telephone accessories such as answering machines, cordless phones, and modems became common household items. The telephone industry itself was turned upside down, all thanks to a little company from Texas.

Nearly 20 years later, the Telecommunications Act of 1996 once again shook up the status quo in the telecommunications industry. As the first major overhaul of telecommunications law in more than 60 years, the Telecommunications Act of 1996 allowed any company to compete in the telecommunications business, effectively ending the local phone service monopoly enjoyed by the regional phone companies. Most importantly for consumers, the Act required local telephone companies to make their wiring network available to competitors. After the Act took effect, hundreds of new companies entered the communications industry, providing everything from local telephone service to specialized network and data communications services.

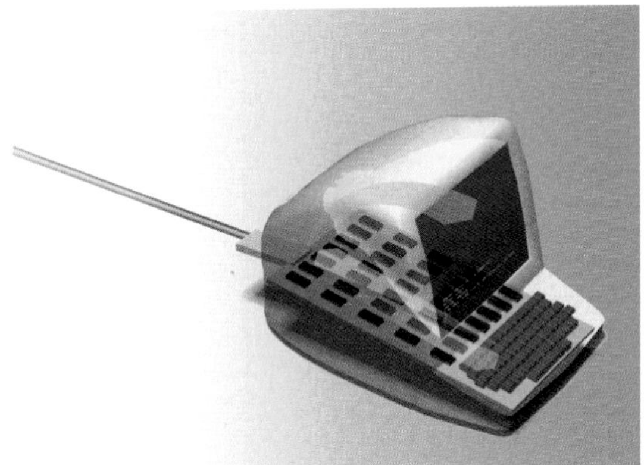

How Punch Cards Worked

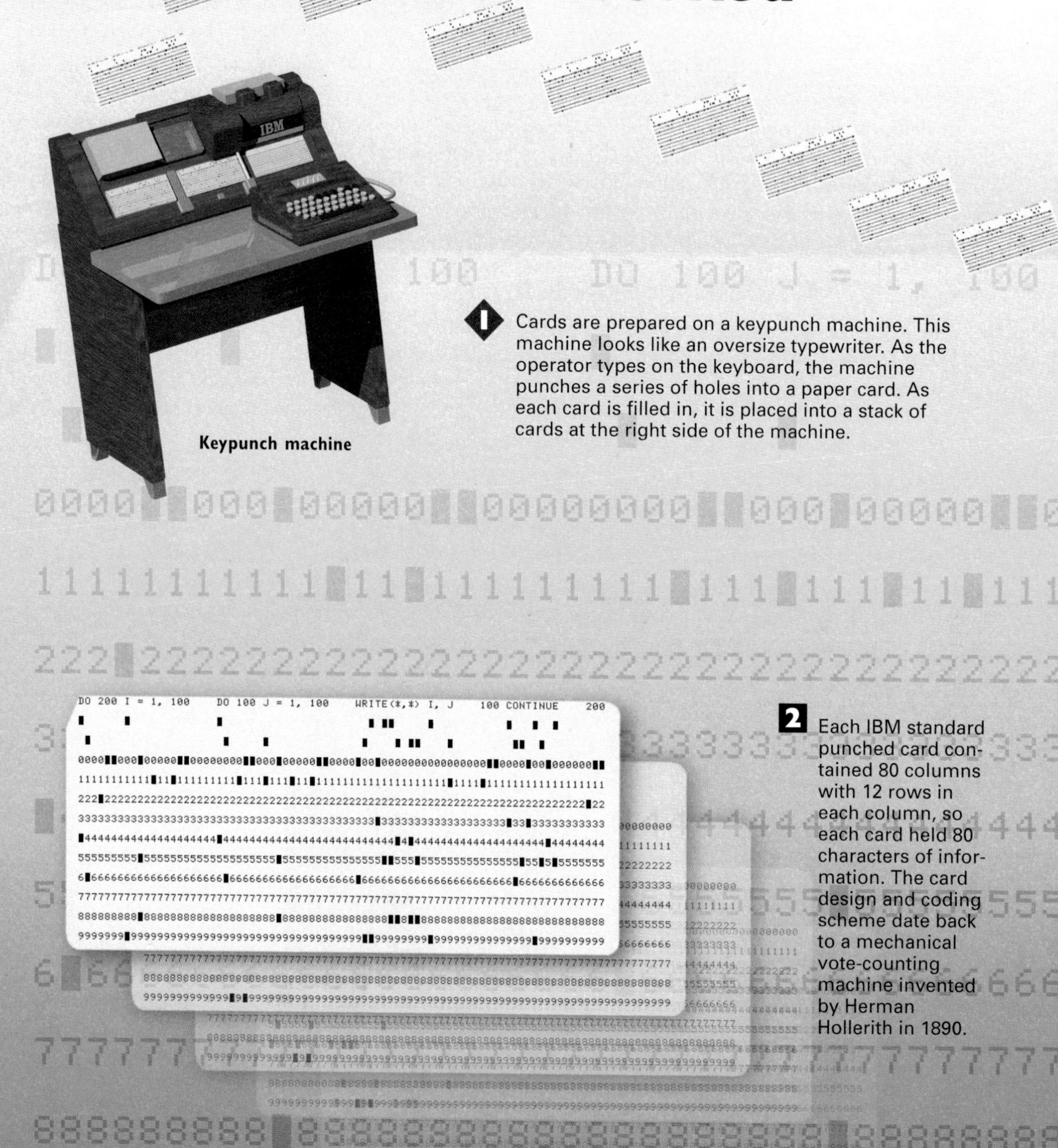

Keypunch machine

1. Cards are prepared on a keypunch machine. This machine looks like an oversize typewriter. As the operator types on the keyboard, the machine punches a series of holes into a paper card. As each card is filled in, it is placed into a stack of cards at the right side of the machine.

2. Each IBM standard punched card contained 80 columns with 12 rows in each column, so each card held 80 characters of information. The card design and coding scheme date back to a mechanical vote-counting machine invented by Herman Hollerith in 1890.

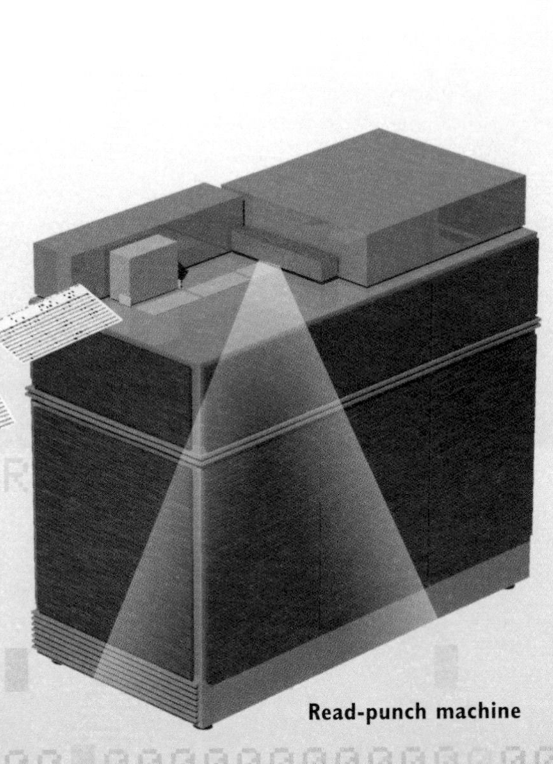
Read-punch machine

Main computer cabinet

3 To enter data into the computer, the stack of punched cards was placed into a card reader, shown here to the left of the main computer cabinet. This machine read each card in sequence and copied the data encoded on the cards into the computer's memory.

Spring-loaded electrical contacts

Side view of punch card

1 0 0 0 1 0 0 0 0

4 Early card readers used a series of electrical contacts to sense the presence of holes in the card. A hole would allow the spring-loaded contacts to pass through the card, completing a circuit. Later designs replaced the electrical contacts with optical sensors.

How Early Terminals Worked

IBM Selectric Terminal

1 Like other printing terminals, the IBM Selectric terminal converted keystrokes into electrical signals. As users typed on the keyboard, the terminal sent a code to the computer to indicate which key was pressed. The computer could also send data to the terminal.

2 Unlike earlier printing terminals, the Selectric used a high-quality printing mechanism that could print upper- and lowercase characters. Instead of the usual array of type levers found in common typewriters and printing terminals, the Selectric used a unique rotating "golf ball" printing element. As data was received from the host computer, the type ball rotated and tilted until the appropriate letter was positioned over the paper.

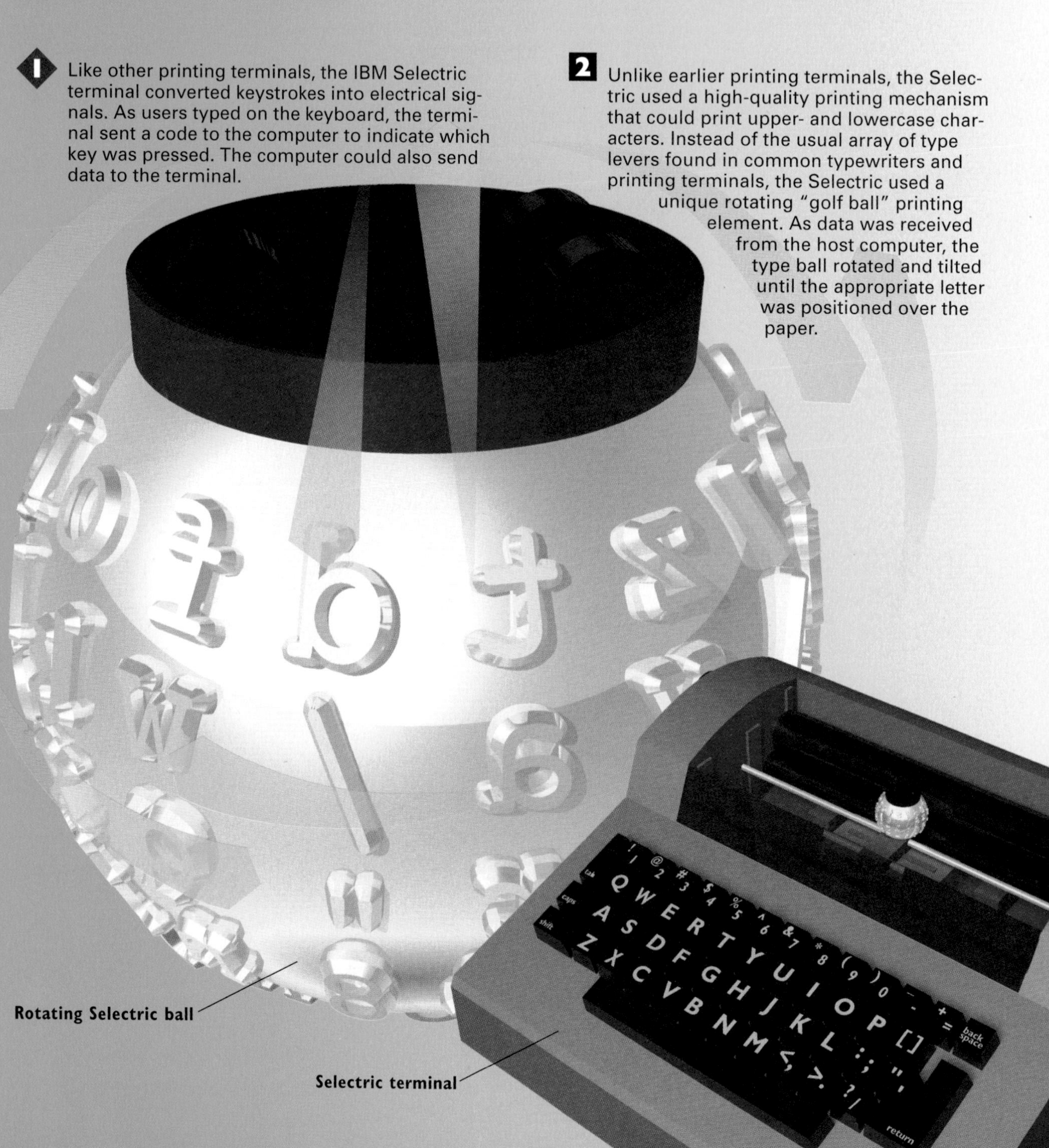
Rotating Selectric ball
Selectric terminal

Early Video Display Terminals

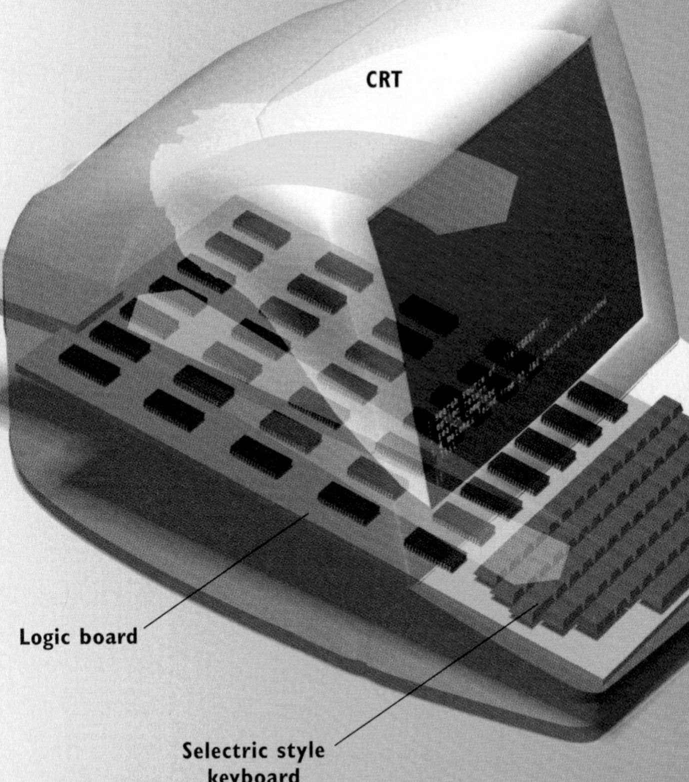
CRT
Logic board
Selectric style keyboard

1 Video Display Terminals, or VDTs, began to replace printing terminals in the 1970s. Like printing terminals, VDTs used a serial data connection between the terminal and a host computer system.

2 VDTs worked much like printing terminals. But instead of printing data on paper, they displayed data on a video screen. A logic board inside the terminal converted typed keystrokes into serial data that was sent to the host computer, and the same board converted incoming data into a video signal that was displayed on the screen.

The Carterfone

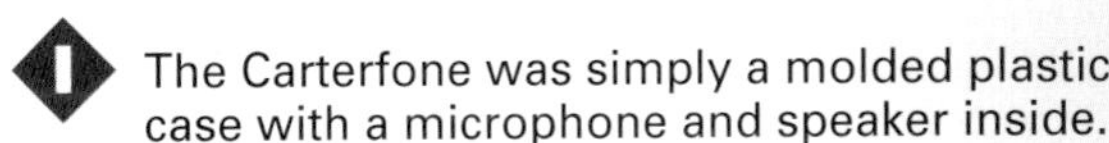

1 The Carterfone was simply a molded plastic case with a microphone and speaker inside.

2 The microphone and speaker were arranged so that when a standard telephone handset was placed into the Carterfone, the Carterfone's speaker "talked" into the telephone's microphone, and vice versa. This arrangement—often called a *phone patch*—provided a nonelectrical connection between a private two-way radio system and the public telephone network.

Incoming audio data
Outgoing audio data

CHAPTER 5 How Data Is Encoded

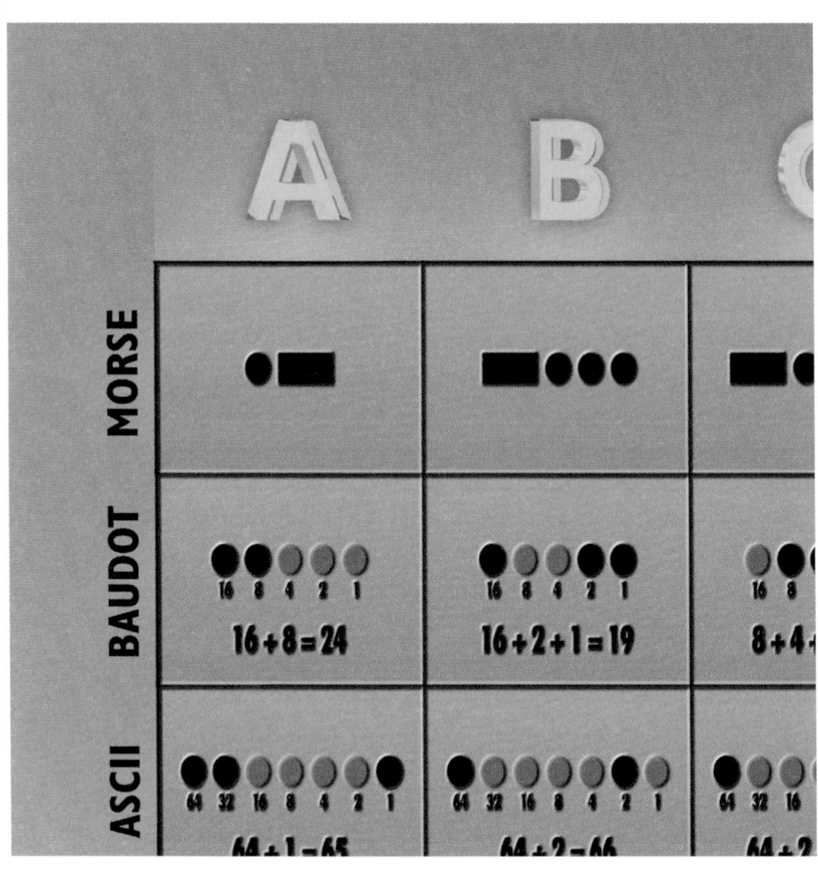
A
B
MORSE
BAUDOT
ASCII
16 8 4 2 1
16+8=24
16 8 4 2 1
16+2+1=19
64 32 16 8 4 2 1
64 32 16 8 4 2 1

LIKE Morse code before it, Emile Baudot's five-level teletypewriter code introduced the world to a faster, more efficient form of communications. Invented in 1870, Baudot's code, with improvements and additions made by English inventor Donald Murray, served as the primary code used in machine-to-machine communications for more than 50 years. But despite its longevity, the Baudot code had several shortcomings.

The Baudot code used five bits of data to represent each transmitted character. Many of the early printing telegraphs discussed in Chapter 1, "How Telegraphs Work," used the Baudot code. A special shift code was used to shift the receiving machine between letters and figures mode. Even with the shift code, the Baudot code could accommodate only uppercase letters.

In 1966, several American computer, teletypewriter, and communications companies collaborated to devise a replacement for the Baudot code. The result of their work is the American Standard Code for Information Interchange, or ASCII. ASCII uses a 7-bit code, allowing it to represent 128 discrete characters without using a shift code. ASCII defines 96 printable characters (the letters A through Z in upper- and lowercase, numbers 0 through 9, and punctuation marks) and also includes several control characters that define nonprinting functions such as carriage return, line feed, and backspace.

Besides offering full upper- and lowercase printing, ASCII also defines a simple error-checking mechanism. An extra bit, called the parity bit, is added to each transmitted character. If the communications circuit is using even parity, the parity bit is set to 0 when there is an even number of bits in the transmitted character. If the circuit is using odd parity, the parity bit is set to 0 when there is an odd number of bits. Although parity checking doesn't provide a means to retransmit corrupted characters, it does provide a simple validity test for received data.

ASCII was widely and readily adopted by most computer and communications equipment vendors worldwide (IBM was the notable exception). Beyond the improvements ASCII offered over Baudot, ASCII provided a well-defined public standard that didn't owe its existence to any one company. As an added bonus, any ASCII-standard computer could, at least in theory, exchange information with any other ASCII system.

IBM, following a long-standing tradition of doing things its own way, did not adopt ASCII. Instead, IBM engineers devised their own code, called EBCDIC, for Extended Binary Coded Decimal Interchange Code. EBCDIC is an 8-bit code, so it can define a total of 256 different characters. This is its one advantage over ASCII. Unlike ASCII, the alphabetic characters in EBCDIC are not sequential, making sorting operations more difficult.

Although it is still widely used in IBM mainframes and minicomputers, EBCDIC never caught on in the non-IBM universe. IBM itself has shunned EBCDIC on several occasions, most notably in the design of the IBM Personal Computer and its successors.

From Morse Code to EBCDIC

Morse—Because Morse code was meant for human ears, it contains data elements of unequal length. The dash is three times the length of the dot, and a period equal to one dot is added between letters, so the receiving operator can discern one letter from the next.

Baudot—The five data elements defining each character of Baudot code (called "bits" today) are of equal length. Because 5 bits allow only 32 combinations, Baudot code uses two special characters called FIGS and LTRS to tell the receiving machine to print the figures character set or the letters set. Only 62 discrete characters result because two characters are found in both sets. Baudot code is uppercase only, and the characters are not in sequential numerical order: For example, A has a value of 24, B is 19, and C is 14.

ASCII—ASCII improves on Baudot code in several key ways. The use of seven data elements, or bits, allows ASCII to represent up to 128 discrete characters: 31 characters are reserved for such special functions as carriage return, backspace, and line feed, and 96 characters are reserved for the letters A through Z in upper- and lowercase, as well as numbers and punctuation marks. ASCII characters are in sequential order: A is 65, B is 66, C is 67, and so on. This facilitates computer manipulation of ASCII text and numbers.

EBCDIC—IBM's EBCDIC uses eight data bits, allowing it to represent 256 discrete characters and symbols, of which 63 characters are reserved for control functions. In this table, A is 193, B is 194, C is 195. However, EBCDIC is not sequential: Its character set—unlike ASCII's—does not follow sequential order. There are gaps between i and j and again between r and s.

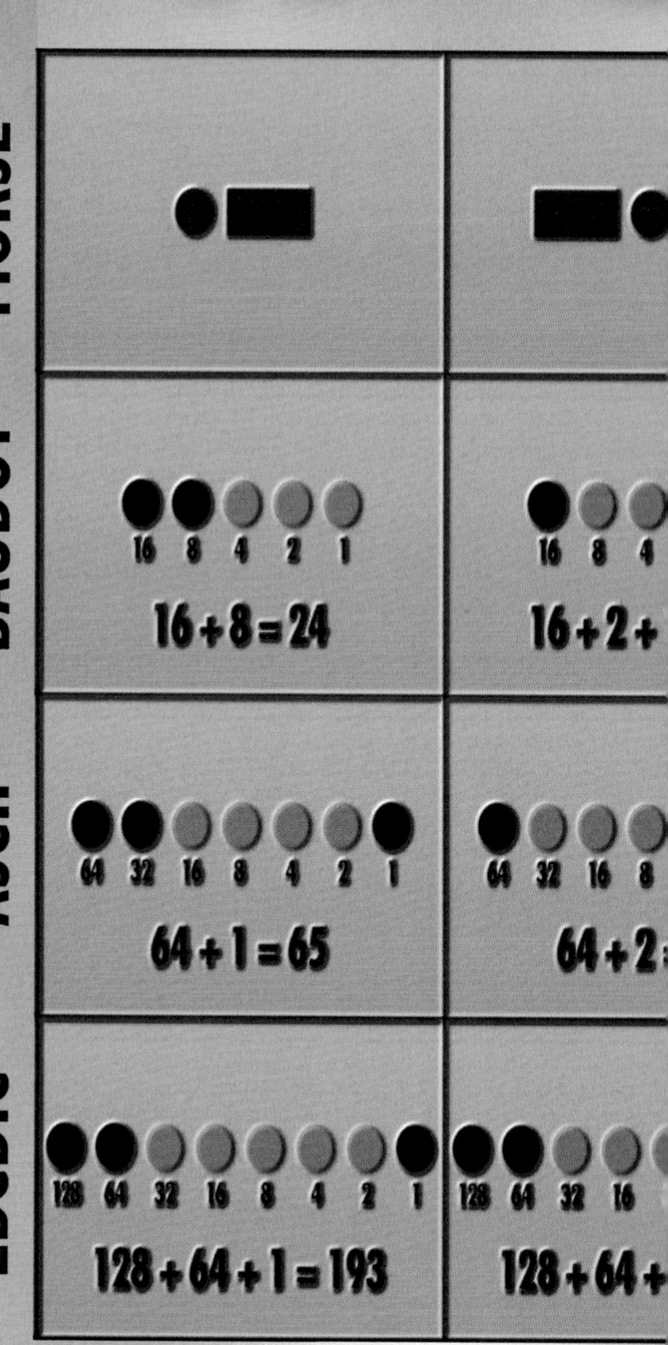
A
MORSE
BAUDOT
16 8 4 2 1
16+8=24
ASCII
64 32 16 8 4 2 1
64+1=65
EBCDIC
128 64 32 16 8 4 2 1
128+64+1=193

● On Bits ● Off Bits

	C	D	E	
	16 8 4 2 1 8+4+2=14	16 8 4 2 1 16+2=18	16 8 4 2 1 16=16	16 16+
1	64 32 16 8 4 2 1 64+2+1=67	64 32 16 8 4 2 1 64+4=68	64 32 16 8 4 2 1 64+4+1=69	64 32 64+
1	128 64 32 16 8 4 2 1 128+64+2+1=195	128 64 32 16 8 4 2 1 128+64+4=196	128 64 32 16 8 4 2 1 128+64+4+1=197	128 64 32 128+6

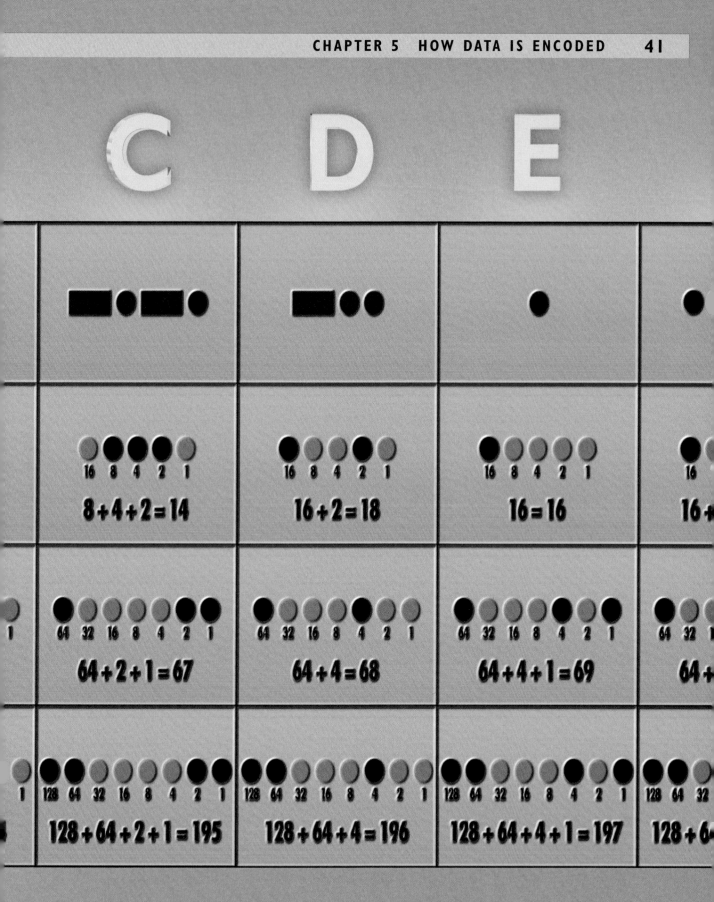

CHAPTER 6 How a Modem Works

RAM
ROM
ROM
Central Processing Unit

THE earliest electronic communications devices—the telegraph and teletypewriter—communicated with one another by exchanging pulsed direct current (DC) signals over a long wire. Modern-day computers and terminals use a much-improved version of this technique, as defined by the RS-232C, Universal Serial Bus (USB), and other serial data communications standards.

Telephones, in contrast, communicate by passing an analog audio signal over the line. The strength and frequency of the signal varies depending on the volume and pitch of the sound being sent. Because the telephone network is designed to carry voice signals, it cannot carry the DC signals used in computer communications.

As the use of computers spread in the late 1950s and early 1960s, a need arose to connect computers and terminals using ordinary telephone lines. AT&T's answer was the Bell 103 modem.

The Bell 103 modem operated at a speed of 300 bits per second. This is painfully slow by modern-day standards, but it was fast enough for the slow-printing terminals of the day. Because it allowed the terminal to be physically separated from the host computer, the modem made computing resources available from virtually anyplace.

The Bell 103 modem uses two pairs of tones to represent the on-and-off states of the RS-232C data line. One pair of tones is used by the modem originating the call, and the other pair is used by the modem answering the call. The modem sends data by switching between the two tones in each pair. The calling modem sends data by switching between 1,070 and 1,270 hertz, and the answering modem sends data by switching between 2,025 and 2,225 Hertz. Newer modems use more and different tones to convey information, but the basic principle remains the same.

Before the Bell system breakup in 1984, AT&T set virtually all modem standards. Bell Labs' engineers designed new modems, and AT&T's Western Electric division manufactured them. Bell licensed the 103 and 212a technology to other companies, but, with few exceptions, all new modem designs came from AT&T. After the breakup, AT&T was no longer in a position to dictate standards to the rest of the industry.

The Bell breakup coincided with the boom years in personal computer growth. By 1984, the personal computer industry was in the midst of a period of phenomenal growth, which began with the introduction of the IBM personal computer in late 1981. The personal computer explosion, coupled with the Bell breakup, presented some unique business opportunities for America's modem manufacturers.

The next major advance in modem technology was the development of the 2,400-bits-per-second modem in 1985. Until 1985, most modem technical standards had come from AT&T's Bell Labs. The 2,400bps standard was created by the CCITT—an industry standards-setting organization comprising members from hundreds of telecommunications companies worldwide. The new modem standard—designated V.22bis—was widely accepted and is still in use today.

The CCITT—now called the International Telecommunication Union-Telecommunication sector ITU-T)—continues to mediate industry standards for modems. Newer ITU-T standards include V.32 (9,600bps), V.32bis (14,400bps), V.34 (33,600bps), V.42 (error control), V.42bis (data compression), and V.90 (56,000bps). Virtually all modems in use today conform to one or more ITU-T standards, assuring compatibility between modems worldwide.

Today's 56,000bps V.90 and V.92 modems represent what is likely to be the end of the road for analog modem development. The laws of physics and the need to maintain compatibility with the existing telephone network represent an insurmountable roadblock to faster analog modems. As we'll see in Chapter 10, several other communication technologies offer faster, more reliable connections.

How a Modem Works

1 There are three distinct signal paths inside a modem. The first of these is the analog audio path, which begins and ends at the telephone line. Most modems—such as the one shown here—have two phone jacks. One jack connects to the phone line, and the other connects to your phone. When the modem is using the line, it disconnects the signal to the phone jack so that you don't pick up the phone and interrupt the modem. For this example, we'll follow the signal path from the phone line to the computer; data sent from the computer to the phone line takes an identical, but opposite, path.

2 Because a modem connects directly to a phone line, it contains an isolation transformer and other protective circuitry required to meet FCC and other regulatory agency standards for telephone devices. Most modems also include a lightning-arrestor circuit.

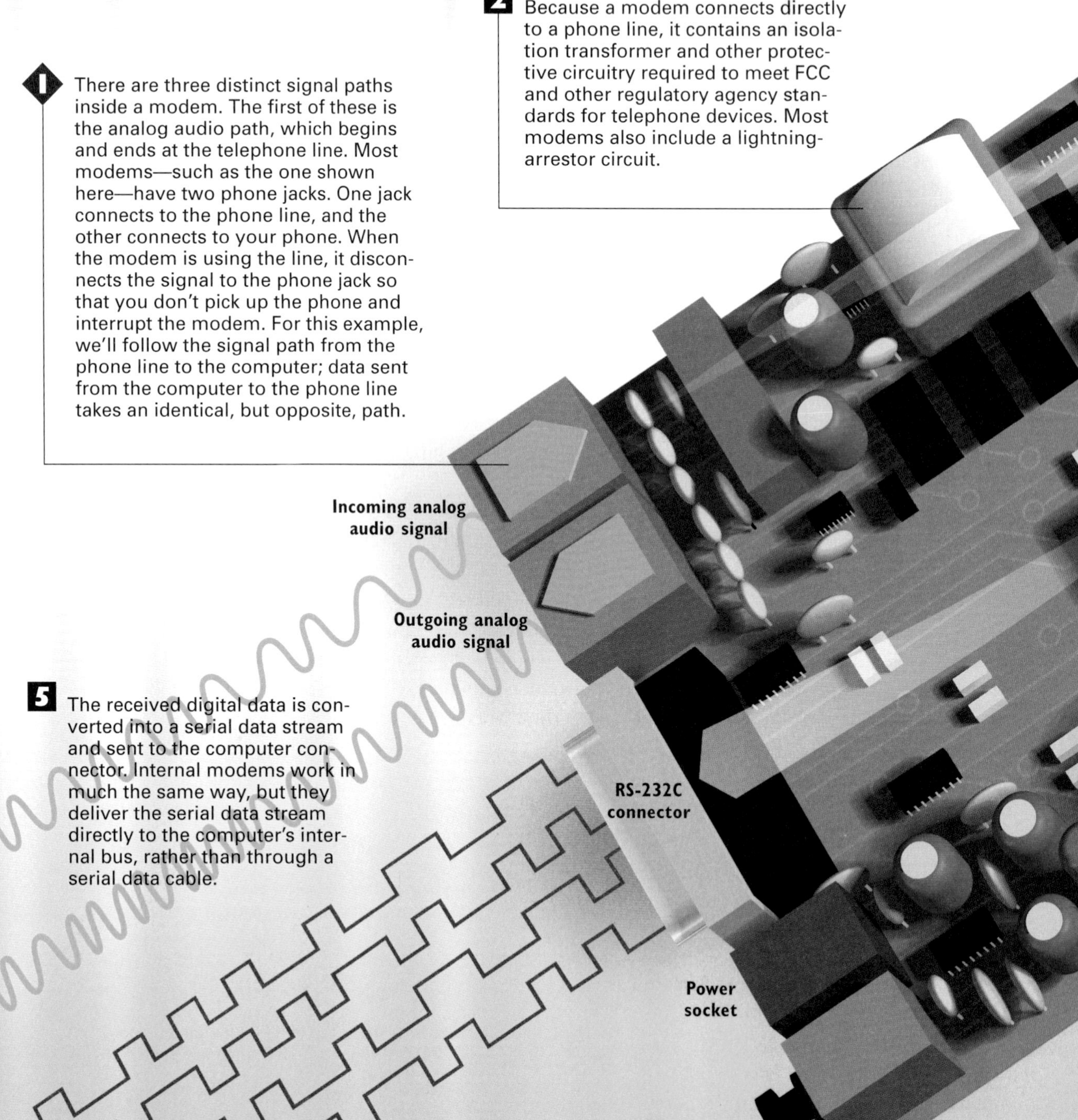
Incoming analog audio signal
Outgoing analog audio signal
RS-232C connector
Power socket
On/off button

5 The received digital data is converted into a serial data stream and sent to the computer connector. Internal modems work in much the same way, but they deliver the serial data stream directly to the computer's internal bus, rather than through a serial data cable.

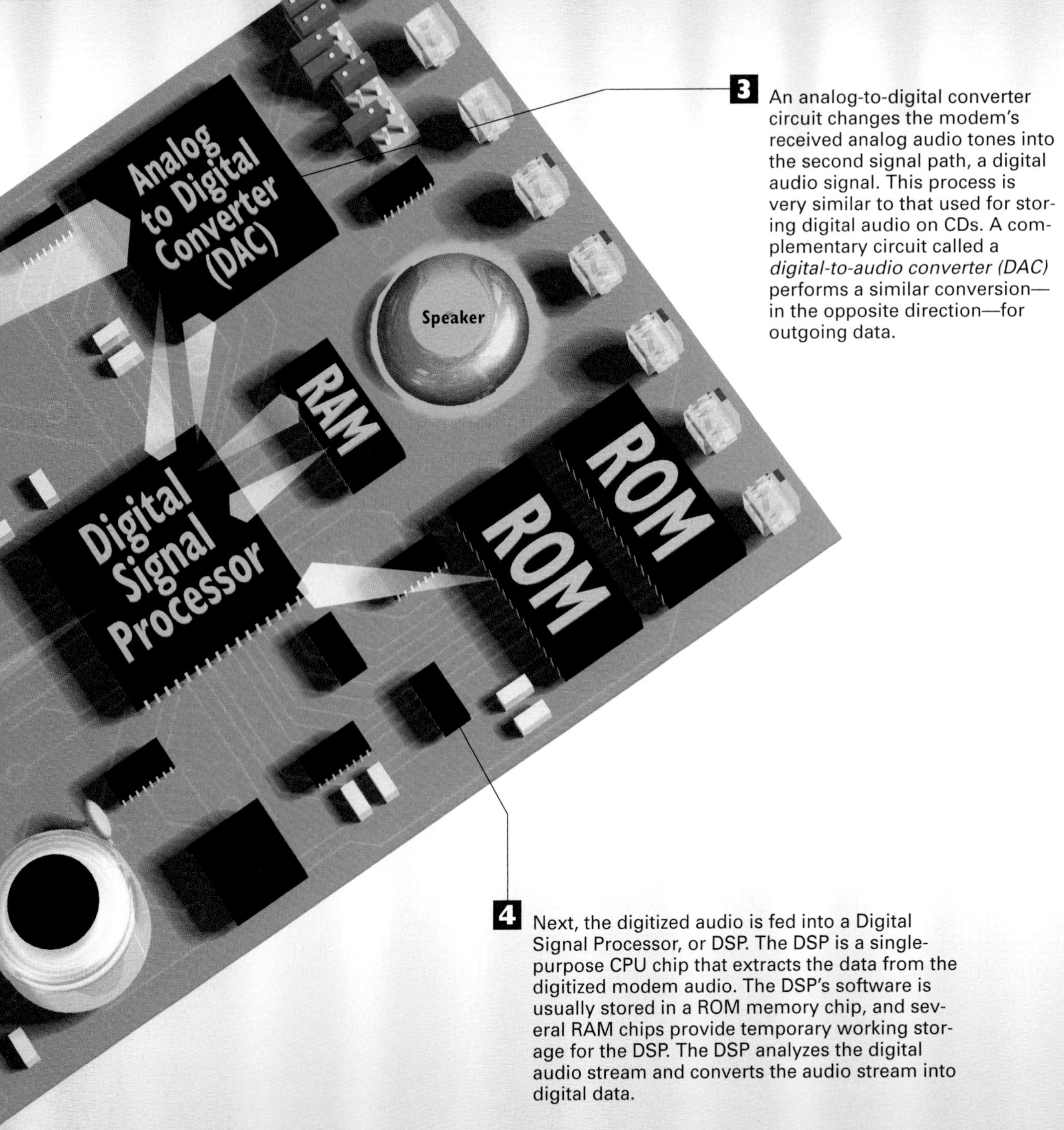
Analog to Digital Converter (DAC)
Speaker
RAM
Digital Signal Processor
ROM
ROM

3 An analog-to-digital converter circuit changes the modem's received analog audio tones into the second signal path, a digital audio signal. This process is very similar to that used for storing digital audio on CDs. A complementary circuit called a *digital-to-audio converter (DAC)* performs a similar conversion—in the opposite direction—for outgoing data.

4 Next, the digitized audio is fed into a Digital Signal Processor, or DSP. The DSP is a single-purpose CPU chip that extracts the data from the digitized modem audio. The DSP's software is usually stored in a ROM memory chip, and several RAM chips provide temporary working storage for the DSP. The DSP analyzes the digital audio stream and converts the audio stream into digital data.

How a Modem Connection Works

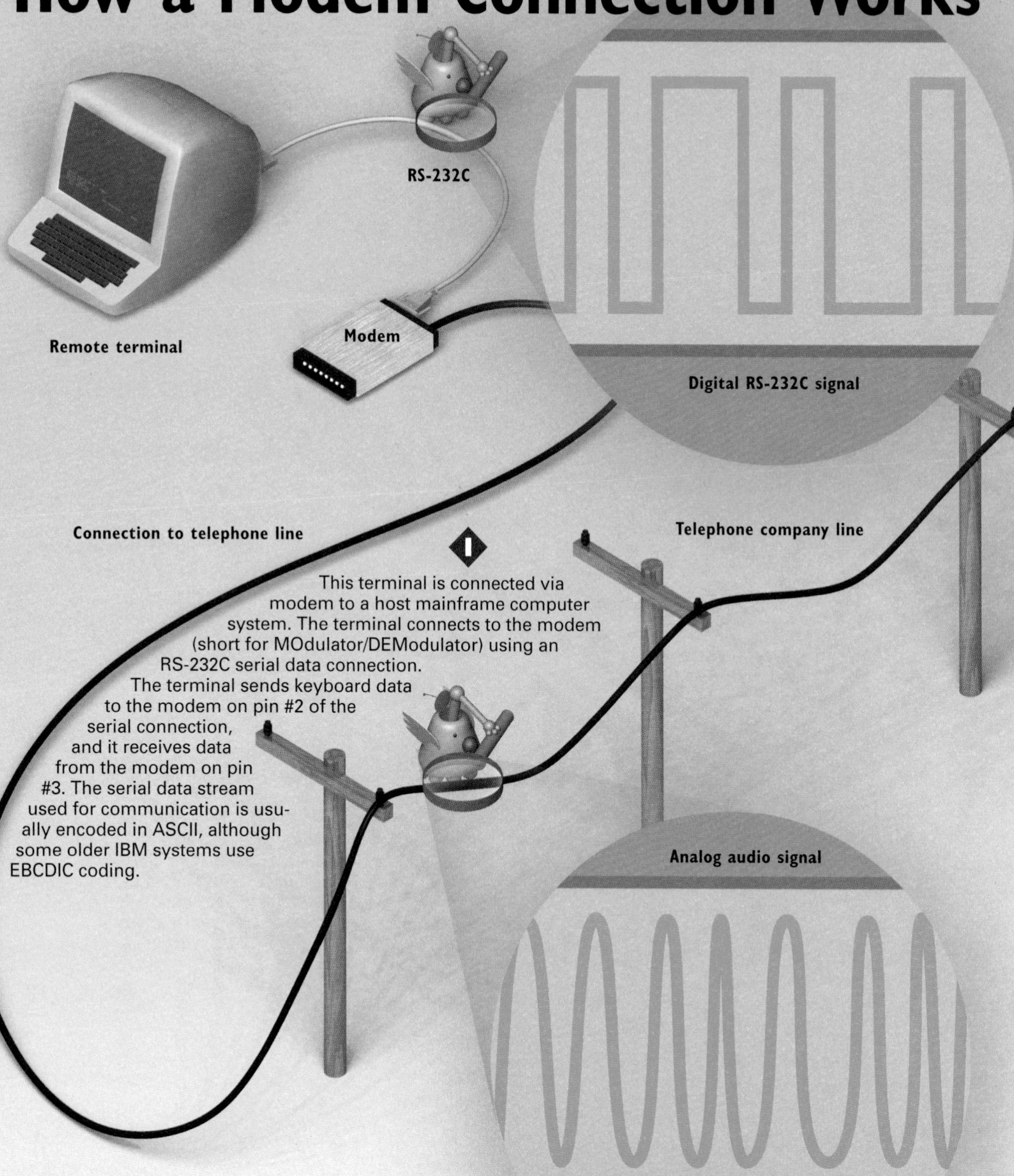
RS-232C
Remote terminal
Modem
Digital RS-232C signal
Connection to telephone line
Telephone company line
Analog audio signal

1 This terminal is connected via modem to a host mainframe computer system. The terminal connects to the modem (short for MOdulator/DEModulator) using an RS-232C serial data connection. The terminal sends keyboard data to the modem on pin #2 of the serial connection, and it receives data from the modem on pin #3. The serial data stream used for communication is usually encoded in ASCII, although some older IBM systems use EBCDIC coding.

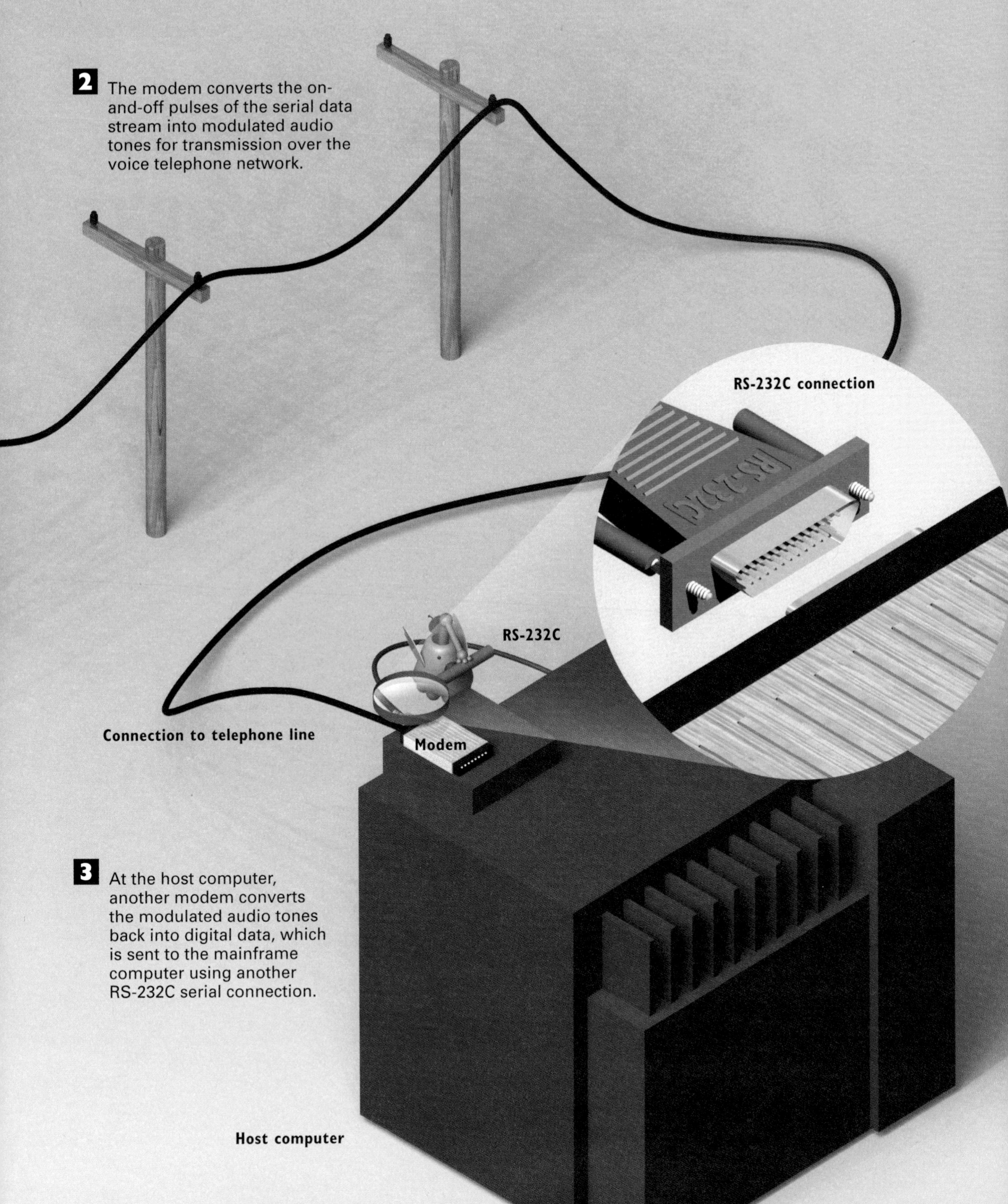
2 The modem converts the on-and-off pulses of the serial data stream into modulated audio tones for transmission over the voice telephone network.
RS-232C connection
RS-232C
Connection to telephone line
Modem
3 At the host computer, another modem converts the modulated audio tones back into digital data, which is sent to the mainframe computer using another RS-232C serial connection.
Host computer

CHAPTER 7 How a Remote Terminal Works

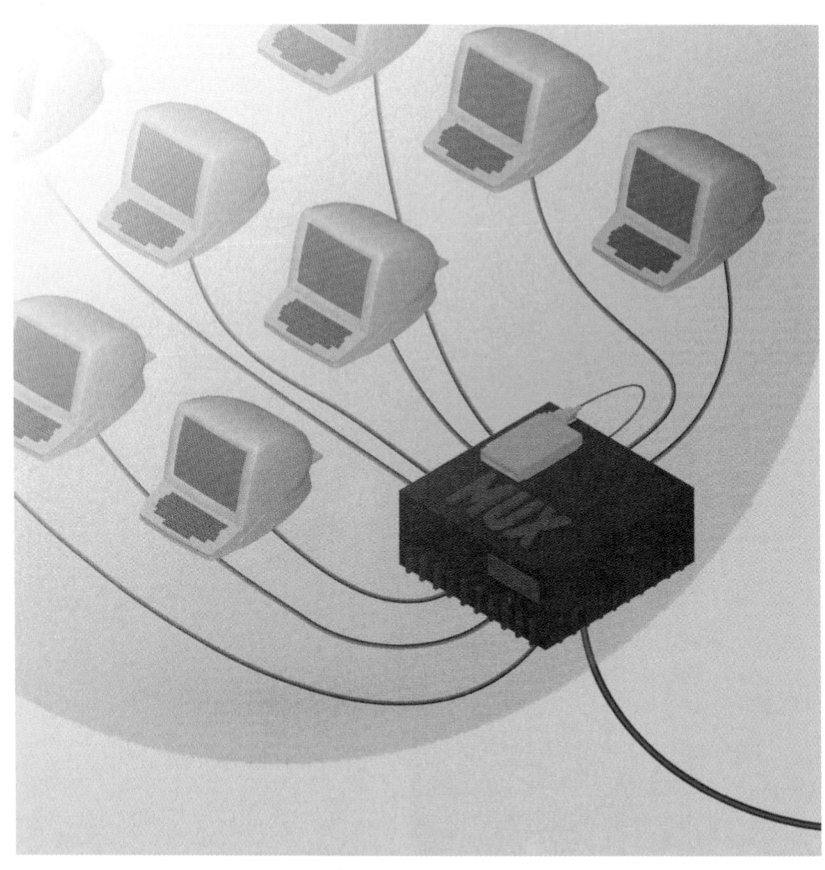
MUX

EARLY computer systems were very large and very expensive. A typical mainframe computer cost millions of dollars and required several hundred square feet of specially air-conditioned office space. In addition to the hardware, early computers required a full-time staff of programmers and technicians to keep them running. Despite the enormous costs involved, thousands of businesses and universities installed mainframe computer systems in the 1960s and 1970s. Many of those systems are still in use today.

One of the major developments of the 1960s in computing technology was the concept of time-sharing. A time-sharing system allows more than one user—often as many as several hundred—to use the same computer simultaneously. Users could run their own programs, and each user interacted with the computer using a terminal. Most of these early mainframe terminals were mechanical teletypewriter units. By the mid-1970s, the video display terminal (VDT) had replaced printing terminals for many applications. Because VDTs often replaced aging teletypewriters, they became known as "glass Teletypes."

In most multiterminal systems, the terminals connected directly to the host computer using a cable. IBM, in typical IBM style, devised its own proprietary system to connect terminals to host computers. This move meant that IBM computers could communicate only with IBM terminals—so users had to buy all of their computers and terminals from IBM. However, other manufacturers, including Digital Equipment Corporation, Data General, and Honeywell, used RS-232C connections between the host and the terminals. And for users located away from the main computer site, terminals equipped with modems could be used to access the host computer. These connections then allowed terminals to move out of the computer room and onto users' desktops.

This seemingly simple relocation had a huge effect on the way people used computers. By allowing hundreds of users to share the same computer system, the cost per user spiraled downward. Suddenly, it made economic sense to use computers for such mundane tasks as accounting, classroom scheduling, and even word processing. Before time sharing, computing was the domain of very large corporations and research institutions. By reducing the cost per user, mainframe computers became affordable for many smaller companies and colleges.

The development of the microprocessor and the accompanying personal computer explosion of the late 1970s began a trend away from terminals and toward desktop computing. In effect, the computing power moved out of the mainframe computer room and onto the users' desktops. As PCs became cheaper and more powerful, it appeared that mainframe computers and the whole idea of a central processing unit were dead.

But in the late 1980s, a new type of time sharing arrived on the scene. A new breed of shared computers called *Application Servers* enables several users to offload specialized tasks onto a shared computer. In effect, these systems do exactly what the time-sharing systems did—they rely on one centralized processor to perform a specific task.

How Host Computers and Terminals Work

Terminal
Statistical Multiplexer (stat mux)
MUX
Leased line

1. A typical mainframe system can accommodate hundreds of users at once. Local users—those users located in the immediate area of the computer system—use terminals connected directly to the host computer system.

2. Branch offices with more than a few terminals employ a device called a *statistical multiplexer*, or *stat mux*. The mux device combines the data traveling to and from several terminals into a single data stream. The multiplexed data stream is connected to a modem, which in turn is connected to a leased phone line. Another mux at the host computer end of the connection separates the data to and from each remote terminal.

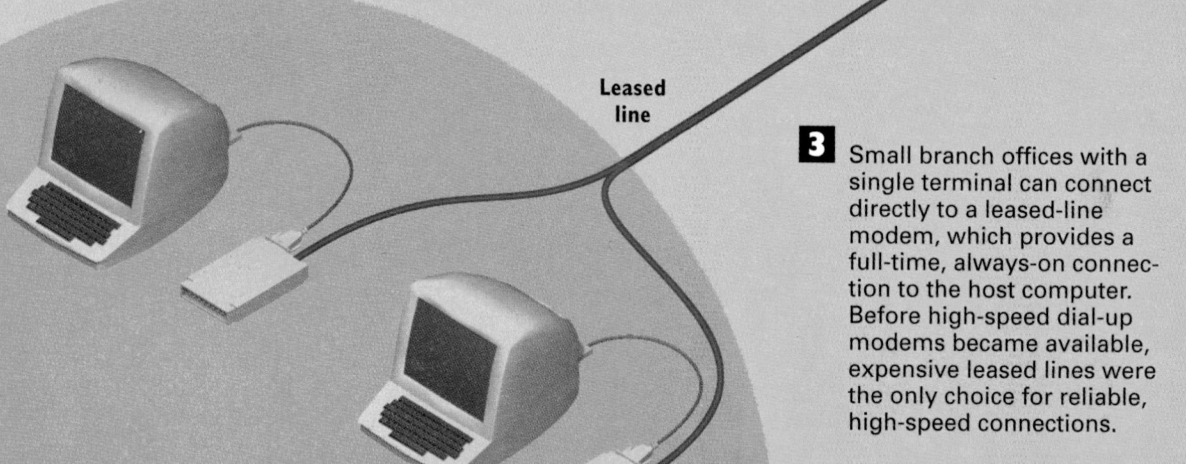
Leased line

3. Small branch offices with a single terminal can connect directly to a leased-line modem, which provides a full-time, always-on connection to the host computer. Before high-speed dial-up modems became available, expensive leased lines were the only choice for reliable, high-speed connections.

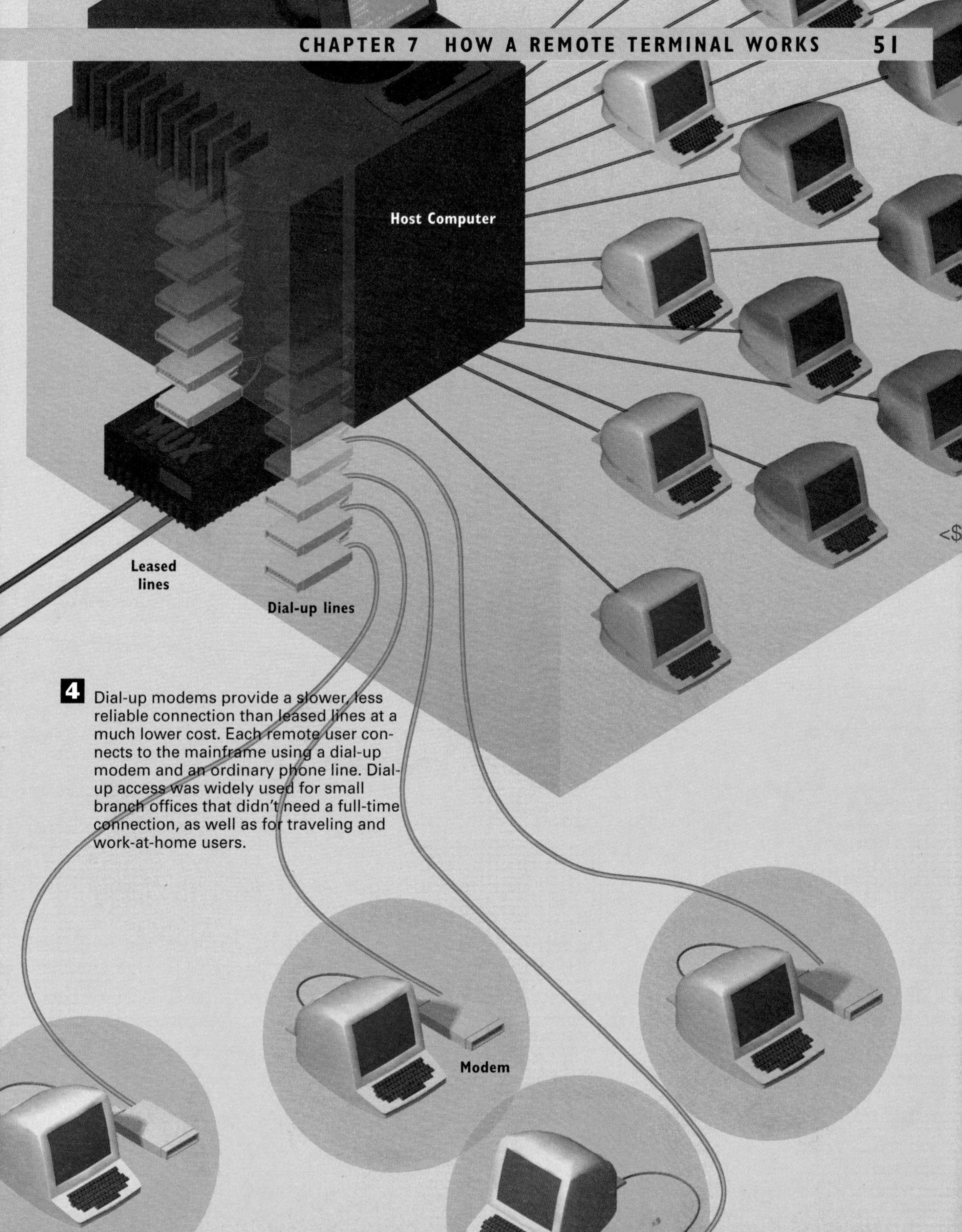
Host Computer
MUX
Leased lines
Dial-up lines
Modem

4 Dial-up modems provide a slower, less reliable connection than leased lines at a much lower cost. Each remote user connects to the mainframe using a dial-up modem and an ordinary phone line. Dial-up access was widely used for small branch offices that didn't need a full-time connection, as well as for traveling and work-at-home users.

CHAPTER

8

How Serial Communication Works

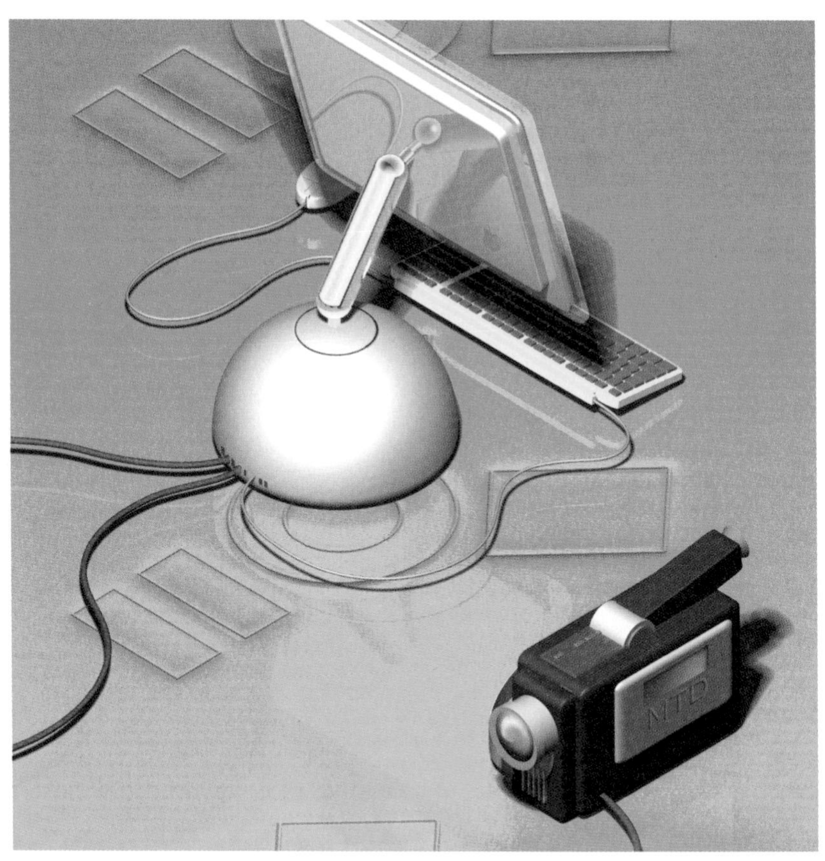

THE earliest electronic communications devices—the telegraph and teletypewriter—communicated by switching on and off voltage on a wire. The voltage used varied according to the equipment in use and the length of the wire involved. The circuit between two machines typically allowed communication in one direction at a time.

Modern high-speed data communications equipment still operates on the principle of switching voltage on and off, but many improvements have been made to the basic communications circuit. Today's RS-232C, Universal Serial Bus (USB), and IEEE 1394 (also called *FireWire*) connections all use a series of on-and-off pulses to send data over a wire.

RS-232C

In 1969, the Electronics Industries Association (EIA) created a standard to define the electrical signaling and cable connection characteristics of a serial port. In an attempt to ensure that one serial device will talk to another, the EIA established Recommended Standard (RS) number 232 in version C, or RS-232C, one of the most common types of communications circuits in use today. The ASCII character set defines what numbers to use for each character, and the RS-232C standard defines a way to move the data over a communications link.

Although it is most commonly used with ASCII characters, RS-232C can also be used to transmit Baudot or EBCDIC data. The RS-232C standard defines the function of the signals in the serial interface, as well as the physical connection used by the interface. This standard defines two classes of serial connections: one for terminals, or Data Terminal Equipment (DTE), and one for communications equipment, or Data Communications Equipment (DCE). A DTE device usually connects to a DCE device.

For example, a personal computer (DTE) can connect to a modem (DCE). The serial port on most personal computers is configured as a DTE port. A standard RS-232C connection normally uses a 25-pin D-shell connector with a male plug on the DTE end and a female plug on the DCE end. This connector is large and bulky, and it contains many connections that aren't necessary for a typical PC-to-modem connection. Most PCs use a smaller, 9-pin connector that eliminates the unnecessary connection.

RS-232C has two major shortcomings. First, it was designed in an era when high-speed devices operated at 9,600 bits per second. Although RS-232C devices can operate at speeds of up to 115,200bps, it can operate at these speeds over only a very short distance. RS-232C worked well enough for relatively slow devices such as modems and printers, but it's too slow to be practical for moving large files, such as those used by digital cameras, photo scanners, and color graphic printers.

Second, despite the complexity of the connection and the large number (nine) of wires needed to make a connection, RS-232C can connect only two devices to each other. If you needed to connect an RS-232C serial printer, mouse, and modem to your computer, you'd need three RS-232C ports on your computer—and three cables to connect the devices.

Faster Serial Connections: USB and FireWire

Two new types of serial interface called *Universal Serial Bus (USB)* and *IEEE 1394*, or *FireWire*, pick up where RS-232C left off. USB and FireWire are serial data communications standards, but the similarity to RS-232C ends there. RS-232C connections provide for two-way interaction between two and only two devices. USB and FireWire can connect dozens of devices to a single computer at once. FireWire supports up to 62 simultaneous connections; USB allows up to 127 devices to share a single connection.

USB and FireWire use smaller cables and connectors than RS-232C, making them easier to handle. Because of their high data speeds, USB and FireWire require very high-quality cable, so the cables themselves are relatively expensive.

Universal Serial Bus

USB devices operate at speeds up to 480Mbps, or about 400 times the speed of the fastest RS-232C connection. As the name infers, the USB connection is a bus; that is, it can connect more than one device (up to 127) at one time. USB connectors are smaller, easier to connect, and use thinner wire than bulky RS-232C cables. USB connections can be hot-plugged, which enables users to connect and disconnect devices without turning off the power or resetting the host computer.

The four-wire USB cable interface uses only two wires for data; the other two wires provide power to small devices such as computer mice, webcams, and modems. This reduces the need for external power supplies and eliminates the need to have separate power cables for each USB-connected device. Larger USB devices such as printers and scanners typically provide their own power.

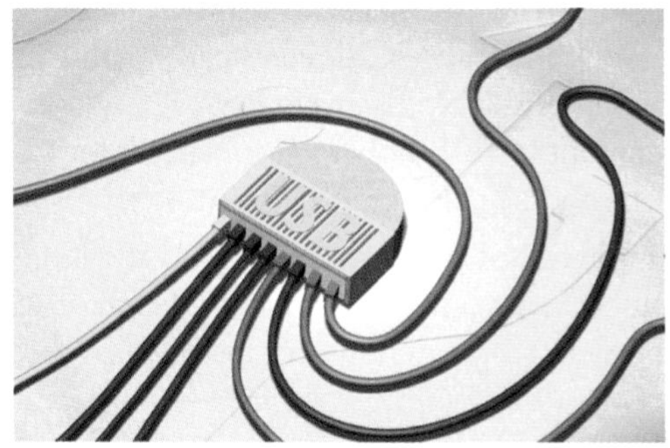
USB

There are thousands of USB devices on the market today, including everything from mice and keyboards to scanners, printers, digital cameras, and modems. USB's small, simple connector, fast transfer speed, and multiple-device capabilities have all but replaced RS-232C in most computing applications. Some computer manufacturers have already eliminated the RS-232C serial interface from their products.

There are two versions of USB in wide use. The original USB 1.1 specification supports speeds up to 12Mbps; the newer USB 2.0 operates at 480Mbps. USB 2.0 provides backward compatibility for USB 1.1 devices, so you can connect USB 1.1 and USB 2.0 devices to the same computer.

FireWire/IEEE 1394/iLink

Like USB, FireWire (also known as IEEE 1394 and Sony iLink) was designed to be a faster, better replacement for serial communications devices. FireWire was originally developed by Apple Computer and Sony Corporation, but the company turned the specification over to the Institute of Electrical and Electronics Engineers (IEEE) to make FireWire an industry standard.

FireWire operates at speeds up to 400Mbps. When it was originally developed in 1995, FireWire was 30 times faster than USB 1.1. USB 2.0, introduced in 2001, increased USB's speed to 480Mbps, so the two technologies are comparable in speed.

Because FireWire was initially much faster than USB, many consumer electronics companies—notably Sony, Canon, and Nikon—adopted FireWire as a way to move video and large digital still images between cameras and PCs. FireWire can also be used to connect external devices such as CD-ROM drives, hard drives, and memory card readers to PCs and Mac computers.

FireWire can also be used to create a small LAN. Microsoft Windows 2000 and Windows XP support FireWire LAN connections. FireWire can operate only over relatively short cables, so it isn't suitable for a buildingwide LAN. Because of its high speed and simple cabling, FireWire is ideal for moving large amounts of data from one computer to another.

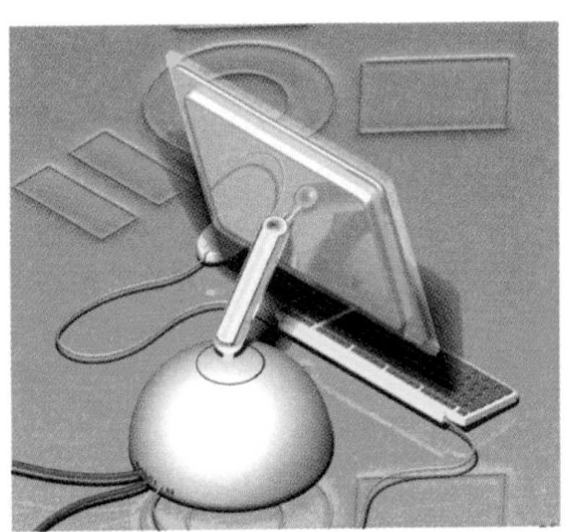

How RS-232C Works

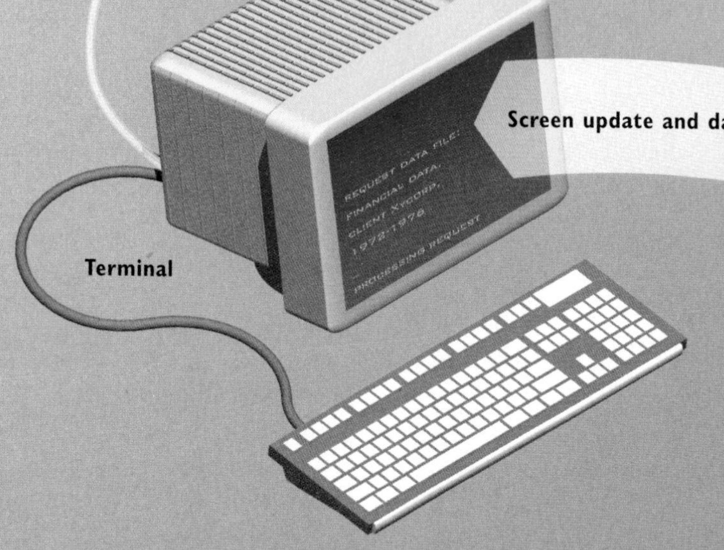
Screen update and data
REQUEST DATA FILE:
FINANCIAL DATA,
CLIENT XYCORP,
1972-1976
PROCESSING REQUEST
Terminal

1. Although it uses a very complex cable and connector, RS-232C is actually very simple.

2. The most important part of the RS-232C connection is the data path. There are two data circuits, one in each direction. Terminal devices (such as a PC) transmit data on pin 2; host computer devices transmit data on pin 3.

3. Signals on pins 4 and 6 let the computer and terminal device tell each other that they are present and powered on. The Data Terminal Ready signal (pin 4) tells the computer that the terminal is connected, and the Data Set Ready signal on pin 6 lets the terminal know that the computer is connected.

DTE connector
(terminal)
RS-232C
1 2 3 4 5
6 7 8 9
RS-232C
DCE connector
(host computer)

4 Two additional signals called *Request to Send* (pin 7) and *Clear to Send* (pin 8) allow the computer and terminal to temporarily stop the flow of data. These signals prevent the computer from sending data before the terminal is ready to receive it and vice versa.

RS-232C cable junction
Data request

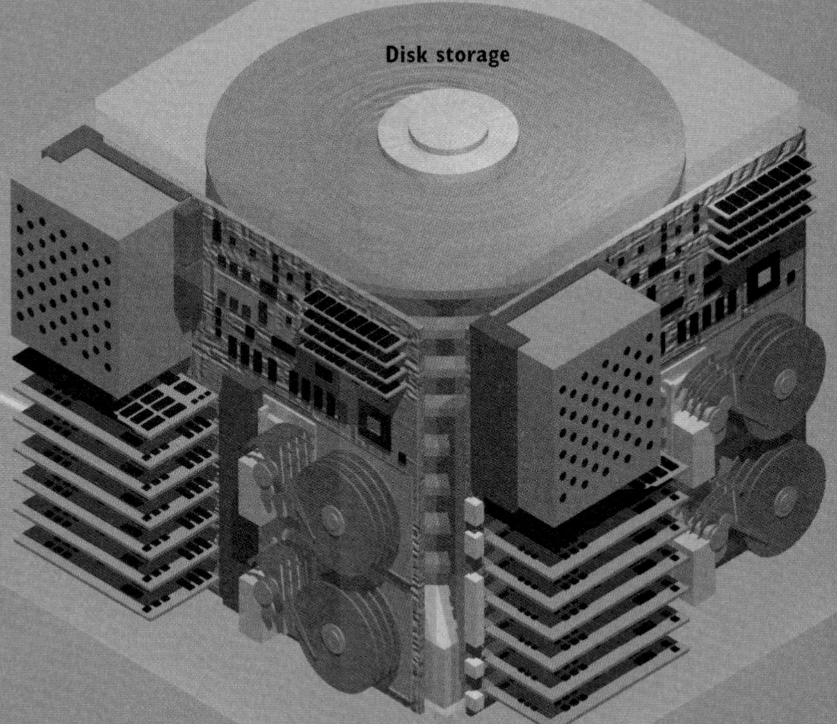
Host computer
Disk storage
Network interface cards

5 The Ring Indicator signal on pin 9 is used in modem-to-computer connections. As the name infers, this signal tells the computer that the phone line attached to the modem is ringing.

How USB Works

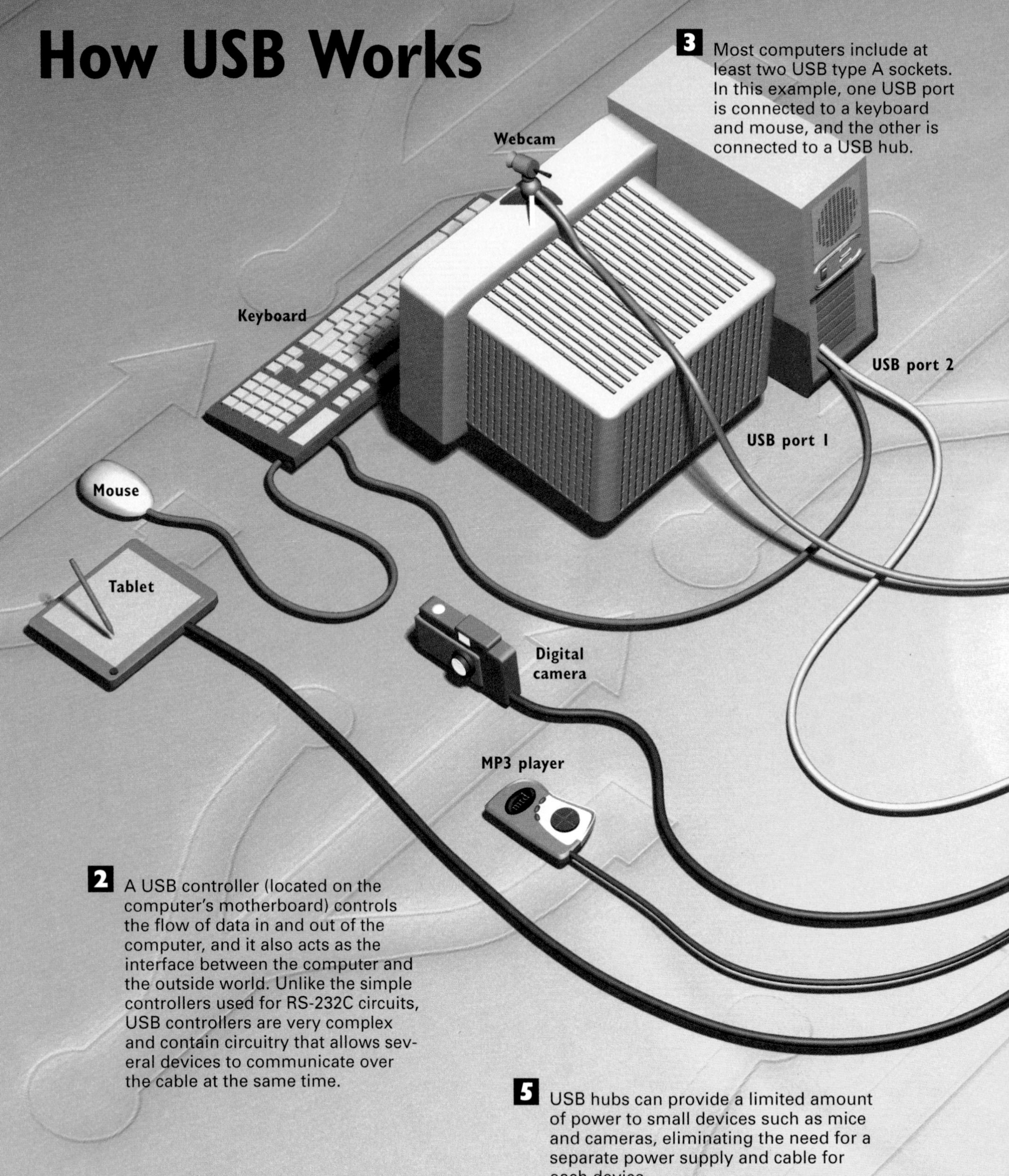
Webcam
Keyboard
USB port 2
USB port 1
Mouse
Tablet
Digital camera
MP3 player

3 Most computers include at least two USB type A sockets. In this example, one USB port is connected to a keyboard and mouse, and the other is connected to a USB hub.

2 A USB controller (located on the computer's motherboard) controls the flow of data in and out of the computer, and it also acts as the interface between the computer and the outside world. Unlike the simple controllers used for RS-232C circuits, USB controllers are very complex and contain circuitry that allows several devices to communicate over the cable at the same time.

5 USB hubs can provide a limited amount of power to small devices such as mice and cameras, eliminating the need for a separate power supply and cable for each device.

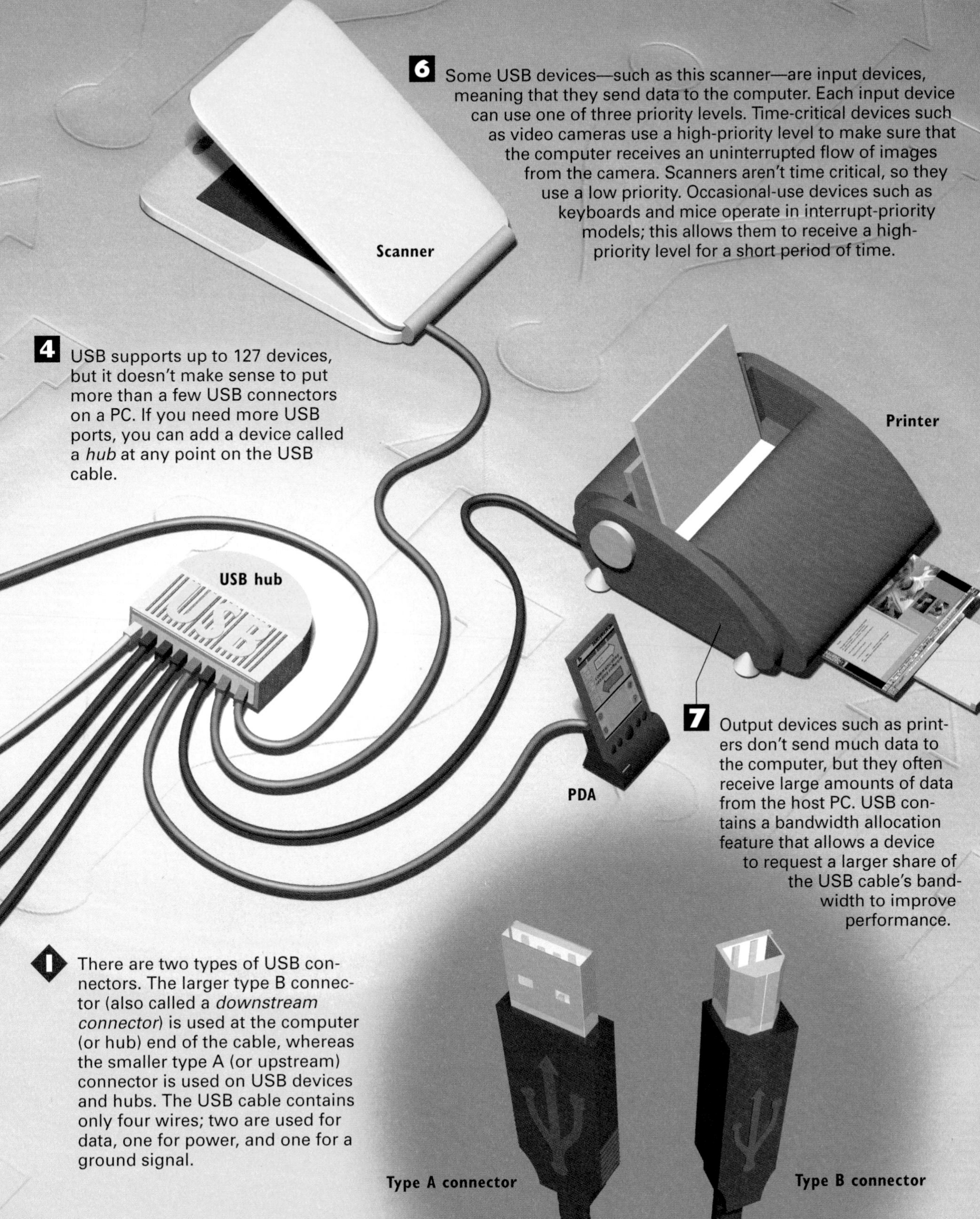
Scanner
Printer
USB hub
PDA
Type A connector
Type B connector

6 Some USB devices—such as this scanner—are input devices, meaning that they send data to the computer. Each input device can use one of three priority levels. Time-critical devices such as video cameras use a high-priority level to make sure that the computer receives an uninterrupted flow of images from the camera. Scanners aren't time critical, so they use a low priority. Occasional-use devices such as keyboards and mice operate in interrupt-priority models; this allows them to receive a high-priority level for a short period of time.

4 USB supports up to 127 devices, but it doesn't make sense to put more than a few USB connectors on a PC. If you need more USB ports, you can add a device called a *hub* at any point on the USB cable.

7 Output devices such as printers don't send much data to the computer, but they often receive large amounts of data from the host PC. USB contains a bandwidth allocation feature that allows a device to request a larger share of the USB cable's bandwidth to improve performance.

1 There are two types of USB connectors. The larger type B connector (also called a *downstream connector*) is used at the computer (or hub) end of the cable, whereas the smaller type A (or upstream) connector is used on USB devices and hubs. The USB cable contains only four wires; two are used for data, one for power, and one for a ground signal.

PC

How FireWire Works

4 Digital Video requires large amounts of data storage, so FireWire-connected hard drives have become very popular. Unlike slower USB 1.1 drives, external FireWire drives operate at speeds comparable to a computer's internal hard drive.

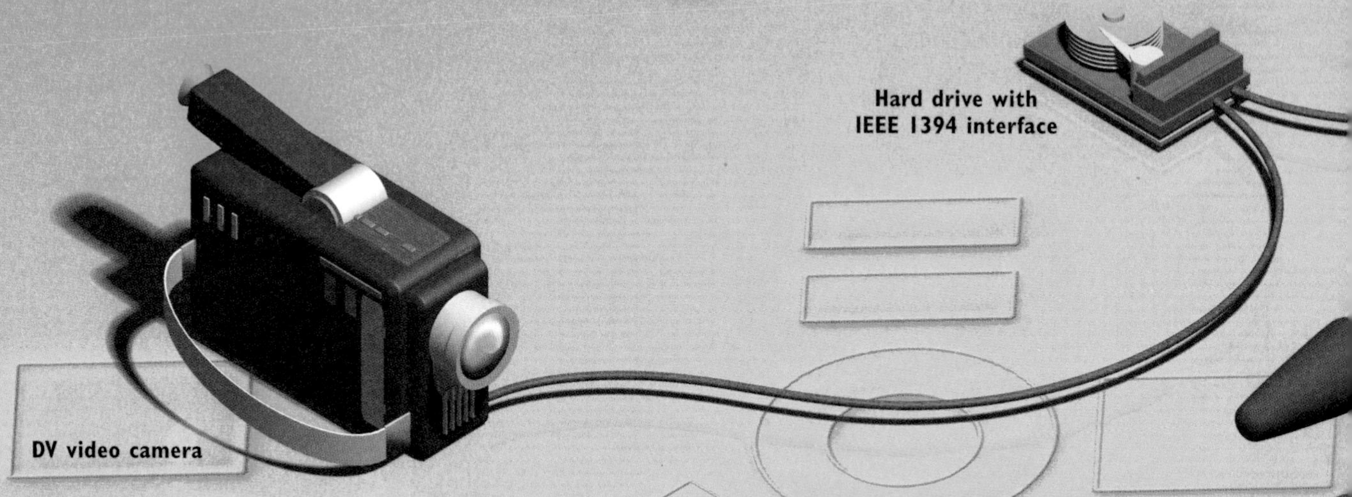

2 FireWire is a peer-to-peer connection technology, so it can be used to connect two or more PCs into a small LAN. In this example, two computers are sharing an external hard drive and a DV video camera.

3 FireWire is widely used to connect digital camcorders and still cameras to PCs. FireWire's fast transfer speed makes it possible to transfer very large digital video files from cameras into PCs for editing.

Hard drive with IEEE 1394 interface

DV video camera

5 FireWire's uses aren't limited to computers. Digital camcorder users can use FireWire to connect two camcorders together without a PC. This arrangement allows users to make copies of digital video files with no loss of quality.

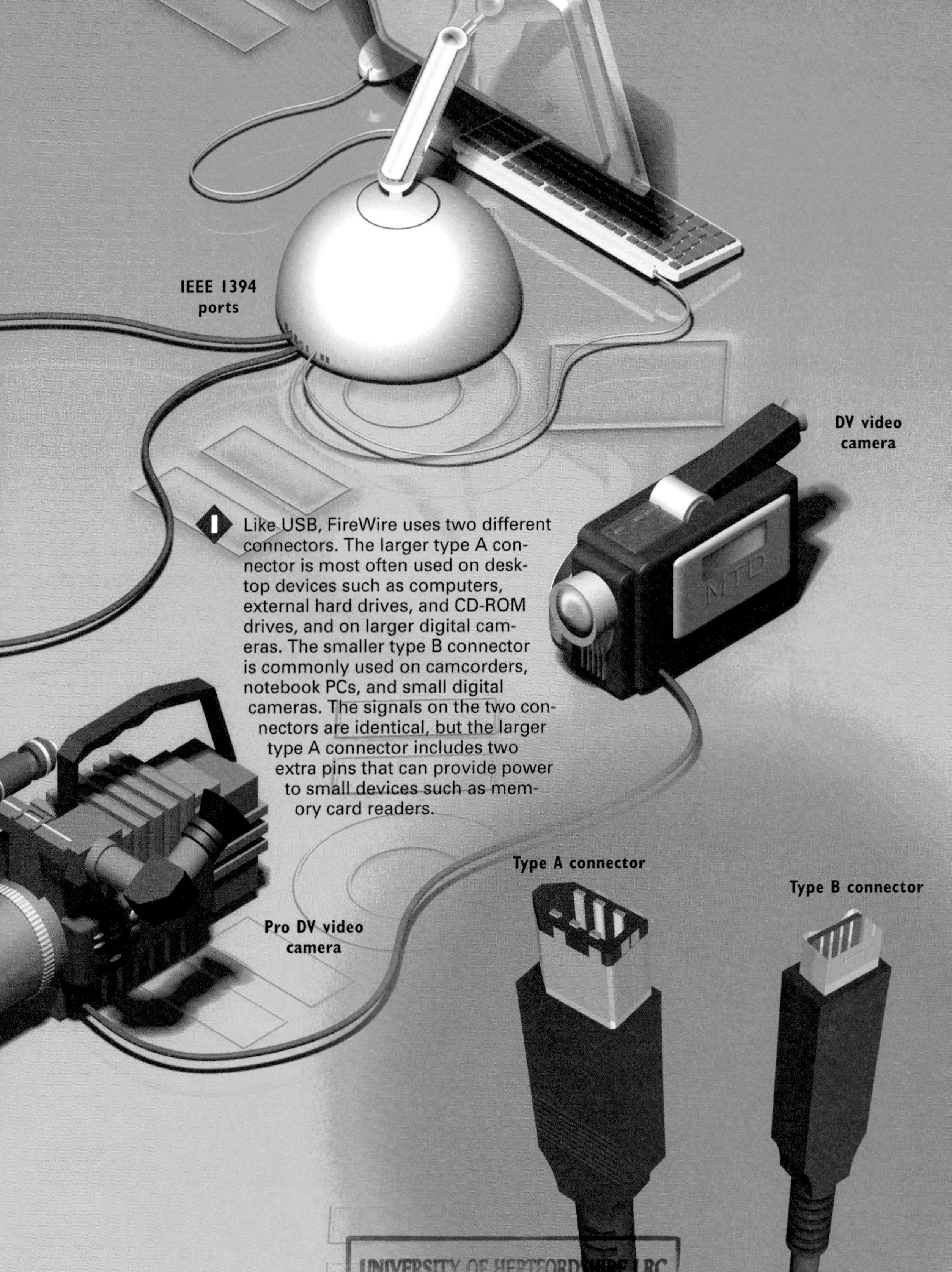
IEEE 1394 ports
DV video camera
Pro DV video camera
Type A connector
Type B connector
MTD

1 Like USB, FireWire uses two different connectors. The larger type A connector is most often used on desktop devices such as computers, external hard drives, and CD-ROM drives, and on larger digital cameras. The smaller type B connector is commonly used on camcorders, notebook PCs, and small digital cameras. The signals on the two connectors are identical, but the larger type A connector includes two extra pins that can provide power to small devices such as memory card readers.

CHAPTER 9 The PC As a Terminal

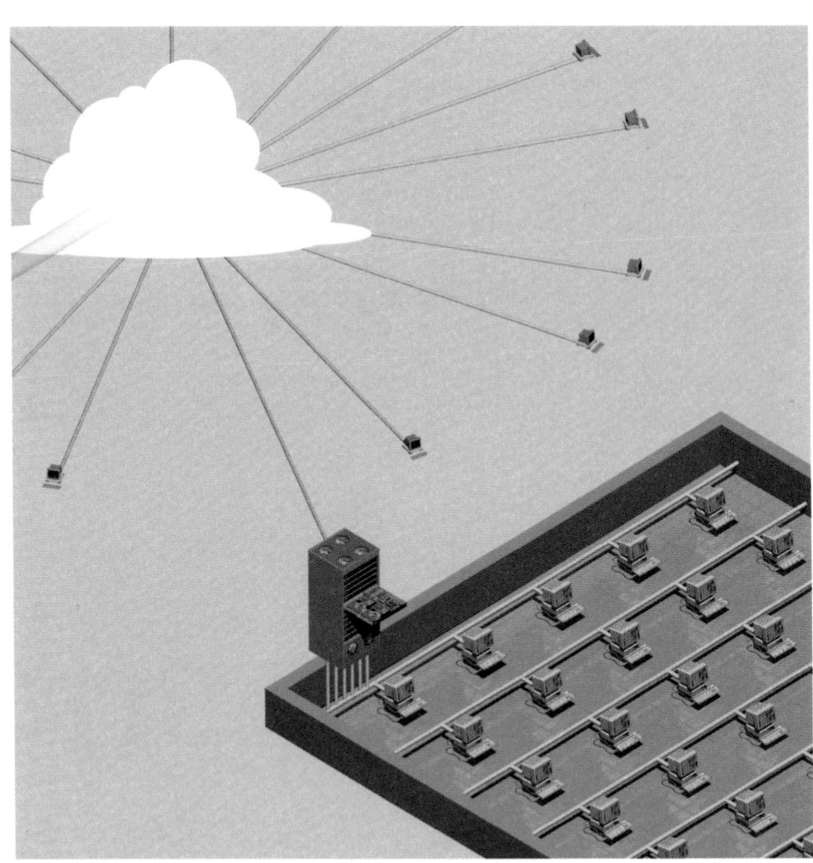

UNLIKE a personal computer, a computer terminal can't do anything unless it is connected to a host computer. When connected, the terminal displays incoming data on the video screen and sends keyboard input to the host computer. Communication with the host computer takes place through the serial interface. The central computer does all the work, and the remote terminals provide a way for users to communicate with the central computer. This type of system is called a *Shared Processor* system.

Personal computers first appeared on the scene in the late 1970s. In many cases, those early personal computers were purchased by medium and large companies, most of which already had a larger computer system. At first, these computers were used as standalone systems; thousands of them were purchased just to run one application such as Lotus 1-2-3, VisiCalc, or WordPerfect.

Today, personal computers are routinely used as the access point to the company's mainframe or minicomputer system. Rather than placing both a personal computer and a terminal on everyone's desk, many companies have retired their terminals and replaced them with computers. With the proper communications software, a personal computer can perform all the functions of a terminal.

Today's desktop PCs have as much or more processing power as the mainframe and minicomputer systems of 10 years ago. As a result, many companies have retired their mainframe and minicomputer systems and replaced them with networks of personal computers. Instead of sharing one large, powerful, and expensive processor on the mainframe, networked systems—also called *distributed computing* systems—spread the computing workload among the PCs on the network. Each PC operates independently of the others, yet any PC can share files, printers, and other resources with the other computers on the network. We'll take a more detailed look at networked computing in Part 3.

Distributed processing systems have many advantages; the most important is that they're often cheaper than a central processor system. They're also more reliable in many ways because no one component is essential to the system's operation. However, distributed systems have their own problems. Because they share the work among dozens or hundreds of PCs, distributed systems require a great deal more maintenance than a central processor system. Networked PCs are often difficult to maintain; each new operating system and application software release must be installed on each and every PC on the network. PCs are also susceptible to computer viruses and user configuration problems, resulting in costly service calls.

In a back-to-the-future effort to blend the best of the distributed and centralized computing worlds, two new computing models have evolved. The thin client and Application Service Provider (ASP) computing models are variations on a similar theme.

Thin Clients—Instead of putting a complete computer on every user's desk, thin client computers provide users with a bare-bones computer with no hard disk, floppy drive, or CD-ROM drive. Network computers must load all their applications over a LAN from a network server, and all work must be saved onto the server's hard drive.

Thin client computing is a hybrid of distributed and centralized computing models. By storing all the programs and data on a central server, network administrators regain control over their organizations' computing resources. Because users can't install programs on their own machines, they can run only authorized software—this greatly reduces the risk of computer viruses. By eliminating local storage, thin clients also provide enhanced data security, because users can't make floppy or CD-ROM copies of files.

Application Service Providers—Despite continually lower computer equipment costs, many large organizations have found their computing costs spiraling out of control. Although the cost of computer hardware continues to fall, many Information Technology directors have found it hard to justify the cost of installing and maintaining a network of PCs.

Application Service Providers (ASPs) attack the cost of ownership issue by providing a complete suite of computing services that a company can purchase on an outsourced basis. An ASP provides client companies with the hardware and software necessary to operate their business, but the ASP's computers and storage equipment are located at the ASP's business location.

PCs As Terminals

The Mainframe Model

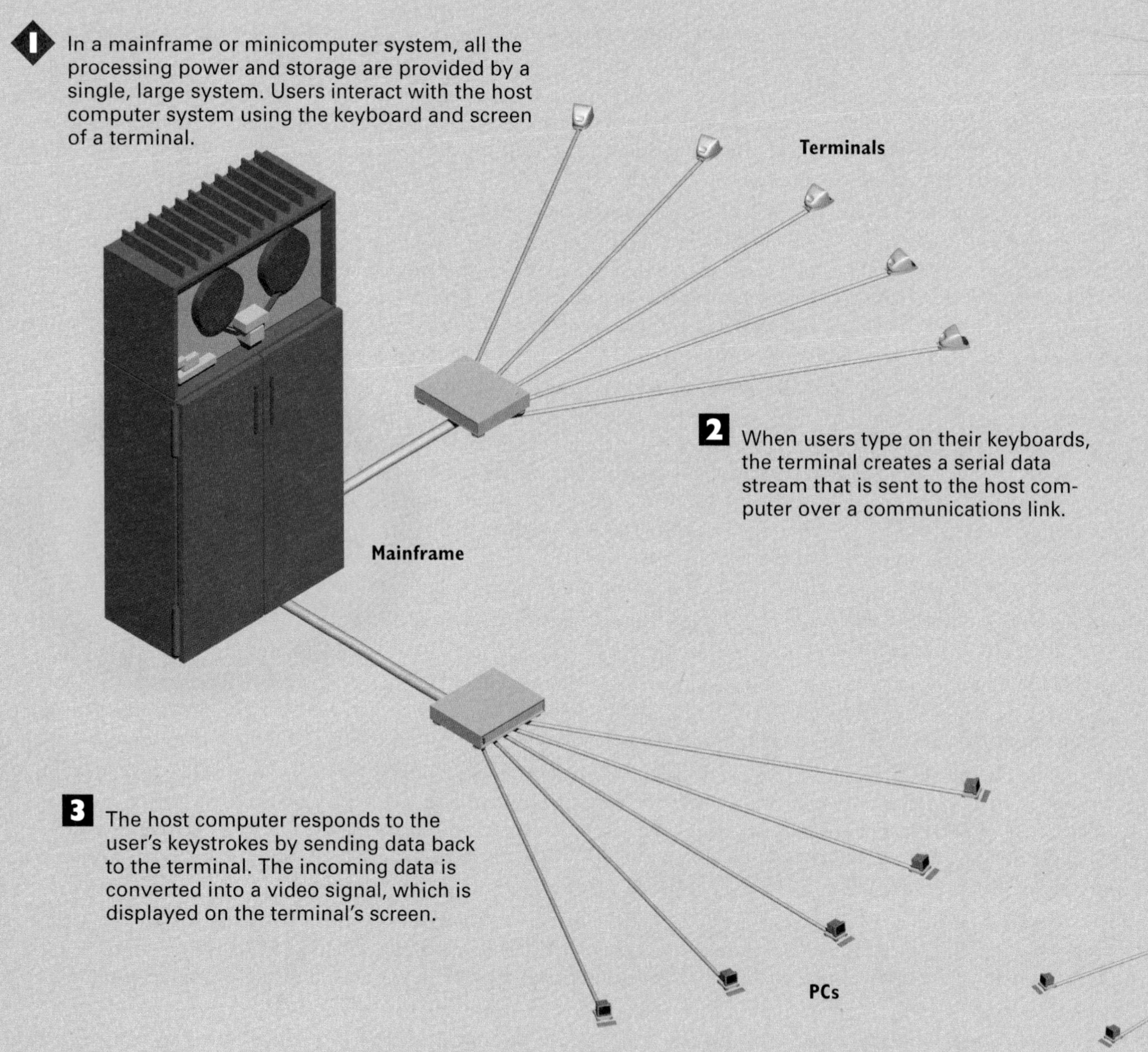
Terminals
Mainframe
PCs

1. In a mainframe or minicomputer system, all the processing power and storage are provided by a single, large system. Users interact with the host computer system using the keyboard and screen of a terminal.

2. When users type on their keyboards, the terminal creates a serial data stream that is sent to the host computer over a communications link.

3. The host computer responds to the user's keystrokes by sending data back to the terminal. The incoming data is converted into a video signal, which is displayed on the terminal's screen.

The Thin Client Model

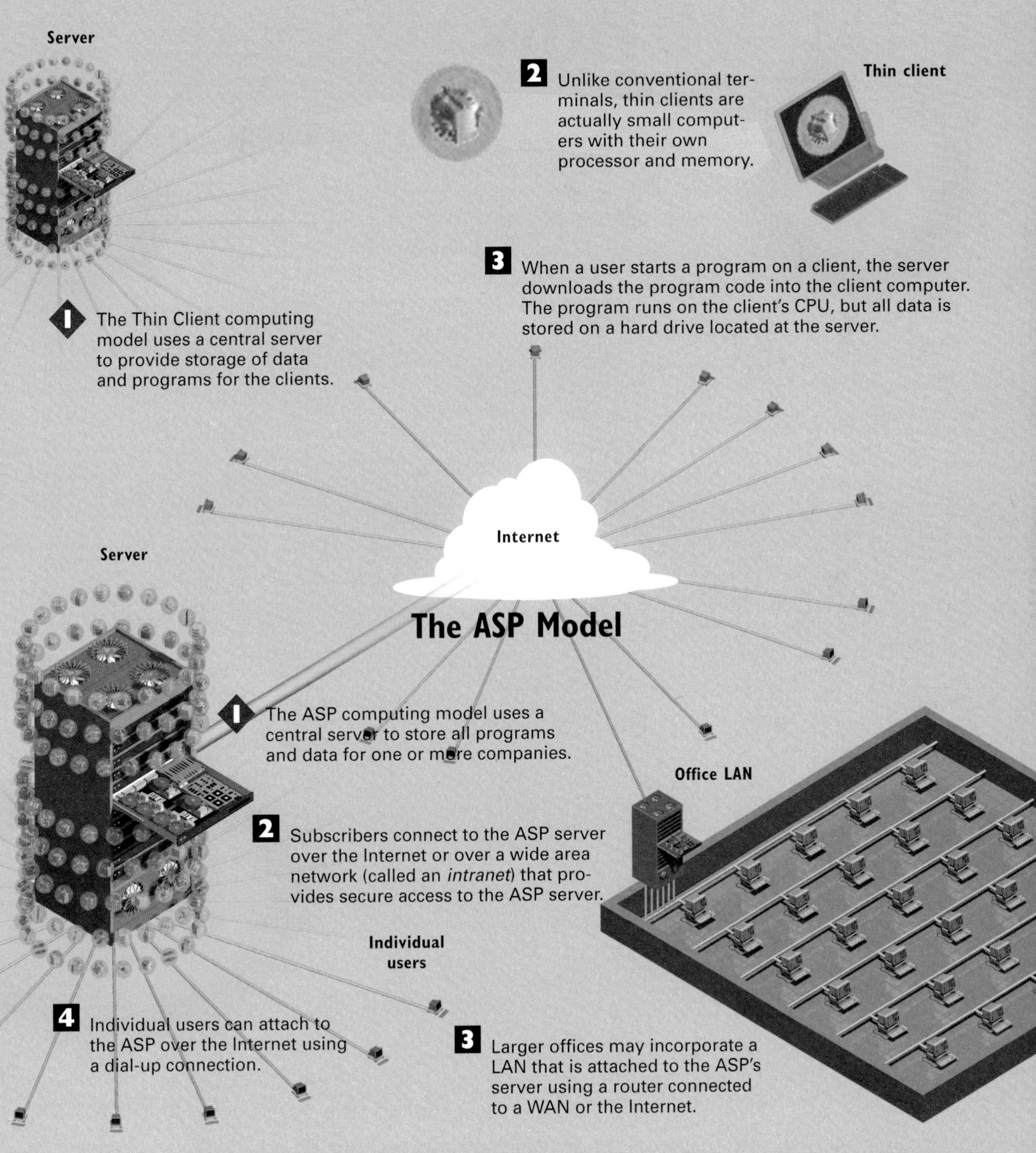
Server
2 Unlike conventional terminals, thin clients are actually small computers with their own processor and memory.
Thin client
3 When a user starts a program on a client, the server downloads the program code into the client computer. The program runs on the client's CPU, but all data is stored on a hard drive located at the server.
1 The Thin Client computing model uses a central server to provide storage of data and programs for the clients.
Internet
Server
The ASP Model
1 The ASP computing model uses a central server to store all programs and data for one or more companies.
Office LAN
2 Subscribers connect to the ASP server over the Internet or over a wide area network (called an *intranet*) that provides secure access to the ASP server.
Individual users
4 Individual users can attach to the ASP over the Internet using a dial-up connection.
3 Larger offices may incorporate a LAN that is attached to the ASP's server using a router connected to a WAN or the Internet.

CHAPTER 10 How Broadband Works

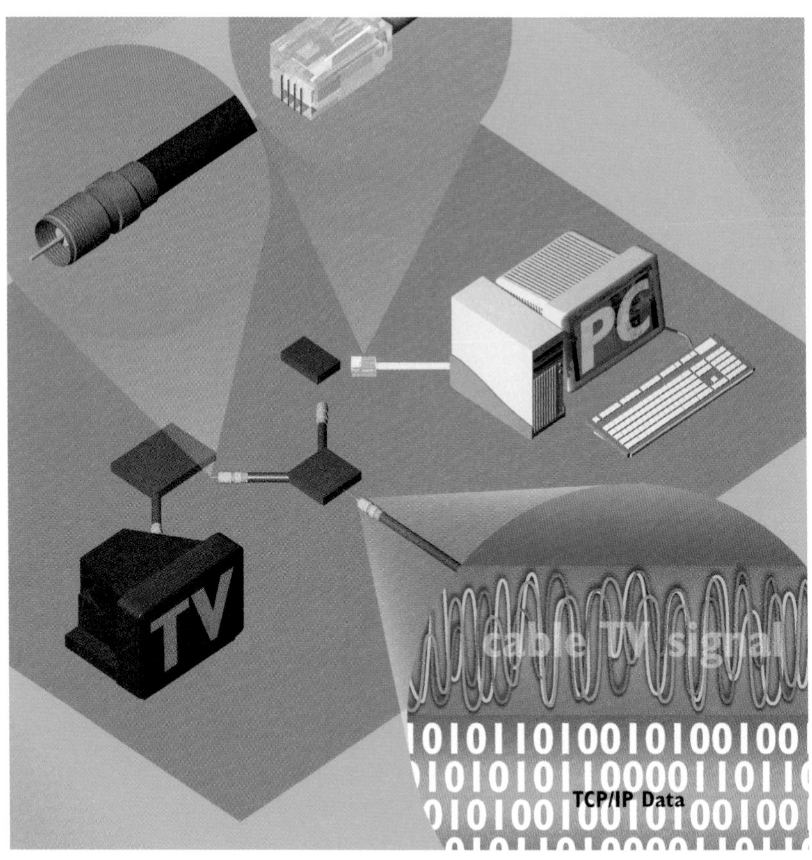
PC
TV
cable TV signal
TCP/IP Data

THE Internet has evolved from a network of a few hundred computers to a global network encompassing millions of computers. At the same time, much of the content on the Internet has evolved from plain text to include graphics, animations, video, and sound. Multimedia content requires more bandwidth than plain text, and several technologies have emerged to provide users with faster, more reliable Internet connections. Those fast connections are collectively called *broadband connections*. Users can choose from a variety of broadband services, including ISDN, DSL, and cable modem technologies.

ISDN—Integrated Services Digital Network (ISDN) was the first broadband technology widely available to consumers. It is an all-digital telephone service that provides reliable voice and data communications using the same wiring as the existing telephone network. ISDN provides two 64Kbps connections that can be combined into one 128,000bps connection. Each of the two 64Kbps channels operates independently of the other, and each channel can be used for voice or data communication. Phones attached to ISDN lines can place and receive calls to conventional analog phones, and most ISDN lines have two phone numbers, one for each of the two channels.

ISDN was developed in the early 1980s, and was quickly and widely adopted in Europe. In the United States, ISDN was not widely available until the early 1990s. Although ISDN's 128Kbps speed seems passé when compared to DSL or cable modem service, it is still faster and more reliable than an analog dial-up modem connection. In many places, a single ISDN line is cheaper than two POTS lines. ISDN is a good choice for Internet connectivity in areas where DSL or cable modem service isn't available.

DSL—Like ISDN, Digital Subscriber Line (DSL) uses the existing telephone network wiring to deliver an all-digital connection. DSL service can share a wire path with a conventional phone line, so you can receive DSL service and conventional phone service on the same wire. Unlike ISDN, DSL provides a single data channel, and that data channel is a dedicated point-to-point circuit, usually used to connect a home or office directly to an Internet service provider.

The data and voice services on a DSL connection don't interfere with one another, so you can place and receive voice calls while your computer is connected to the Internet. DSL service is typically provided by your local telephone company, although many Internet service providers (ISPs) also offer DSL services.

There are several different varieties of DSL, but the most common type for home and small office use is Asymmetrical DSL, or ADSL. As the name implies, ADSL connections are faster in one direction than the other. The faster, inbound part of the connection is used to deliver Internet content to your PC, whereas the slower outbound connection sends your keystrokes, mouse clicks, and outbound email to the Internet.

Most DSL service providers offer several different speed options, with the faster lines commanding higher prices. Typical ADSL speeds are 768Kbps or 1.5Mbps downstream and 128Kbps or 256Kbps upstream.

Cable Modem—Cable modem service delivers multimegabit data speeds using your local cable company's cable TV network. Originally developed as an entertainment technology, cable modem service is widely available from most cable providers.

Unlike the telephone network, which uses a discrete pair of wires to connect each individual phone line to the telephone network, cable TV is a shared medium. Instead of running a separate cable to each home, cable TV systems operate over a single cable. This allows the cable company to provide the same signal to all the subscribers, but it also means that you'll be sharing the cable's Internet bandwidth with all the other users in your neighborhood. Like ADSL, cable modem service is usually asymmetrical. Typical cable modem services provide 1.5Mbps to 2Mbps downstream, and 128Kbps upstream.

How ISDN Works

1 ISDN service operates over conventional twisted-pair telephone wiring. Unlike POTS, the ISDN signal is all digital. Voice traffic on an ISDN line travels as digitally encoded data, not as an analog audio signal.

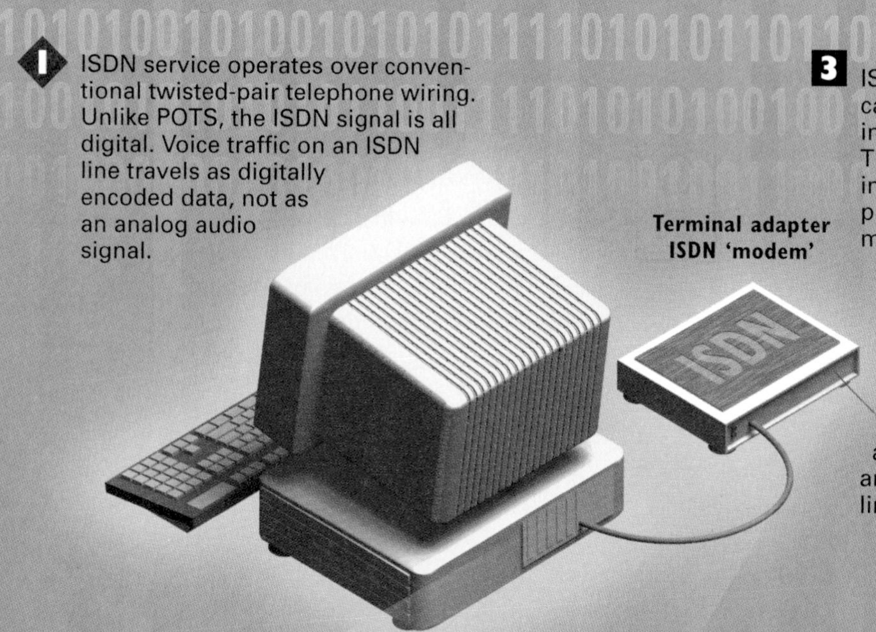
Terminal adapter
ISDN 'modem'
ISDN

3 ISDN users must have a device called a *terminal adapter*, also (and incorrectly) called an *ISDN modem*. The terminal adapter provides an interface between the user's computer and the ISDN line, much as a modem does on analog phone lines. Because ISDN lines are digital, there is no analog-to-digital conversion process as there is in a conventional modem. Most terminal adapters provide one or two phone jacks that allow users to use standard analog phones, fax machines, and answering machines on the ISDN line.

4 The terminal adapter contains an RS-232C serial interface that attaches to a serial port on the user's PC. In order to connect to the Internet or to another ISDN user, the PC must dial a number to connect the call. ISDN calls connect much more quickly than standard modems, usually in less than a second.

ISDN
Power
Telephone line
RS-232C to computer

4

B channel
64 kbits

B channel
64 kbits

D channel
16 kbits

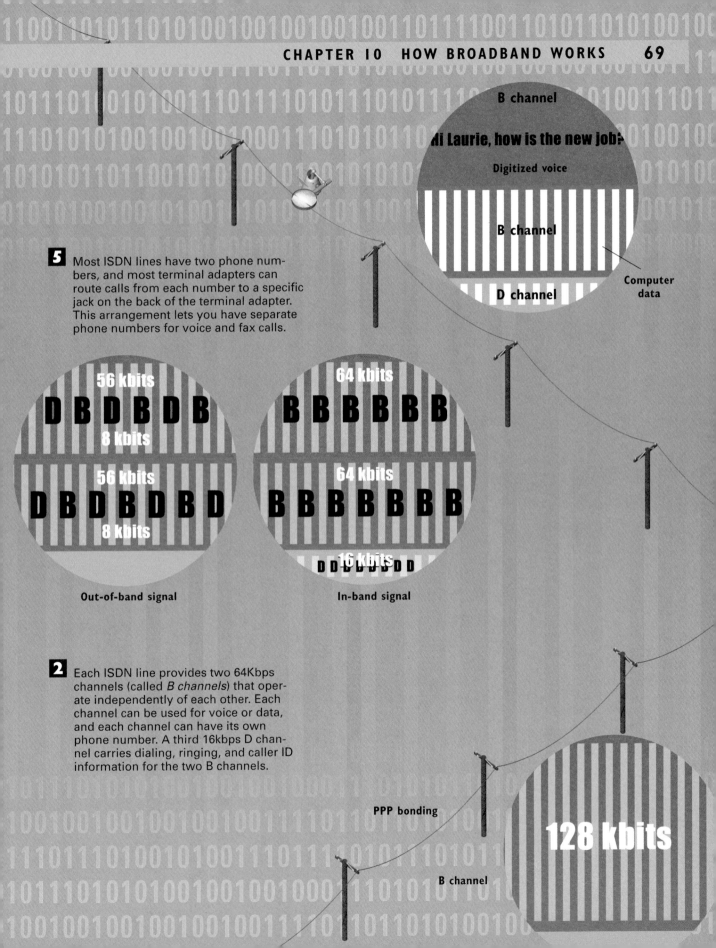

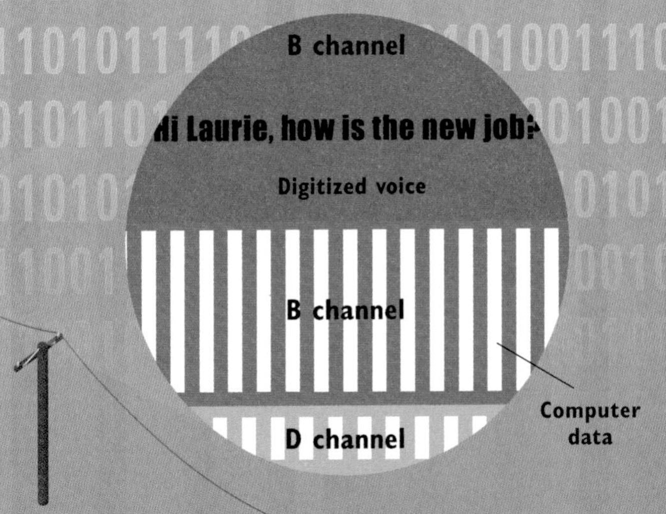

B channel
Hi Laurie, how is the new job?
Digitized voice
B channel
D channel
Computer data

5 Most ISDN lines have two phone numbers, and most terminal adapters can route calls from each number to a specific jack on the back of the terminal adapter. This arrangement lets you have separate phone numbers for voice and fax calls.

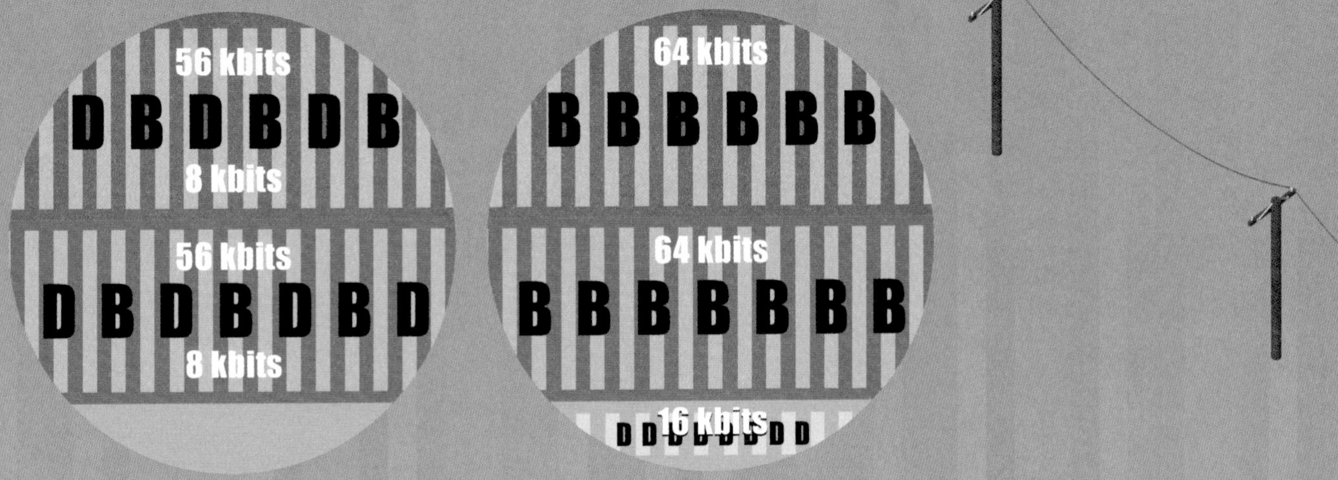

56 kbits
D B D B D B
8 kbits
56 kbits
D B D B D B D
8 kbits
Out-of-band signal
64 kbits
B B B B B B
64 kbits
B B B B B B B
16 kbits
D D D D D D D D
In-band signal

2 Each ISDN line provides two 64Kbps channels (called *B channels*) that operate independently of each other. Each channel can be used for voice or data, and each channel can have its own phone number. A third 16kbps D channel carries dialing, ringing, and caller ID information for the two B channels.

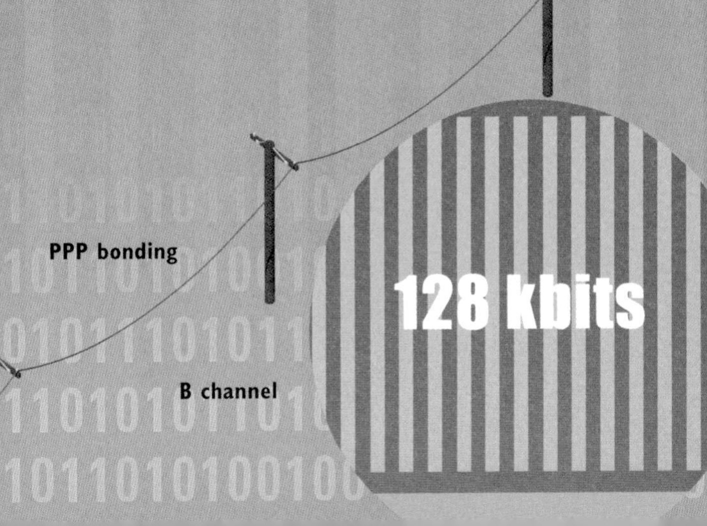

PPP bonding
128 kbits
B channel

How ADSL Works

Filter

2 The splitter has separate connections for the phone line, the DSL modem, and the analog phones. The filtered analog signal is connected to the existing house or office wiring, just like a conventional phone line.

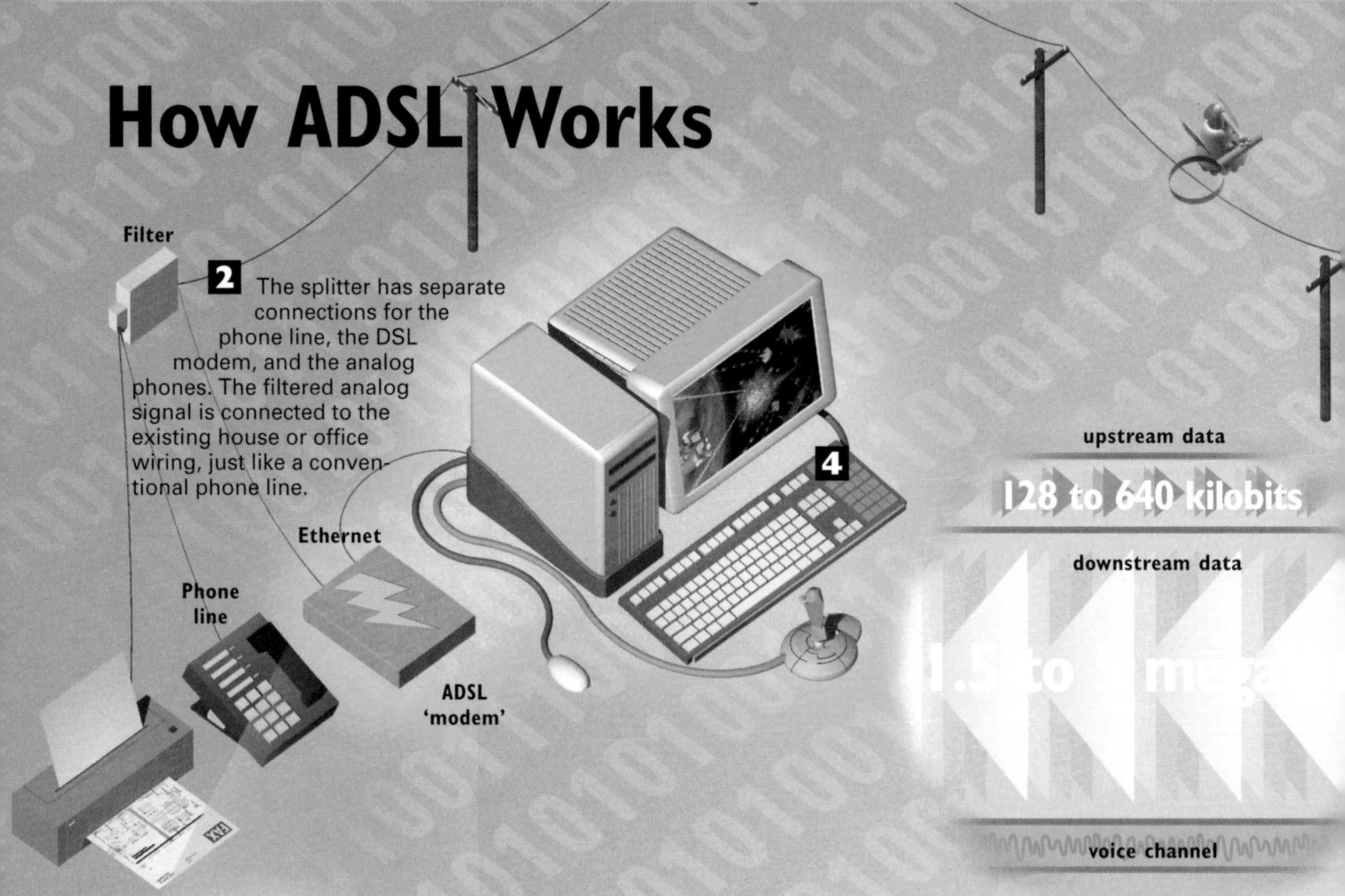

4

Ethernet

Phone line

ADSL 'modem'

upstream data

128 to 640 kilobits

downstream data

voice channel

Ethernet

3 The unfiltered DSL signal is connected to the DSL modem. Like an analog modem, a DSL modem provides an interface between the phone line and the user's computer.

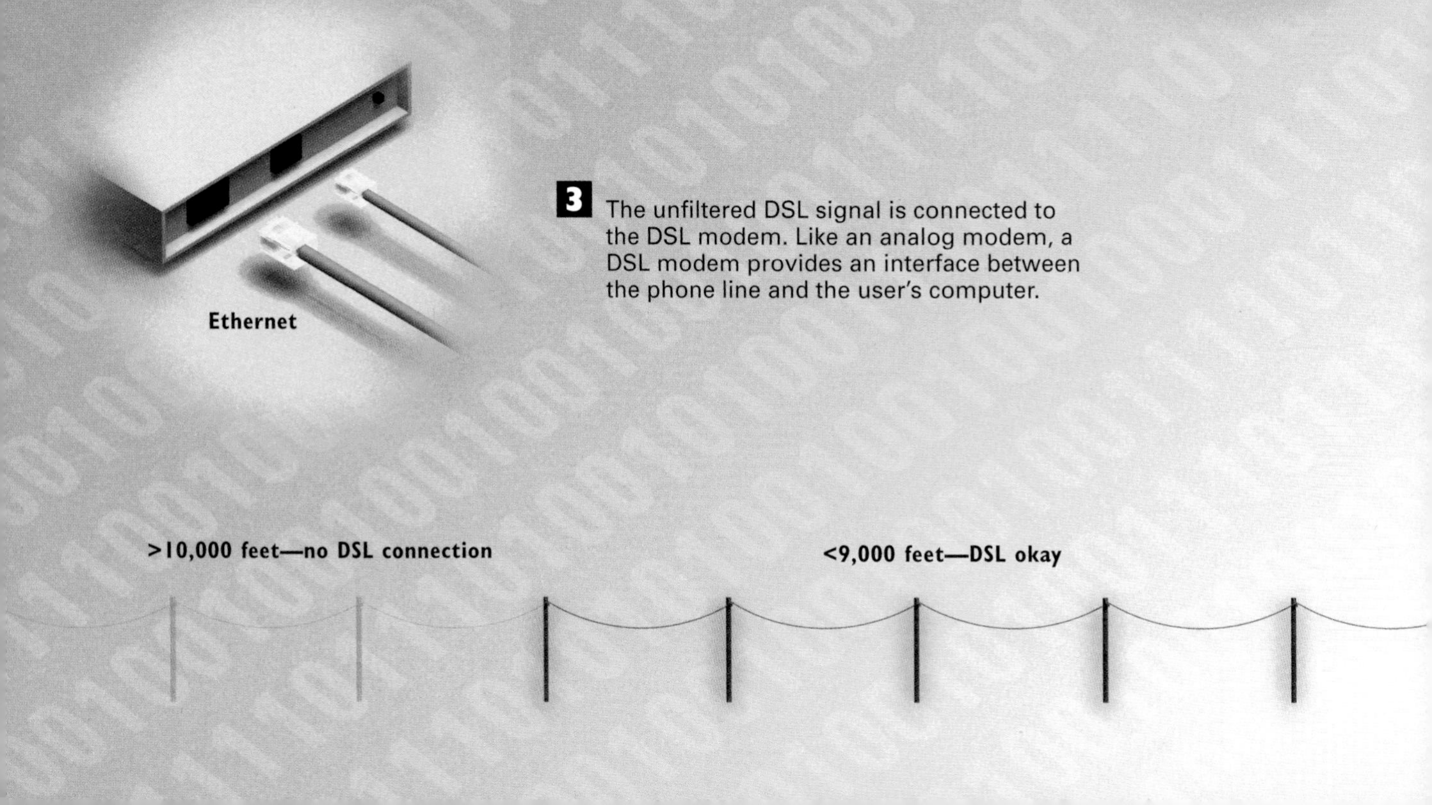

>10,000 feet—no DSL connection

<9,000 feet—DSL okay

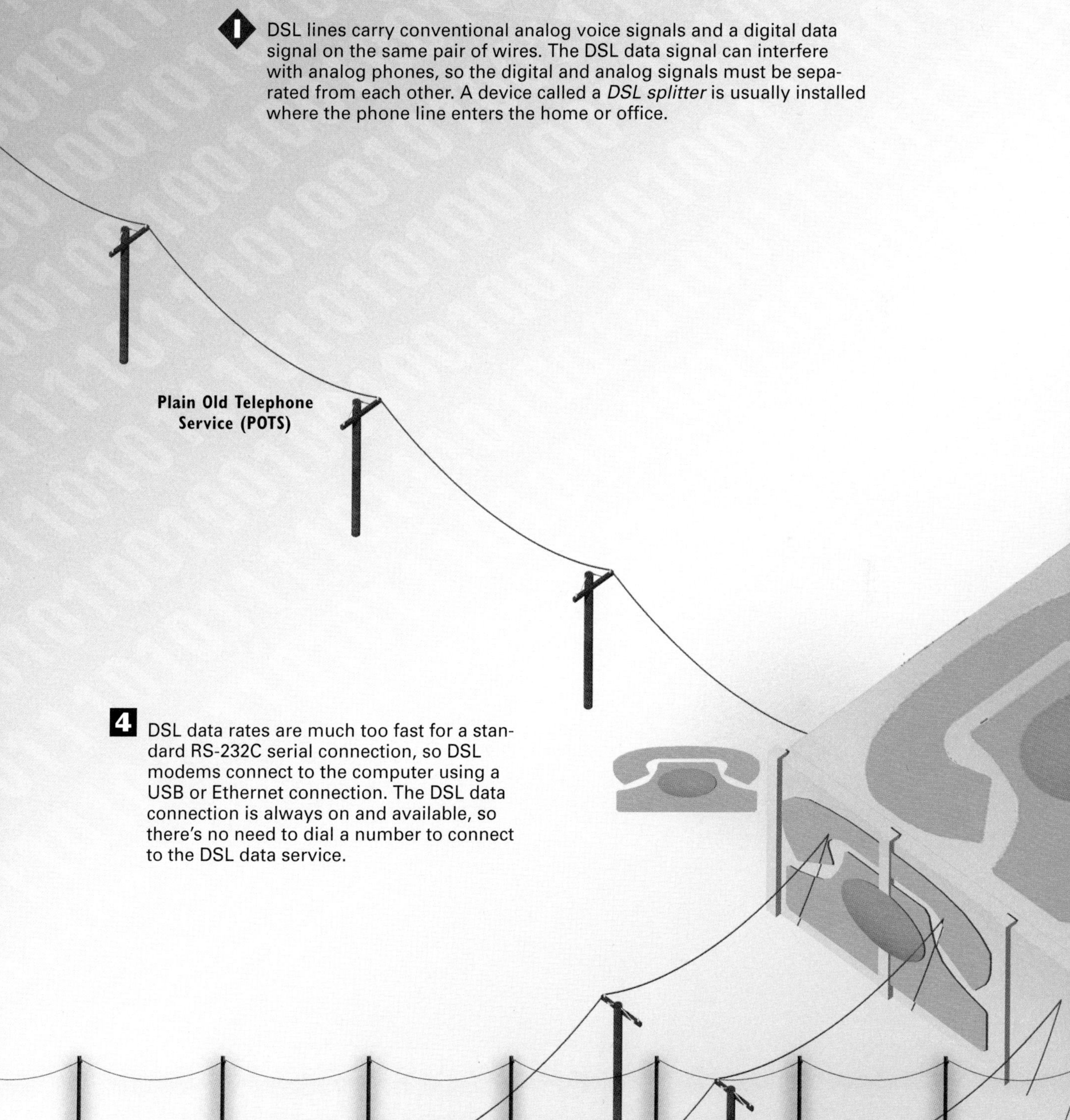
Plain Old Telephone Service (POTS)

1. DSL lines carry conventional analog voice signals and a digital data signal on the same pair of wires. The DSL data signal can interfere with analog phones, so the digital and analog signals must be separated from each other. A device called a *DSL splitter* is usually installed where the phone line enters the home or office.

4. DSL data rates are much too fast for a standard RS-232C serial connection, so DSL modems connect to the computer using a USB or Ethernet connection. The DSL data connection is always on and available, so there's no need to dial a number to connect to the DSL data service.

How Cable Modems Work

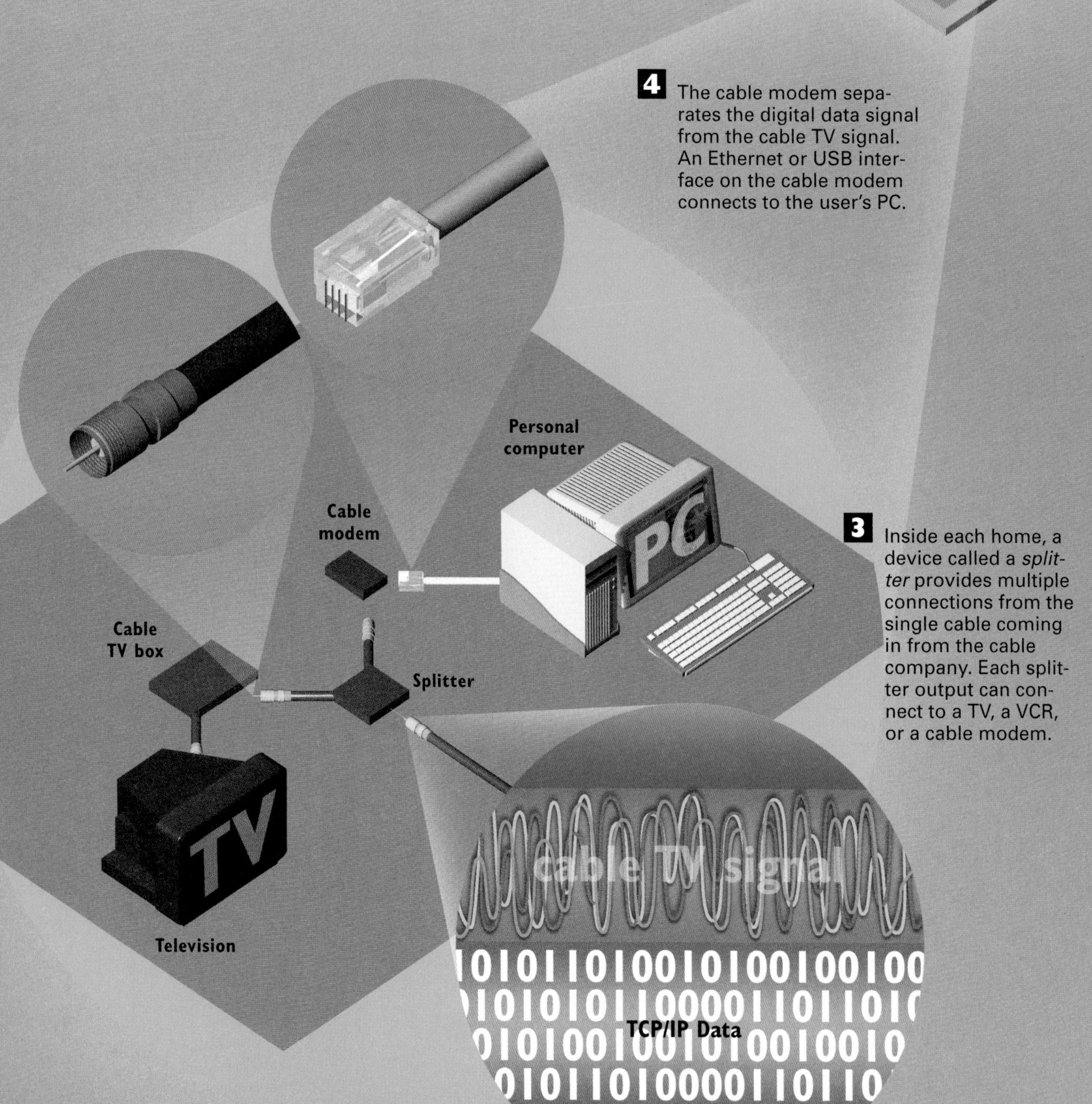
Personal computer
Cable modem
Cable TV box
Splitter
Television
TV
PC
cable TV signal
TCP/IP Data

4 The cable modem separates the digital data signal from the cable TV signal. An Ethernet or USB interface on the cable modem connects to the user's PC.

3 Inside each home, a device called a *splitter* provides multiple connections from the single cable coming in from the cable company. Each splitter output can connect to a TV, a VCR, or a cable modem.

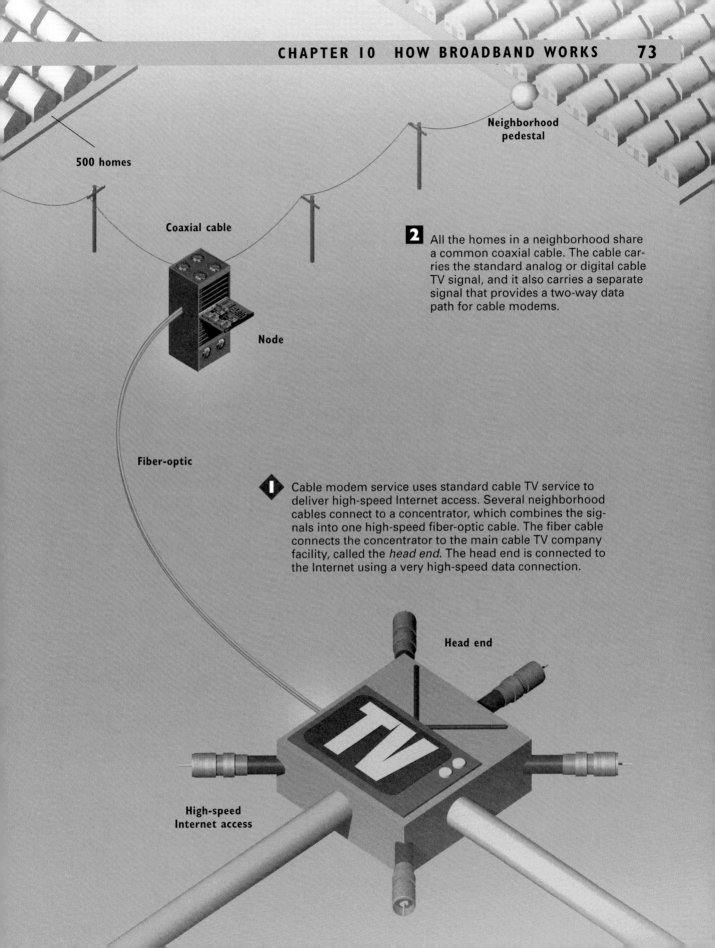

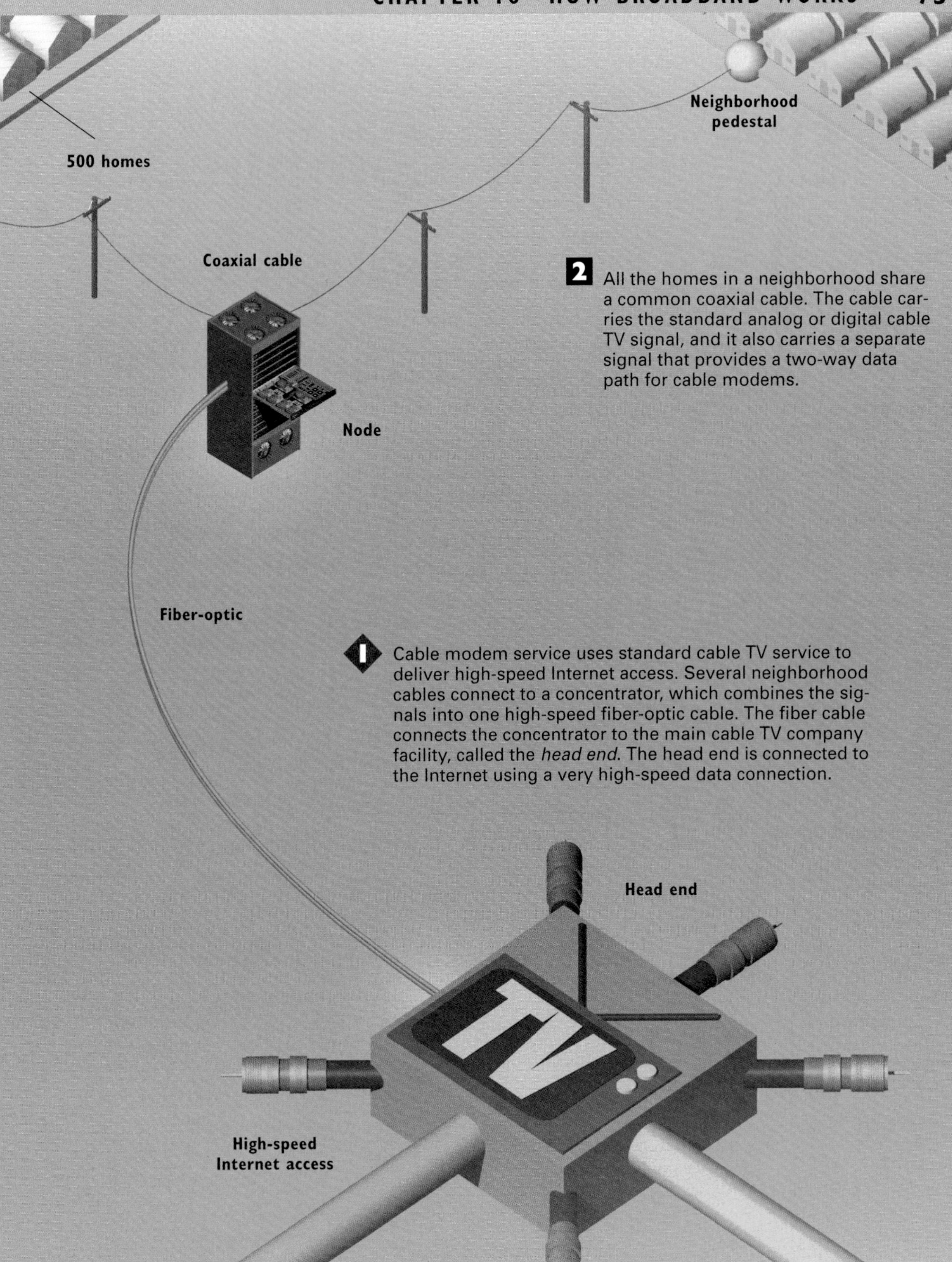
500 homes
Neighborhood pedestal
Coaxial cable
Node
Fiber-optic
Head end
High-speed Internet access

2 All the homes in a neighborhood share a common coaxial cable. The cable carries the standard analog or digital cable TV signal, and it also carries a separate signal that provides a two-way data path for cable modems.

1 Cable modem service uses standard cable TV service to deliver high-speed Internet access. Several neighborhood cables connect to a concentrator, which combines the signals into one high-speed fiber-optic cable. The fiber cable connects the concentrator to the main cable TV company facility, called the *head end*. The head end is connected to the Internet using a very high-speed data connection.

CHAPTER 11

How Computer Telephony Integration Works

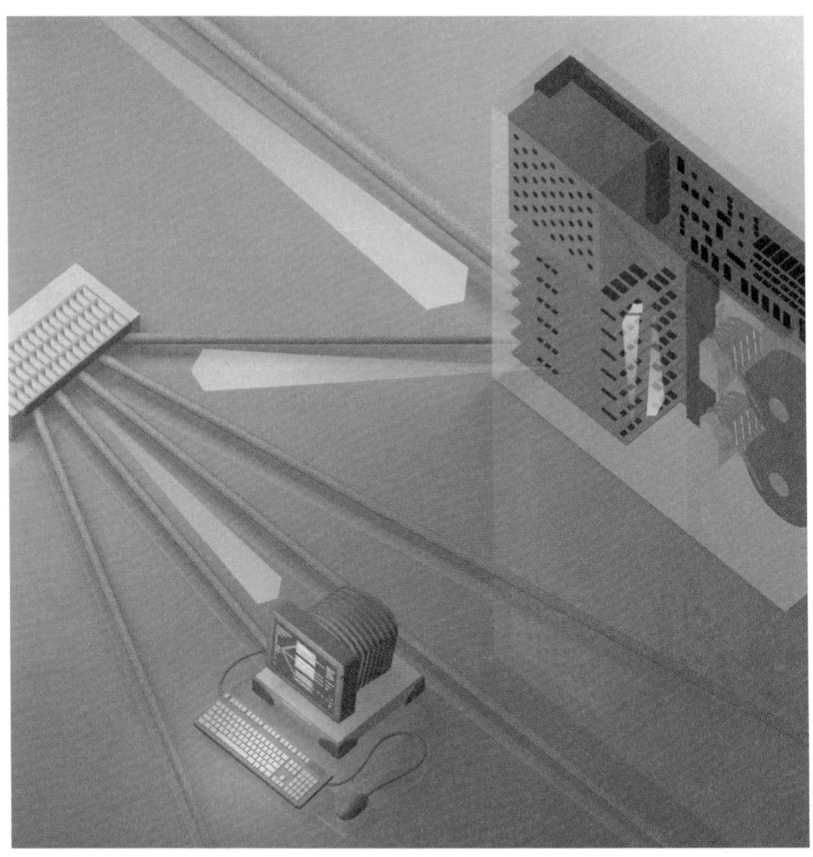

VOICE *over IP (VoIP)* and *customer relationship management (CRM)* are important topics for businesses of every size. The networking technology behind both VoIP and CRM is called *Computer Telephony Integration (CTI)*. If you want to sound smart about this stuff, you need to pronounce "Telephony" correctly. It's te-LEFF-in-nee, not tell-a-phony.

The term *Computer Telephony Integration* describes ways of linking telephones and computers to gain productivity. CTI makes your small business appear to be a multinational corporation to callers. CTI takes several forms. As an application, CTI includes CRM functions. CRM integrates telephone and computer systems into call centers that handle support and sales activities in modern organizations of many kinds. As a networking technology or transport service, CTI includes the many VoIP services available today.

Corporate call center is the term used to describe the workplaces of people such as reservation clerks, order takers, and 911 operators. A CTI device performing a function known as *call routing* sends incoming calls to the right place. You know this as "Press 1 for new accounts, press 2 for support," and so on. Call routing equipment can make decisions based on the telephone number of the originating caller. If the caller is a repeat customer, the clerk sees a pop-up screen identifying the caller and detailing any current account information before saying "Hello."

Modern e-business techniques change a "call center" into a "contact center." Guided by CRM application programs, the contact center workers use email, fax, Web site connections, and any other available resources to interact with customers. CRM programs track the history and status of every customer interaction and help workers give customers personalized service.

VoIP is the second piece of CTI. VoIP puts voice and fax over Internet connections for greater flexibility and lower cost. VoIP can work within a company to carry voice and fax calls between branch office telephone systems. In international calling, VoIP services bypass the high tariffs imposed on telephone connections by some countries. This saves money for both businesses and private individuals. VoIP is also used by cable television companies that offer residential voice and fax telephone services in competition to the local telephone company.

How Incoming Call Routing Works

Caller dials
a number

1. The process of call routing begins when a caller dials into the system.

2. The telephone company completes the call and sends the telephone number of the caller to the destination between the first and second ring. The ID block can also include name and geographical information, but systems vary. The CTI system takes the ID information and passes it to an application program before answering the incoming call.

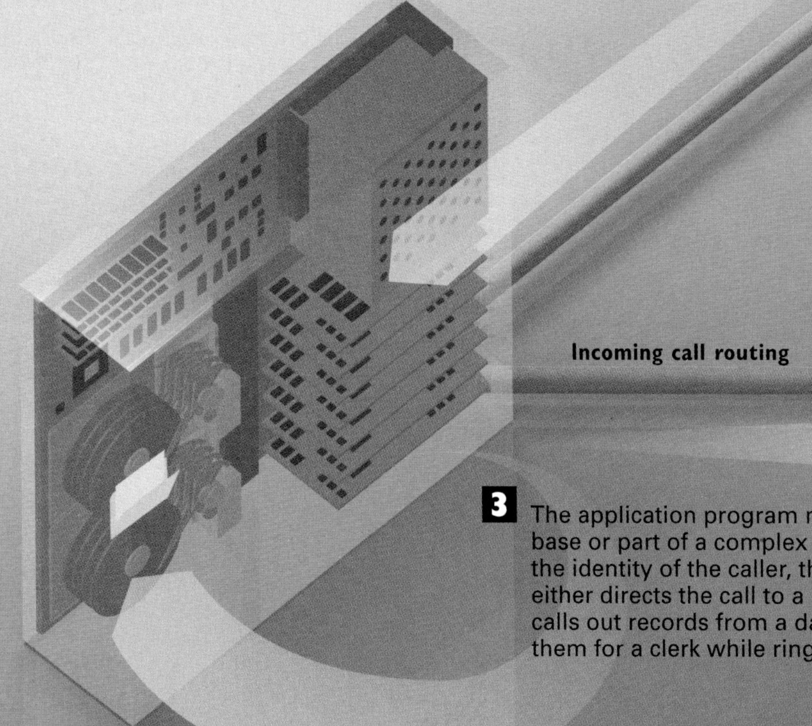
Caller records and
account history
Incoming call routing

3. The application program might be a simple database or part of a complex CRM suite. Based on the identity of the caller, the application program either directs the call to a recorded message or calls out records from a database and displays them for a clerk while ringing the clerk's phone.

5 The telephony server aggregates commands from different computers and programs and passes them to the PBX. At the PBX, these commands initiate, terminate, and forward calls. Similarly, call control information from the PBX can cross the LAN to get call routing information.

4 The CTI system allows the exchange of signals, called *call control commands*, between computers and the private branch exchange (PBX) telephone switch inside the company or enterprise. The call control commands flow from programs or keyboard inputs across a local area network to a computer acting as a telephony server.

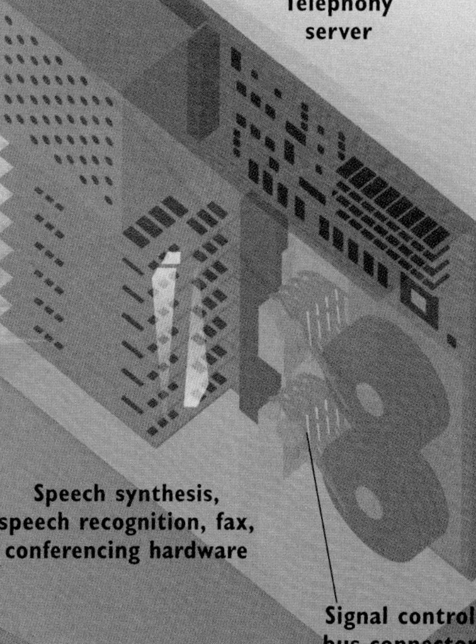
Desktop telephone
Telephone circuits
Telephony server
Call control commands
LAN wiring hub
Telephone switch to LAN interface
LAN cable
Speech synthesis, speech recognition, fax, conferencing hardware
Signal control bus connector
Desktop PC

6 On the other side of the system, speech synthesis and recognition devices generate messages, recognize spoken commands, and interact with computer programs to control and route calls and to pass information such as customer identification. These features are often used in reservation and ordering systems.

How Voice Over IP Works

1 Voice over IP digitizes voice calls and uses various means to send them across the Internet. Cable Internet service providers attach telephones to their cable modems to provide local telephone access.

Digitized voice or fax packets

Can you hear me?

Call completion and digitized voice packets

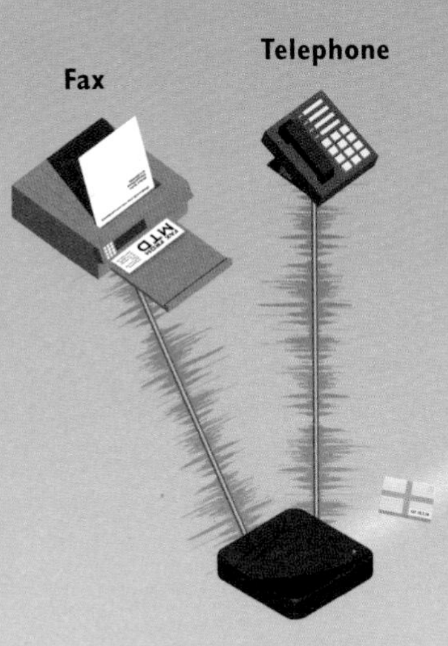
Fax
Telephone

Internet Service Provider Country A

Here is your call completion information

2 Some VoIP services connect from computer to computer. "Callers" must register with the service to complete connections.

VoIP connection box or cable modem with a telephone jack

Computer

Audio headset

Call Registration Service

The Internet

Sounds great!

3 VoIP carriers "hop off" the Internet to connect to Public Switched Telephone Networks around the world. These carriers can avoid costly local tariffs.

Internet Service Provider Country B

Domestic Public Switched Telephone Network – Country B

Telephone

Fax

VoIP telephone

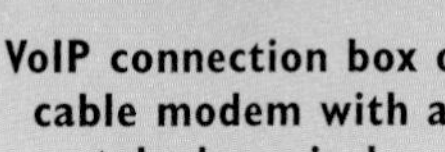
VoIP connection box or cable modem with a telephone jack

Telephone

How Multiplexed Voice, Fax, and Data Work

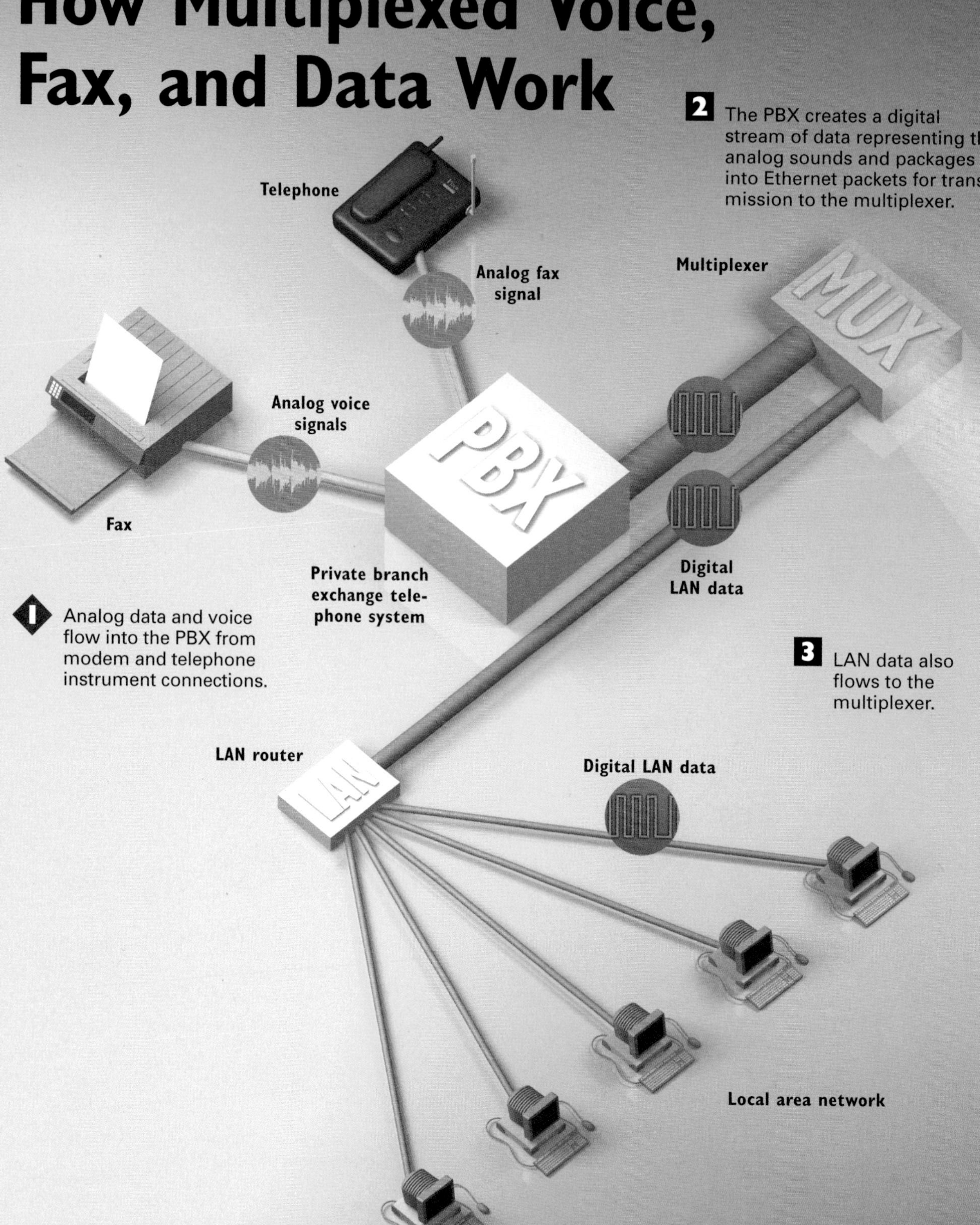
Telephone
Analog fax signal
Multiplexer
MUX
Analog voice signals
PBX
Fax
Private branch exchange telephone system
Digital LAN data
LAN router
LAN
Digital LAN data
Local area network

1 Analog data and voice flow into the PBX from modem and telephone instrument connections.

2 The PBX creates a digital stream of data representing the analog sounds and packages it into Ethernet packets for transmission to the multiplexer.

3 LAN data also flows to the multiplexer.

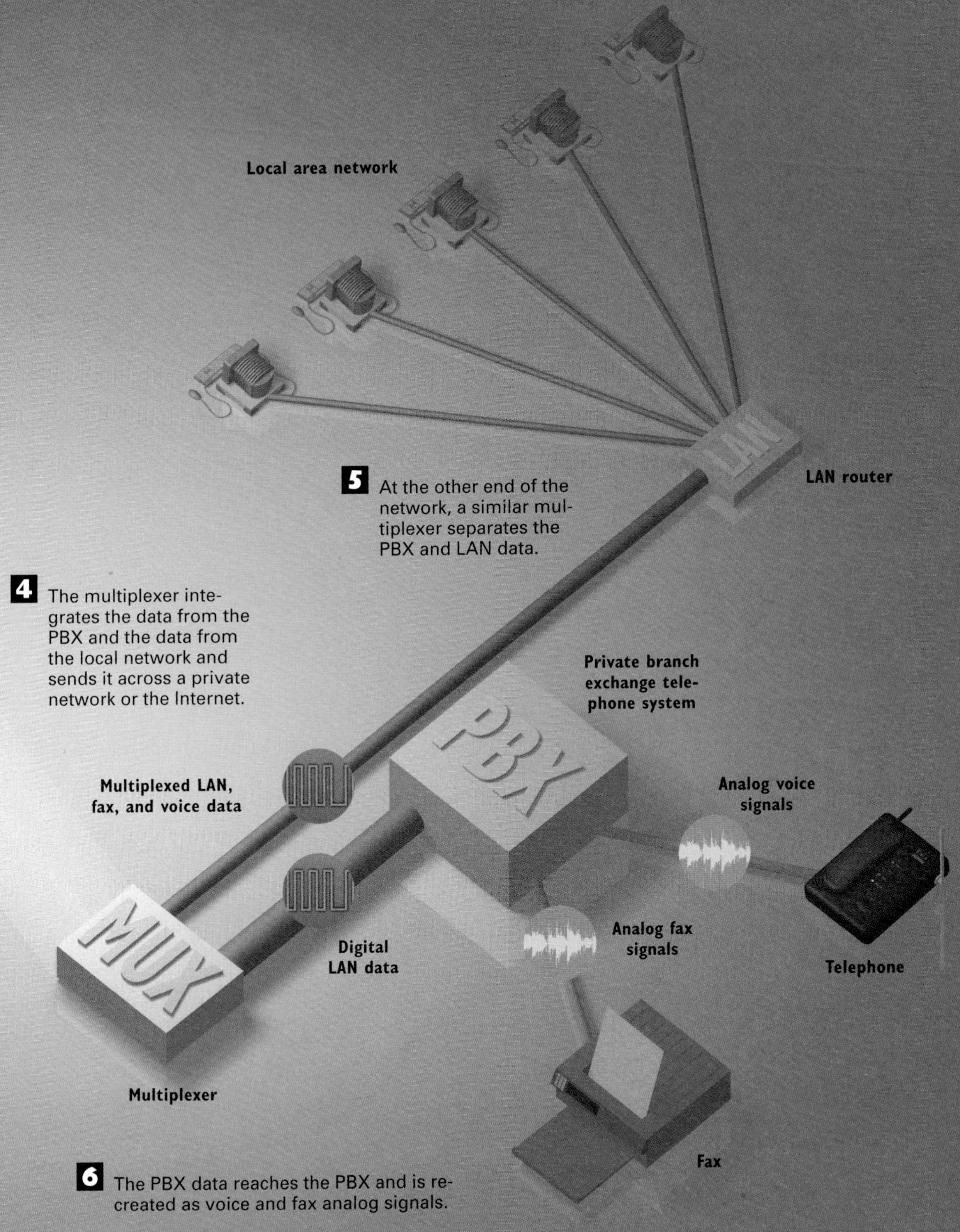
Local area network
LAN
LAN router
PBX
Private branch exchange telephone system
Multiplexed LAN, fax, and voice data
Analog voice signals
Telephone
MUX
Digital LAN data
Analog fax signals
Multiplexer
Fax

5 At the other end of the network, a similar multiplexer separates the PBX and LAN data.

4 The multiplexer integrates the data from the PBX and the data from the local network and sends it across a private network or the Internet.

6 The PBX data reaches the PBX and is recreated as voice and fax analog signals.

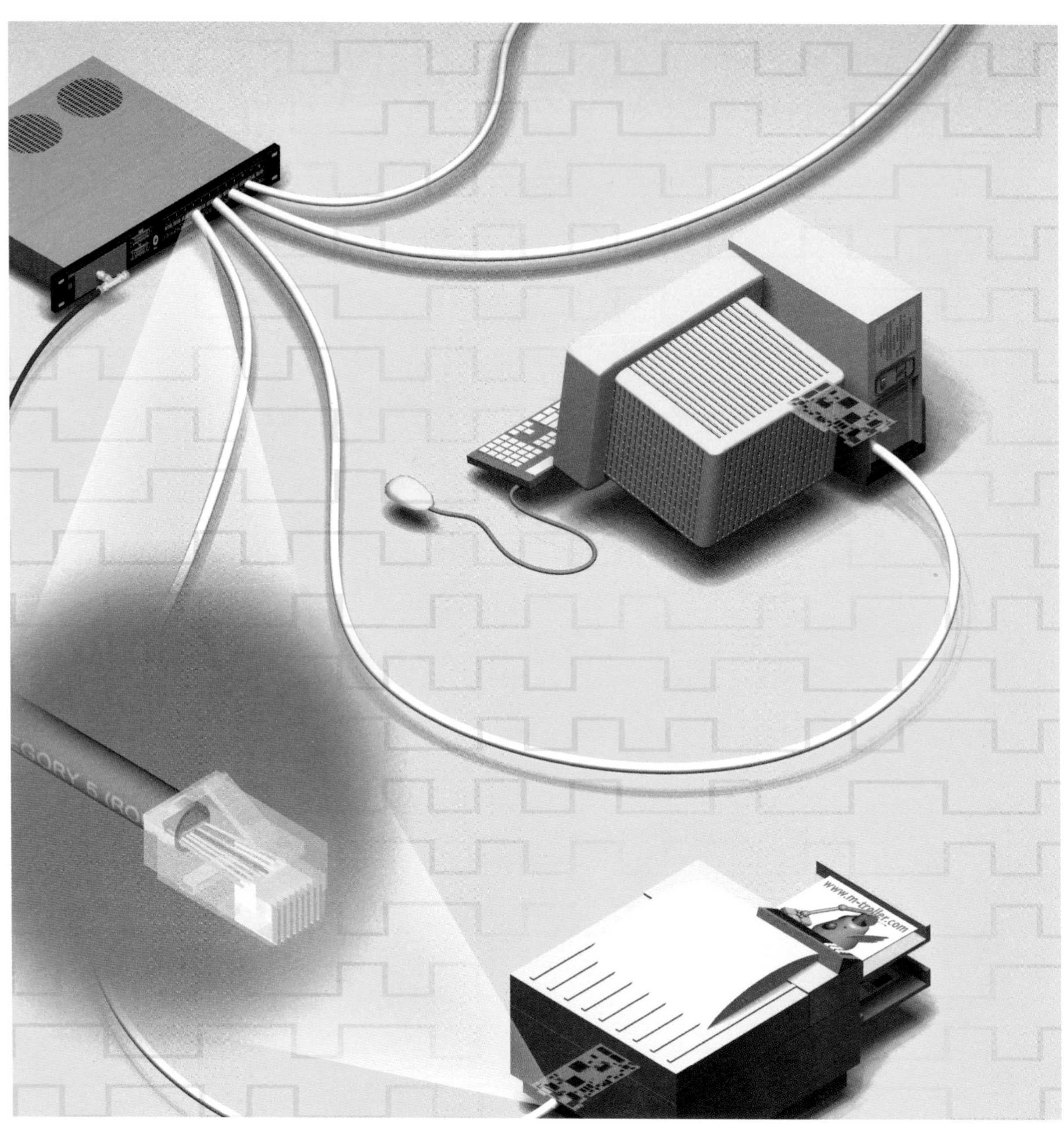
www.m-troller.com

LOCAL AREA NETWORKS (LANS)

NETWORKS are for sharing—sharing things such as word processing and spreadsheet files, printers, communications links to distant computers and networks, and electronic mail systems is the function of a network. Every sharing activity, from carpools to bank lines, has its own rules. In networking, we call these rules *standards* and *protocols*. Standards describe how things should be; typically, they set a minimum performance level. Protocols are sets of rules and agreements; protocols describe how things interact. The key to understanding networking is understanding the standards and protocols that make it possible to interoperate without losing or abusing the files and devices we share across the LAN.

In this section, we'll talk about standards, protocols, and sharing. The standards and protocols for computer interoperation emerged only in the early 1980s. Three separate streams fed the growth of networking technology: IBM, the U.S. Department of Defense, and the Xerox Palo Alto Research Center (PARC). Later, other industry and professional organizations, particularly the Institute of Electrical and Electronics Engineers (IEEE), played an important part in developing standards.

In the 1970s, the U.S. Department of Defense (DoD), faced with an inventory of computers from different manufacturers that could not interoperate, pioneered the development of protocols for network software that works on more than one make and model of computer. The major set of protocols established by the DoD is the Transmission Control Protocol/Internet Protocol (TCP/IP). As the titles infer, these protocols are agreements on how transmission takes place across networks. Companies, particularly those who wanted the federal government's business, wrote software that conformed to those protocols. The government also commissioned the creation of networking software conforming to the TCP/IP standards and placed that software in the public domain.

At about the same time, IBM began making public the standards and protocols it used at that time for its own proprietary computer systems. The standards included detailed descriptions of cabling and the protocols were designed to ensure accurate communications under heavy loads. This work by IBM led others to emulate IBM's techniques and raised the level of the quality of network development in the entire industry.

IBM and Digital Equipment Corporation developed ways for a few large computers to interoperate over local networks in the 1970s, but the most important work on LANs for a large number of computers was done at the Palo Alto Research Center (PARC) of Xerox Corporation in the late 1970s and early '80s. At PARC, an important set of standards and protocols called *Ethernet* was conceived and developed to the point of becoming a commercial product.

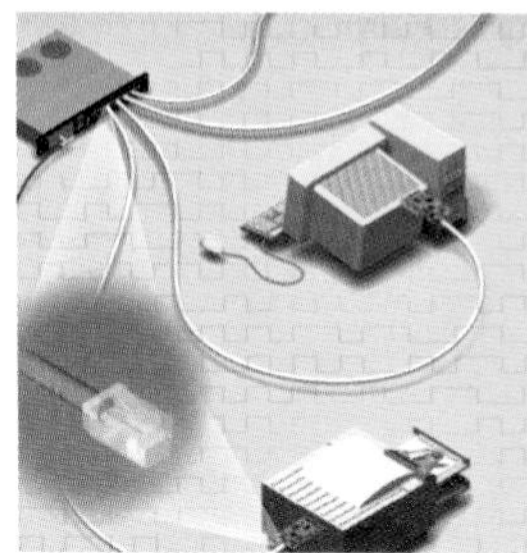

The early local area network architectures combined inflexible hardware specifications with strict protocol descriptions. Specific types of copper cable, specific cable connectors, one physical configuration, and certain software functions were bundled together in each LAN definition. Because of the government and industry push for flexibility, however, the single simple set of specifications and descriptions for each type of network has expanded to include different types of cables, configurations, and protocols. Active committees from many industry and governmental organizations have published protocols describing the finest details of how computers interconnect and communicate. Buyers will not invest in equipment that doesn't conform to widely accepted standards. Today, you can mix and match hardware and software to create a customized network and still stay within a network system specification supported by products from many different companies.

Over a short few decades, the computer network industry has made incredible progress in performance, cost, reliability, and interoperability. We assume that products from different manufacturers will interoperate. We take high reliability and high performance for granted. These benefits come from simultaneous industry cooperation on standardization and competition on features and cost.

The network evolution has swept through telephone technology, computer hardware design, software design, and even workgroup sociology. Today, both computers and buildings come with their networking components in place. If you have new equipment and a new building, you can add the software of your choice, plug a cable into a wall jack, and interoperate across LAN. Wireless networks—both high-speed local networks and slower mobile wireless networks—link portable computers with the central business location. Modern networks intermix handwritten and typed words, voice, and sound with graphics and video conferencing on the same cable. Networks make it possible for organizations to abandon the top-down management structure in which a lot of information was held at the top and to move to a flatter, more responsive structure in which information is shared and widely available.

The networking developments of decades support many things we now take for granted. The Internet is actually a set of applications built on top of interoperable and ubiquitous networking products. Many people access the Internet through corporate or even home local networks. Automatic teller machines, cell phone systems, and credit card authorization machines all use basically the same networking technology as they process our service requests. Telematics, the use of automation in automobiles, depends on networking between dozens of processors in high-end cars. Networking products make up a large part of the new biology. Decoding genomes and modeling cellular operations wouldn't be possible without networks. Networks change the way we work and live, so now let's find out how they work!

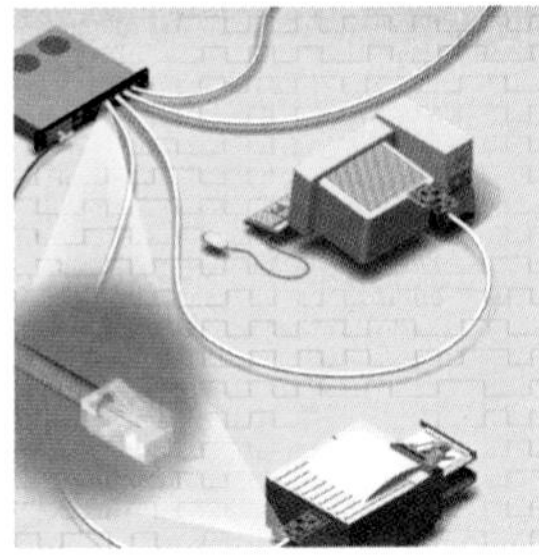

CHAPTER 12 How Local Area Networks Work

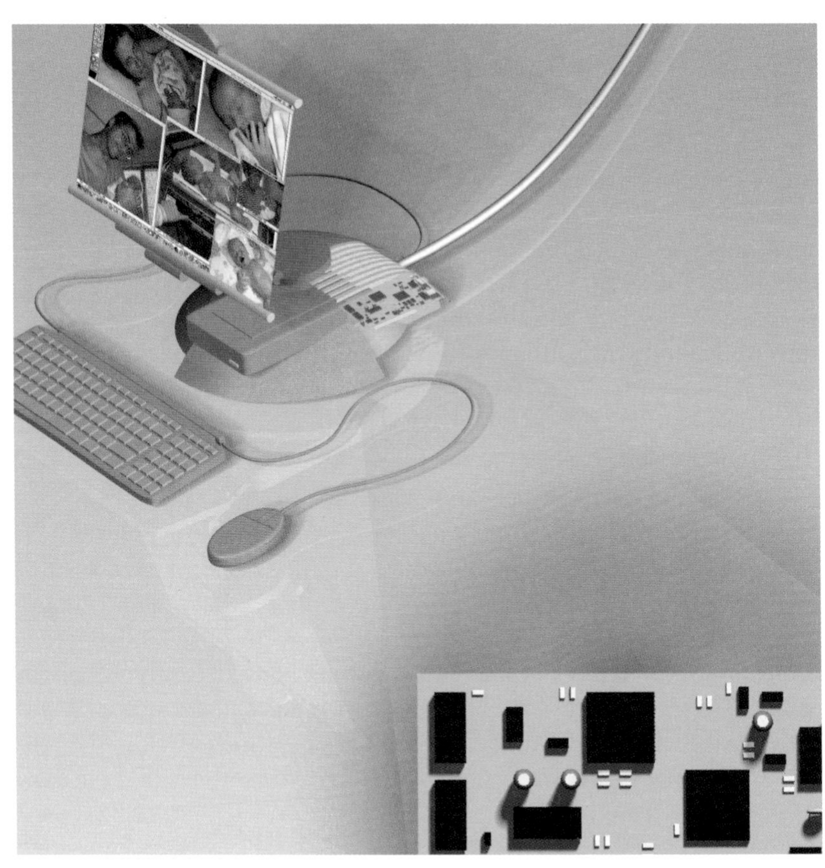

LET'S begin our investigation of networks by looking at the components of a network to see how they relate to one another and connect together. Then, we'll go inside each network component to see how it works.

The four major components of a network include operating system network services, networked peripherals, a network interface card, and network cabling.

Operating System Network Services—Modern operating systems such as Unix, Linux, Windows, the MacOS, and Solaris contain a series of special functions for networking. Because modern multitasking operating systems can perform many tasks nearly simultaneously, these networking functions run as *processes* within the operating system. Some of these processes give computers the capability to share files, printers, and other devices across the network. Computers that share their resources are called *servers*. Other functional programs, giving the capability to use those shared resources, are called *clients*. It is common to have client and server software running in the same computer so that you can use the resources on other computers while other people make use of your shared disk space, printers, or communications devices.

Networked peripherals—In 1991, a new category of products called *networked peripherals* became generally available. These include printers and modems with their own network connections. These devices have their own internal specialized processors to run networking server software, so they don't have to be directly attached to a PC. Application programs running on client Macintosh computers and PCs can use a networked printer or storage as if it were locally attached instead of being somewhere else on the LAN.

Network interface card—The low-powered digital signals inside a computer aren't powerful enough to travel long distances, so a device called a *network interface card* changes the signals inside the computer into more powerful signals that can go across the network cable. After the network interface card takes the data from the computer, it has the important jobs of packaging the data for transmission and acting as a gatekeeper to control access to the shared network cable.

Network cabling—The computers in modern networks can send messages in the form of electrical pulses over copper cable of several different kinds, over fiber-optic cable using pulses of light, or through the air using radio or light waves. In fact, you can combine all of these techniques into one network to meet specific needs or to take advantage of what is already installed. Modern network cabling installations use a central wiring hub, typically called a *switch*, that can isolate cable problems and improve reliability.

How a LAN Works

Network cabling

1 Network functions performed by operating system processes package data for transmission, control the transmission, recognize servers and clients, control security, and perform many other functions. In today's modern networks, these functions conform to the TCP/IP standard protocols. Software processes conforming to the IP protocol package the data, and functions conforming to the TCP protocol control the transmissions.

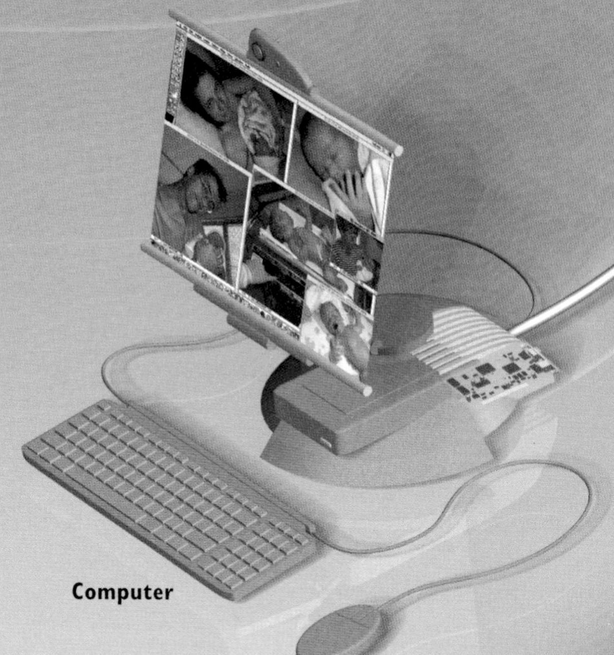

Computer

2 Network interface cards, abbreviated as NICs and called *Nicks*, link the computer to the network cable system. The card controls the flow of data between the computer's internal data bus and the serial stream of data on the network cable. Some computers come with their own network interface cards on the motherboard, and some interface adapters attach to a computer's USB port, but they are usually added to the PC's expansion bus. The vast majority of interface cards in use today conform to the Ethernet standard protocols.

Network interface card

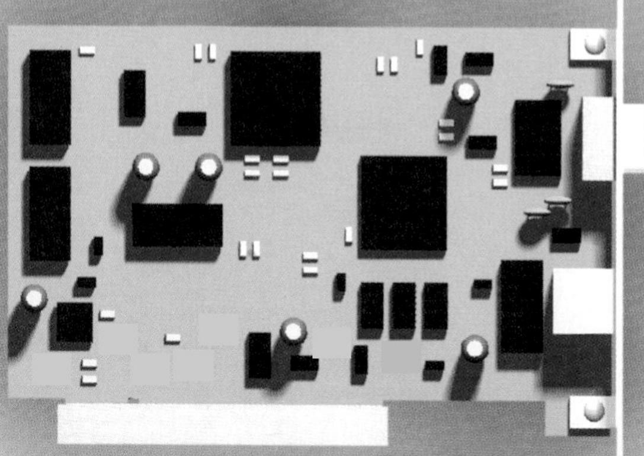

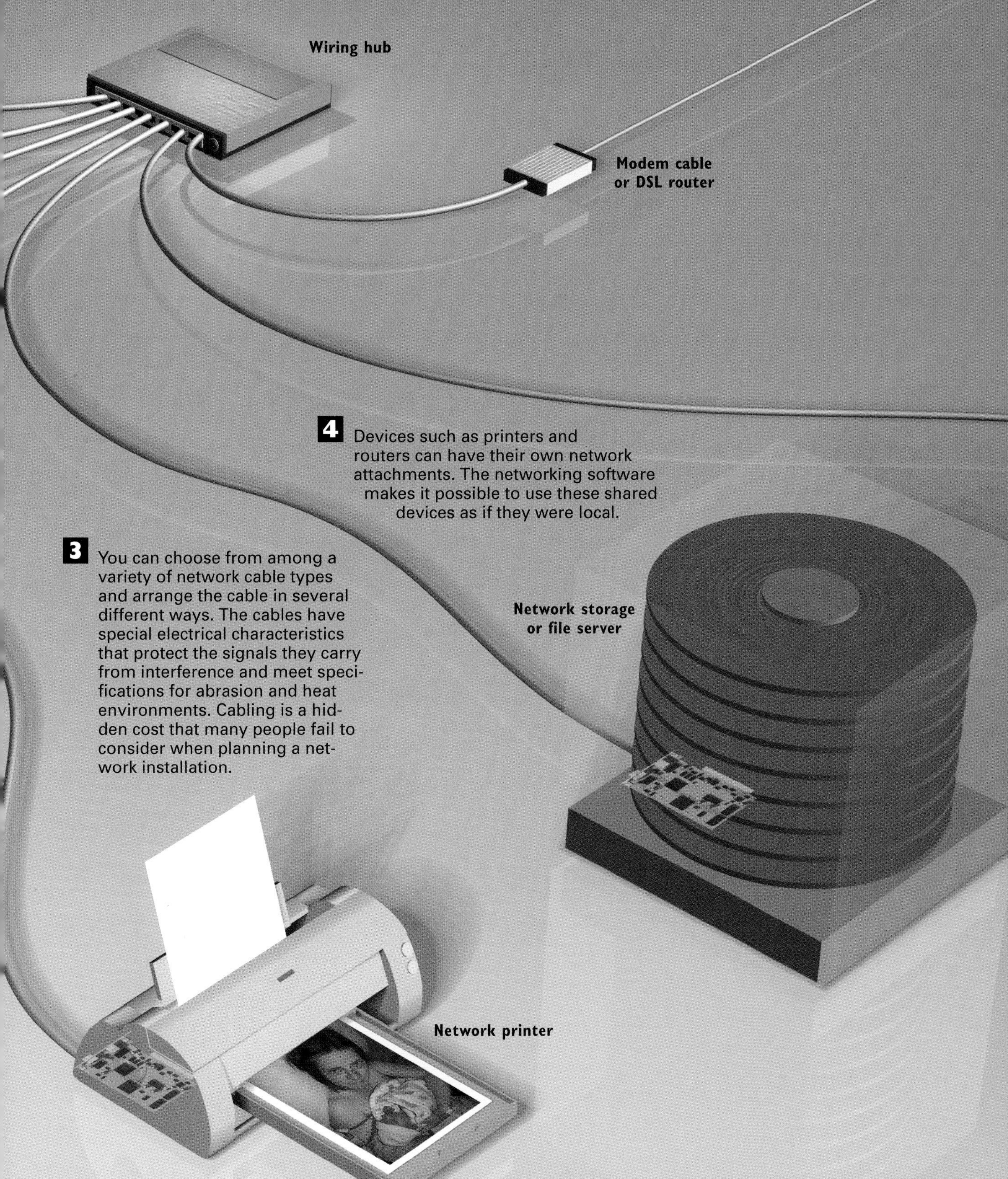
Wiring hub
Modem cable or DSL router
Network storage or file server
Network printer

4 Devices such as printers and routers can have their own network attachments. The networking software makes it possible to use these shared devices as if they were local.

3 You can choose from among a variety of network cable types and arrange the cable in several different ways. The cables have special electrical characteristics that protect the signals they carry from interference and meet specifications for abrasion and heat environments. Cabling is a hidden cost that many people fail to consider when planning a network installation.

CHAPTER

13

How Networking Operating Systems Work

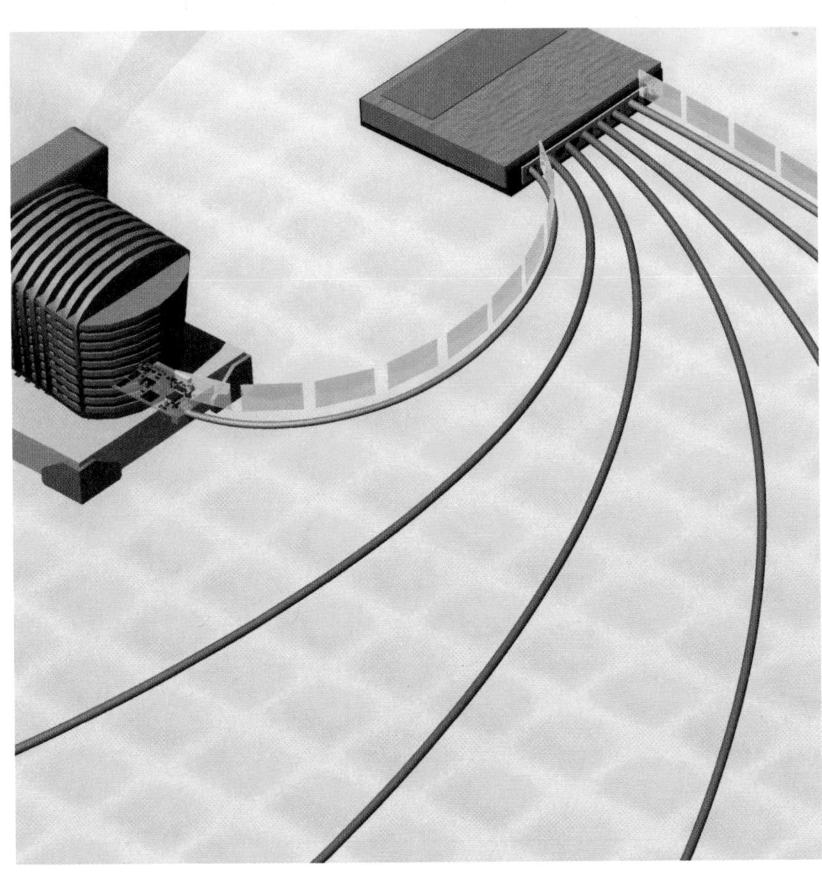

COMPUTER operating systems such as Linux, Unix, Windows, and others contain many small programs or processes able to perform specialized tasks. The networking processes are among the most complex because they have to package, account for, hold, accept, and process information at high speed while checking every step for accuracy. They integrate with and mediate between fast processes inside the computer and the comparatively slow connections outside the computer. The networking processes often use the power of special function chips contained on network interface cards or in other hardware to handle encryption and security.

Within a network, computers that share their hard disk drives, attached peripherals such as printers and CD-ROM drives, and communications circuits are generically called *servers*. The term *server* has grown to include Web servers, special forms of security servers, and other devices that deliver services to clients across a network. Servers inspect service requests for proper authentication and authorization, check for conflicts, and then provide the requested service.

File servers store files created by application programs such as databases. In some configurations, the file servers might also hold the application programs themselves. A file server is a computer that has access to a large hard-disk storage area. File servers provide reliability because they often include specialized redundant hardware such as dual power supplies and they provide security because they are often kept in locked rooms with special security and environmental controls. An important function of the file server component of the operating system is to control multiple simultaneous access to the same data file. The file server software allows shared access to specific segments of the data files under controlled conditions.

Print servers accept print jobs sent by any authorized user across the network. Although even the fastest print jobs still typically take a few seconds per page, *spooling* the print jobs (saving them in a disk file) is a critical function of the print server software. The print server software also reports the status of jobs waiting for printing and recognizes the priorities assigned to specific users.

Client software works inside a device such as a personal computer or a handheld. It routes requests from application programs and from the keyboard out to file servers and other types of servers on the network. A principal element of the client software is a process called a *redirector*. As its name infers, the redirector captures requests for service it has been programmed to recognize and routes them out of the computer and across the network for service.

Communications processes package data from the client computer, send it across the network, and receive incoming data with appropriate addresses and packaging. These processes work according to specific protocols for addressing, ensuring delivery, and ensuring accuracy. Suites of network communications protocols include Apple Computer's Apple File Protocol (AFP), the Microsoft NetBIOS Extended User Interface (NETBEUI), and Novell's Sequential Packet Exchange and Internetwork Packet Exchange (SPX and IPX). TCP/IP is used on both local area and wide area networks, including the Internet.

The network *interface card driver* software works between the network interface card and the network communications software. (You'll sometimes hear network administrators discuss the problem of having the proper *drivers*.) At one time, you had to generate a special configuration of the network operating system for every make and model of LAN adapter on the market. Today, adapter manufacturers and operating system manufacturers work together to include drivers for a wide variety of interface cards within the libraries included in the operating systems. However, finding the appropriate driver for some operating systems such as Linux or Solaris is still a potential problem.

How Networking Software System Requests Work

1 Networking software allows many computers acting as clients to share the resources of a few computers acting as servers. In this example, client computers send requests for service to different servers. At each step, networking software formats the data for transmission, packages it for delivery, controls the transmission, checks for proper permission, and constantly checks for errors. In this example, the network uses Ethernet for electrical signaling and packet construction, TCP for transmission control, and IP for addressing.

2 The dedicated file server could hold word processing files, database files, Web pages, or the files from any other application. When the network adapter and network communications software deliver a request for file access, the security process checks to make sure the client placing the request has been granted access to the file. Once validated, the request goes to the file service processes. This software mediates simultaneous requests for the same data, finds the data, and sends it back to the requesting client computer.

3 The networking client software in this client computer allows application programs to use disk drives, printers, and other resources as if they were directly attached to the computer. In this case, an application program—perhaps a word processing program or a spreadsheet—has a job to print. The print job goes from the application to Windows with instructions to print on a specific printer port such as LPT3. The redirector process is programmed to send any print jobs addressed to LPT3 out through the networking software and NIC to a specific networked printer. The network communications software packages the print data within an IP packet, wraps it with TCP transmission control, and then inserts it into an Ethernet packet for electrical transmission across the network cable.

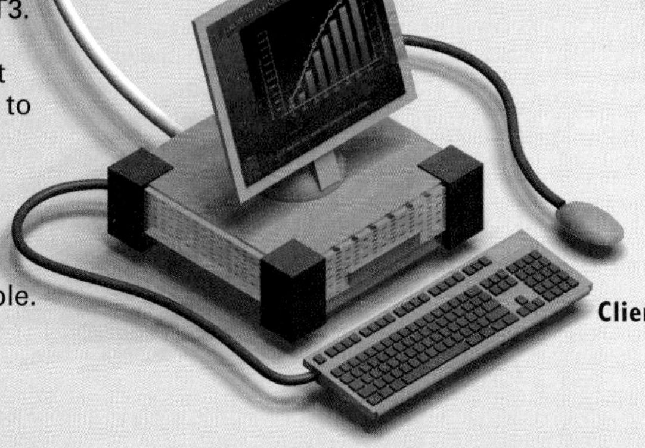

Save file
Dedicated file server
Network printer data
Client computer

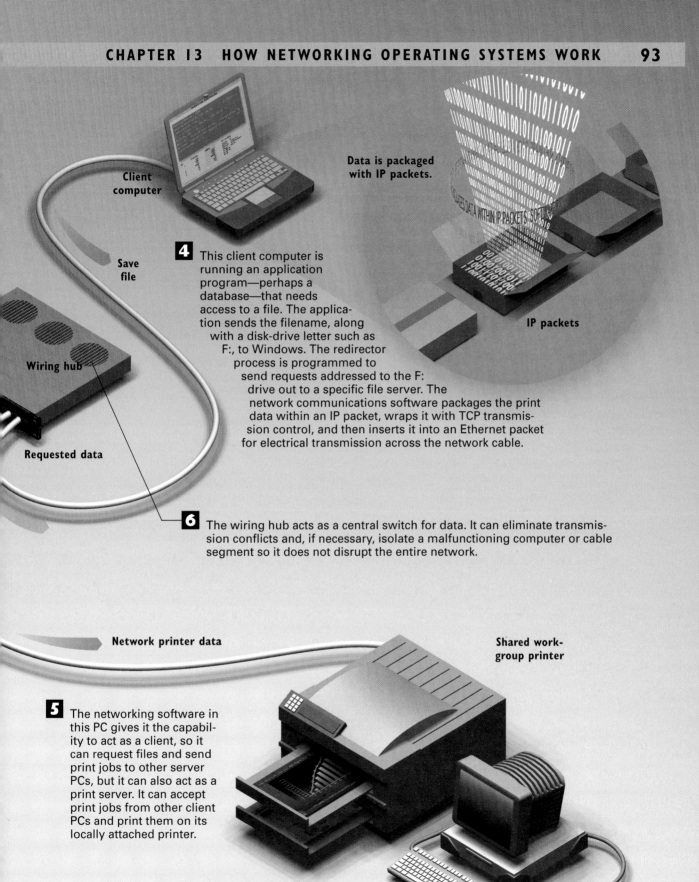

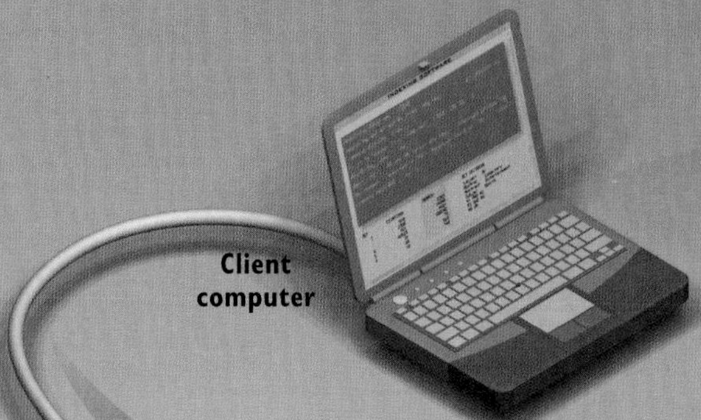

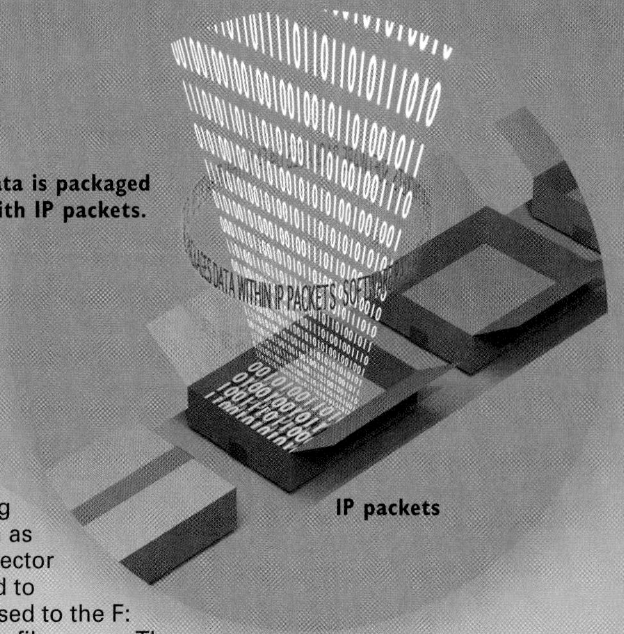

Client computer

Data is packaged with IP packets.

Save file

4 This client computer is running an application program—perhaps a database—that needs access to a file. The application sends the filename, along with a disk-drive letter such as F:, to Windows. The redirector process is programmed to send requests addressed to the F: drive out to a specific file server. The network communications software packages the print data within an IP packet, wraps it with TCP transmission control, and then inserts it into an Ethernet packet for electrical transmission across the network cable.

IP packets

Wiring hub

Requested data

6 The wiring hub acts as a central switch for data. It can eliminate transmission conflicts and, if necessary, isolate a malfunctioning computer or cable segment so it does not disrupt the entire network.

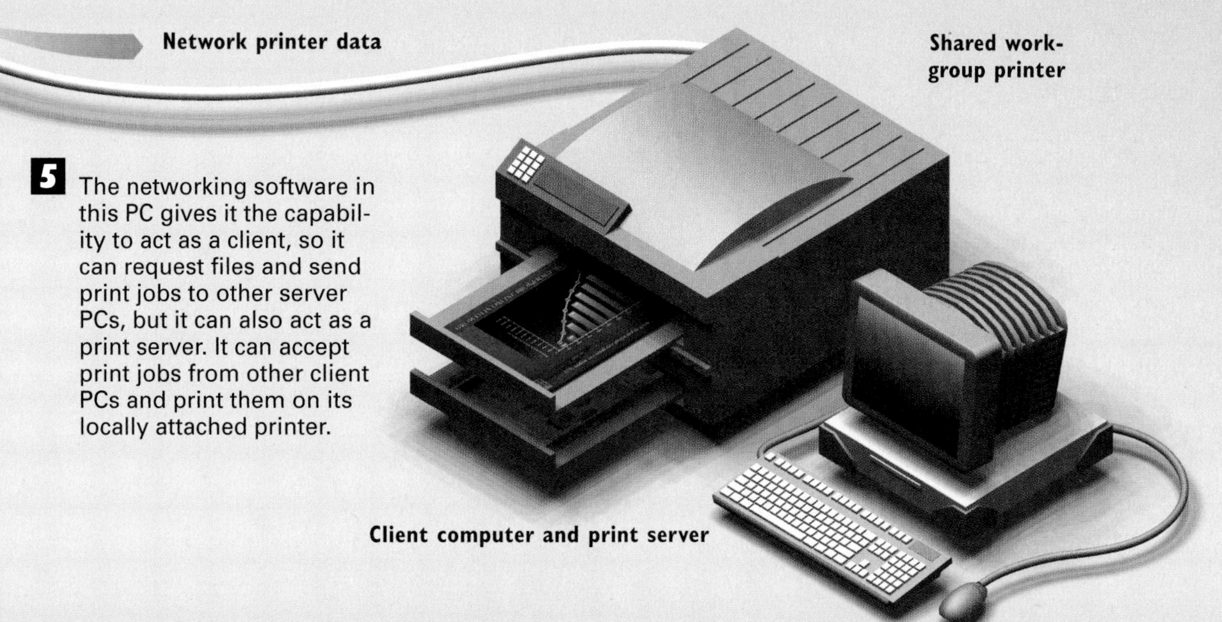
Network printer data
Shared work-group printer
Client computer and print server

5 The networking software in this PC gives it the capability to act as a client, so it can request files and send print jobs to other server PCs, but it can also act as a print server. It can accept print jobs from other client PCs and print them on its locally attached printer.

How Networking Software Data Packaging Works

Windows

Open file

1. Network software packages requests from the keyboard and from applications in a succession of data "envelopes" for transmission across the network. In this example, networking software running within Microsoft Windows detects that a service request should be redirected to a server, packages a directory request in an IP packet, appends TCP transmission controls, and sends it to the LAN adapter. The LAN adapter further packages the request into an Ethernet frame. Each data "envelope" contains its own addressing and error control information.

2. Devices along the network examine both the Ethernet address (called the *media access control*, or *MAC-layer address*) and the IP address of each packet. Some network devices, such as switches, take actions or grant permissions based on the MAC-layer address and others, such as routers, take actions based on the IP address.

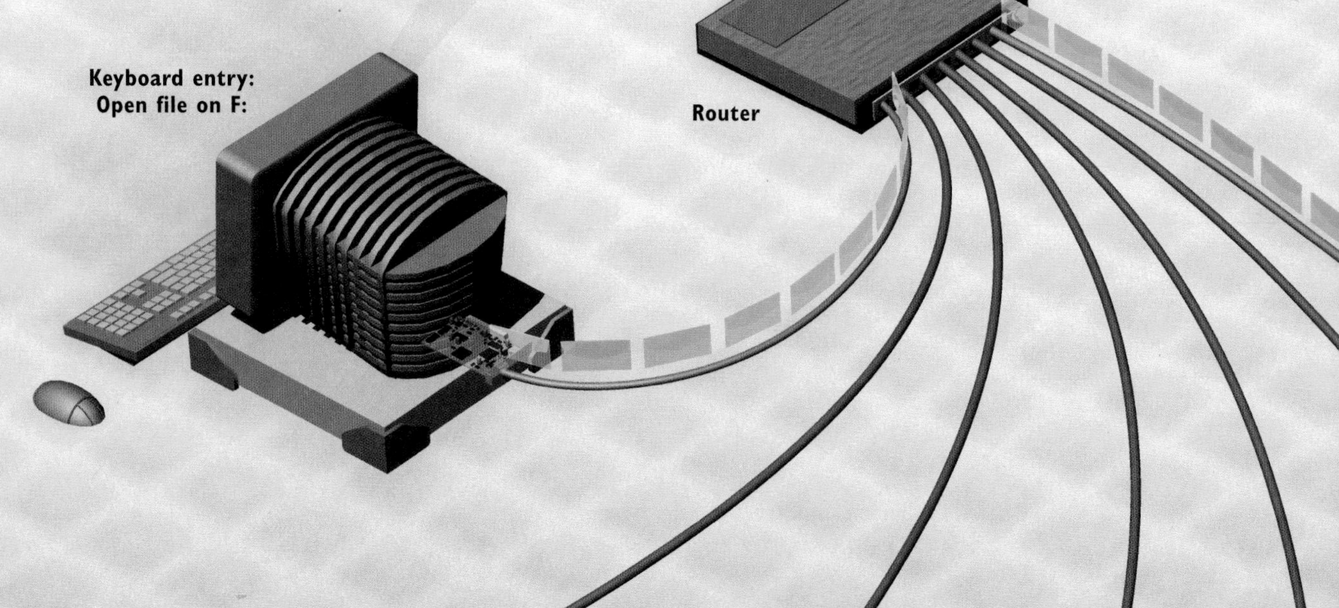
Keyboard entry:
Open file on F:
Router

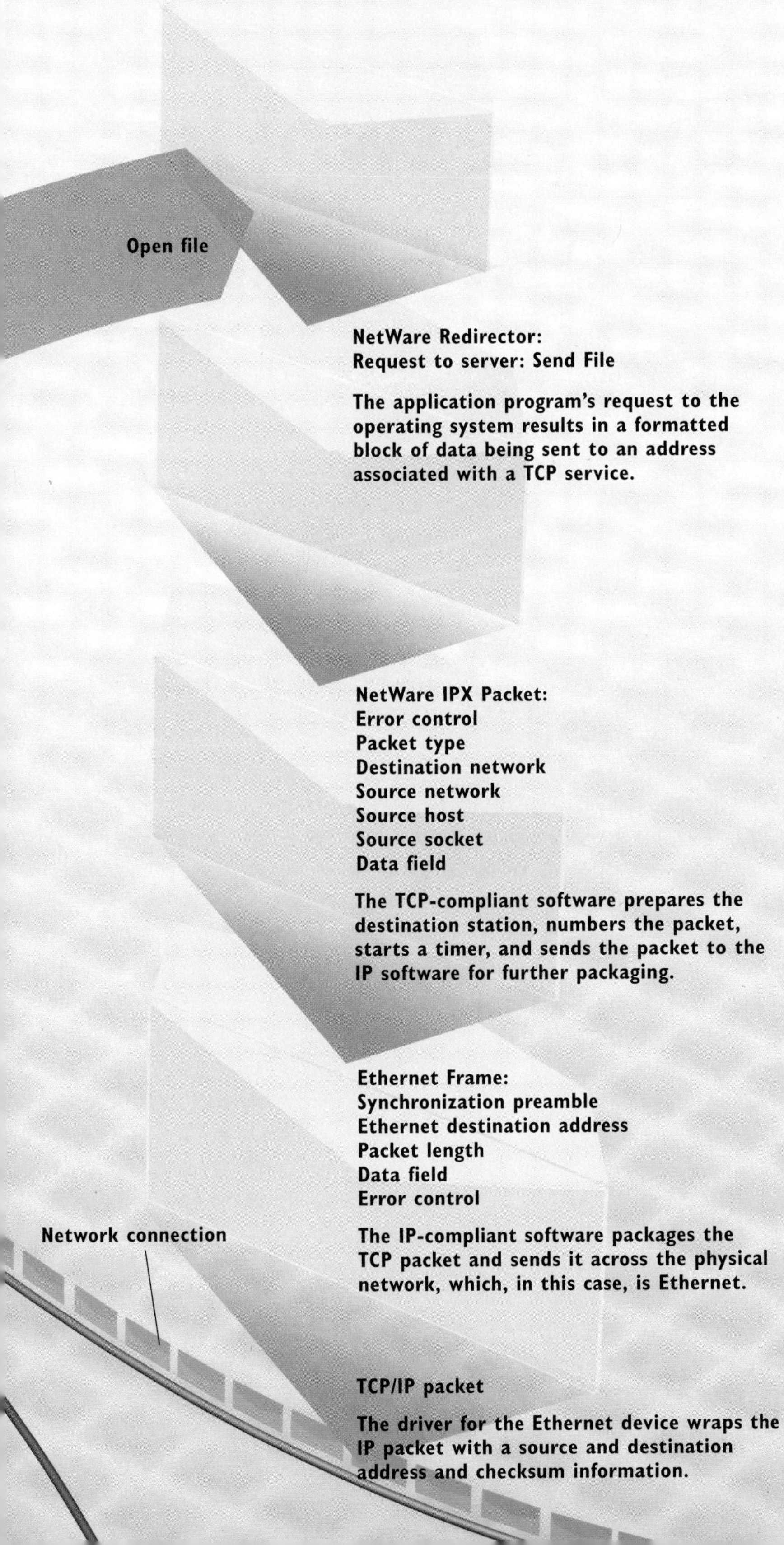

Open file

NetWare Redirector:
Request to server: Send File

The application program's request to the operating system results in a formatted block of data being sent to an address associated with a TCP service.

NetWare IPX Packet:
Error control
Packet type
Destination network
Source network
Source host
Source socket
Data field

The TCP-compliant software prepares the destination station, numbers the packet, starts a timer, and sends the packet to the IP software for further packaging.

Ethernet Frame:
Synchronization preamble
Ethernet destination address
Packet length
Data field
Error control

Network connection

The IP-compliant software packages the TCP packet and sends it across the physical network, which, in this case, is Ethernet.

TCP/IP packet

The driver for the Ethernet device wraps the IP packet with a source and destination address and checksum information.

3 At the destination server, the envelopes are unwrapped by networking software processes and put into order. Then, it presents the original request to the server operating system for action. The presence of these layers of software allows detailed management of the flow of data across the network. The management increases reliability and raises overall efficiency.

CHAPTER 14

How Network Interface Cards Work

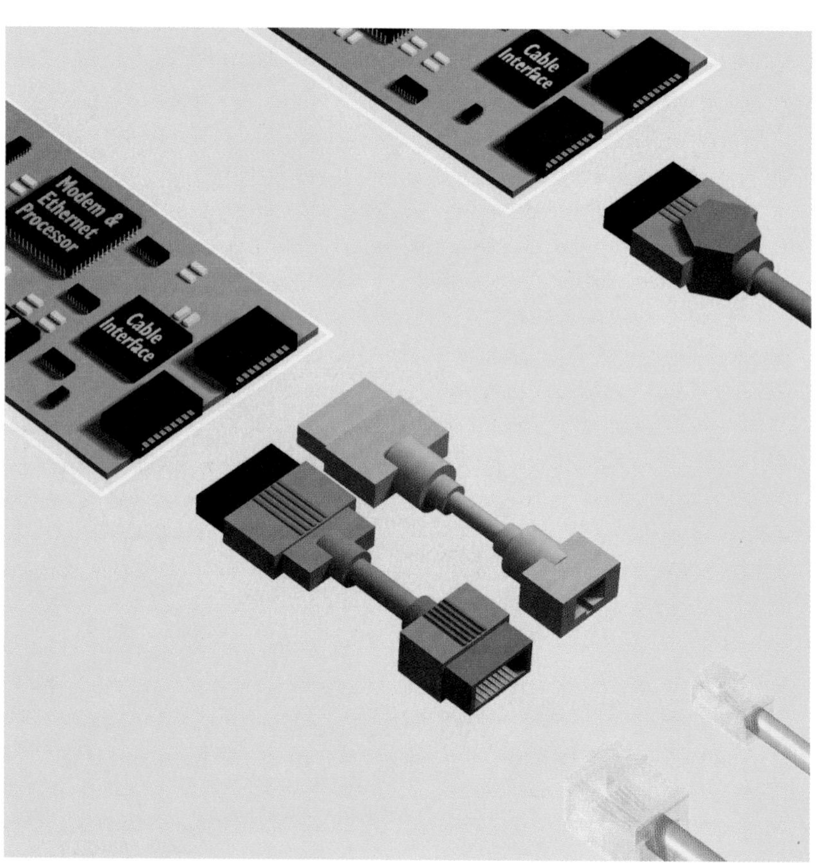
Cable Interface
Modem & Ethernet Processor
Cable Interface

THE network interface card (NIC), or *LAN adapter*, as it's also called, functions as an interface between the computer and the network cabling, so it must serve two masters. Inside the computer, it moves data to and from the computer's random access memory. Outside the computer, it controls the flow of data in and out of the network cable system. An interface card has a specialized port that matches the electrical signaling standards used on the cable and the specific type of cable connector. In between the computer and the cable, the interface card must buffer the data (for the computer is typically much faster than the network) and change the form of the data from a wide parallel stream coming in at 32 bits at a time to a narrow stream moving one bit at a time in and out of the network port. Now it is also common for computers to come with an internal NIC on the motherboard. NICs might also attach through a computer's Universal Serial Bus (USB) port or to a PC Card slot.

This job requires on-board processing power and LAN adapters have processors specially designed for the task. A wide variety of companies including Intel, National Semiconductor, and Texas Instruments sell special-purpose processors and supporting chips for network adapters. Some NICs also have on-board processors to handle intensive tasks such as encryption. Other on-board features might include virus checking, the creation of specialized management reports, and even the capability to wake up the computer through a command delivered across the network. This wake-on-LAN is useful for conducting remote maintenance and management tasks.

On the network cable side, the LAN adapter performs three important functions: It generates the electrical signals that go over the network cable, it follows specific rules controlling access to the cable, and it makes the physical connection to the cable. Adapters for Ethernet and Token-Ring both use the same basic system of electrical signaling over the cable. Surprisingly, the signals on these high-speed computer cables aren't very different from the early Morse code or Baudot teletype code. Wireless LANs are very popular, but despite their apparent differences, wireless NICs are very similar to their cabled cousins. They access a shared transmission media, although without a cable, and translate between parallel and serial data streams just like NICs attached to a cable.

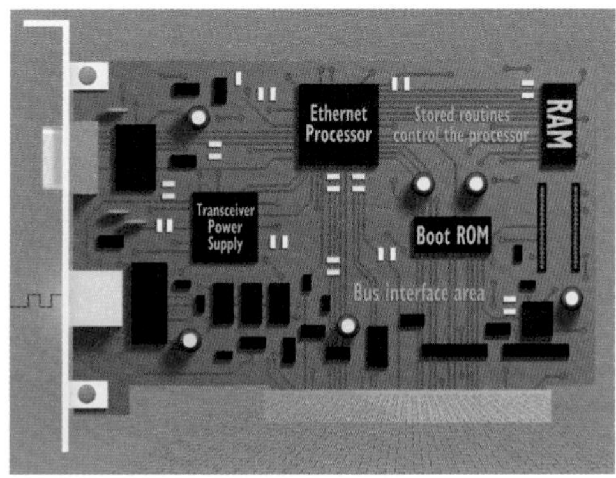
Ethernet Processor
Stored routines control the processor
RAM
Transceiver Power Supply
Boot ROM
Bus interface area

How Internal NICs Work

1 A network interface card uses a specialized processor and routines stored in read-only memory. This processor receives instructions from processes running in the host computer to retrieve data from the contents of specific shared-memory locations within the host computer. These memory locations hold data packaged according to specific protocols such as TCP/IP. The NIC uses the computer's fast expansion bus to access the shared memory as parallel data. The processor then uses a series of its own specialized storage locations called *shift registers* to change the parallel data into a serial stream. The serial stream is packaged into groups of specific length (usually frames of 1,518 bytes, but other sizes are used) for transmission over the slower cable. The NIC's processor rearranges and buffers the data while handling the interface to the computer and the interface to the cable.

2 This parallel-to-serial and fast-to-slow conversion is a necessary trade-off caused by distance. The laws of physics dictate that when signals cross long distances, they weaken and become more susceptible to interference, so there is a trade-off between speed and accuracy. Modern networks are getting faster—reaching gigabit-per-second signaling speeds—but the highest network speeds are still only 10% or so of the average speed of data handling within a common PC.

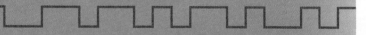

4 You must select a network interface card that matches your computer's data bus and the network cable. The Peripheral Component Interface (PCI) bus has emerged as the standard for NICs. On the PC side, it can theoretically allow a data transfer rate of 133.33 MBps. It sends data across 32 parallel connections and the LAN adapters must repackage that data into one serial stream.

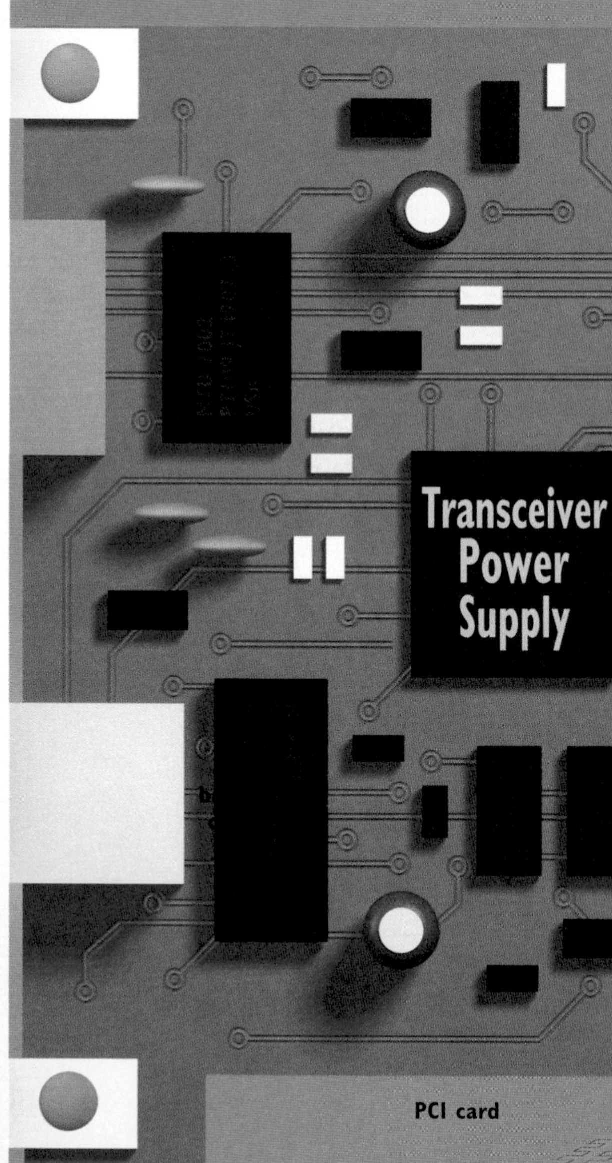
Transceiver Power Supply
PCI card

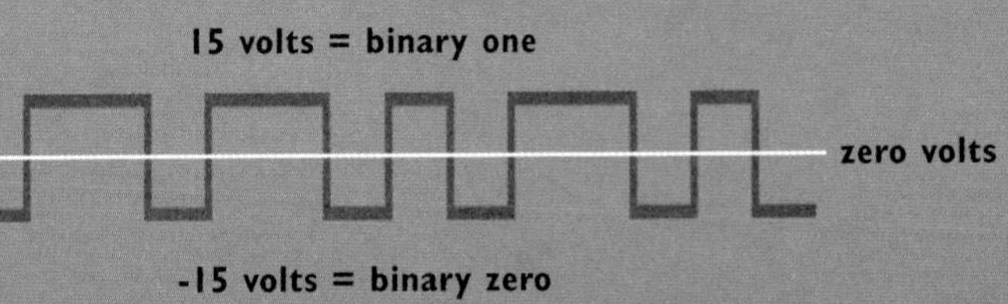
15 volts = binary one
zero volts
-15 volts = binary zero

3 A technique called *Manchester encoding* provides a way to transmit zeros and ones using direct current voltage pulses that range from -15 to +15 volts. Under this technique, a change in the voltage level from zero volts to +15 volts represents a binary 1 in the message stream. A change from zero volts to -15 volts represents a binary zero. At the receiving end, the LAN adapters use a device called a *digital phased locked loop*, typically contained within a chipset, to translate each change in the voltage level as a bit in a digital stream.

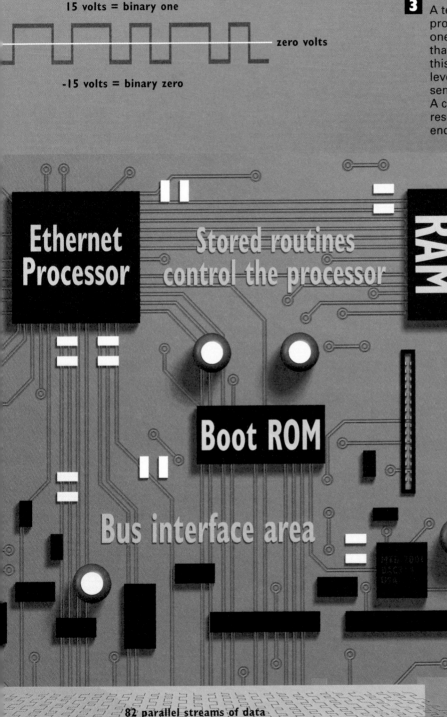

Ethernet Processor

Stored routines control the processor

RAM

Boot ROM

Bus interface area

82 parallel streams of data

5 The technique the adapters use to control access to the cable and the type of cable connectors are attributes of the network architecture, such as Ethernet or Token-Ring, that you choose. We'll describe those architectures more thoroughly in the following pages, but you should know that you'll have to buy adapters with the right connectors and the right protocols for access into the network cable.

6 The processor uses a series of its own specialized temporary storage locations called *shift registers* to change the parallel data into a serial stream. The serial stream is packaged into groups of specific length (usually frames of 1,518 bytes) for transmission over the cable.

How PC Card Adapters Work

1 Laptop and handheld computers often use credit-card–size LAN adapters that fit into special accessory slots. The standards for these adapters have changed and the names of the standards have changed drastically, so it's sometimes difficult to keep them straight. PCMCIA stands for *Personal Computer Memory Card International Association*. PCMCIA is the overall standard for expansion slots in laptop computers, PDAs, and other small devices. Cardbus is an evolved version of PCMCIA and almost all new network interface cards conform to the Cardbus standard. Under this standard, Cardbus Type II (single thickness) cards can support bandwidth up to 50MBps, whereas Type III (double thickness) cards support 100MBps bandwidth. In comparison, the standard PCMCIA cards support only about 8MBps. Cardbus slots are backward compatible with PCMCIA cards, but Cardbus cards require Cardbus slots to reach optimal performance.

2 The Cardbus and PCMCIA devices use 68-pin plugs and sockets to link to the host device. A specialized controller inside the host device manages the card slot and helps to identify the card so the operating system can load the correct drivers.

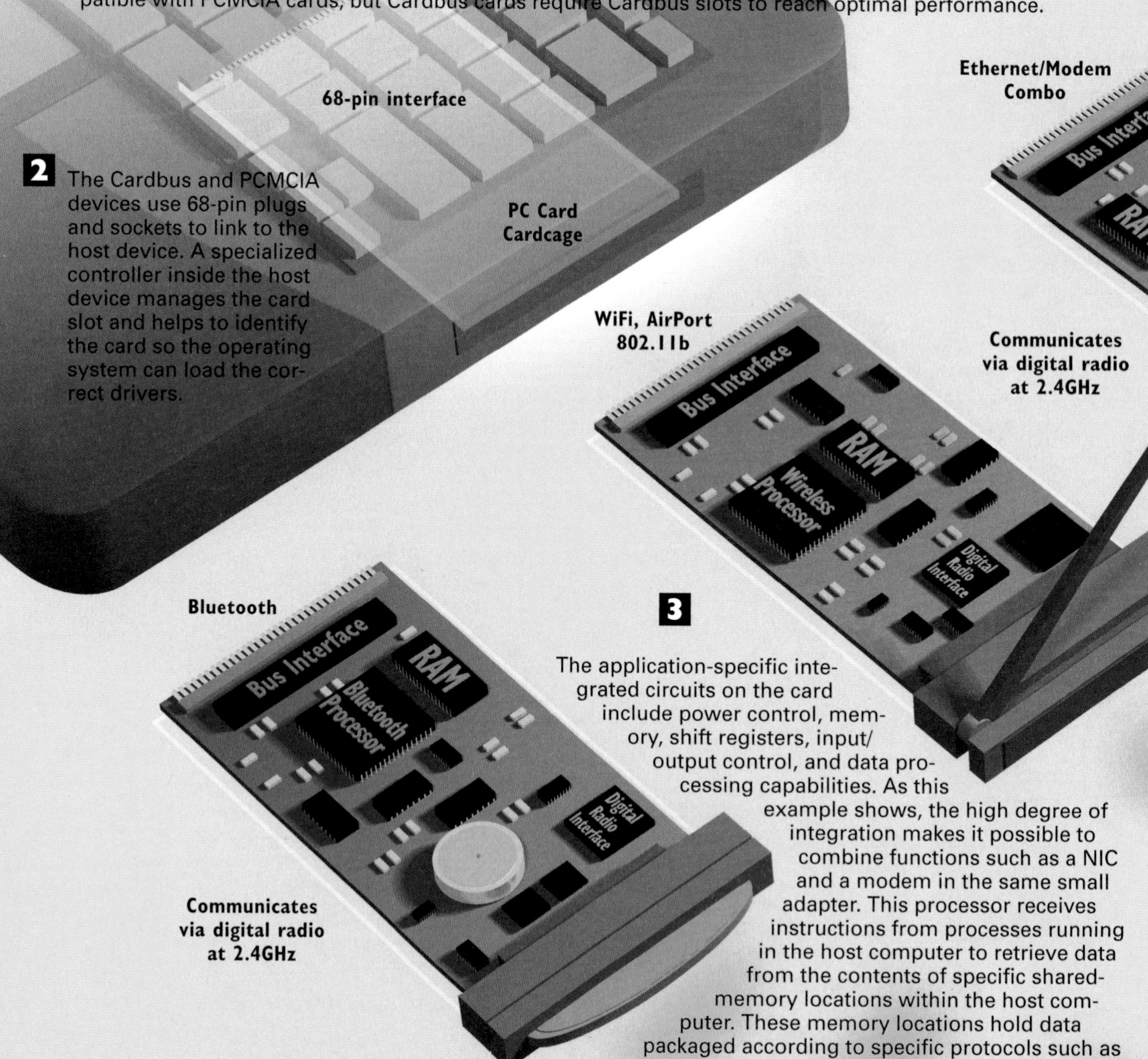
68-pin interface
PC Card Cardcage
Ethernet/Modem Combo
Bus Interface
RAM
WiFi, AirPort 802.11b
Communicates via digital radio at 2.4GHz
Bus Interface
RAM
Wireless Processor
Digital Radio Interface
Bluetooth
Bus Interface
RAM
Bluetooth Processor
Digital Radio Interface
Communicates via digital radio at 2.4GHz

3 The application-specific integrated circuits on the card include power control, memory, shift registers, input/output control, and data processing capabilities. As this example shows, the high degree of integration makes it possible to combine functions such as a NIC and a modem in the same small adapter. This processor receives instructions from processes running in the host computer to retrieve data from the contents of specific shared-memory locations within the host computer. These memory locations hold data packaged according to specific protocols such as TCP/IP. The NIC uses the computer's fast expansion bus to access the shared memory as parallel data.

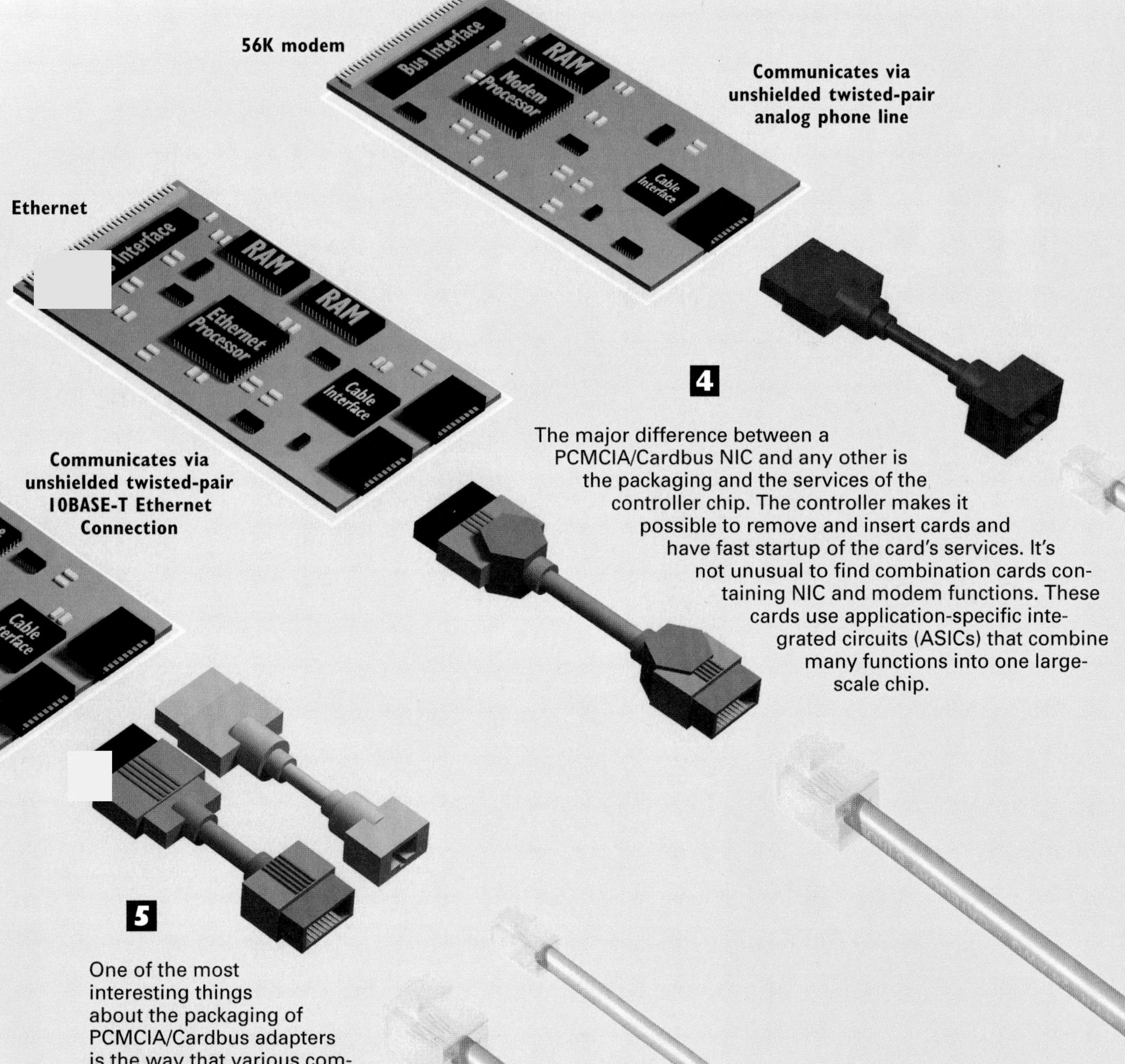
56K modem
Bus Interface
RAM
Modem Processor
Cable Interface
Communicates via unshielded twisted-pair analog phone line
Ethernet
RAM
RAM
Ethernet Processor
Cable Interface
Communicates via unshielded twisted-pair 10BASE-T Ethernet Connection
Cable Interface

4

The major difference between a PCMCIA/Cardbus NIC and any other is the packaging and the services of the controller chip. The controller makes it possible to remove and insert cards and have fast startup of the card's services. It's not unusual to find combination cards containing NIC and modem functions. These cards use application-specific integrated circuits (ASICs) that combine many functions into one large-scale chip.

5

One of the most interesting things about the packaging of PCMCIA/Cardbus adapters is the way that various companies handle the cable connections. If the designer puts full size connectors on the card, the second slot is blocked for many types of cards. Some companies have fold-out jacks or special cable extensions that make it possible to have a cable connection and still make use of the second available slot.

CHAPTER 15 How Network Cables Work

To: Mail Server
(24.2.3.33)

IN the mid-1990s, the networking industry settled on Ethernet as the common standard for local area networks. Before that time, ARCnet and Token-Ring competed with Ethernet. You'll still find ARCnet in retail stores, and high-reliability applications such as brokerage houses use Token-Ring. Interestingly, new standards for cabling have emerged that override the standards of each networking scheme. In the following pages, we'll illustrate the classic wiring configurations associated with each scheme, and we'll also illustrate the *structured wiring system* that has overtaken the classic configurations.

The network cable, or *media*, is a single thread of copper or glass that links all of the nodes on the network, but that can only can carry the signals from one network interface card at a time. Every LAN architecture needs a media access control (MAC) scheme so adapters can take turns transmitting into the cable.

In an Ethernet network, the adapters share the common cable by listening before they transmit and only transmitting during a break in the traffic when the channel is quiet—a technique called *carrier-sense multiple access with collision detection (CSMA/CD)*. Under the collision detection part of the scheme, if two stations begin to transmit at the same time, they detect, stop, and retry.

Token-Ring adapters use a much more complex control scheme called *token-passing*. Token-Ring adapters must gain permission to transmit into a cable system that forms a complete electrical loop. Under this technique, the active adapters negotiate to determine a master adapter. The master initiates a special message called a *free token*. When an interface card receives a free token, it changes the free token into a data packet and sends it to the next station for relay. After the addressed interface card receives the message and returns it to the originating interface card, that card initiates a new free token and the process begins again.

ARCnet adapters use a somewhat similar control scheme. A master adapter, designated by the highest number set into an adapter, maintains a table of all active adapters and polls each adapter in turn, giving it permission to transmit.

Until the mid-1990s, each networking scheme had its own type of specialized cable. New installations use standard cables and connectors. Ethernet has almost completely nosed out Token-Ring and ARCnet, but many older schemes still exist. Some older LAN adapters that are still in service have connectors for various kinds of cables. Older Ethernet installations use coaxial cable and *T-connectors*. Others have connectors for a 15-pin socket for more complex external *transceivers* like fiber optic. Token-Ring adapters have a 9-pin connector for shielded twisted-pair wire. However, unshielded twisted-pair wire has become the standard for all modern installations, and include a plastic rectangular jack similar to those found on telephones.

Modern network cable installations conform to specifications for structured wiring systems issued by the Electronic Industries Association and Underwriters Laboratories. This architecture uses wire without an external shield of copper braid, but each pair of wires is twisted together at about six turns per inch. The twisting cancels electric currents, absorbed from power cables and other outside sources, that can mask the network signals. Structured wiring systems improve reliability by using dedicated spans of wire from each node to a central wiring hub. The hub or switch automatically disconnects malfunctioning interface cards and defective wire spans so they don't degrade the rest of the network.

UTP cable systems are graded according to categories established by the Electronic Industries Alliance/Telecommunications Industry Association (EIA/TIA) that describe the quality of the components and installation techniques. Category 5e is the minimum typical specification. Category 6 and 7 specifications exist, but they aren't widely installed. Networking adapters evolved to do more with less. Modern Gigabit Ethernet adapters can reliably use Category 5e cabling over reasonable distances. Today, the choices are between Cat5e cabling or fiber. Fiber is preferred only on runs of over a hundred meters and in building environments with extreme electrical noise.

These cable standards describe the size of the wires, spacing, positioning, insulation, and the construction of the connectors. These factors control electrical characteristics such as resistance, capacitance, and inductance, which, in turn, affect the way signals degrade as they travel across the cable. They also control susceptibility to *crosstalk*—electric currents between wires in the same cable—and outside electrical fields caused by power lines, motors, relays, radio transmitters, and other devices.

Fiber optic network interface cards read pulses of laser light. They have become so sophisticated that they can discriminate between color groups, so network designers can create sub-networks on the same cable by dividing them into color bands.

Your network's operating system and network interface cards can be changed in a few hours. But changing the cabling requires weeks of work. Cable selection and installation are important steps in designing a network that will serve you economically and reliably for years. Study the options and carefully specify your needs.

Unshielded Twisted Pair

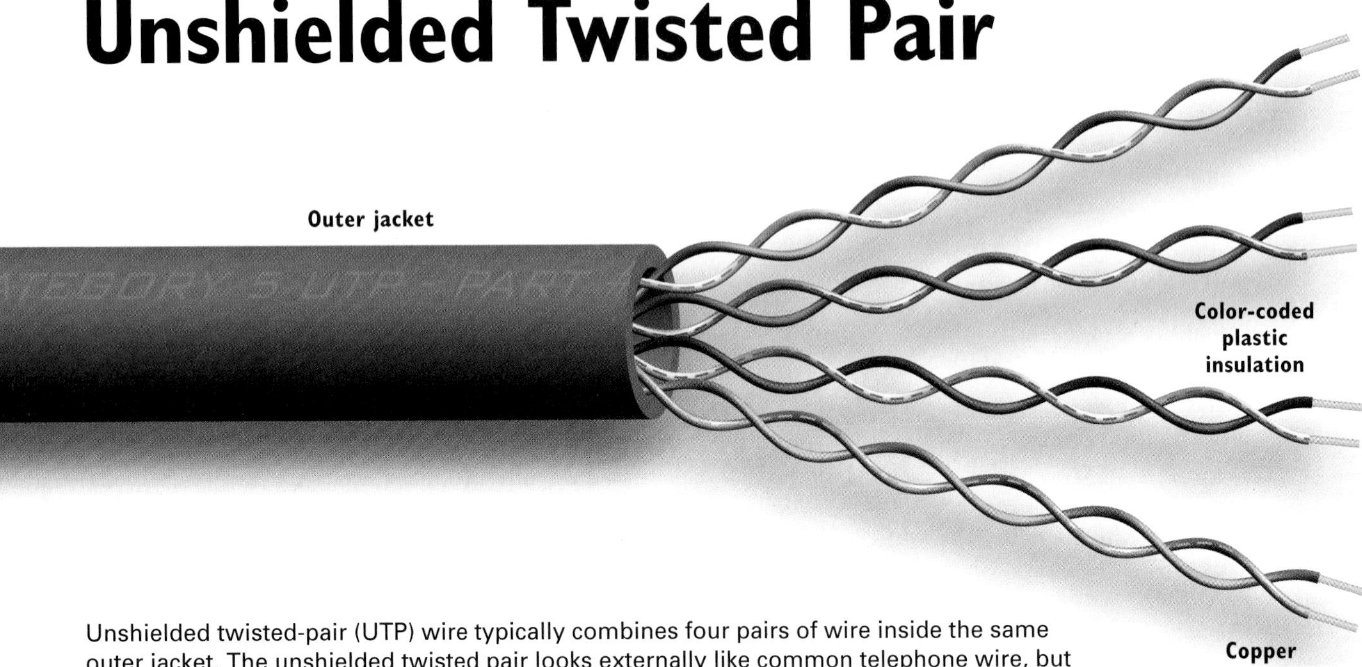
Outer jacket
CATEGORY 5 UTP – PART #
Color-coded plastic insulation
Copper conductor

Unshielded twisted-pair (UTP) wire typically combines four pairs of wire inside the same outer jacket. The unshielded twisted pair looks externally like common telephone wire, but telephone wire lacks the twisting and other electrical characteristics needed to carry data. Each pair is twisted with a different number of twists per inch. The twisting cancels out electrical noise from adjacent pairs and from other devices in the building such as motors, relays, and transformers and it reduces the amount of crosstalk or mutual interference from signals traveling on different pairs of wires.

In typical 10- or 100-Megabit-per-second Ethernet installations, the blue and white/blue pair and the green and white/green pair are the only ones used. Each network adapter transmits using signals composed of plus and minus voltages imposed on the orange and green wires and receives signals as voltages imposed on the white/green and white/orange wires. In most installations, the other wires are used as spares. Gigabit Ethernet installations use all the wires. UTP cable attenuates signals and doesn't keep out noise as effectively as shielded cables or fiber-optic cable, but its range of about 100 meters meets most local network needs. UTP is produced in bulk without expensive braids or shields, so it is very affordable.

SPEED & THROUGHPUT
FAST ENOUGH

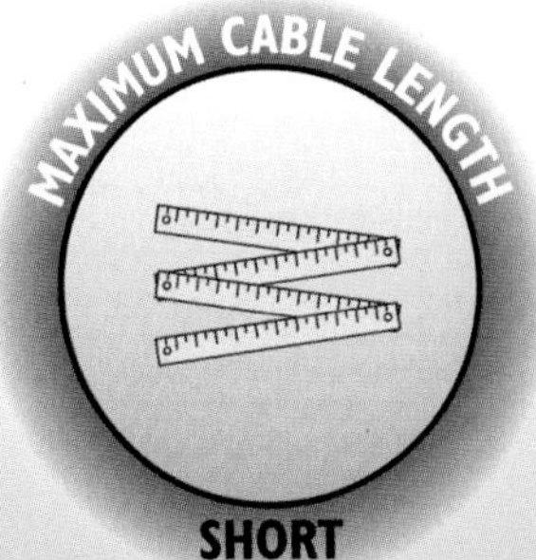
MAXIMUM CABLE LENGTH
SHORT

RJ-45 connector
MEDIA & CONNECTOR SIZE
SMALL

AVERAGED COST PER NODE
LEAST EXPENSIVE

Coaxial Cable

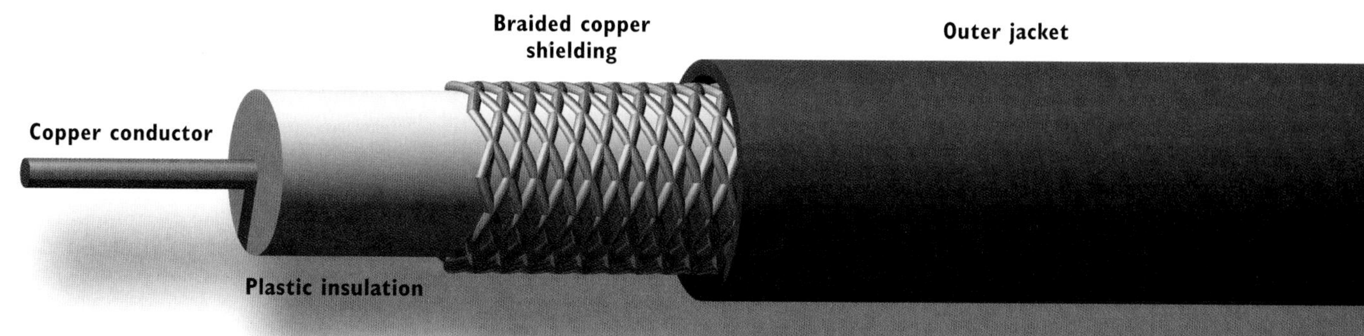
Braided copper shielding
Outer jacket
Copper conductor
Plastic insulation

Coaxial cable gets its name because the two conductors, a center wire and a copper braid shield, share the same center axis, so they are coaxial. This cable relies on the woven copper braid to shield the center conductor from outside electrical currents. A thick plastic insulator separates the center conductor from the shield and keeps the two conductors a specific distance apart. An external jacket covers the copper braid.

The Ethernet and ARCnet specification both include coaxial cable, but they each call for a different type of cable. These signaling schemes impose signals as plus and minus voltages between the center conductor and the outer shield. Coaxial cable is heavy and it uses a lot of materials, but it is made in such bulk for use in radio systems that the overall cost is moderate. Special devices called *line drivers* can send data at hundreds of megabits per second for thousands of feet over coaxial cable. This technique is used to cross campuses with computer networks and to extend services such as DSL into neighborhoods. As a general guideline, the maximum data rate falls in inverse proportion to the square of the distance: You can get one-fourth the data rate at twice the distance.

SPEED & THROUGHPUT
FAST ENOUGH

MAXIMUM CABLE LENGTH
MEDIUM

BNC connector
MEDIA & CONNECTOR SIZE
MEDIUM

AVERAGED COST PER NODE
INEXPENSIVE

Shielded Twisted Pair

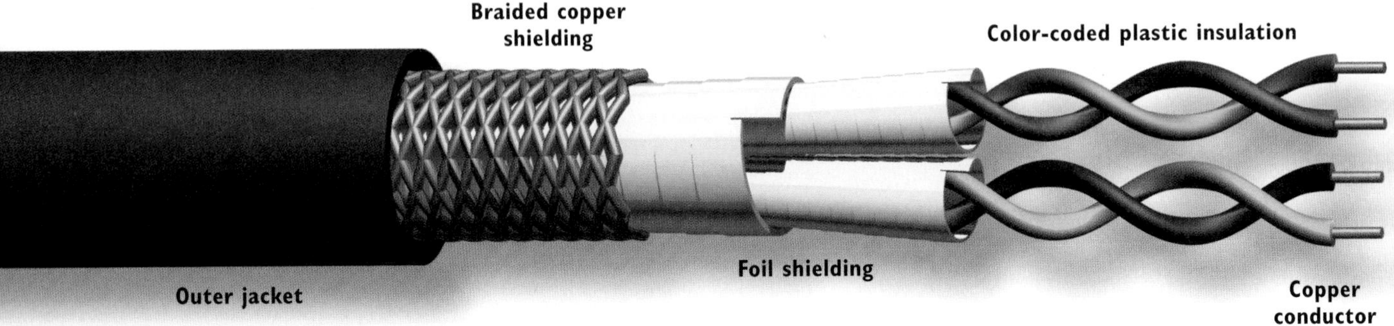
Braided copper shielding
Color-coded plastic insulation
Foil shielding
Outer jacket
Copper conductor

The original design of the Token-Ring networking system aimed at extremely high reliability. The initial specification called for shielded twisted-pair wire (STP) using a woven copper braid, a foil wrap, and internal twisting of the pairs to provide a high degree of protection from outside electrical currents. However, the combination creates an expensive cable. Newer Token-Ring adapters use unshielded twisted pair and work fine in all but the most hostile electrical noise environments.

In shielded twisted-pair wire, the signals ride between the wires in the pairs. The shield is not a part of the signaling circuit. STP requires large connectors to accommodate the signal leads and to properly terminate the shield. The range of this cable is limited by the network specification on signal timing, not by the cable's attenuation of signals. Because of the cost and bulk of STP, long-distance data connections usually go over fiber-optic or coaxial cable.

SPEED & THROUGHPUT
VERY FAST

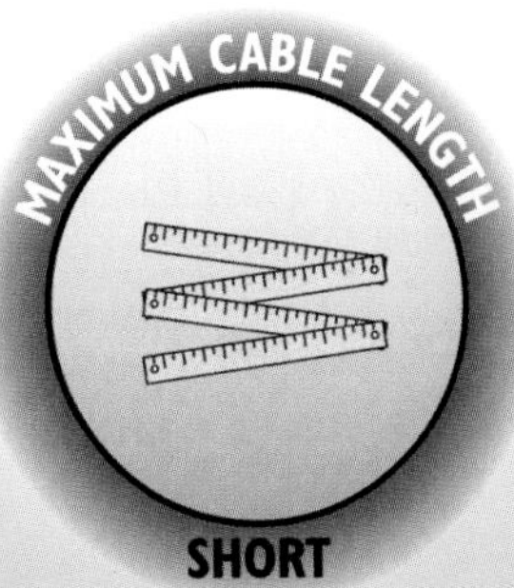
MAXIMUM CABLE LENGTH
SHORT

IBM data connector

MEDIA & CONNECTOR SIZE
LARGE

AVERAGED COST PER NODE
EXPENSIVE

Fiber-Optic Cable

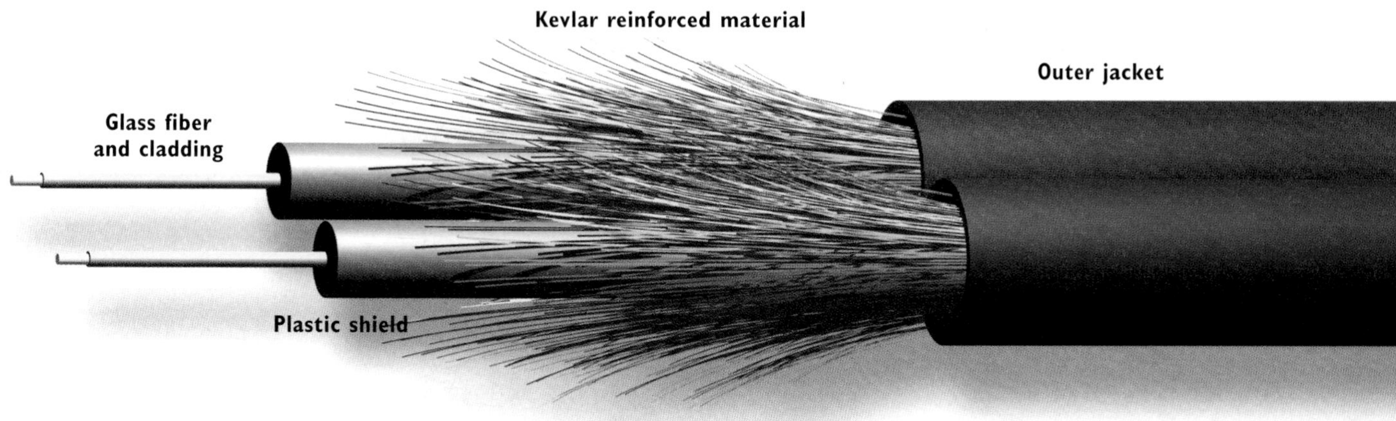
Kevlar reinforced material
Outer jacket
Glass fiber and cladding
Plastic shield

Fiber-optic cable consists of Kevlar fibers (for strength) and a reinforcing layer of plastic surrounding a glass strand. Because the signals it carries are pulses of light conducted over threads of glass, fiber-optic cables aren't bothered by outside electrical currents. Special connectors make an optically pure connection to the glass fiber and provide a window for laser transmitters and optical receivers. Because they are free of interference, the light pulses travel for miles without losing appreciable strength.

Each glass strand passes signals in only one direction, so a cable has two strands in separate jackets. Fiber-optic cables can carry data at high signaling speeds over long distances. Designers can trade lower speed for greater distance and breakthroughs seem to come with semiannual regularity, but hundreds of megabits per second over hundreds of miles is now possible. The major challenge in using fiber optics is the cost of connectors and the difficulty in making connections and splices because of the need for the precise alignment of the fibers.

SPEED & THROUGHPUT
FASTEST POSSIBLE

MAXIMUM CABLE LENGTH
VERY LONG

Fiber-optic connector

MEDIA & CONNECTOR SIZE
TINY

AVERAGED COST PER NODE
MOST EXPENSIVE

How Ethernet Networking Works

T-connector
with
terminator
Terminator
T-connector
BNC
connector
T-connector
T-connector
Thin Ethernet
coaxial cable

1 In an Ethernet network, the adapters share the common cable by listening before they transmit and transmitting only during a break in the traffic when the channel is quiet—a technique called *carrier-sense multiple access with collision detection* (CSMA/CD). Ethernet networks can have several different cabling schemes. On the left, you see computers connected by a cable that runs from interface card to interface card. This linear bus or Thin Ethernet configuration saves cable and is easy to install in small groups, but if the cable breaks at any point, it disrupts network operation of all the computers on that cable. Thin Ethernet uses a T-shaped coaxial connector at each interface card. Each end of the coaxial cable has a terminator, which absorbs signals when they reach the ends of the cable and prevents their reflection.

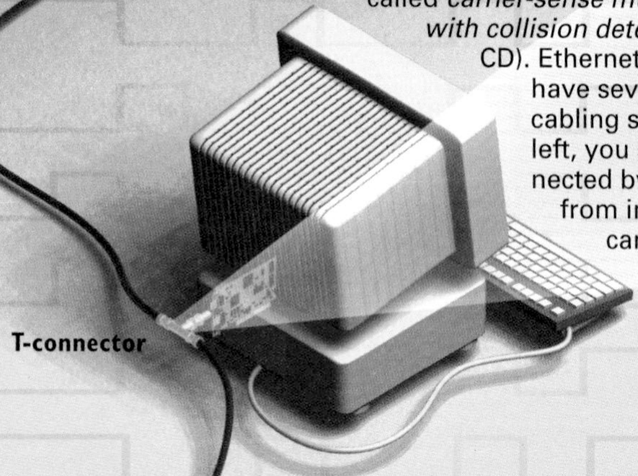

2 In a linear bus, the computers share the cable using a technique called *Carrier Sense Multiple Access (CSMA)*. If the NIC senses signals on the cable, it waits for a quiet period to transmit. Because the nature of network traffic is that it happens in bursts, most cable systems have almost 90% quiet times, so CSMA is an adequate system in typical networks.

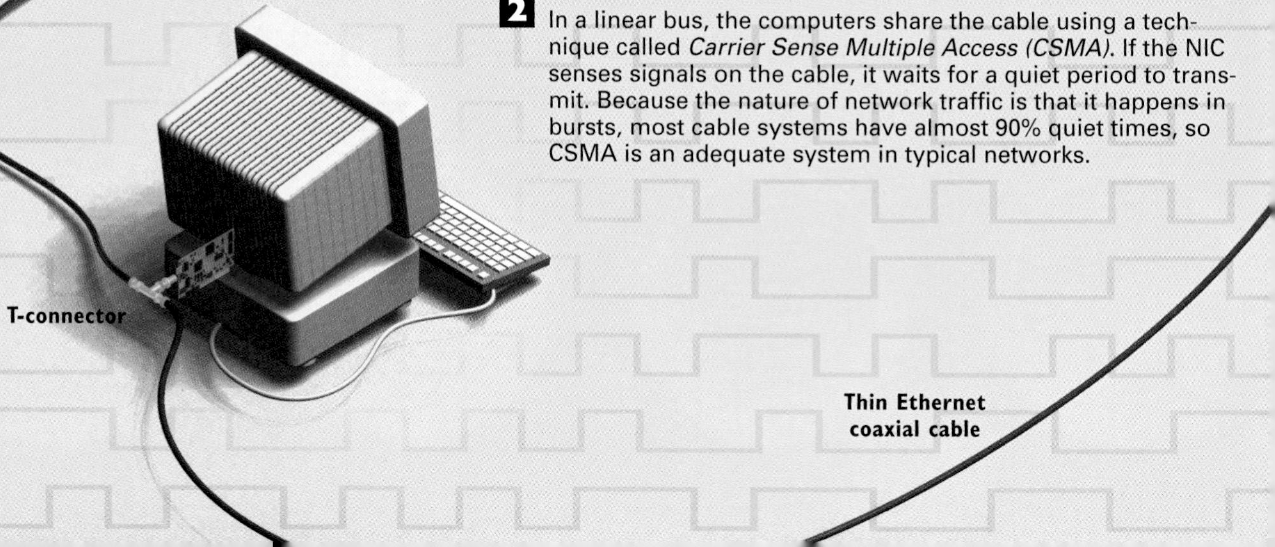

3 On the right side, you see that each network station has a direct connection to a central point. Until the late 1990s, this central device was called a *hub*. The hub was simply a convenient physical device for making connections. If one cable run was broken or shorted, the hub could isolate it from the network to prevent a total disruption. In the mid 1990s, it became economical to use switches in this position instead of simple hubs.

PC card network interface

Wiring Hub

4 In the late 1990s, the cost of centralized devices called *switches* dropped to the point where it no longer made sense to buy hubs. Switches do sophisticated routing of Ethernet packets based on destination addresses. A switch knows the MAC addresses of each connected device and sends a packet on to only the destination device. So, CSMA sharing is less important and the overall load on the network goes down significantly. In this example, the switch connects to the thin Ethernet linear bus of coaxial cable and has a strip of connectors for unshielded twisted-pair wire.

Unshielded twisted-pair wire used in 10BASE-T, 100BASE-T, and gigabit Ethernet configurations.

5 The Ethernet configuration using unshielded twisted-pair wire is known as 10BASE-T because it uses 10-megabit-per-second (Mbps) signaling speed, direct current, or baseband, signaling, and twisted-pair wire. This configuration includes a central wiring hub with special circuitry to isolate malfunctioning segments of the network. Unshielded twisted-pair wire uses a small plastic connector called an *RJ-45 connector* at each end of the wire. Gigabit Ethernet networks use the same UTP cabling with upgraded hubs and adapters.

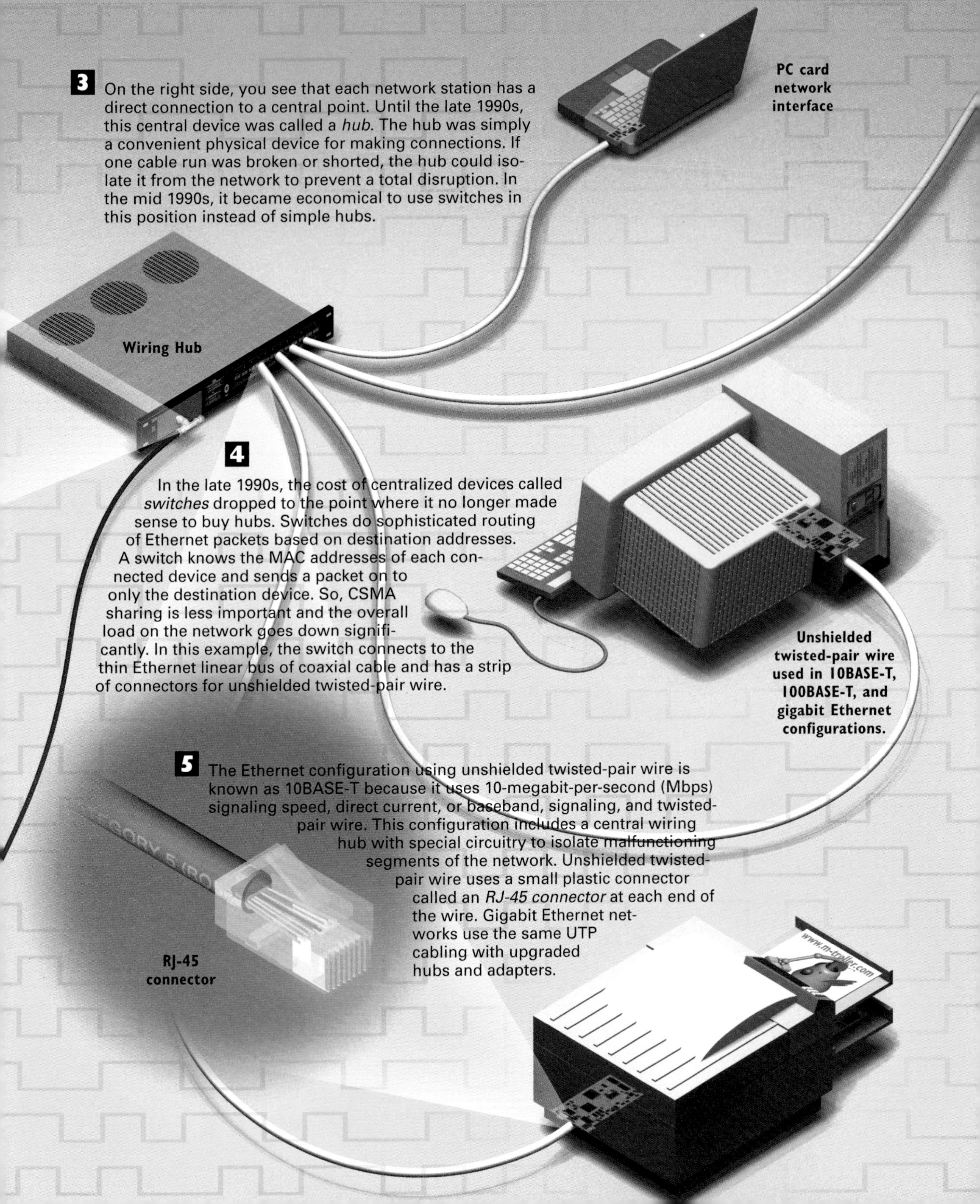

RJ-45 connector

How Token-Rings Work

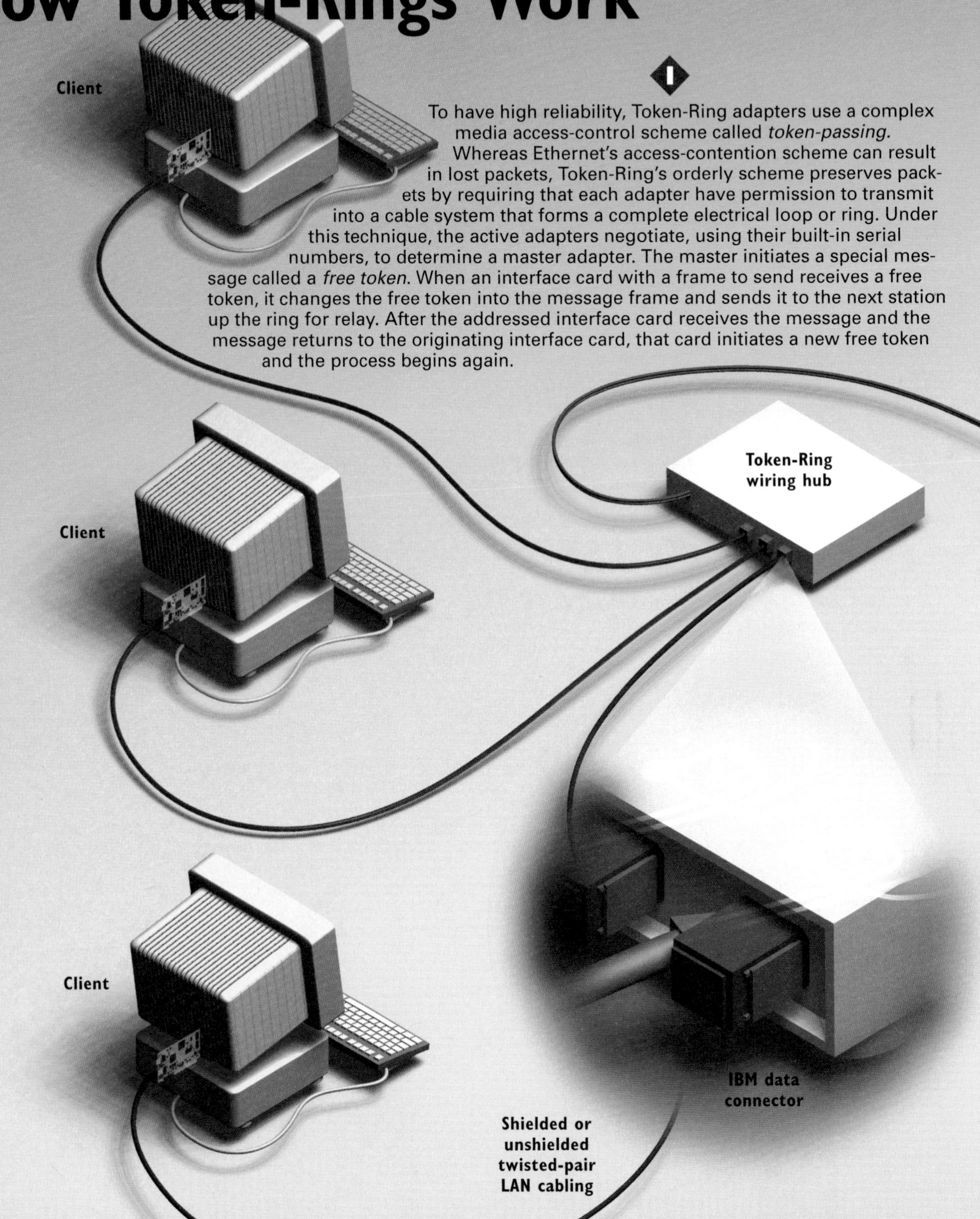
Client
Client
Client
Token-Ring wiring hub
IBM data connector
Shielded or unshielded twisted-pair LAN cabling

1

To have high reliability, Token-Ring adapters use a complex media access-control scheme called *token-passing*. Whereas Ethernet's access-contention scheme can result in lost packets, Token-Ring's orderly scheme preserves packets by requiring that each adapter have permission to transmit into a cable system that forms a complete electrical loop or ring. Under this technique, the active adapters negotiate, using their built-in serial numbers, to determine a master adapter. The master initiates a special message called a *free token*. When an interface card with a frame to send receives a free token, it changes the free token into the message frame and sends it to the next station up the ring for relay. After the addressed interface card receives the message and the message returns to the originating interface card, that card initiates a new free token and the process begins again.

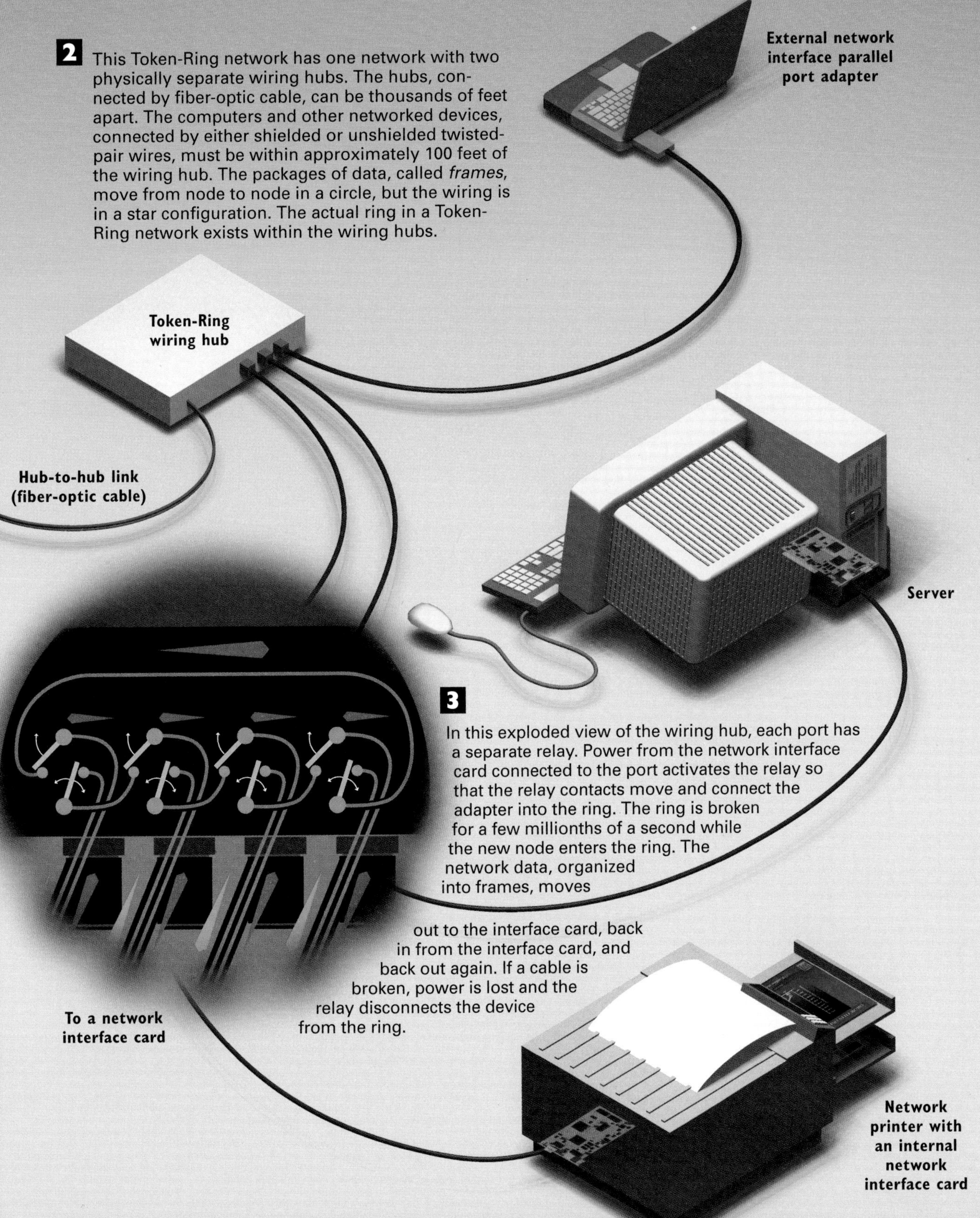
External network interface parallel port adapter
Token-Ring wiring hub
Hub-to-hub link (fiber-optic cable)
Server
To a network interface card
Network printer with an internal network interface card

2 This Token-Ring network has one network with two physically separate wiring hubs. The hubs, connected by fiber-optic cable, can be thousands of feet apart. The computers and other networked devices, connected by either shielded or unshielded twisted-pair wires, must be within approximately 100 feet of the wiring hub. The packages of data, called *frames*, move from node to node in a circle, but the wiring is in a star configuration. The actual ring in a Token-Ring network exists within the wiring hubs.

3 In this exploded view of the wiring hub, each port has a separate relay. Power from the network interface card connected to the port activates the relay so that the relay contacts move and connect the adapter into the ring. The ring is broken for a few millionths of a second while the new node enters the ring. The network data, organized into frames, moves out to the interface card, back in from the interface card, and back out again. If a cable is broken, power is lost and the relay disconnects the device from the ring.

How Structured Wiring Systems Work

Router

Wiring closet

Router

Wiring closet

Router

Main distribution frame

Network administrator console software

1 A network is never any more reliable or efficient than its cable system allows it to be. The labor and materials invested in a cable system can make it the most expensive part of a modern network. All new network installations of any size use a structured wiring system because it provides a standardized way to wire a building for all types of networks. If you understand how this structured system works, you can better understand how your network fits into your building.

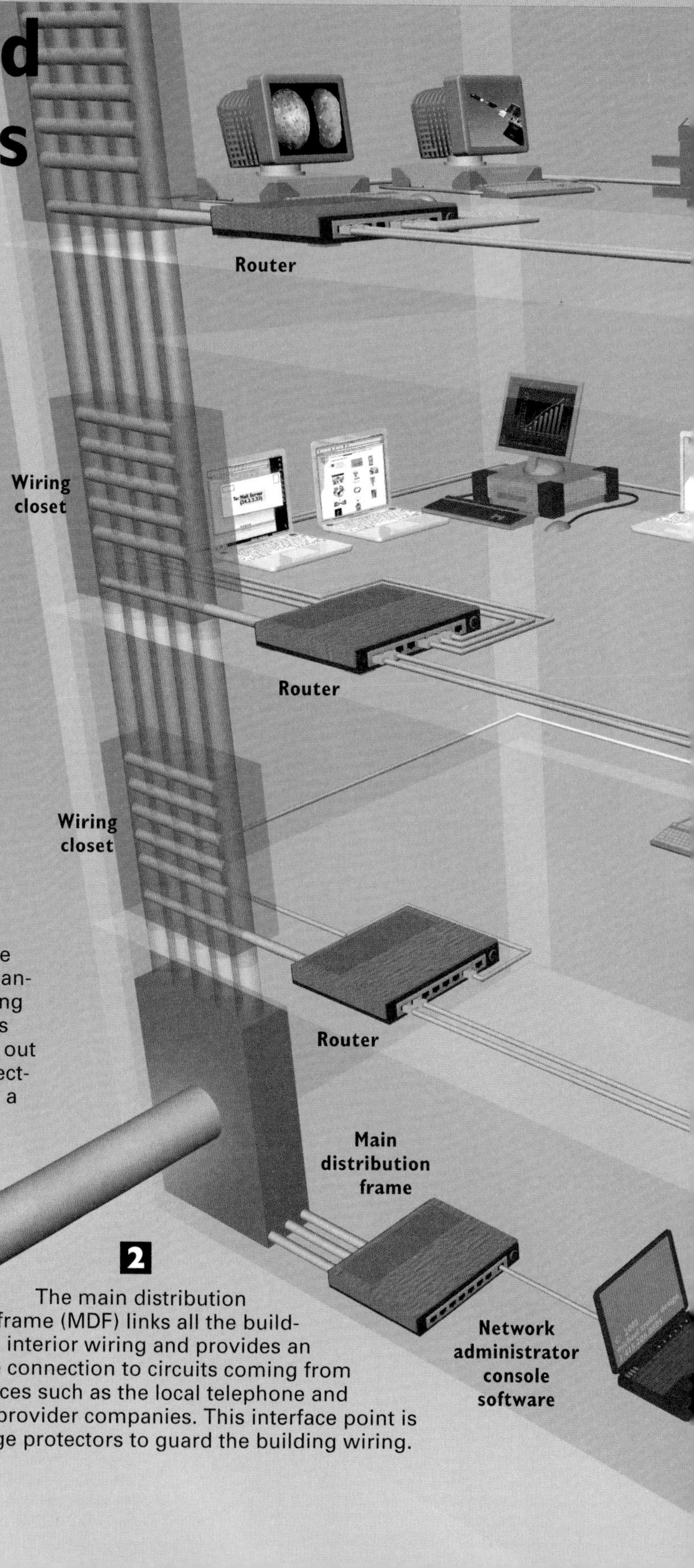

2 The main distribution frame (MDF) links all the building's interior wiring and provides an interface connection to circuits coming from outside sources such as the local telephone and Internet service provider companies. This interface point is equipped with surge protectors to guard the building wiring.

3 Vertical cables carry the Internet and private network connections up to cross-connect panels in wiring closets on each floor. The wiring closet is the place where hubs and switches interconnect to the horizontal cables going out to the office floor. The vertical cables connecting the building floors are required to have a special flame-resistant jacket for fire and smoke protection and they are often fiber-optic cables so they have greater resistance to outside electrical interference.

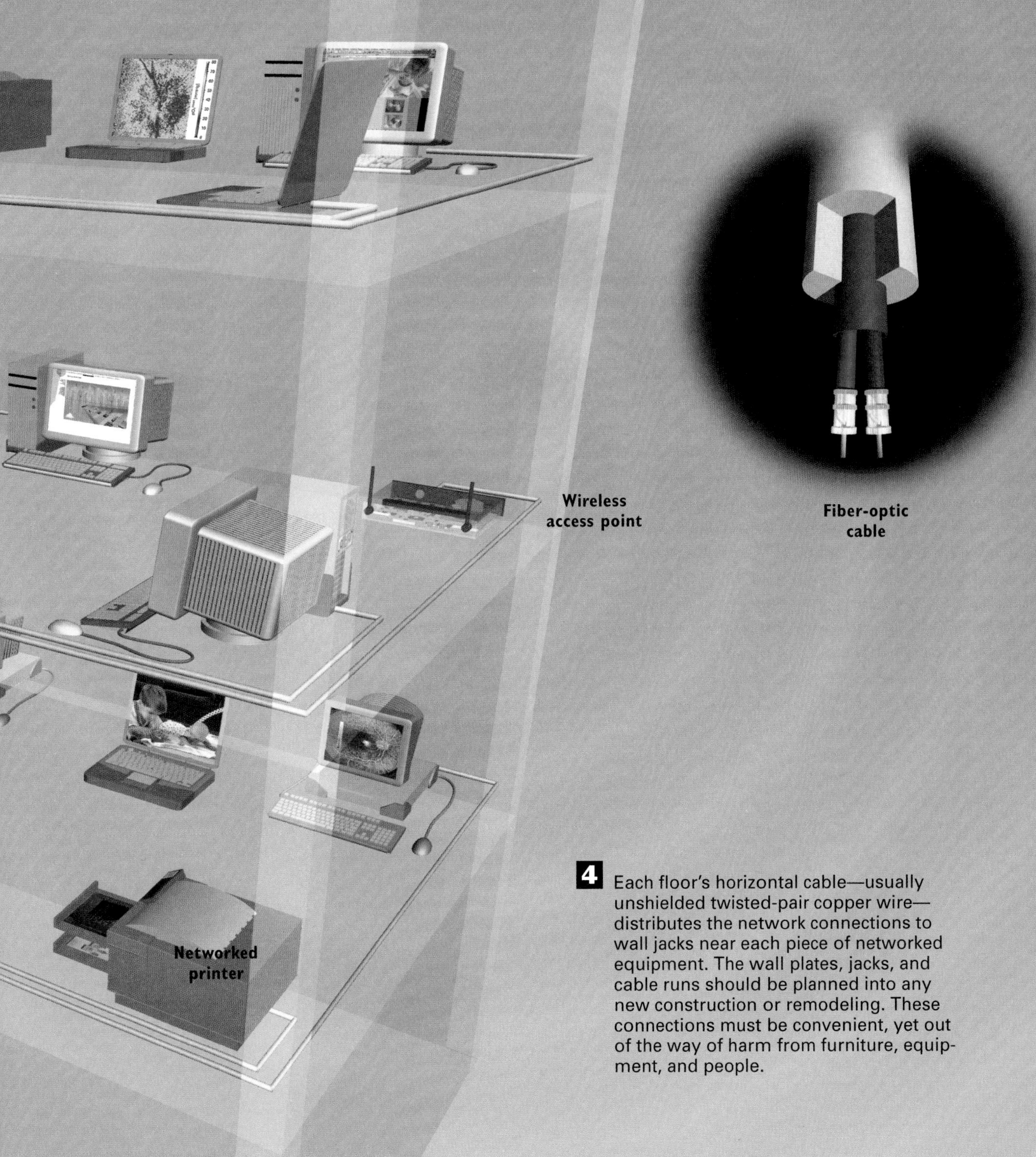
Wireless access point
Fiber-optic cable
Networked printer

4 Each floor's horizontal cable—usually unshielded twisted-pair copper wire—distributes the network connections to wall jacks near each piece of networked equipment. The wall plates, jacks, and cable runs should be planned into any new construction or remodeling. These connections must be convenient, yet out of the way of harm from furniture, equipment, and people.

How UTP Connectors Work

The type of RJ-45 connectors used in UTP-structured cable plans are the weakest links in the system. It's useful for you to know what a proper connector looks like. It's also useful to be able to tell a normal connector from a crossover connector used on a patch cable.

The RJ-45 connectors typically used in structured wiring plans follow a specific color scheme specified by EIA Standard 568-B. When you look at the connector with the tab away from you, pin 1 is on the top. The wire code uses the terms "tip" and "ring," left over from the old switchboard wiring schemes.

10Mbps Ethernet uses pairs 1 and 3. The remaining pairs are spares and might not be present in all cables. Gigabit Ethernet requires all pairs.

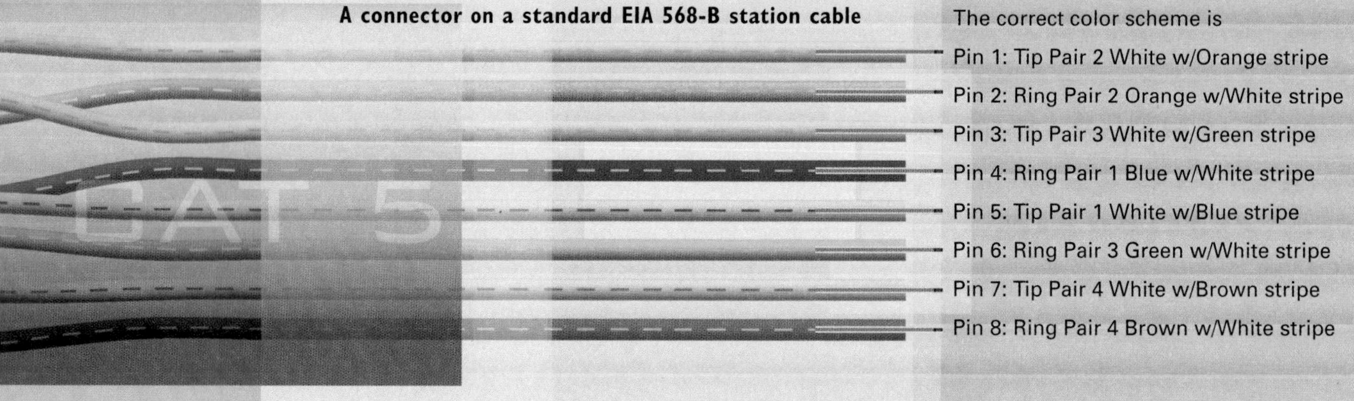
A connector on a standard EIA 568-B station cable
CAT 5
The correct color scheme is
Pin 1: Tip Pair 2 White w/Orange stripe
Pin 2: Ring Pair 2 Orange w/White stripe
Pin 3: Tip Pair 3 White w/Green stripe
Pin 4: Ring Pair 1 Blue w/White stripe
Pin 5: Tip Pair 1 White w/Blue stripe
Pin 6: Ring Pair 3 Green w/White stripe
Pin 7: Tip Pair 4 White w/Brown stripe
Pin 8: Ring Pair 4 Brown w/White stripe

Some network connections might require a different configuration. This is particularly true of direct connections that would typically go through a switch, such as between two PCs or between a router and a PC. These connections made without a hub or switch use a *crossover cable*. As the name implies, pairs of wires cross over at one end of the cable in order to keep the matching tip and ring connections. Most crossover cables are marked as such on their jackets. You can always tell by comparing the connectors at each end of the cable. If both connectors follow the standard color pattern, it is a normal station cable. But, if the end connectors have different color sequences from each other, it's likely a crossover cable. You can usually quickly notice that the Orange wire is out of place.

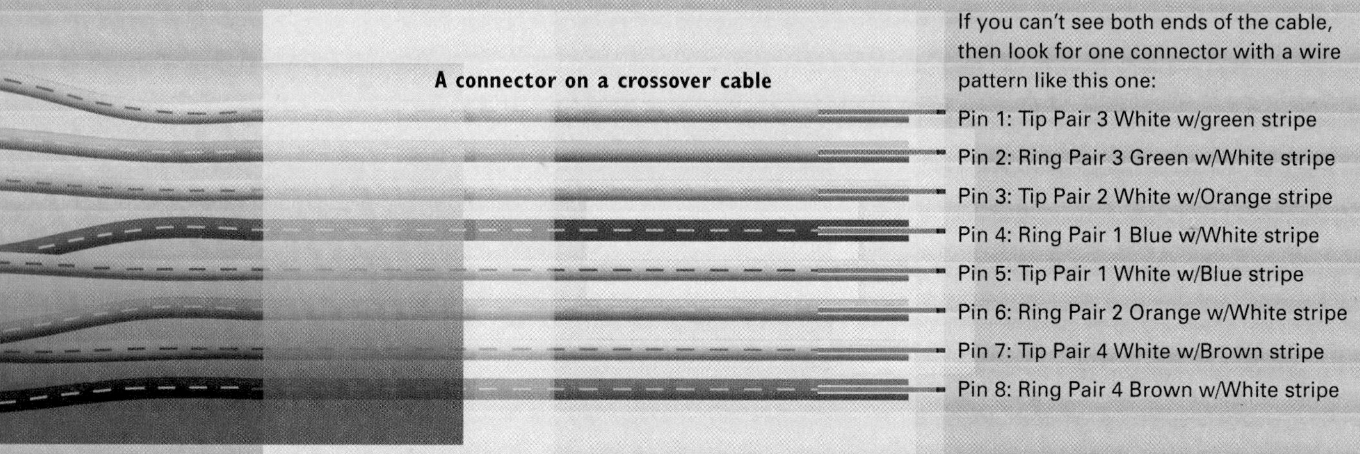
If you can't see both ends of the cable, then look for one connector with a wire pattern like this one:
A connector on a crossover cable
Pin 1: Tip Pair 3 White w/green stripe
Pin 2: Ring Pair 3 Green w/White stripe
Pin 3: Tip Pair 2 White w/Orange stripe
Pin 4: Ring Pair 1 Blue w/White stripe
Pin 5: Tip Pair 1 White w/Blue stripe
Pin 6: Ring Pair 2 Orange w/White stripe
Pin 7: Tip Pair 4 White w/Brown stripe
Pin 8: Ring Pair 4 Brown w/White stripe

It is often more economical and convenient to create your own cables and connectors. Many retail stores sell bags of connectors, cable on reels, and tools. The three tools you need are

- cable stripper
- sharp pair of wire cutters
- crimping tool

Here are the steps to creating your own station and crossover cables:

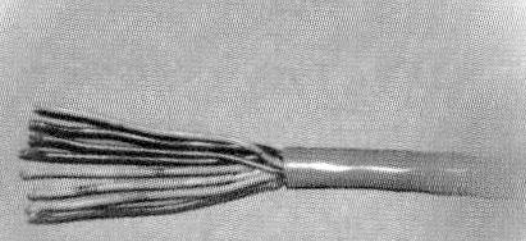

Use a cable stripper to remove about 1″ of the outer jacket from the cable.

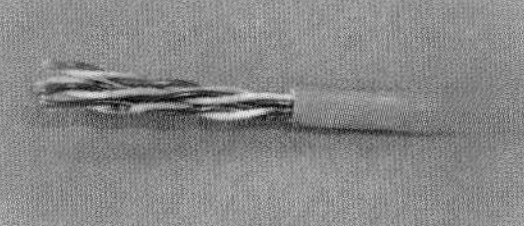

Remove the underlying polyester fiber with the wire cutters.

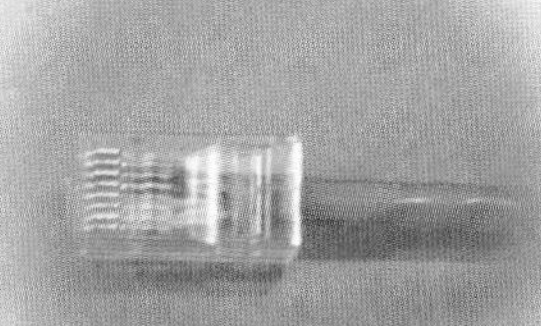

Separate and smooth the wire pairs so that you have eight individual wires, and arrange them in the proper order.

Trim the wires straight across so they extend 5/8″ from the cable jacket.

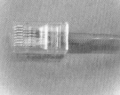

Place the RJ-45 connector over the wires so they stay in the correct order. The cable jacket should extend 3/16″ into the connector.

Insert the connector into the crimping tool without letting any wires slip back out of the connector.

Squeeze the handles of the crimping tools firmly once and then squeeze again a second time.

CHAPTER 16 How Wireless Networks Work

COMPUTERS are becoming smaller, lighter, more portable, and less expensive every year. And every year, computer users increasingly rely on networks—and on the Internet in particular—as sources of information and communication. For many home and business users, the network connection has become as important as the computer itself.

Today's laptop computers and Personal Digital Assistants (PDAs) can run for many hours or even several days on a battery charge, so they are free of the physical constraints of an AC power cord. But until recently, portable computing devices often remained tethered in one place, their mobility limited by a length of Ethernet cable.

Wireless networks are about freedom—the freedom to use your computer wherever and whenever you want. The wireless networking products of just a few years ago were slow, power-hungry, expensive, and unreliable. Not surprisingly, the early adopters of these products were corporations and universities.

Thanks to a huge consumer demand for better wireless networks, users can now choose from a broad variety of inexpensive wireless products that offer connection speeds, security, and reliability rivaling those of wired networks. Wireless networking has become so pervasive that many laptops and PDAs come with built-in wireless network adapters as standard equipment, and Intel makes an entire line of laptop CPU chips with built-in wireless networking.

The first wireless networking products were designed to provide network connectivity for corporate computer users within a small, well-defined area—most often within the confines of a conference or meeting room. As is often the case with new technologies, several manufacturers offered competing—but not compatible—wireless networking systems. Eventually, the major wireless equipment makers adopted a common, interoperable standard called Wi-Fi, short for Wireless Fidelity.

Early wireless systems often cost $800 or more per room, plus an additional $500 per computer for the necessary wireless network cards. Despite the high costs, many home users found wireless networks to be just what they needed to share an Internet connection, files, and printers among several computers in their homes.

Equipment makers quickly realized that there was a huge demand for wireless home networks—and not just for laptop users. For years, the major network equipment manufacturers had been trying to tap into the home market, but the difficulty and expense of running Ethernet cables kept a lid on home network sales. Wireless networks don't need cables, thus eliminating a major roadblock for home network sales. As a bonus, many corporate computer users already had company-provided wireless adapters for their portable PCs.

The result has been an avalanche of wireless network products designed specifically for the home market. Many of these products are "one box" solutions that combine a router/firewall for Internet connection sharing, a small Ethernet switch to connect wired desktop PCs, and a wireless access point to connect laptop computers and other wireless devices. These products are designed to be simple to set up and operate, and they are very inexpensive—often less than $100.

Now that wireless has reached into the workplace and the home, several companies and organizations are extending the reach of wireless networks to the rest of the world. Many airports, hotels, and coffee shops now offer wireless network connections. Some of these are free; others are fee-based. We're not sure how the economics of this new business opportunity will play out, but we are sure that public wireless Internet access (commonly called "hotspots") are here to stay.

The original cellular telephone network was designed at AT&T in the 1960s, based on FM radio technology dating back to the 1930s. The first cellular networks were deployed in the early 1980s, and demand for cellular telephone service greatly exceeded projections. Cellular equipment manufacturers responded to the demand by using digital encoding technologies. Compared to analog FM radio, digital cellular technologies provide clearer, more reliable service for users. These technologies allow wireless telephone operators to serve more customers with fewer expensive towers. Most importantly, digital cellular services provide better protection against fraudulent use and eavesdropping than their analog counterparts.

How Wireless Networking Works

1 Wireless Local Area Network (WLAN) systems extend the reach of a wired network to include wireless laptops and PDAs within a room or building. Virtually all wireless LANs operate using one of several IEEE 802-series standards: 802.11a, 802.11b, and 802.11g, collectively known as the Wi-Fi standards. These standards define a method for transporting Ethernet network signals using a digital radio link instead of a physical Ethernet cable. Wireless LANs use a device called an *access point* that provides wireless coverage for a limited area. The access point provides a bridge between an existing Ethernet LAN and all of the wireless-equipped computers within range of the access point. Wi-Fi networks use complex data encoding schemes similar to those used in GPS satellites and advanced digital cellular telephone networks to send data across the radio link. The radios in these systems use *differential phase shift keying* to impose the data onto the radio signal.

Client computer
MAC address: AA2947487
Okay—you are on the list!

3 Access points broadcast their names and invite client computers to link. A single access point can connect to many clients at the same time. Each client has a unique identifier called a MAC address that enables the access point to tell one client from another. If a client is within range of several access points, it chooses the one with the best signal strength.

2 The range of Wi-Fi access points varies, but each access point typically covers a radius of 200–300 feet—and often much less. You can cover an entire building or campus by using multiple access points attached to the LAN.

Wireless access point
Encryption key
Encrypted data stream
Key accepted
Connected
Client computer
Client computer
They are talking, I am waiting

5 Wireless network encryption comes in two forms: the older *Wired Equivalency Privacy (WEP)* and the newer *Wi-Fi Protected Access (WPA)*. Both use the RC4 encryption algorithm, which is known as a *stream cipher*. A stream cipher operates by using mathematical operations to create a pseudorandom stream of data from a key of 40 or 128 bits. The transmitting device mixes the payload data with the pseudorandom stream to produce an encrypted data stream. WEP encryption had a security weakness that made it possible for a determined hacker to learn the encryption key. WPA automatically generates a new unique encryption key periodically for each client, and it does so several times a second. This makes it much more difficult to break into a WPA-protected wireless LAN.

6 As the name implies, a wireless repeater extends the range of an existing LAN. It does this by listening to all of the traffic coming from a specific access point while simultaneously re-transmitting the data on another channel. Conversely, the repeater listens for traffic from client PCs on one channel and re-transmits the data back to the access point on the AP's own channel.

Wireless
access point

4 Security across wireless links is important, so wireless LANs use authentication and encryption to maintain security. In the simplest and most effective form of authentication, an access point will only connect to clients having specific MAC address numbers. MAC addresses are burned into client adapter card chipsets during manufacture and are very difficult to mimic. More complex authentication schemes use public key authentication systems, including smart cards and biometric scanning, to confirm the identity of the user.

Router/
wiring hub

Effective
range limit

7 The clients share the radio spectrum in almost exactly the same way they share an Ethernet cable: by listening for an open channel before transmitting.

Effective
range limit

Planning and Installing a Wireless LAN

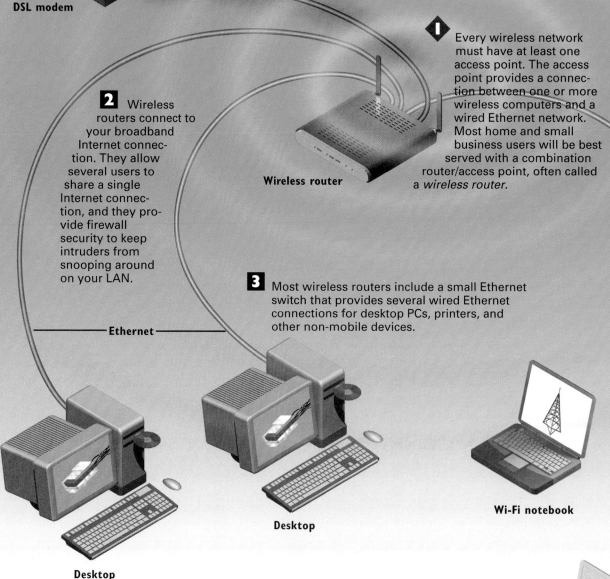

Cable or DSL modem

1 Every wireless network must have at least one access point. The access point provides a connection between one or more wireless computers and a wired Ethernet network. Most home and small business users will be best served with a combination router/access point, often called a *wireless router*.

Wireless router

2 Wireless routers connect to your broadband Internet connection. They allow several users to share a single Internet connection, and they provide firewall security to keep intruders from snooping around on your LAN.

3 Most wireless routers include a small Ethernet switch that provides several wired Ethernet connections for desktop PCs, printers, and other non-mobile devices.

Ethernet

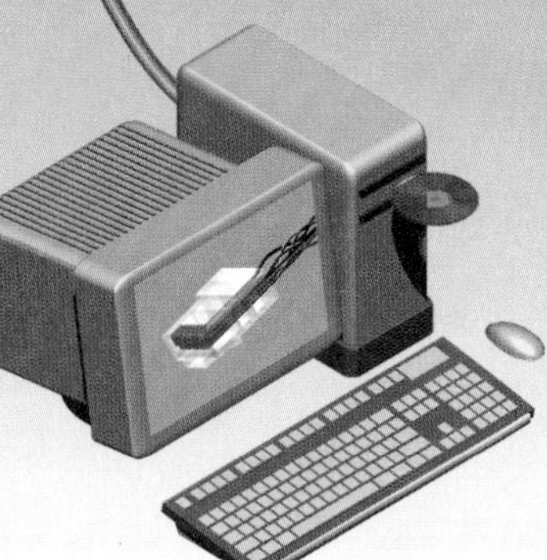

Desktop

Desktop

Wi-Fi notebook

Wi-Fi device out of range

Main wireless router coverage area

Second AP's coverage area

Wi-Fi notebook

Wi-Fi notebook

5 Larger wireless networks require use of more than one access point. It is a good idea to locate multiple access points so that there is some overlap in the coverage area of adjacent access points; this allows users to move from one area to another with no loss of connectivity.

Ethernet

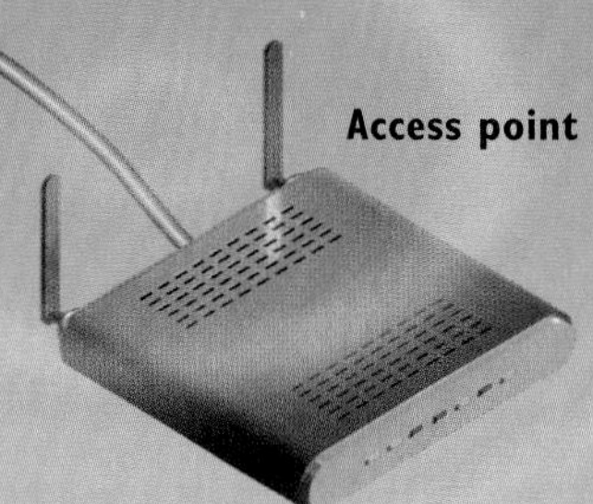

Access point

4 A single access point provides wireless connectivity for all of the computers within a limited area. The range of wireless access points and wireless routers varies widely and can be affected by nearby objects.

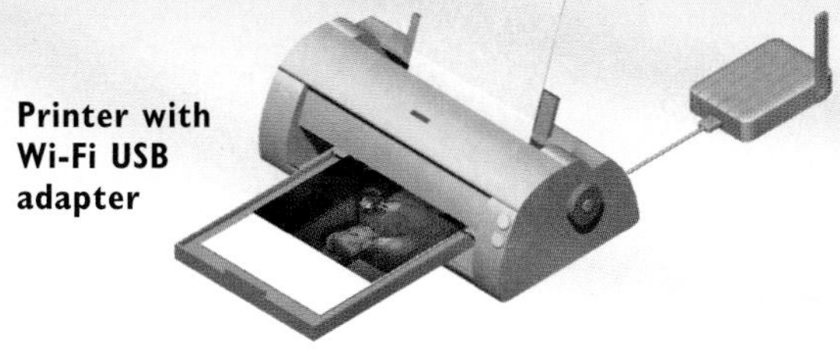

Printer with Wi-Fi USB adapter

Wi-Fi notebook

How Bluetooth Works

I'm a phone—can I connect to the Internet?

GSM cell phone

1. Named for a Viking king, Bluetooth is a new wireless system designed to link a wide variety of devices within a very small area—typically no more than 10 meters (about 30 feet). Think of Bluetooth as a replacement for the cables you have in your office and in your computer travel bag. Typical applications include linking a cell phone or PDA to a laptop, but Bluetooth will have other uses in kitchens, recreation rooms, and automobiles.

I'm a fax machine.

2. Because it's likely that an office building or even an airplane in flight will contain many Bluetooth devices operating simultaneously, the system has to include techniques for recognizing each device within its own private network and for handling the effects of radio frequency congestion. Bluetooth uses a radio transmission technique called *spread-spectrum frequency hopping* centered on a frequency of 2.45GHz. That same frequency band is used by many portable devices such as baby monitors and portable phones. A Bluetooth device changes between any of 79 individual randomly chosen frequencies 1,600 times per second. This means that even if two or more devices hop onto the same frequency, their collision will last only a few milliseconds. Software techniques allow the devices to reconstruct data lost in collisions and to avoid frequencies that might be jammed by radio signals from portable phones, portable speakers, or other non-Bluetooth radio devices.

3. When Bluetooth-equipped devices come within range of one another, they pass identification information called *inquiry access codes (IACs)*. Devices can be set up with a variety of recognition schemes by users and manufacturers. In the most basic form, a device can be set as general discoverable, limited discoverable, or nondiscoverable. General discoverable devices will respond to any inquiry access code, but limited-discoverable devices will respond to IACs only from specified units. If devices recognize each other, they exchange status and control information and synchronize into a *piconet*. The members of the piconet change frequencies in unison so they avoid other piconets that may be operating in the same area. Synchronized devices also agree on what kind of data transmission to use.

I'm a PC.

Notebook computer with Bluetooth card

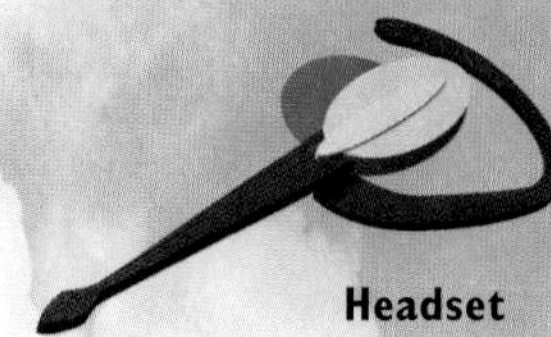
Headset
I can send and receive audio files.

4 For voice, Bluetooth can send data two ways at 64Kbps. This speed allows several simultaneous conversations. If, as is common, the system is moving a lot of data in one direction, Bluetooth can adapt to transmit at speeds up to 721Kbps on the downlink and 57.6Kbps on the uplink.

5 Within the piconet, different nodes adopt different roles to smooth the transmission flow. Under certain conditions of data flow, a master station may assume control and designate when slave stations can transmit. The master/slave roles are temporary and are based on the order of entry into the network and on the work to be done.

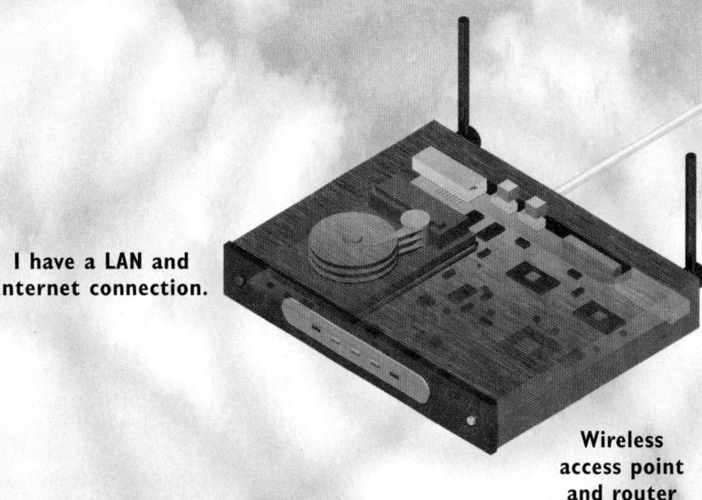
I have a LAN and Internet connection.
Wireless access point and router

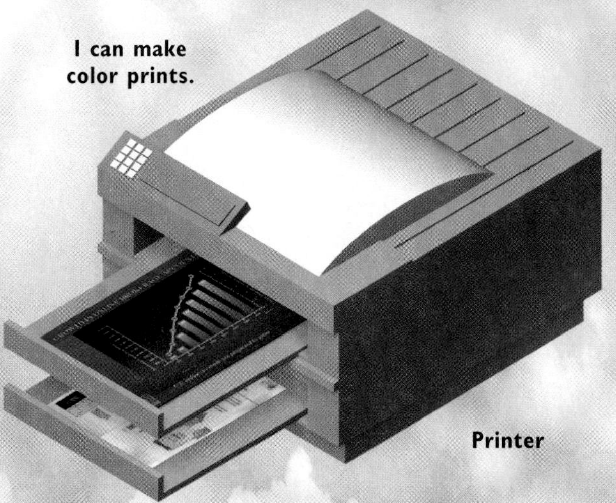
I can make color prints.
Printer

6 Devices within the same piconet exchange additional information about their capabilities and functions called *Service Class ID*. Cameras have certain types of information they transmit, cars have a different information package, soft drink machines have a different package, and so on. The members of the Bluetooth piconet learn about and adapt to one another in this way.

How Wireless Phones Work

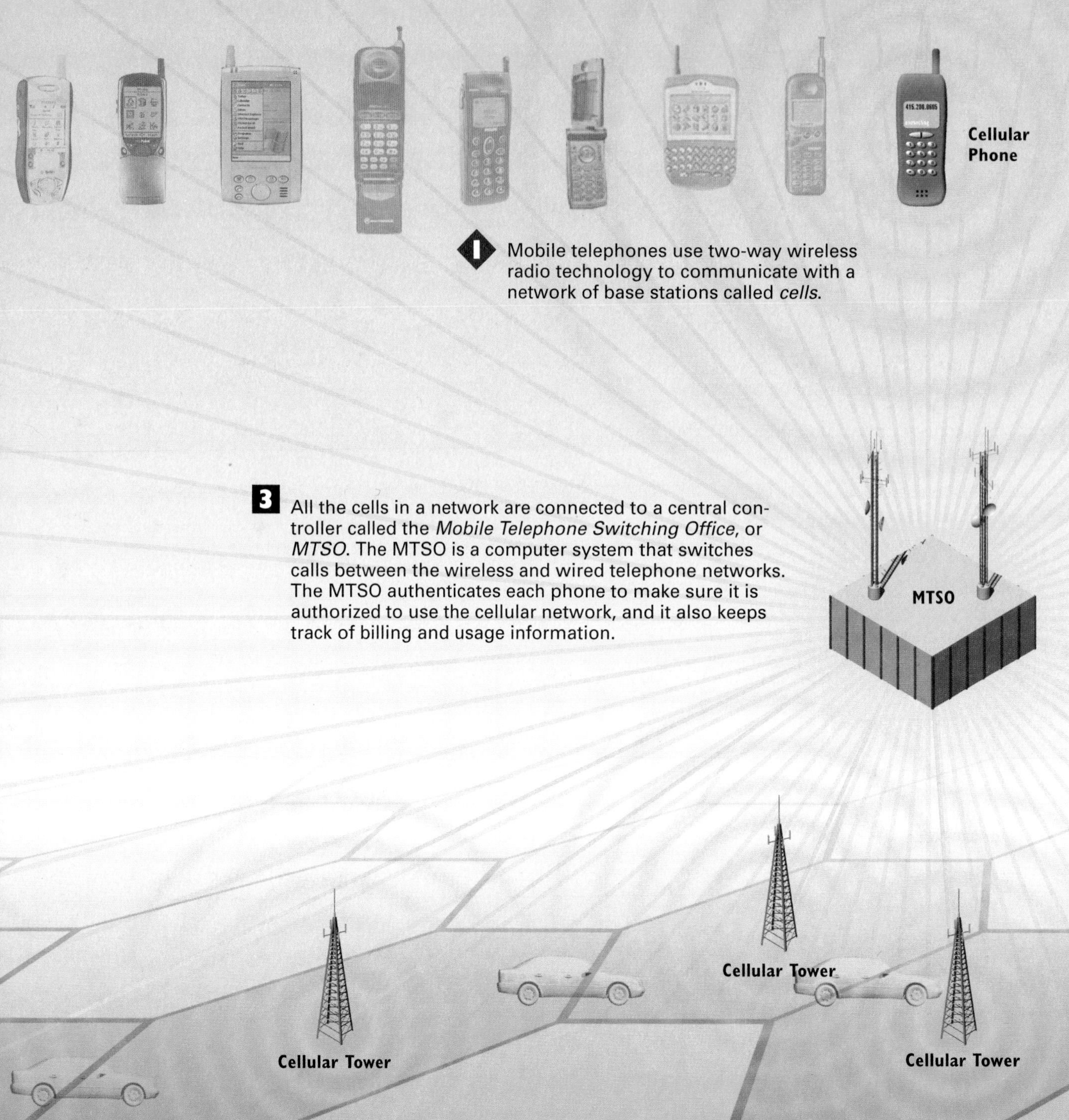
Cellular
Phone
MTSO
Cellular Tower
Cellular Tower
Cellular Tower

1 Mobile telephones use two-way wireless radio technology to communicate with a network of base stations called *cells*.

3 All the cells in a network are connected to a central controller called the *Mobile Telephone Switching Office*, or *MTSO*. The MTSO is a computer system that switches calls between the wireless and wired telephone networks. The MTSO authenticates each phone to make sure it is authorized to use the cellular network, and it also keeps track of billing and usage information.

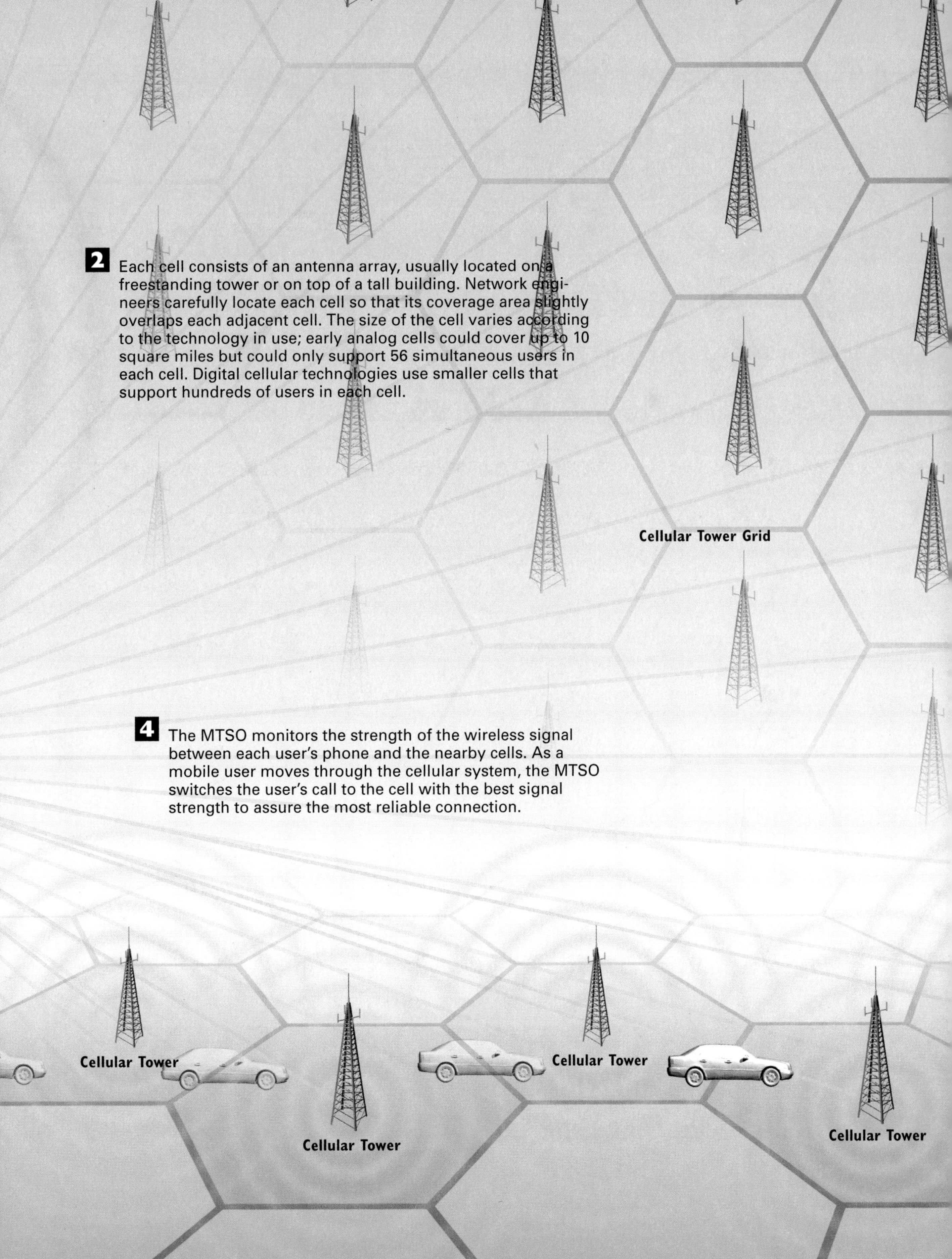
Cellular Tower Grid
Cellular Tower
Cellular Tower
Cellular Tower
Cellular Tower

2 Each cell consists of an antenna array, usually located on a freestanding tower or on top of a tall building. Network engineers carefully locate each cell so that its coverage area slightly overlaps each adjacent cell. The size of the cell varies according to the technology in use; early analog cells could cover up to 10 square miles but could only support 56 simultaneous users in each cell. Digital cellular technologies use smaller cells that support hundreds of users in each cell.

4 The MTSO monitors the strength of the wireless signal between each user's phone and the nearby cells. As a mobile user moves through the cellular system, the MTSO switches the user's call to the cell with the best signal strength to assure the most reliable connection.

CHAPTER

17

How Server-Based LANs Work

DO you keep all of your eggs in one basket or tuck them into many different safe spots? The consolidated and distributed philosophies of resource management each have its benefits. Clustering resources keeps them under tight control, but makes them all vulnerable to a single disaster. Distributing them makes them less vulnerable as a group, but more vulnerable individually. Clustering can limit growth whereas distribution can limit quality control. Also, each philosophy has its own unique cost factors.

Those are the arguments behind two important schools of thought in networking. On one hand, you have a philosophy that is known variously as *server-based*, *network-based*, and *Web-based* computing; there are only differences in distance among those terms. On the other hand, you have a philosophy known as *peer-to-peer (P2P)* computing. P2P leverages the largely unused power of desktop computers and is increasing in importance. In this chapter, we'll describe the approaches to server-centric computing. The next chapter describes peer-to-peer systems.

Functionally, there are four types of servers; file servers, print servers, application servers, and communications servers. You might ask about a Web server, but a Web server is simply a combination of an application server backed up by a file server. In larger installations, Web servers are physically divided in just that way. Today, routers are the most common kind of communications server.

At the extreme deployment of server-based computing, the client computers need modest processing power and little local data storage capacity. A Web-equipped phone or PDA is a good example. The file servers hold the data, application servers run the applications, and the clients have only to present the results. The advantages of this arrangement include lower equipment and management costs for the client and centralized control over valuable data. The fallacy of the arrangement is that all clients are getting simultaneously more powerful and less expensive. So, most real networks use centralized storage and applications where it makes sense and still run many programs and store a lot of data on local desktop clients.

Web-based computing is an extension of server-based computing that takes advantage of the widespread availability of the Internet. In this concept, files and programs are commodities that users share and lease from a central information utility. In effect, Web-based computing is a marketing application of the technology of server-based computing.

How Server-Based LANs Work

1 A large and powerful computer system is the heart of a server-based network. The networked client computers use the file, print, and communications services of the central server. This diagram shows a typical configuration for a small network of up to several dozen clients. In larger networks, the single computer might be a cluster of processors sharing a clustered data storage system. This architecture is robust, powerful, and complex, and incurs a significant installation cost.

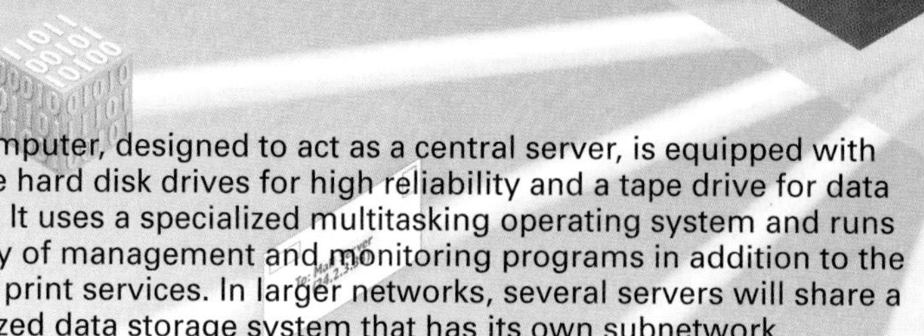
Server

3 This computer, designed to act as a central server, is equipped with multiple hard disk drives for high reliability and a tape drive for data backup. It uses a specialized multitasking operating system and runs a variety of management and monitoring programs in addition to the file and print services. In larger networks, several servers will share a centralized data storage system that has its own subnetwork.

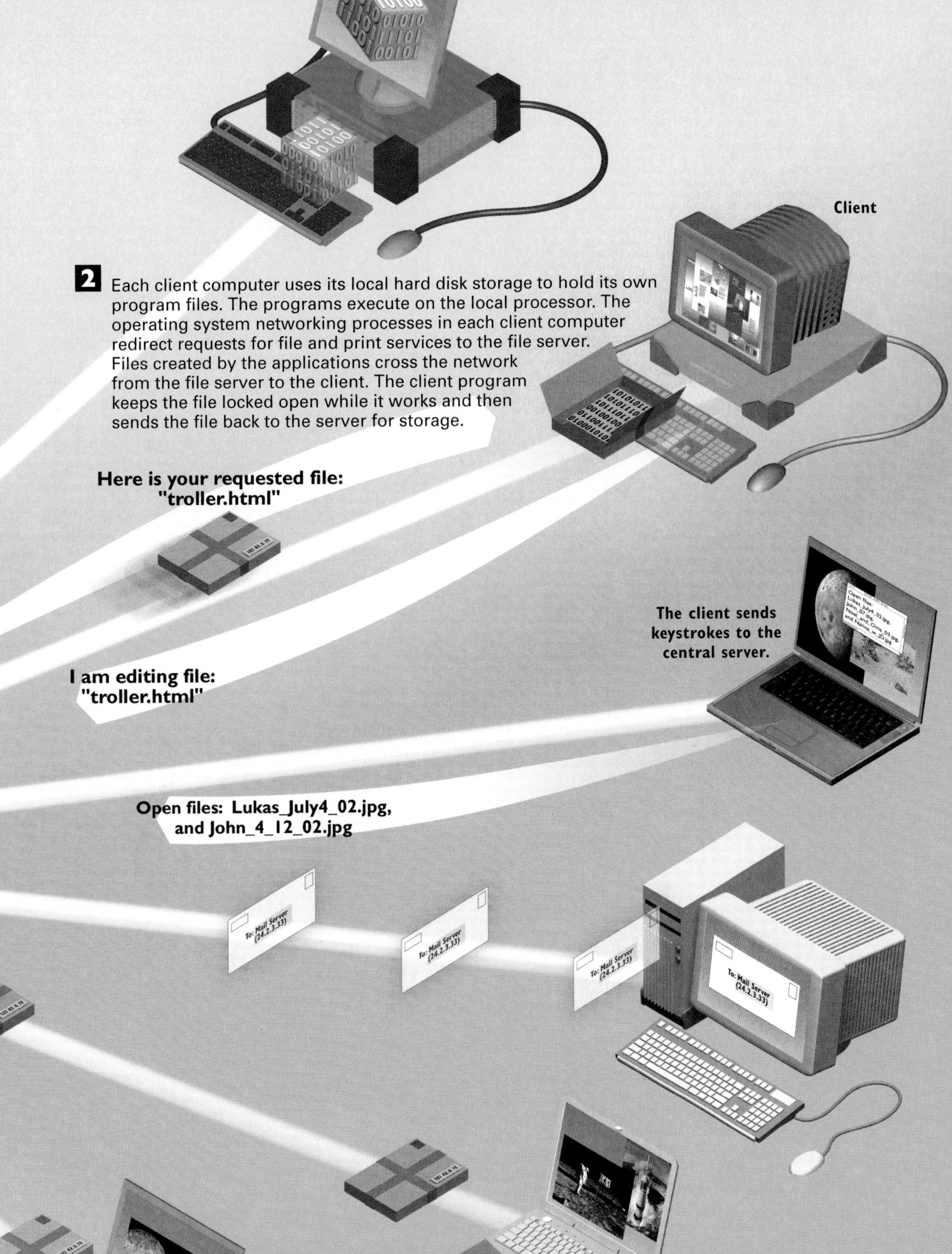
Client
Here is your requested file: "troller.html"
The client sends keystrokes to the central server.
I am editing file: "troller.html"
Open files: Lukas_July4_02.jpg, and John_4_12_02.jpg
To: Mail Server (24.2.3.33)
To: Mail Server (24.2.3.33)
To: Mail Server (24.2.3.33)
To: Mail Server (24.2.3.33)

2 Each client computer uses its local hard disk storage to hold its own program files. The programs execute on the local processor. The operating system networking processes in each client computer redirect requests for file and print services to the file server. Files created by the applications cross the network from the file server to the client. The client program keeps the file locked open while it works and then sends the file back to the server for storage.

How Thin Clients Work

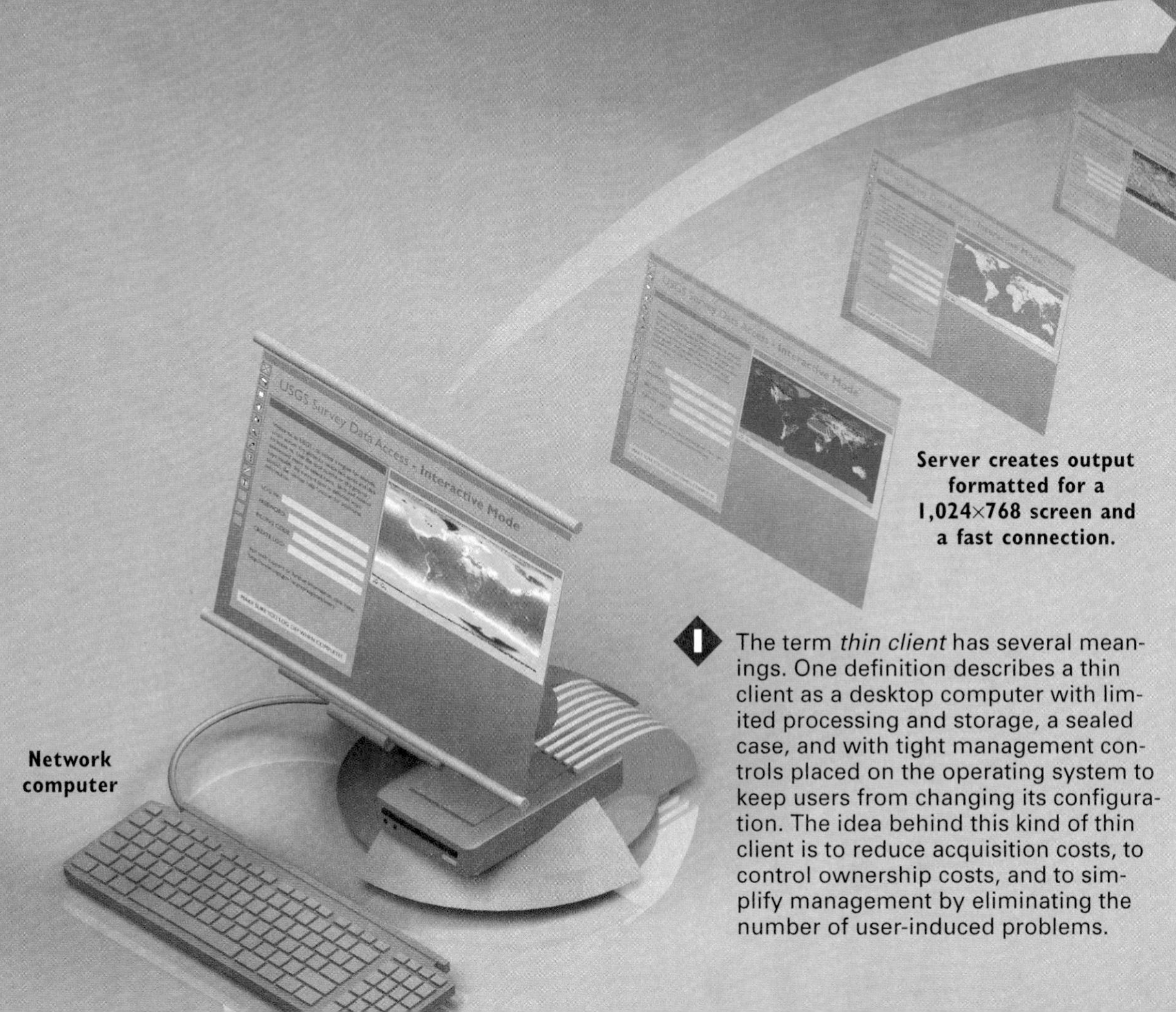
Server creates output formatted for a 1,024×768 screen and a fast connection.
Network computer

1 The term *thin client* has several meanings. One definition describes a thin client as a desktop computer with limited processing and storage, a sealed case, and with tight management controls placed on the operating system to keep users from changing its configuration. The idea behind this kind of thin client is to reduce acquisition costs, to control ownership costs, and to simplify management by eliminating the number of user-induced problems.

RAID
RAID

3 Specialized servers process requests for information and format replies to match the screen, keyboard, memory, and communications capabilities of each client. The servers might parse text into 40-character lines, eliminate graphics, and change menus to meet the capabilities of a specific client device.

Server creates output formatted for a small screen and a slow connection.

2 The term also applies to devices that have a small amount of processing power, limited memory, and only the capability to run a browser and a Java engine. A PDA or Web-equipped cell phone is a good example of this type of thin client. These devices are limited by their size and power source. Because of their processing limitations and their small screens and keyboards, they rely on specialized servers to process and package data into forms they can handle.

GSM phone

How Server-Based Computing Works

1 Server-based computing is a system that runs desktop applications—everything from word processing to personnel programs—on a central shared server. The client computer runs only a simple program that accepts the screens produced by the shared server. This arrangement makes it easy to manage and upgrade applications while centrally applying security, virus protection, and other functions.

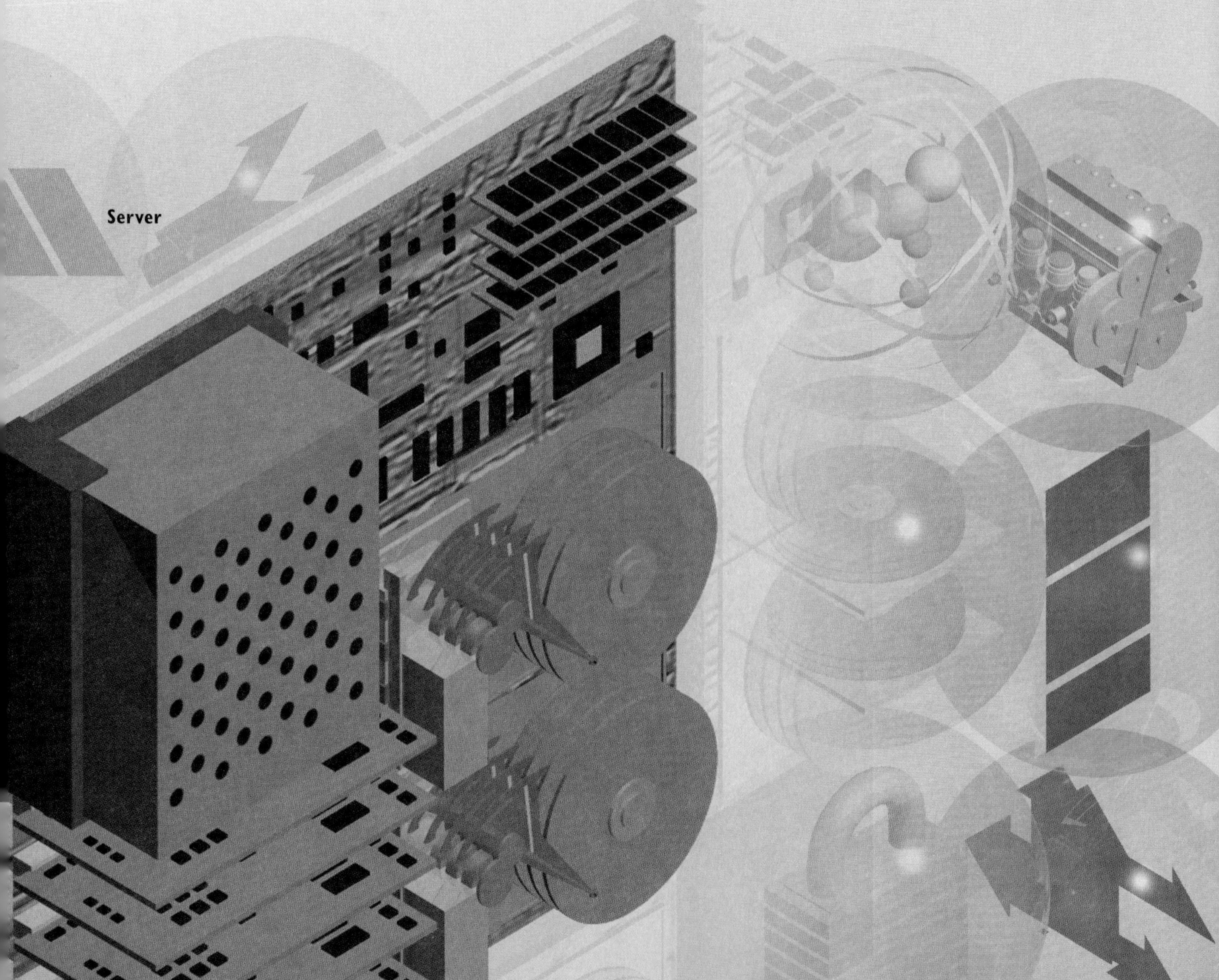
Server

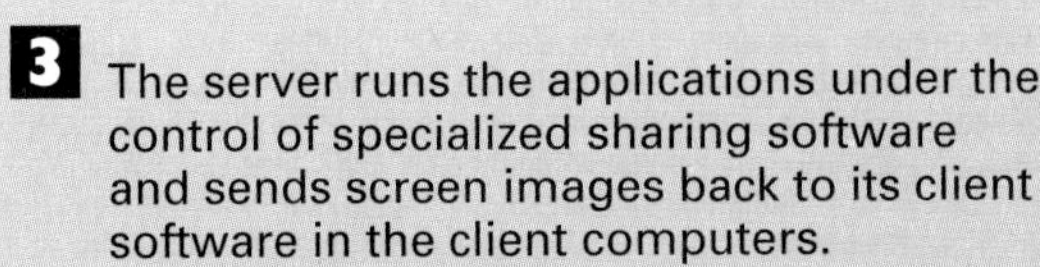

3 The server runs the applications under the control of specialized sharing software and sends screen images back to its client software in the client computers.

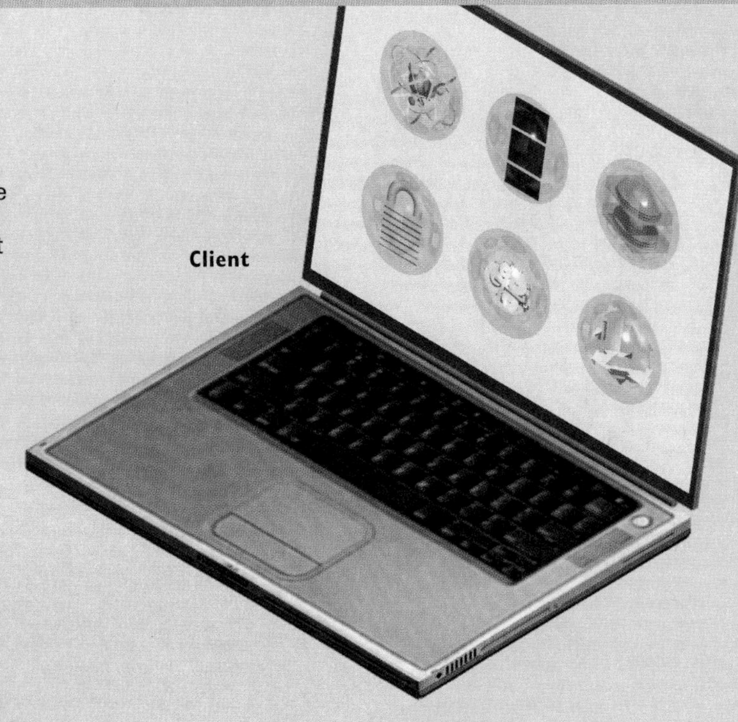
Client

2 The client sends keystrokes to the central server.

4 End users have the power of a full suite of application software installed on their computers, but the software resides in the server.

5 The word processing, database, and other common desktop programs execute in this shared server under the control of specialized software.

CHAPTER

18 How Peer-to-Peer Networks Work

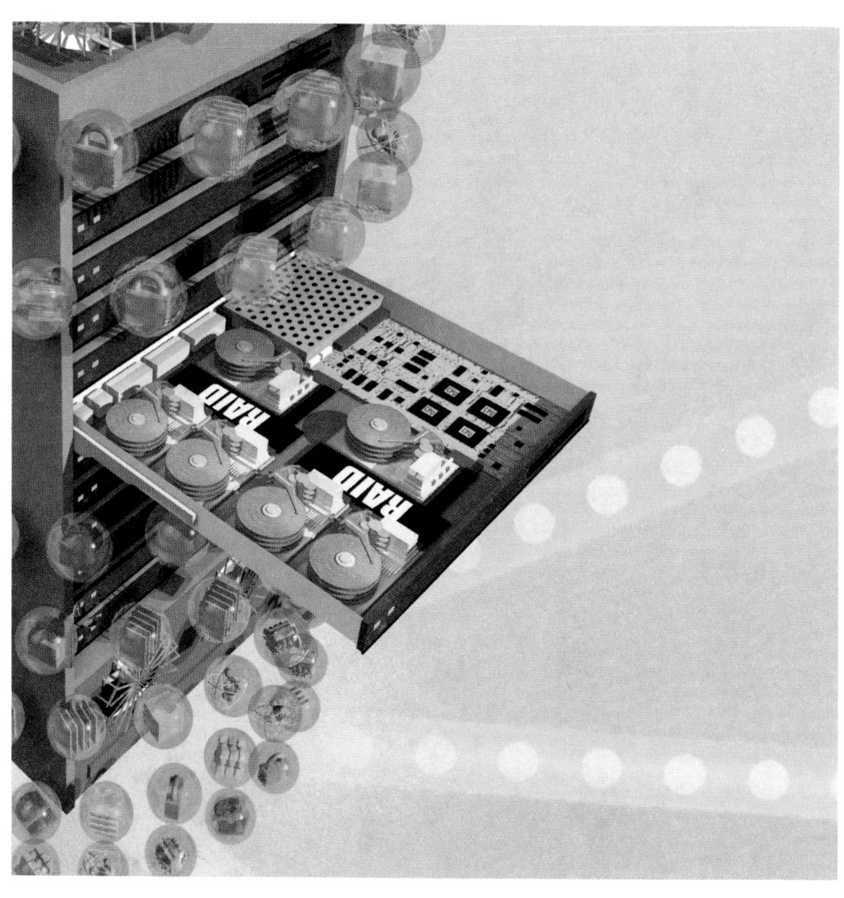
RAID
RAID

IN the last chapter, we described server-based networks that have specific roles and configurations for each device. There are clients, servers, and connections. In this chapter, we'll describe the advantages and disadvantages of peer-to-peer (P2P) networks that don't rely on strictly defined servers. The P2P strategy shares the processing power and storage capacity of networked computers even while they run application programs.

Peer-to-peer networking makes sense because personal computers seem to defy the laws of gravity—their power goes up while their prices go down or at least stay the same. Most computers spend much of their time idling, so why not share that processing power?

Napster, the music-sharing service, was the first P2P system to reach public attention, but the idea has been around for a long time. Distributed computing has been used to search databases of radio signals for signals from extraterrestrials and to unravel the genetic codes of plants and animals.

Most P2P systems have a form of central control, but some don't. If there is a large number of nodes, more than a few dozen, it's most efficient to use a central naming server to match contributing nodes with the work to be done. In the naming server model, contributing nodes post information on the naming server showing their resources available for sharing and a network address. After making a match through the naming server, nodes pair off and make a direct connection across a network or the Internet to exchange files or process applications. This arrangement allows for ad hoc sharing among a large population.

In other P2P systems, it's necessary for nodes to know one another's network address in advance. This technique is very useful for corporate or enterprise networks. This kind of P2P sharing might be done among a group of handheld computers using wireless networking at a job site or at the scene of an emergency. It might also be used to implement workgroup sharing and collaboration within a company for people using a variety of devices.

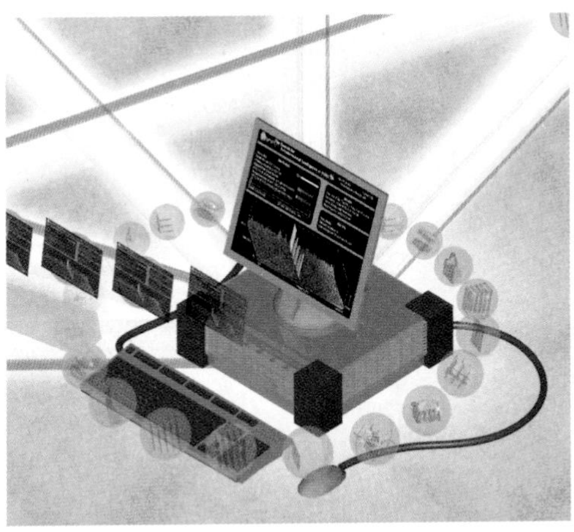

How Peer-to-Peer Works with a Name Server

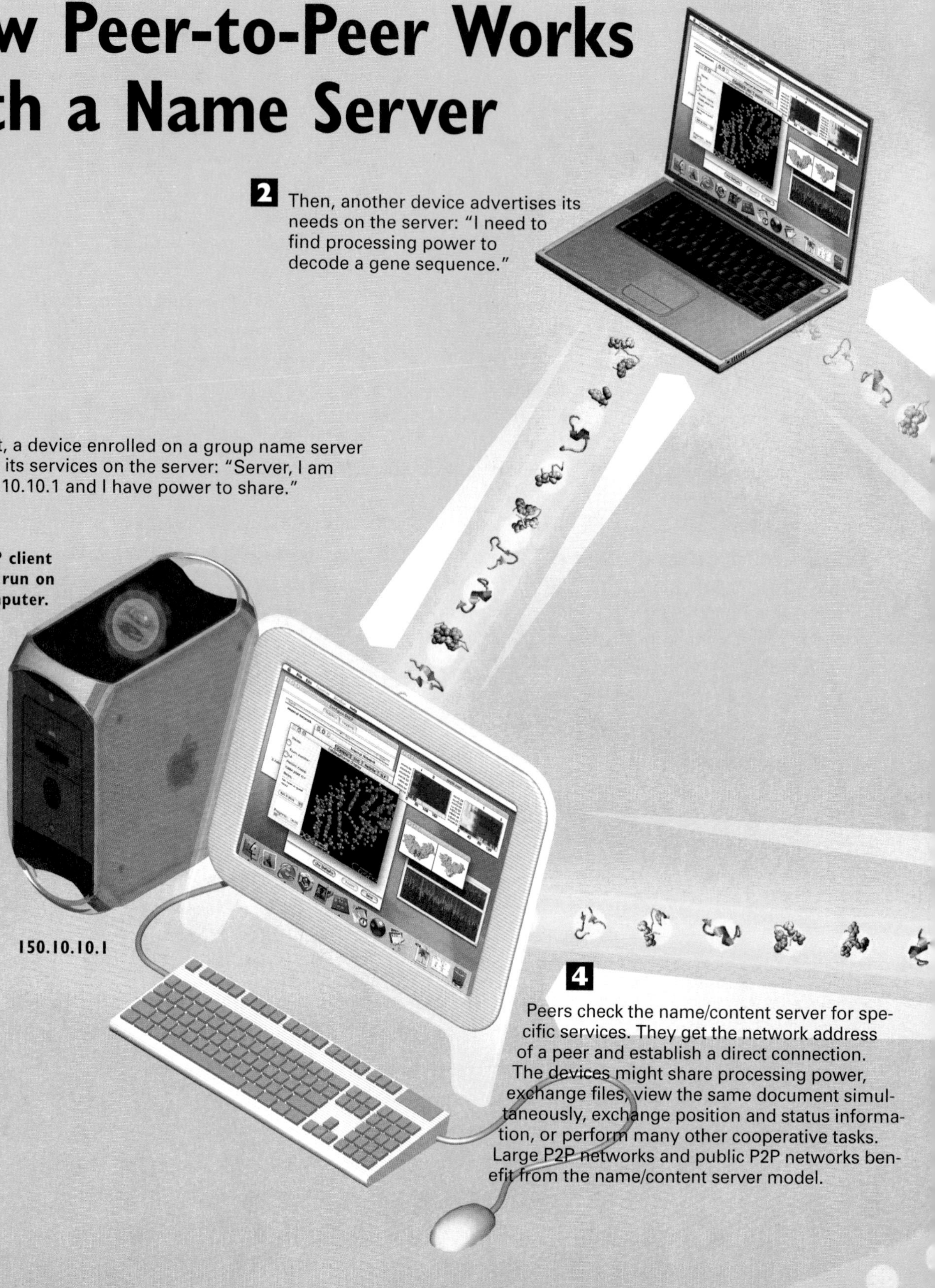

2 Then, another device advertises its needs on the server: "I need to find processing power to decode a gene sequence."

1 First, a device enrolled on a group name server lists its services on the server: "Server, I am 150.10.10.1 and I have power to share."

Small P2P client programs run on each computer.

150.10.10.1

4 Peers check the name/content server for specific services. They get the network address of a peer and establish a direct connection. The devices might share processing power, exchange files, view the same document simultaneously, exchange position and status information, or perform many other cooperative tasks. Large P2P networks and public P2P networks benefit from the name/content server model.

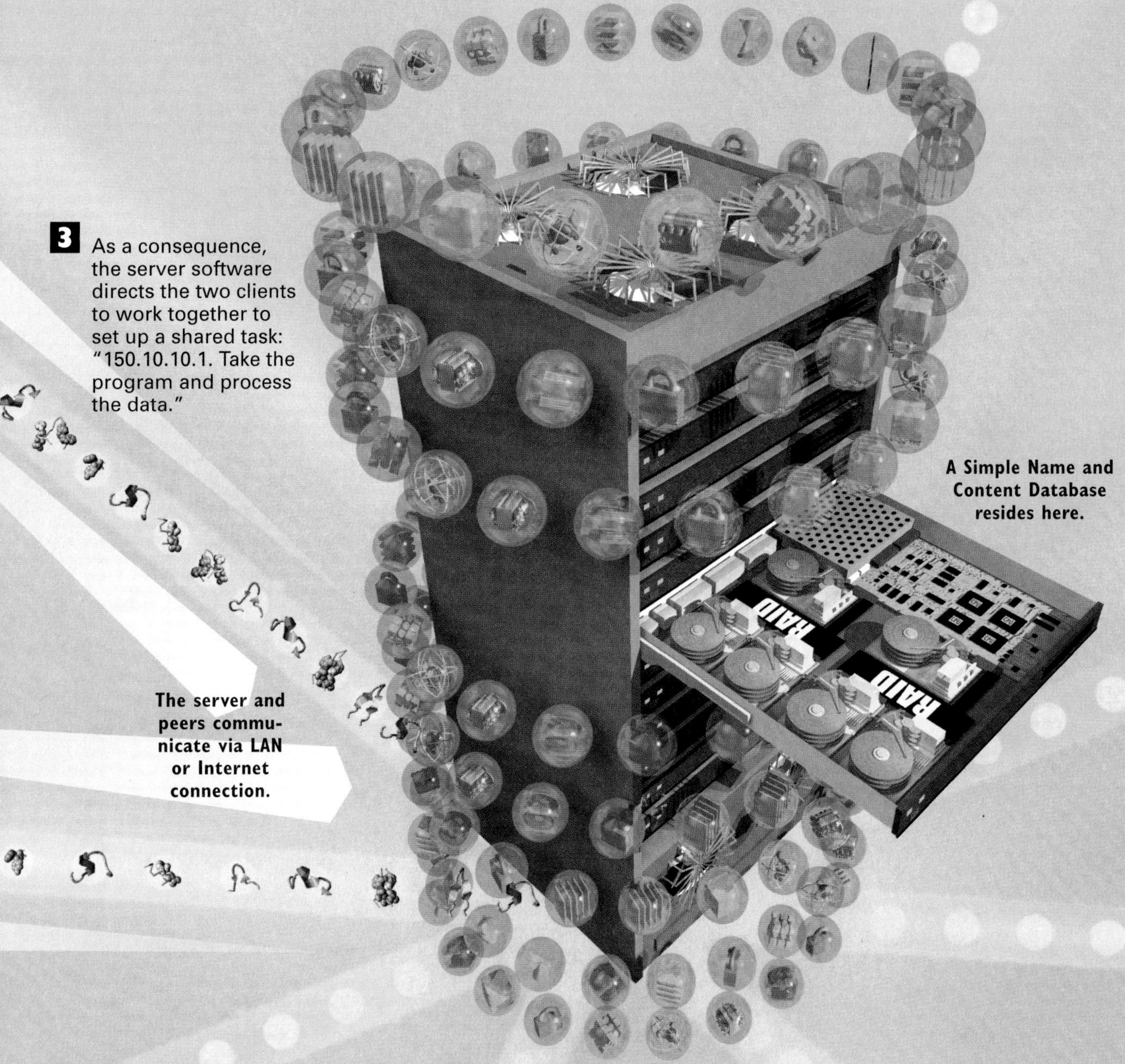
RAID
RAID

3 As a consequence, the server software directs the two clients to work together to set up a shared task: "150.10.10.1. Take the program and process the data."

A Simple Name and Content Database resides here.

The server and peers communicate via LAN or Internet connection.

Many different kinds of distributed computing applications can be stored on the server and shared with peers as needed.

How Peer-to-Peer Works Without a Server

Node 110.10.2.2

1 Nodes regularly advertise capabilities and needs. Here a node with a capability queries a node within the P2P group that previously advertised a need within the group: "Node 110.10.2.1, are you there? I have processing power to share."

3 After processing, the more powerful node completes the task: "Nodes 110.10.2.5 and 110.10.2.7, here is a picture and status information from 110.10.2.3."

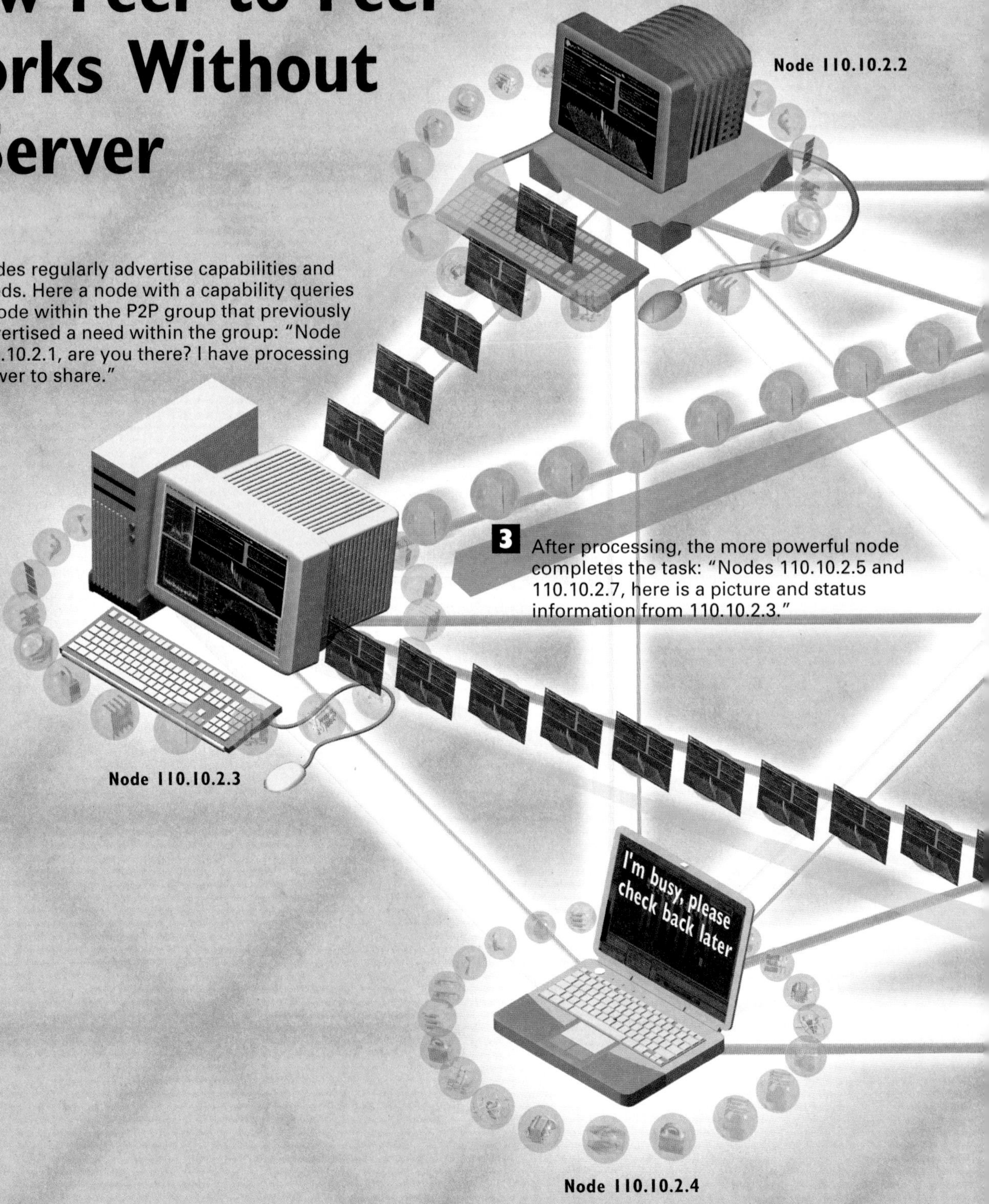

Node 110.10.2.3

I'm busy, please check back later

Node 110.10.2.4

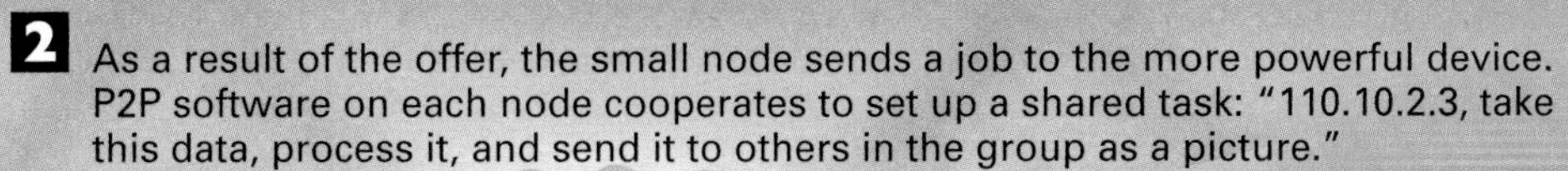

2 As a result of the offer, the small node sends a job to the more powerful device. P2P software on each node cooperates to set up a shared task: "110.10.2.3, take this data, process it, and send it to others in the group as a picture."

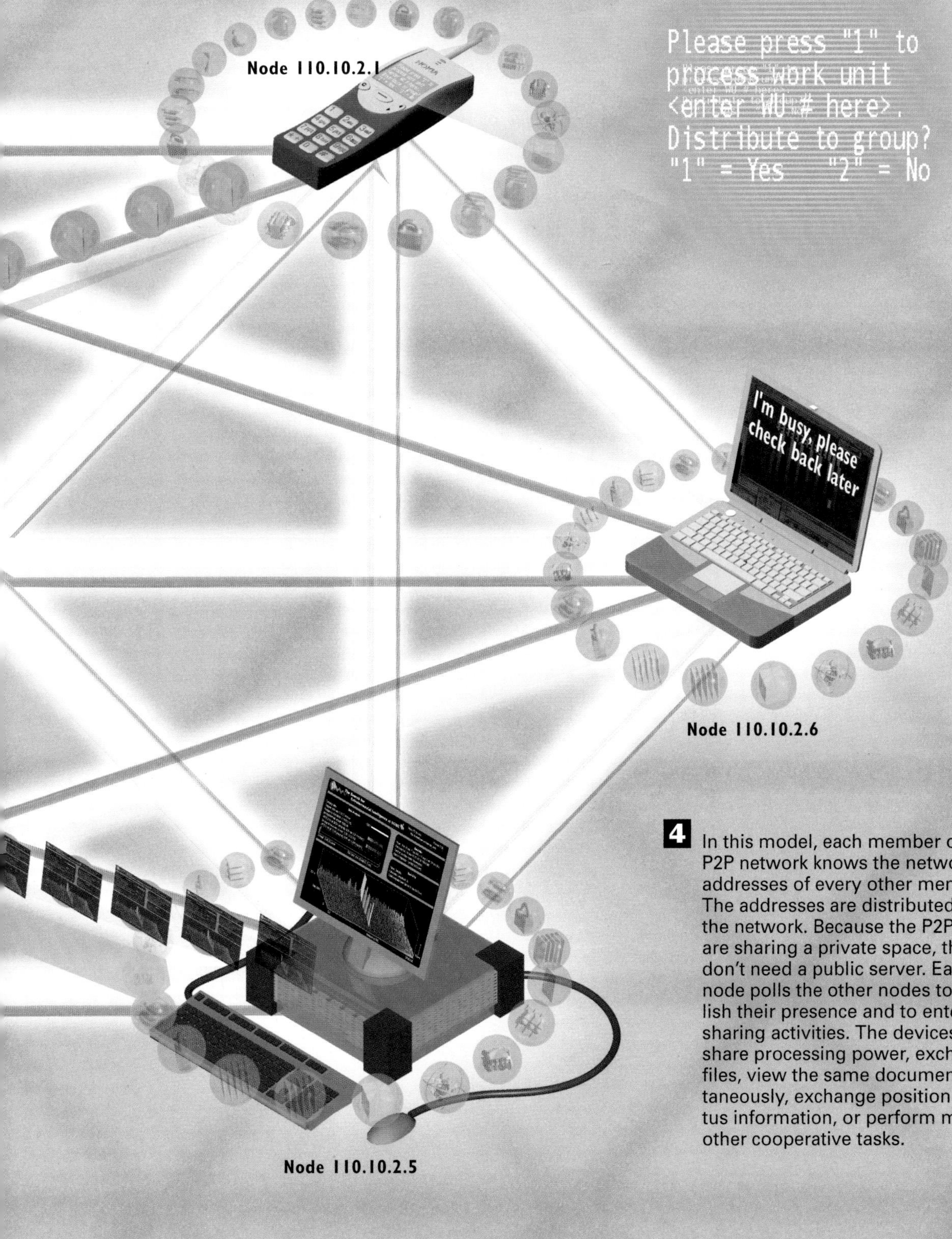

Please press "1" to process work unit <enter WU # here>. Distribute to group? "1" = Yes "2" = No

Node 110.10.2.1

I'm busy, please check back later

Node 110.10.2.6

Node 110.10.2.5

4 In this model, each member of the P2P network knows the network addresses of every other member. The addresses are distributed outside the network. Because the P2P nodes are sharing a private space, they don't need a public server. Each P2P node polls the other nodes to establish their presence and to enter into sharing activities. The devices might share processing power, exchange files, view the same document simultaneously, exchange position and status information, or perform many other cooperative tasks.

CHAPTER

19 How Enterprise Network Systems Work

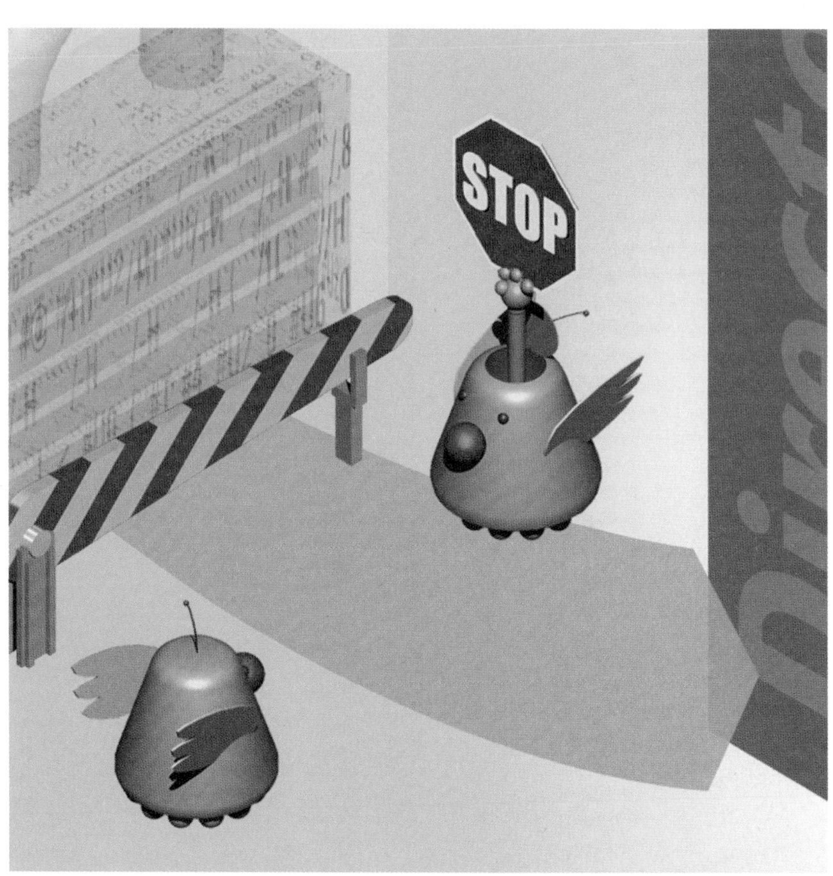
STOP

WE generally use the term *enterprise network* to refer to systems with more than about 500 active users. The physical size of networks makes them difficult to effectively manage by walking around. Along with size, another defining feature of an enterprise network is its importance to the organization. If an enterprise network malfunctions, the organization suffers severe operating difficulties.

Enterprise networks must meet the strategic needs of the organization, the tactical needs of the users, and the practical needs of the network managers. They must be secure, robust, and affordable. They must be easy to use and practical to manage.

The basis of a robust and survivable network is network storage. Applications can be reloaded and run on many servers, but the data of the organization is often irreplaceable. Storage Area Networks can provide the reliability to meet the needs of many organizations.

Users need a way to navigate around the network. Managers of big networks need a way to see and control devices without actually touching them. The tools that help users and managers include network performance monitoring and management, directory services, and single sign-on. These tools help reduce personnel and training costs while building the infrastructure needed to support modern organizations.

Network management systems include many functions such as performance monitoring, inventory reporting, information consolidation, and the ability to make configuration changes on the fly. Small performance monitoring programs, known as *agents*, run in servers, switches, routers, and in special monitoring tools scattered around the network. Inventory monitoring programs take a snapshot of a computer when it starts up and report any changes. The *Simple Network Management Protocol (SNMP)* sets the standard for management operations and reporting. Under the SNMP architecture, agents monitor their devices and gather statistical information in a format known as a *management information base* (*MIB*, rhymes with bib). A central *management console program* polls the agents on a regular basis and downloads the contents of the MIBs.

The management console programs compile the downloaded MIB data into useful information in the form of system diagrams, graphs, and reports. The console programs compare the statistics to preset standards and, if necessary, issue alerts and reports on unusual conditions. Console programs can dial a telephone number and issue alerts through pagers. Managers can use the console programs to reset and even turn off remote devices.

In many ways, large networks are an amalgamation of many smaller local area networks. Individual LANs often reside within functional workgroups or within branch offices. The majority of the program activity, file requests, and print requests stay within that workgroup or office. The combined system shares resources such as high-speed access to the corporate network and to the Internet, specialized security devices for protection and authentication, central storage and backup, extensions to wireless and portable devices, and directory services designed to make life easier for users.

Large enterprise networks benefit from a shared network service called *single sign-on*. The goal of single sign-on is to simplify the life of every network user and manager. On most networks, users have to log on to a desktop, the file server, the print server, the mail server, and maybe even the secure firewall. After that, they log on to the applications they use every day. Add online shopping, more email accounts, and a stockbroker, and each person can juggle a dozen passwords. An IS manager can automate some of those interactions with a logon script, but then how do users get to anything if they're not at their own computers? The ability to have a single sign-on available from anywhere is a goal for users and IS managers, but it isn't easy to achieve.

The pieces of a single sign-on system include authentication, to prove the identity of each user, and a directory service, to provide each user with entry into each appropriate resource. As our diagram describes, the authentication component identifies the user, the public key encryption and certification component verifies the user to the directory service, and the directory service interfaces the user to the resource.

Whereas directory services identify resources, certificate services and the public key infrastructure (PKI) assure that the appropriate people use them. Think of PKI's trust management much like the government granting a passport, or the department of motor vehicles granting a driver's license. In both cases, a trusted entity issues a document that identifies a person and some associated rights. As long as you believe in the trusted entity, you can believe in the individual.

An organization called the *certificate authority* (CA) serves as the trusted entity that identifies individuals or companies and issues a digital certificate tied to those entities. When an individual establishes identity with a CA, the CA's server generates a unique signature key and encryption key pairs in the form of certificates that include the individual's name. The certificates contain the CA's private key to establish authenticity.

How do you prove who you are regardless of where you are? That proof depends on personal authentication services. Personal authentication services use ID/password pairs, challenge response tokens, biometrics, or other devices to ensure a positive ID.

Hardware-based challenge/response mechanisms use electronic card devices to generate unique one-time pass-codes. When the cards are issued, they're associated with an ID that triggers a password request. They provide excellent, but somewhat expensive, authentication.

A broad area of technology called *biometrics* uses encoded versions of your physical voice, eye, face or hand attributes to uniquely identify you. The installation process associates your ID with your biological attributes. The system uses those attributes to verify your identity.

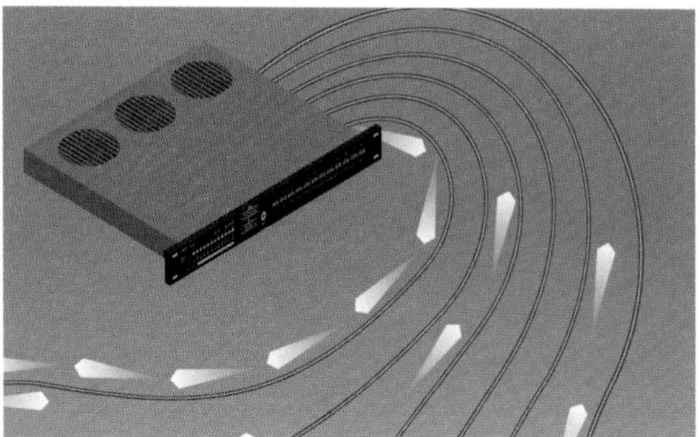

Creating single sign-on from anywhere isn't simple, but it's valuable. Soon we will provide individuals with an electronic identity bubble that identifies them to any resource from a cash machine and gas pump to a cell phone. But, once corporate users are identified and authenticated, what do they see? How do you provide simple access to applications once you're past the sign-on phase?

A directory service is key to finding and entering services across a large network. Bringing a directory service to life is a big project. It requires careful planning because changing a directory name structure is more difficult than setting it up the first time. The directory service interacts between the authentication service and the applications to make sure that the right people have access to the right data, files, and devices at the right time. It's a complex system, but it significantly simplifies life for the user.

Modern enterprise storage systems comprise a complete sub-network within the network. *Storage Area Networks (SANs)* consist of multiple specialized storage devices with their own interconnections. Designers can cluster storage devices in one physical area and connect them with extremely high-speed gigabit or even 10-gigabit networks. Or they can distribute storage devices in different physical locations to enhance survivability. In any case, the storage appears as one contiguous local asset to the applications using the data.

Distributed storage systems enhance business survivability in the event of disasters or business interruptions. Because storage area networks can have parts scattered in different physical locations, the total system is less vulnerable to loss. Business restoration actions become easier when the organization can do business from anywhere it can access the SAN.

When you're planning an enterprise network, it pays to take a long-term perspective. The payback for the investment takes years, but the right management and access services can immediately provide higher productivity and efficiency.

How Storage Area Networks Work

1. The Storage Area Network (SAN) has many sub-elements that work together to store data economically while making it available quickly.

2. The SAN uses internal connections with 1–10 Gigabit speeds. Application servers access the SAN through special high-speed switches.

SAN high-speed switch

3. SAN links extend the SAN functions to different geographical areas.

SAN link

Tape storage subsystem

4. Tape storage systems provide long-term information storage required by laws and regulations.

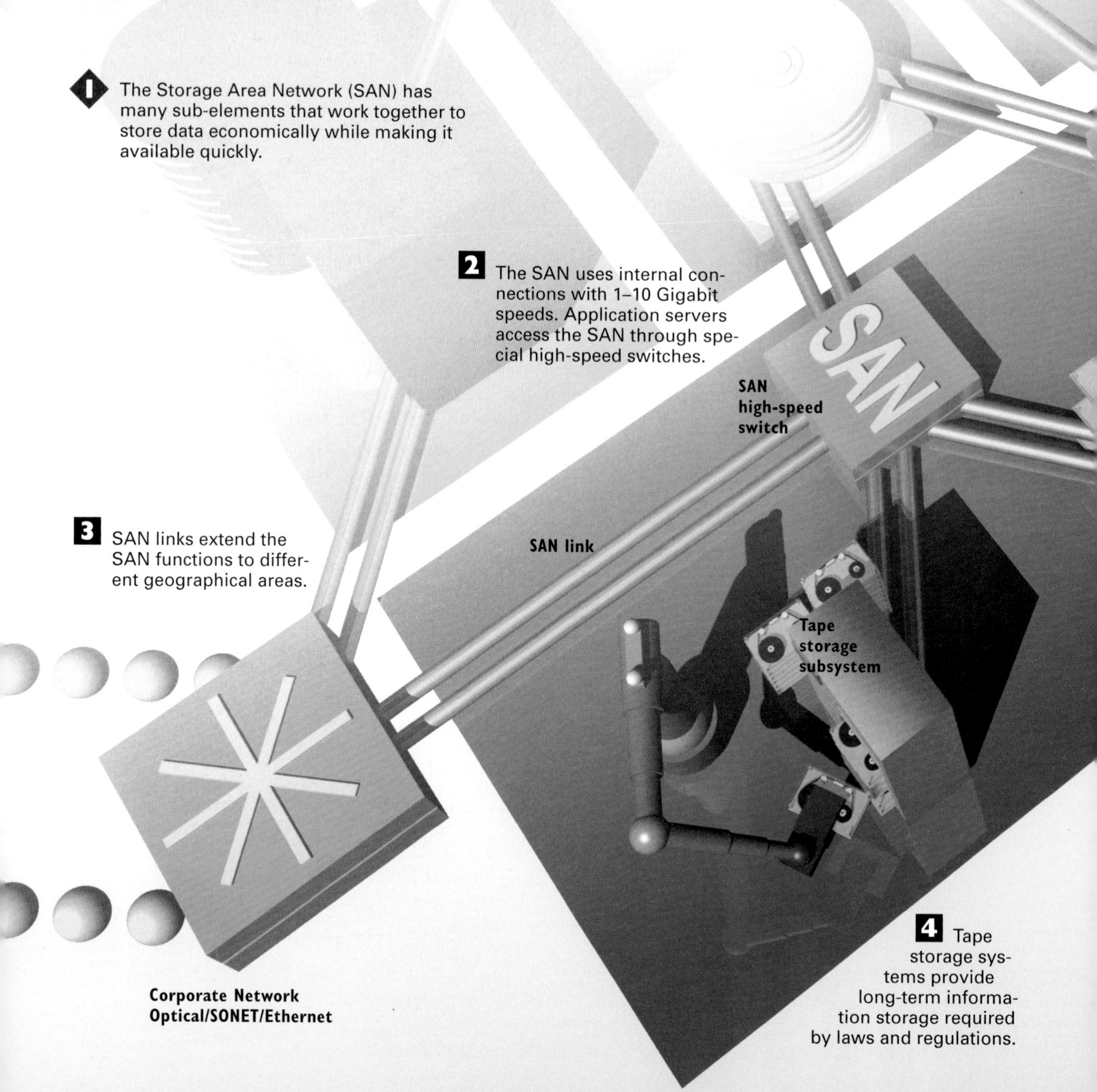

Corporate Network Optical/SONET/Ethernet

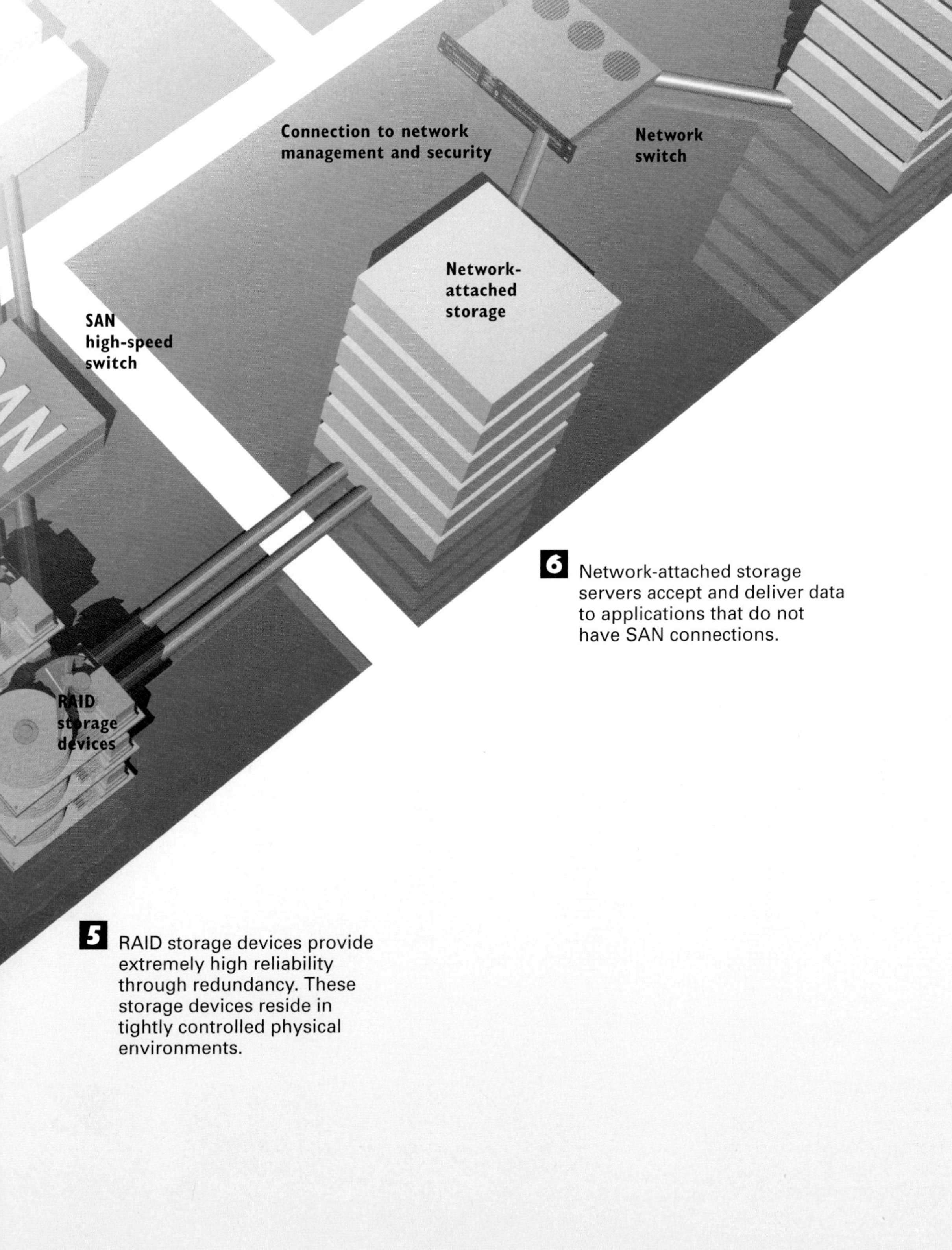
Connection to network management and security
Network switch
Network-attached storage
SAN high-speed switch
RAID storage devices

6 Network-attached storage servers accept and deliver data to applications that do not have SAN connections.

5 RAID storage devices provide extremely high reliability through redundancy. These storage devices reside in tightly controlled physical environments.

How Storage Area Networking Builds Business Continuity

Application server optimization
Wireless mobile access
Cache
ID server
Operations
Secondary data center
VoIP
Mainframe
SAN
Corporate Network Optical/SONET/Ethernet

4 The secondary data center's storage system is part of the overall SAN. Data elements are replicated automatically based on age and activity.

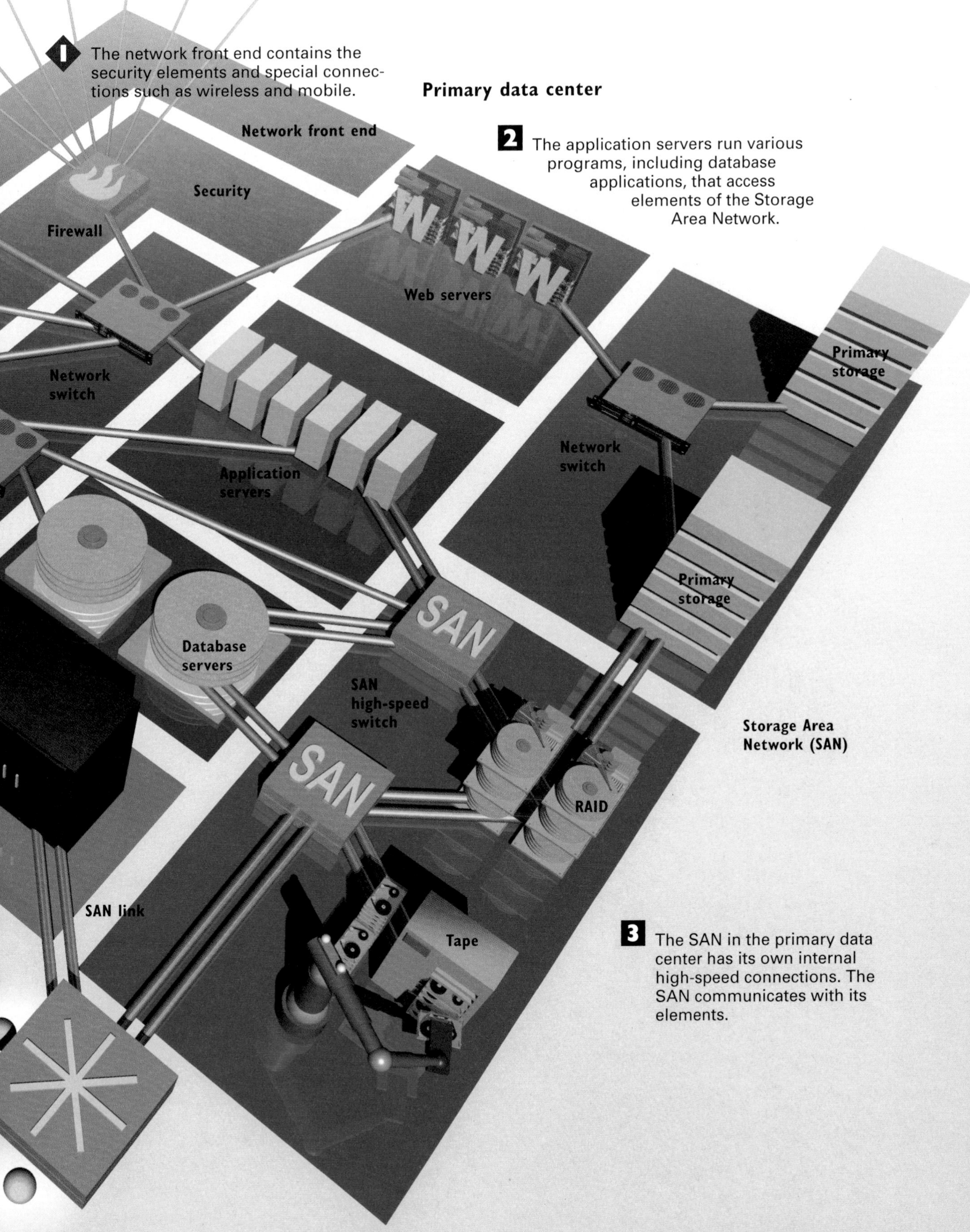
1 The network front end contains the security elements and special connections such as wireless and mobile.
Primary data center
Network front end
2 The application servers run various programs, including database applications, that access elements of the Storage Area Network.
Security
Firewall
Web servers
Primary storage
Network switch
Network switch
Application servers
Primary storage
Database servers
SAN
SAN high-speed switch
SAN
Storage Area Network (SAN)
RAID
SAN link
Tape
3 The SAN in the primary data center has its own internal high-speed connections. The SAN communicates with its elements.

How Network Management Systems Work

1 A management program uses messages conforming to the Simple Network Management Protocol (SNMP) to poll the agent programs running in various network devices. When the agents reply, the SNMP console program aggregates the information and presents it graphically.

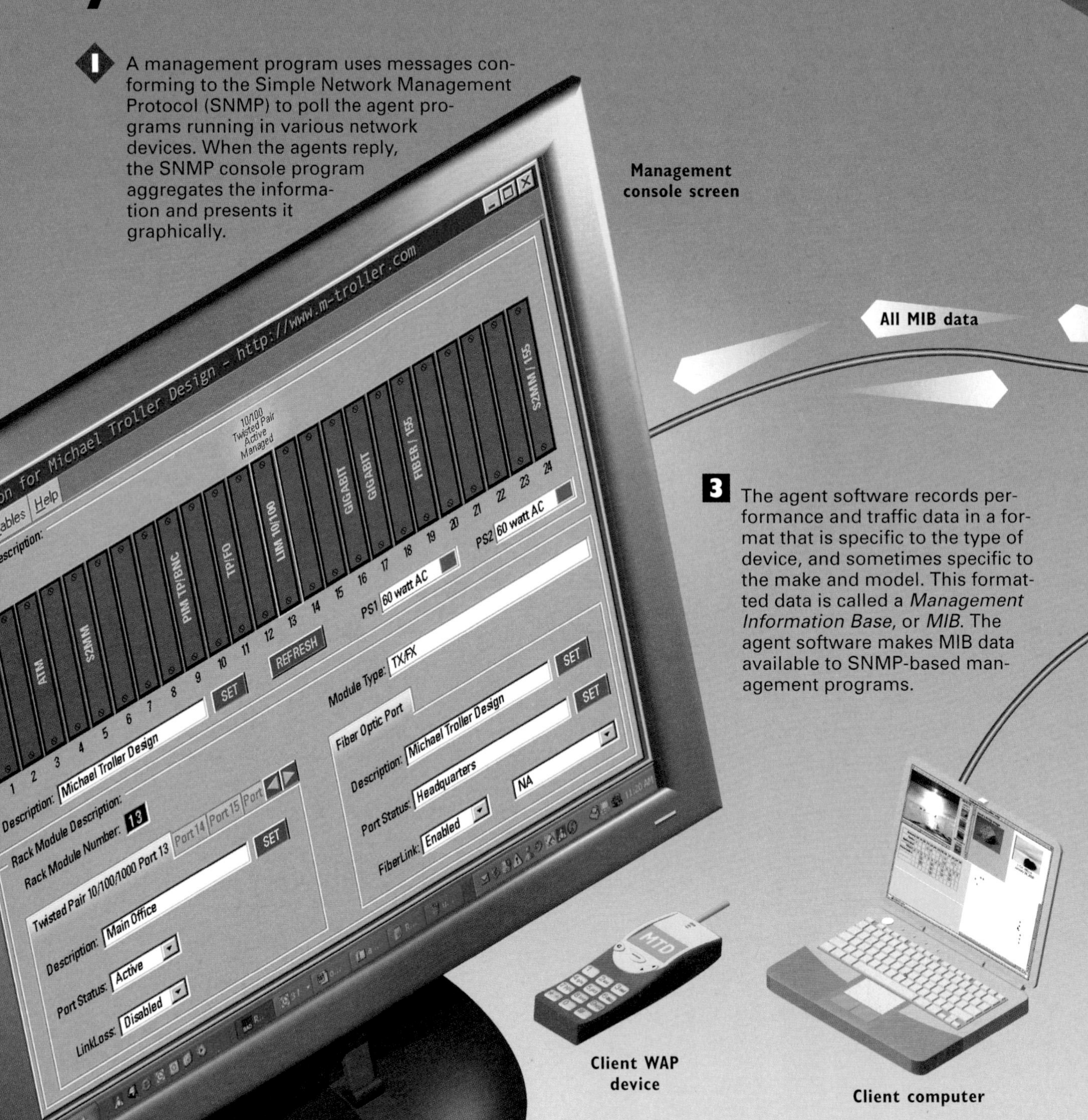

Management console screen
All MIB data
Client WAP device
Client computer

3 The agent software records performance and traffic data in a format that is specific to the type of device, and sometimes specific to the make and model. This formatted data is called a *Management Information Base*, or *MIB*. The agent software makes MIB data available to SNMP-based management programs.

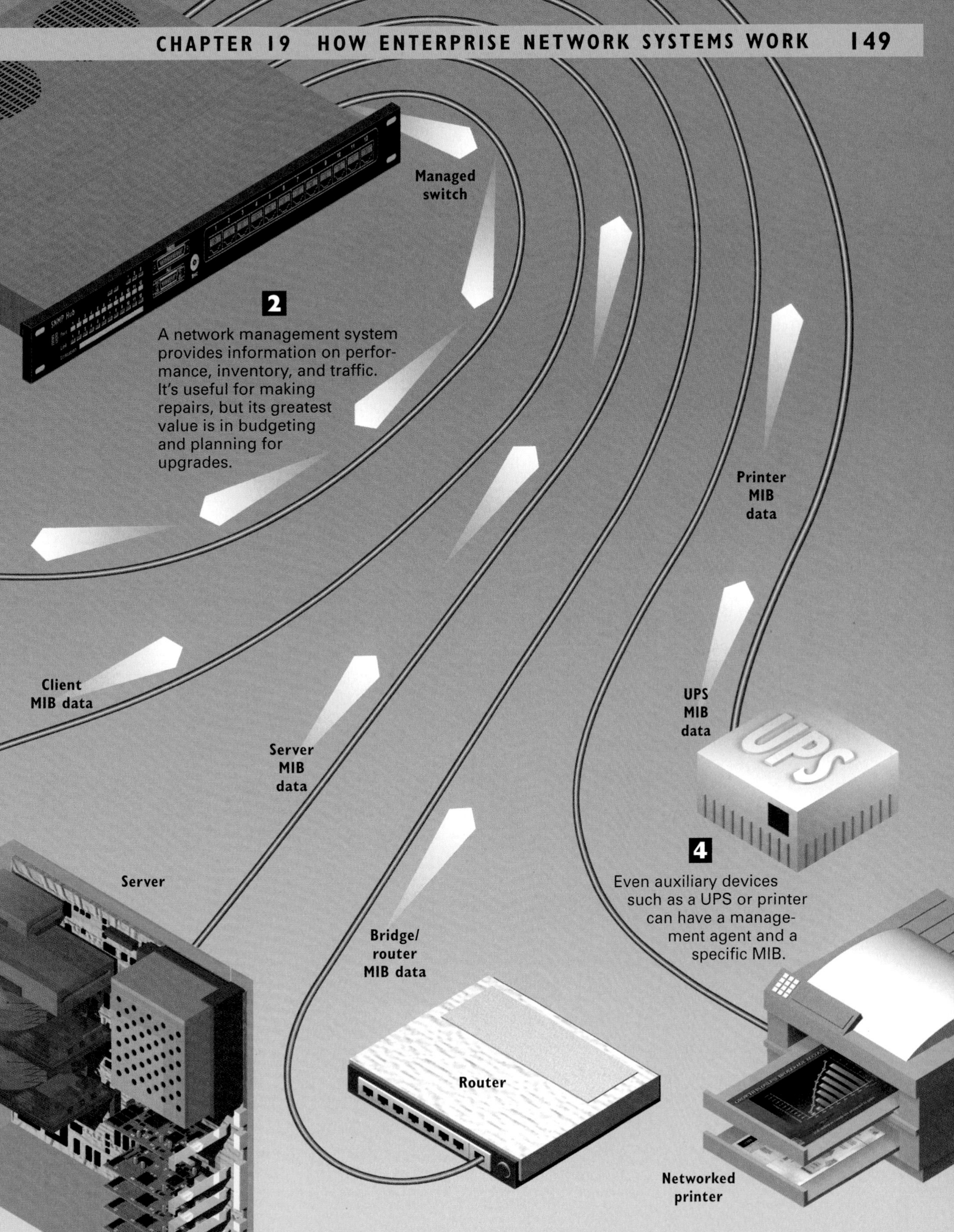
Managed
switch
SNMP Hub
Client
MIB data
Server
MIB
data
Printer
MIB
data
UPS
MIB
data
UPS
Server
Bridge/
router
MIB data
Router
Networked
printer

2 A network management system provides information on performance, inventory, and traffic. It's useful for making repairs, but its greatest value is in budgeting and planning for upgrades.

4 Even auxiliary devices such as a UPS or printer can have a management agent and a specific MIB.

How Enterprise Network Systems Work

Centralized server facility

Switch

1 Located in a physically and environmentally protected and secured data center, the Centralized Server Facility contains redundant equipment with high-quality monitoring and management features. Workgroup and branch office servers replicate and update shared databases held on the central servers.

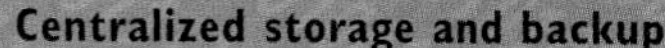
Centralized storage and backup

2 A centralized storage and backup facility stores less frequently used files and maintains a current backup of heavily used files. This storage area network is shared storage for all central servers.

3 Programs running on computers in workgroup LANs can access a local server for commonly used files, but they will reach out through the corporate network for centrally stored files and specialized services.

Router

7 All applications check with the central security server and its related directory services to provide the proper level of access to designated users.

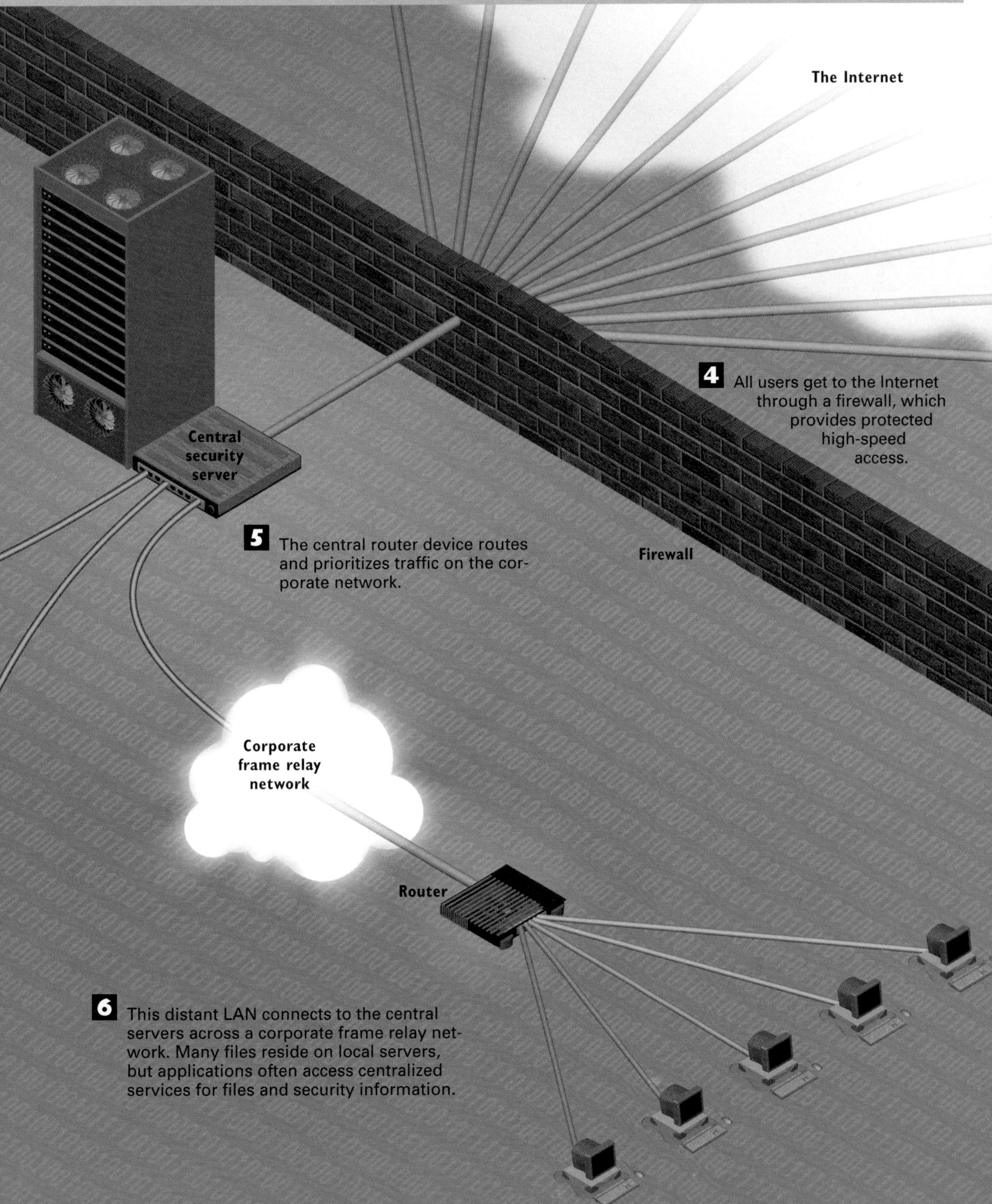
The Internet
Central security server
Firewall
Corporate frame relay network
Router

4 All users get to the Internet through a firewall, which provides protected high-speed access.

5 The central router device routes and prioritizes traffic on the corporate network.

6 This distant LAN connects to the central servers across a corporate frame relay network. Many files reside on local servers, but applications often access centralized services for files and security information.

How Enterprise Single Sign-On Works

1 Individuals prove who they are through strong authentication that combines what they know (password) with what they have (smart card or token) or with what they are (biometric measurements).

Password

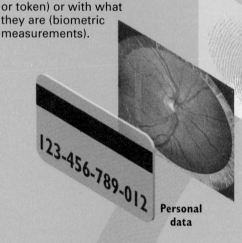

123-456-789-012

Biometrics

Personal data

4 Encrypted certificate says, "I am me and these guys verify it!"

Certificate issued to
Michael D. Troller
Checksum verification:
485201439571 0319

Encrypted certificate

2 The authentication information goes to a central security server.

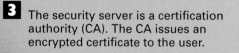

Certificate Authority
Certificate Authority

3 The security server is a certification authority (CA). The CA issues an encrypted certificate to the user.

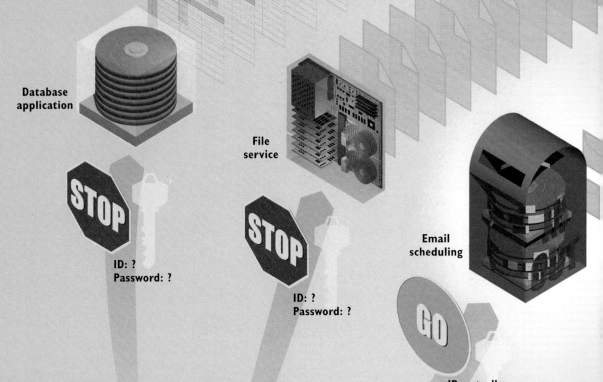

Database
application
STOP
ID: ?
Password: ?

File
service
STOP
ID: ?
Password: ?

Email
scheduling
GO
ID: mtroller
Password: xxx xx xxx

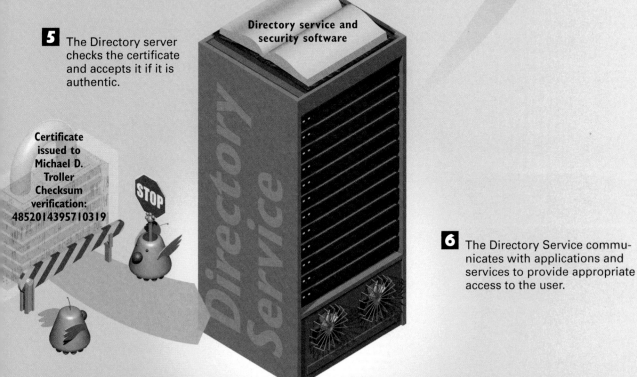

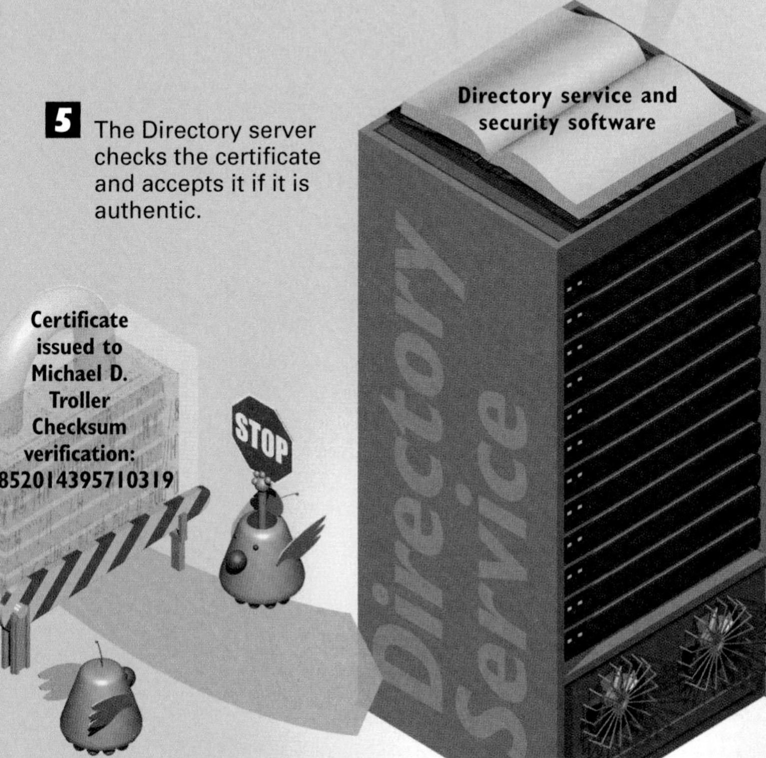
Directory service and
security software
Directory
Service
Certificate
issued to
Michael D.
Troller
Checksum
verification:
4852014395710319
STOP

5 The Directory server checks the certificate and accepts it if it is authentic.

6 The Directory Service communicates with applications and services to provide appropriate access to the user.

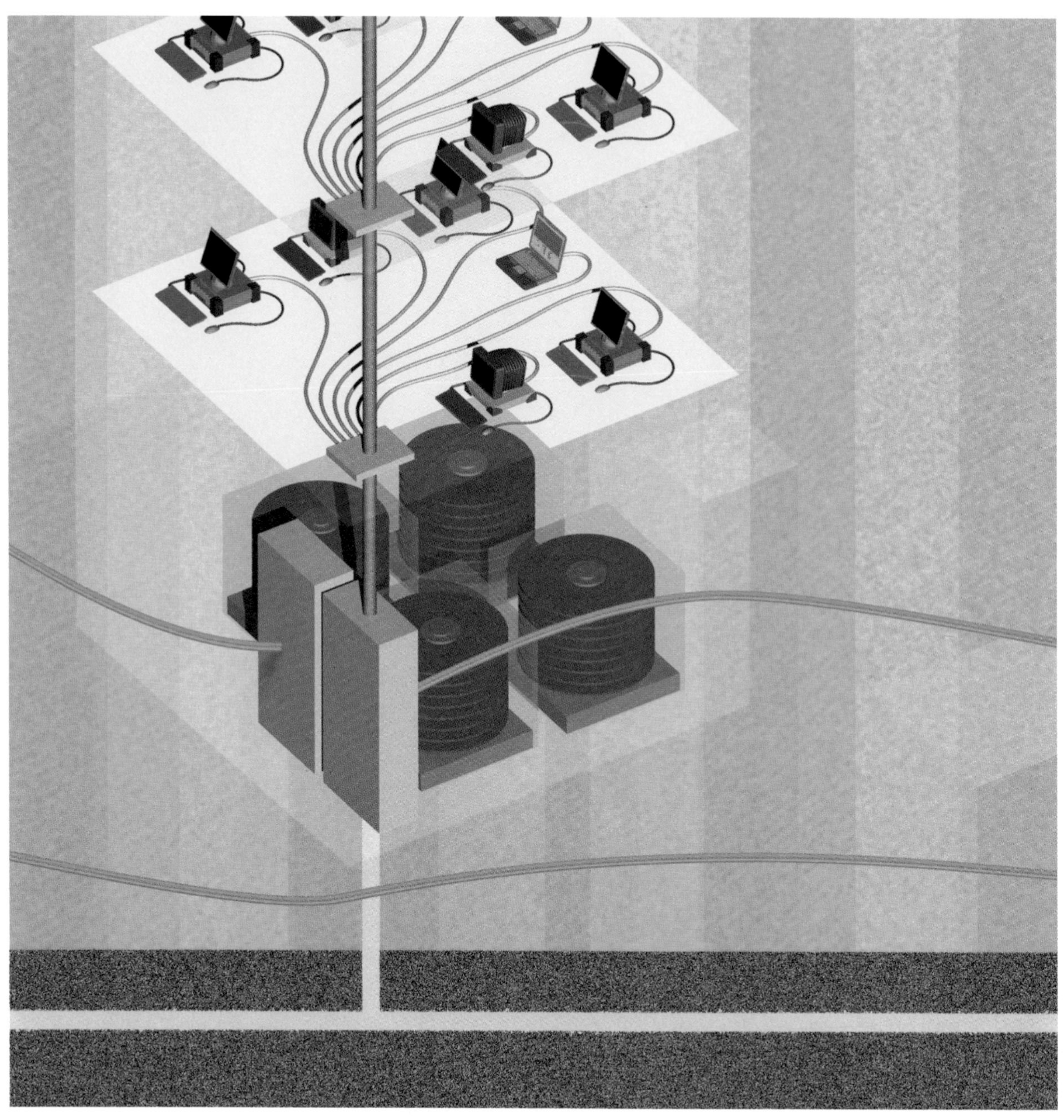

LINKS BETWEEN LANS

INFORMATION is the raw material, inventory, and processed product of many modern organizations. Computer networks are the production line, distribution system, and even the retail point of sale for the information products generated by many organizations and businesses. Corporate networks act as local, regional, and international distribution systems for modern commerce.

If local area networks (LANs) are similar to the in-house production lines of manufacturing plants then computer networks that cover the distances between cities and countries are the roads and rail lines of modern businesses. Long-distance data networks, called *metropolitan area networks (MANs)*, and wide area networks (WANs) are the equivalent of the trucking, rail, barge, and air freight systems needed to support smokestack industries.

Because many organizations must move a lot of data over distances greater than a few thousand feet, the industry developed several techniques for extending and linking LANs. The techniques you select to link LAN segments depend on the distance and speed needed, the network communications protocols in use, and your business's philosophy regarding leasing versus owning facilities.

Just as some manufacturing companies own their own trucks and boxcars, and others contract for all transportation services, some organizations own their MAN and WAN facilities and others lease these specialized services from commercial suppliers. Many organizations set up their own microwave, light beam, or fiber-optic transmission systems to carry data around a metropolitan area or campus. Organizations can use the transportation tunnels under many cities to install their own fiber-optic cable systems between their offices or stores and major customers and suppliers. Metropolitan telephone and cable television companies also supply LAN-to-LAN connections under several types of business arrangements. However, when the connections extend beyond the metropolitan area, organizations typically lease circuits from suppliers such as the long-haul telephone carriers.

When you lease circuits for links between LANs, you have many options. The three general technical categories of leased services are circuit-switched, full-period, and packet-switched. Circuit-switched services are those with a dial tone—for example, switched-56 digital services and the Integrated Services Digital Network (ISDN). The equipment dials a connection, transfers data, and hangs up when it completes the transaction. Full-period services, such as leased telephone lines, provide a circuit dedicated to your use full time. Packet-switched systems allow multipoint connections for bursts of short packets. Packet-switched networks are also called *X.25 networks* after an older packet-switching standard; today, these networks commonly use a newer standard called *frame relay*.

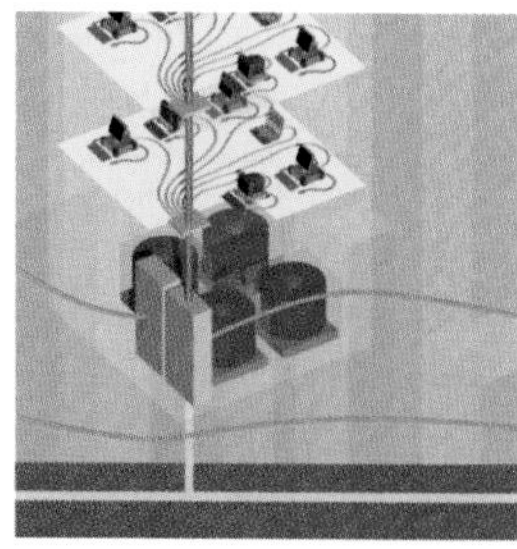

Leasing a circuit to link LAN segments typically will cost thousands of dollars a month. The cost is determined by the maximum signaling speed desired and sometimes by the distance. Therefore, it makes sense to invest in network portal devices for both ends of the link that can use the expensive circuit to maximum efficiency.

Network traffic typically follows specific paths and travels within a group of people with common business interests—a workgroup. However, some traffic also flows between workgroups. Putting all workgroups on the same cable and letting them communicate without restrictions consume the available resources of the cable. Organizations with busy networks can use network portal devices called *bridges* that link workgroup LANs while exercising discrimination over the traffic passing between them.

A router is a more complex portal device than a bridge and has a greater capability to examine and direct the traffic it carries. Routers are somewhat more expensive to buy and require more attention than bridges, but their more robust features make them the best choice for a portal between a LAN and a long-distance link.

A router reads the destination address of the network packet and determines whether it is on the same segment of network cable as the originating station. If the destination station is on the other side of the bridge, the bridge sequences the packet into the traffic on that cable segment.

Routers read the more complex network addressing information in the packet or token and can add more information to get the packet through the network. For example, a router might wrap a network service request in an "envelope" of data containing routing and transmission information for transmission through an X.25 packet-switched network. When the envelope of data comes out the other end of the X.25 network, the receiving router strips off the X.25 data, formats it for Ethernet, and sequences it on its attached LAN segment.

Routers make very smart connections between the elements of complex networks. Routers can choose from redundant paths between LAN segments and they can link LAN segments using very different data packaging and media access schemes.

A new technology, Asynchronous Transfer Mode (ATM), is becoming more important as network traffic includes more time-sensitive video and digitized sound data. ATM uses very small packets. If one packet is lost, it's forgotten. No time is used attempting to resend the lost data.

All of these techniques and devices combine to create today's corporate networks, networks for entertainment and for finance, and the global Internet.

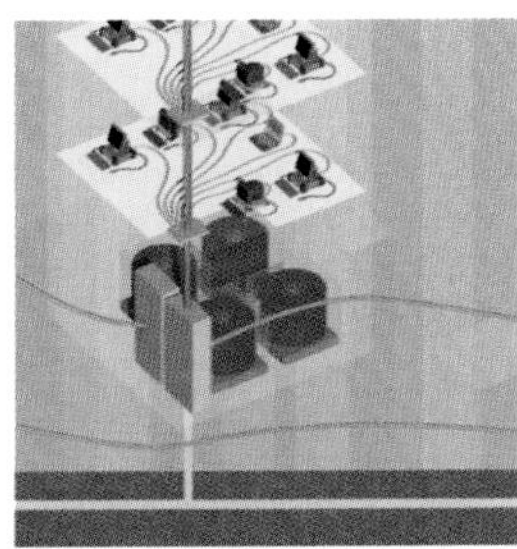

CHAPTER

20

How Routers, Switches, and Firewalls Work

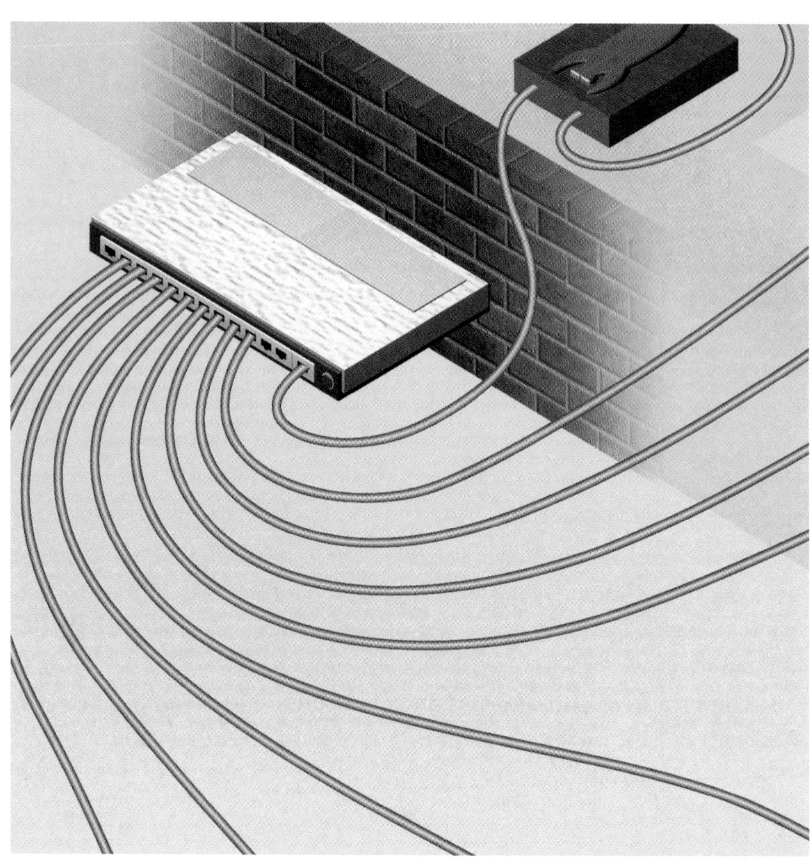

JUST as manufacturing plants have mailrooms and shipping docks, local area networks have specified places where the local and long-distance services meet. Bridges, routers, and switches are tools that are used to connect Local Area Networks into larger Wide Area Networks such as the Internet.

Ethernet Bridges—Bridges are simple devices that are typically used to connect two LANs over a private communications link. Bridges read the destination address of each Ethernet packet—the outermost envelope around the data—to determine where the data is headed, but they do not look inside the packet or frame to read IP addresses. If the destination address isn't on the local LAN, the bridge hands the data off to the LAN at the other end of the communications link.

IP Routers—Routers are more complex devices that are usually used to connect a LAN to a larger network. Unlike bridges, routers dig more deeply into the envelopes surrounding the data to find the destination for the data packet. The router reads the information contained in each packet or frame, uses complex network addressing procedures to determine the appropriate network destination, discards the outer packet or frame, and then repackages and retransmits the data.

Routers act as a safety barrier between network segments and often contain firewall services to protect the LAN from hackers, snoopers, and other intruders.

Ethernet Switches—Early Ethernet networks used simple devices called *hubs* to connect several computers into a LAN. A hub has multiple Ethernet connections, one for each device connected to the LAN. When a hub receives data from any of the devices on the LAN, it retransmits the data to all the other devices on the LAN. This "shotgun" approach is effective but inefficient.

Switches look and work much like hubs, but they make more efficient use of LAN bandwidth. They use simple logic to detect the destination of a packet and send the packet to a specific port on the switch, rather than to every port on the switch. This simple action speeds LAN throughput and greatly reduces LAN congestion.

There are two major types of switches. Layer 2 switches operate by examining the Ethernet address of the data packets, whereas more sophisticated Layer 3 switches examine the destination IP address of the data.

Network Address Translation—As we saw in Chapter 16, "How TCP/IP Works," each device connected to the Internet must have a unique IP address. But it can be expensive and time-consuming to assign a unique address to every computer on a LAN. DHCP helps conserve addresses by assigning addresses on the fly, as computers connect to and disconnect from the LAN. Network Address Translation (NAT) goes a step further by allowing many computers to share a single, public IP address. NAT is widely used in small routers designed for the home and small office markets.

NAT also provides a first-line defense between a private LAN and the public Internet. Because the computers on a NAT LAN aren't directly connected to the Internet, they are protected from hackers and other intruders. NAT Networks typically use special nonroutable IP addresses that are reserved for private networks.

Firewalls—Unless you've spent the past few years on a desert island, you've probably read news reports about hackers breaking into computers to steal data or deface Web pages. Although the inevitable finger is usually pointed at lax security measures or an obscure flaw in a network operating system, the real problem lies with the IP protocol itself.

IP was designed to be an open protocol that allows any IP device to freely connect to any other. In the early days of the Internet, it was common practice for every user to leave his or her files open for sharing on the Internet. This practice made perfect sense at the time, because most Internet users were college professors, students, and researchers who were sharing research data and information over the Internet.

As the Internet moved into the business and personal lives of millions of users, security became a major issue. In the real world, a firewall is a hardened, fire-resistant wall designed to keep a fire contained within a building. In the Internet world, a firewall is a special type of router designed to keep intruders out of a private network while allowing the free, unrestricted flow of authorized data to and from a network.

How Hubs and Switches Work

1 Ethernet hubs are simple and inexpensive, and they work fine on small networks. Hubs contain several Ethernet ports that are effectively connected together.

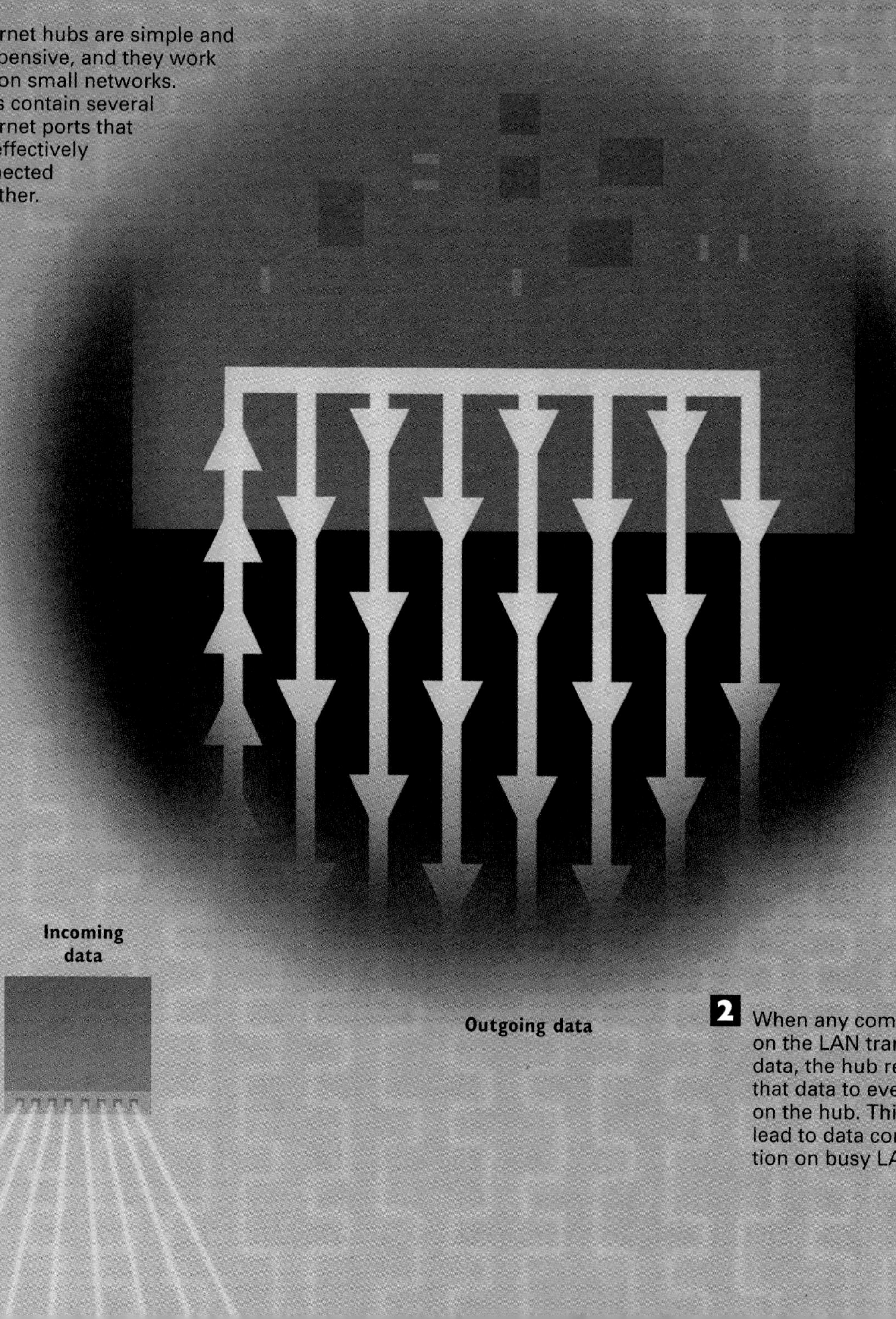

Incoming data

Outgoing data

2 When any computer on the LAN transmits data, the hub repeats that data to every port on the hub. This can lead to data congestion on busy LANs.

3 Like hubs, switches also feature multiple Ethernet ports. But switches also contain some intelligence that allows them to make decisions on where to send LAN traffic.

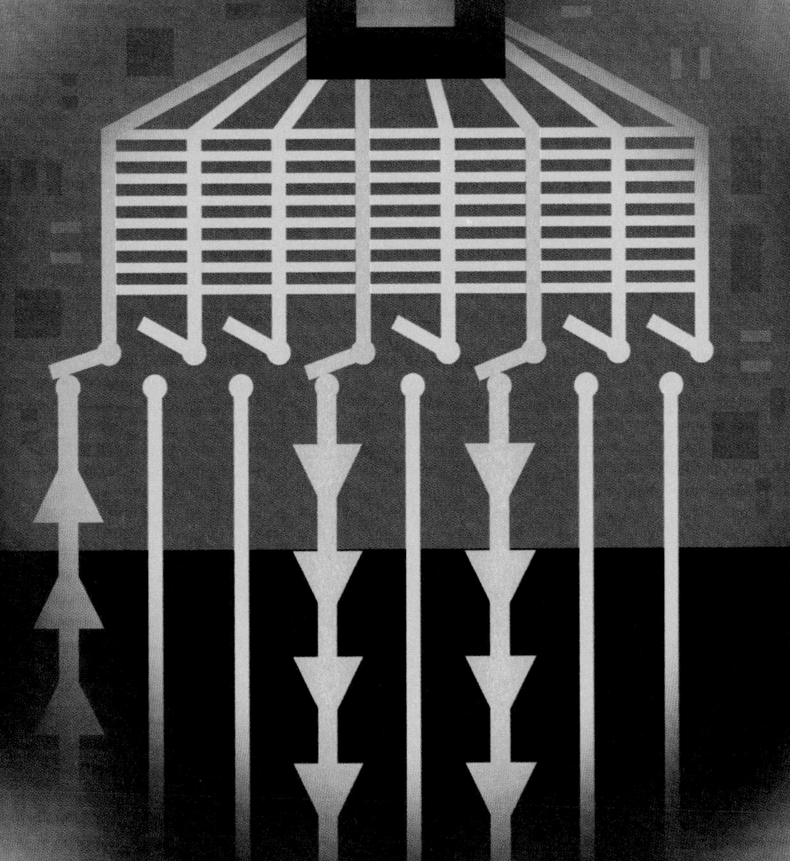

Incoming data
Outgoing data

4 As each computer transmits data, the switch examines the destination address of the data. The switch forwards the data to the appropriate port on the switch, without sending the same data to the rest of the computers connected to the switch.

How Routers Work

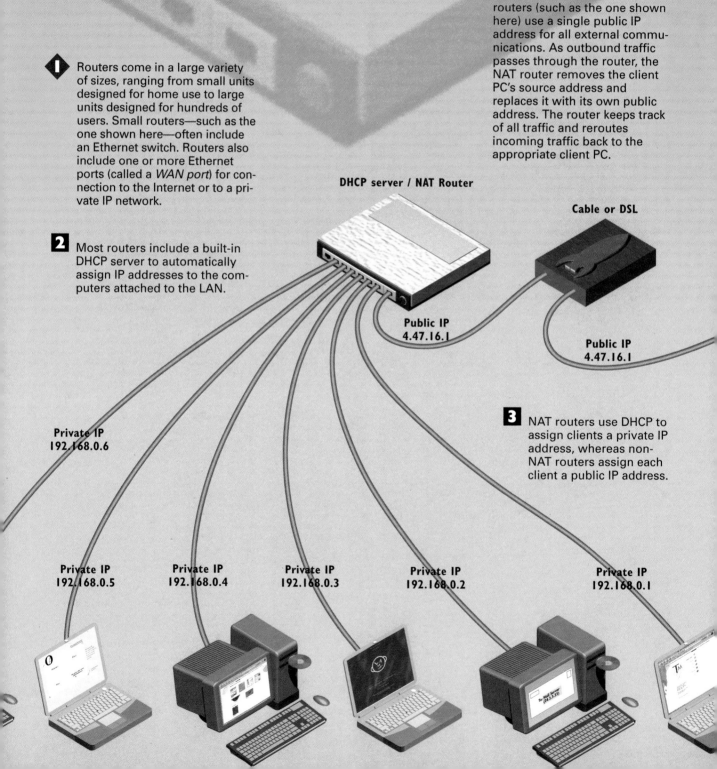

1. Routers come in a large variety of sizes, ranging from small units designed for home use to large units designed for hundreds of users. Small routers—such as the one shown here—often include an Ethernet switch. Routers also include one or more Ethernet ports (called a *WAN port*) for connection to the Internet or to a private IP network.

2. Most routers include a built-in DHCP server to automatically assign IP addresses to the computers attached to the LAN.

3. NAT routers use DHCP to assign clients a private IP address, whereas non-NAT routers assign each client a public IP address.

4. The router acts as a gateway for traffic between the LAN and the external IP network. NAT routers (such as the one shown here) use a single public IP address for all external communications. As outbound traffic passes through the router, the NAT router removes the client PC's source address and replaces it with its own public address. The router keeps track of all traffic and reroutes incoming traffic back to the appropriate client PC.

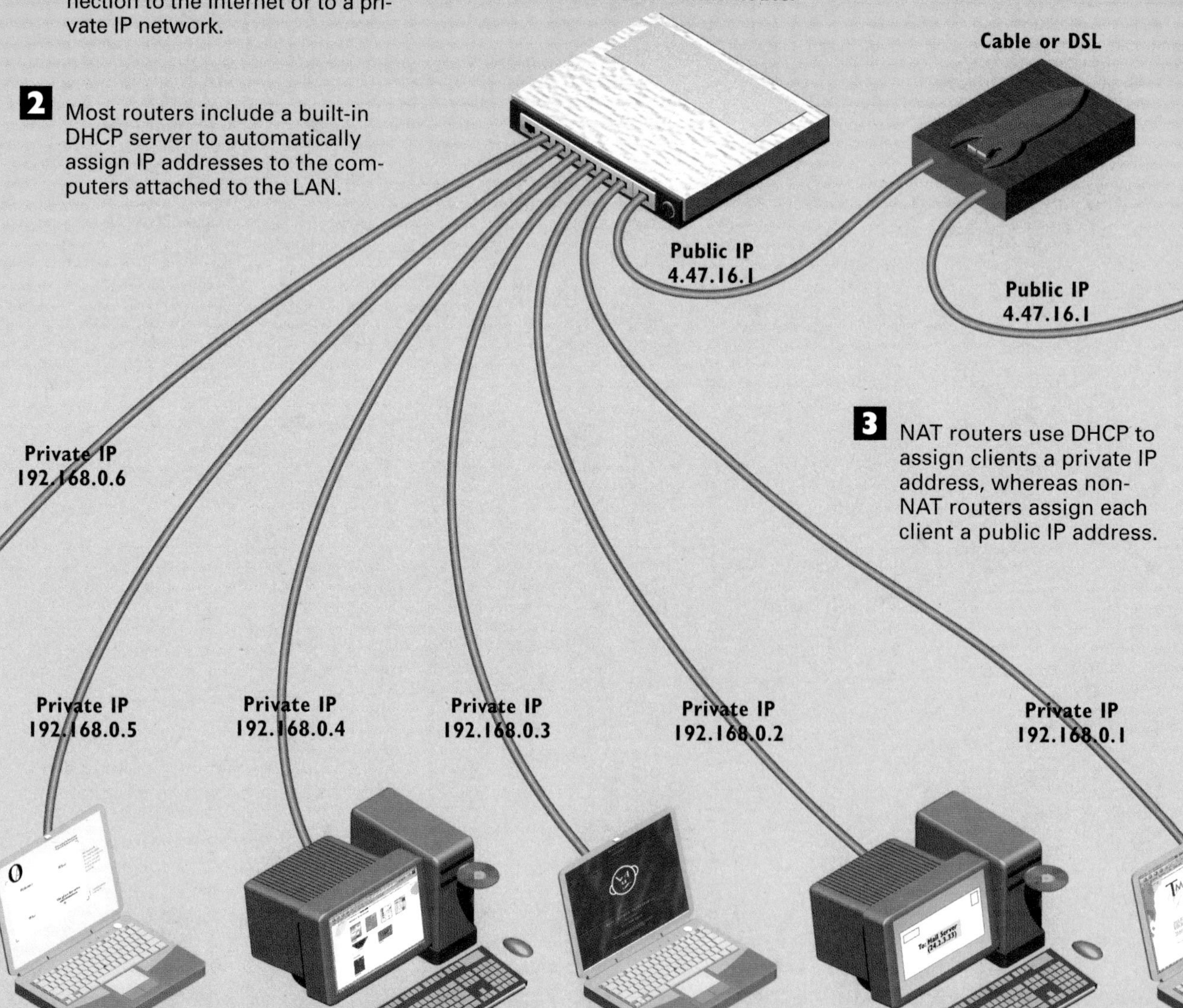
DHCP server / NAT Router
Cable or DSL
Public IP
4.47.16.1
Public IP
4.47.16.1
Private IP
192.168.0.6
Private IP
192.168.0.5
Private IP
192.168.0.4
Private IP
192.168.0.3
Private IP
192.168.0.2
Private IP
192.168.0.1

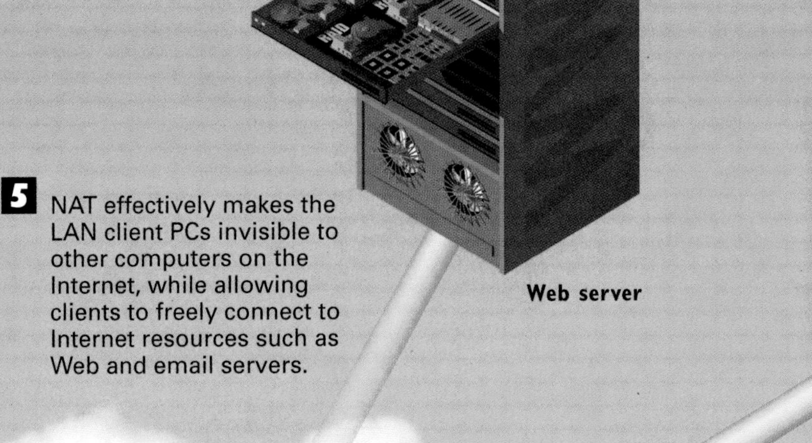
Web server

5 NAT effectively makes the LAN client PCs invisible to other computers on the Internet, while allowing clients to freely connect to Internet resources such as Web and email servers.

Mail server
The Internet

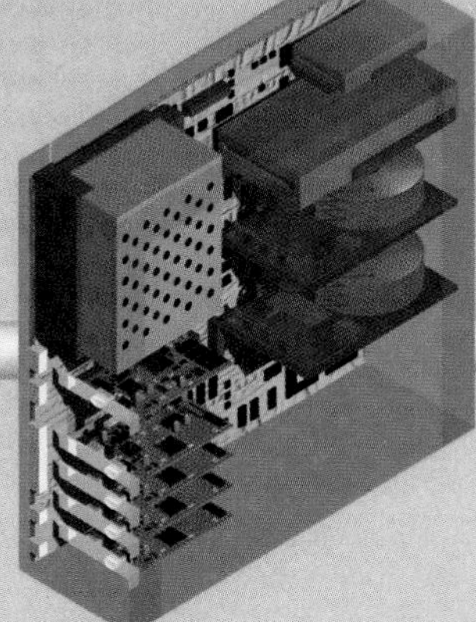
Web server
Hacker
ACCESS
DENIED

6 Hackers attempting to connect to the router or to a PC attached to the router won't see anything because the router blocks unexpected incoming traffic.

How Firewalls Work

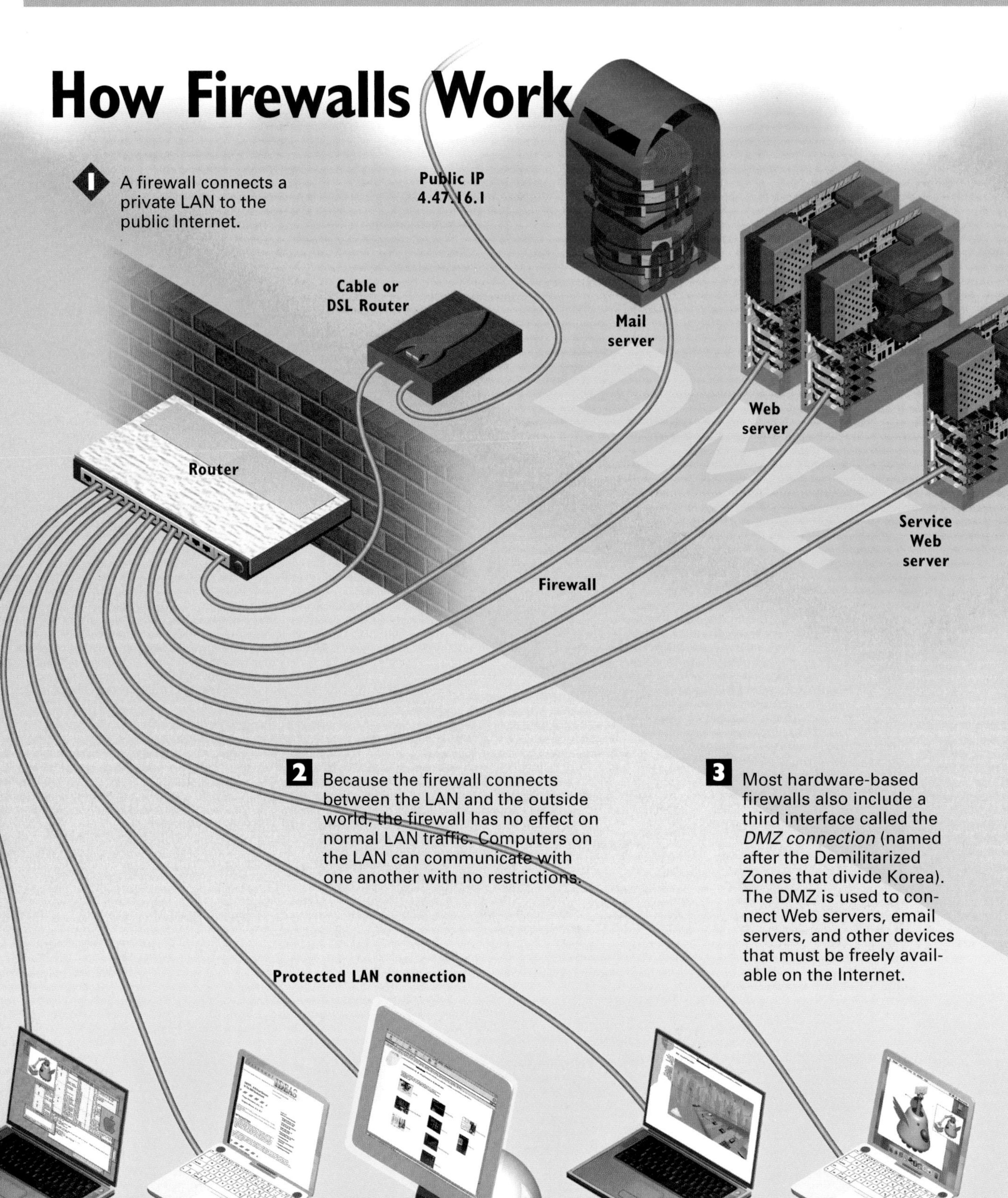
Public IP
4.47.16.1
Cable or
DSL Router
Mail
server
Web
server
Router
Service
Web
server
Firewall
DMZ
Protected LAN connection

1. A firewall connects a private LAN to the public Internet.

2. Because the firewall connects between the LAN and the outside world, the firewall has no effect on normal LAN traffic. Computers on the LAN can communicate with one another with no restrictions.

3. Most hardware-based firewalls also include a third interface called the *DMZ connection* (named after the Demilitarized Zones that divide Korea). The DMZ is used to connect Web servers, email servers, and other devices that must be freely available on the Internet.

The Internet

4 Clients on the protected LAN can access Internet resources such as Web and email servers, as long as that access is allowed by the current firewall settings. Network administrators can program the firewall to block certain types of traffic such as Instant Messenger, Peer file sharing, and network game programs.

5 Client computers on the Internet can access public Web and email servers connected to the firewall's DMZ port. As traffic arrives from the Internet, the firewall inspects each packet and allows traffic into the firewall only if it was requested by a client computer on the protected LAN.

Web server

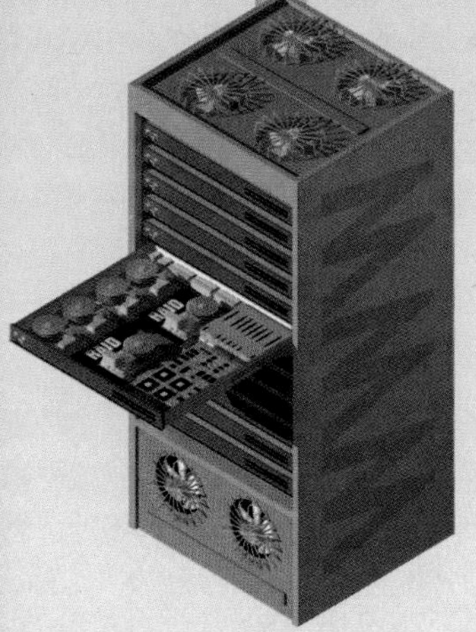

Web client

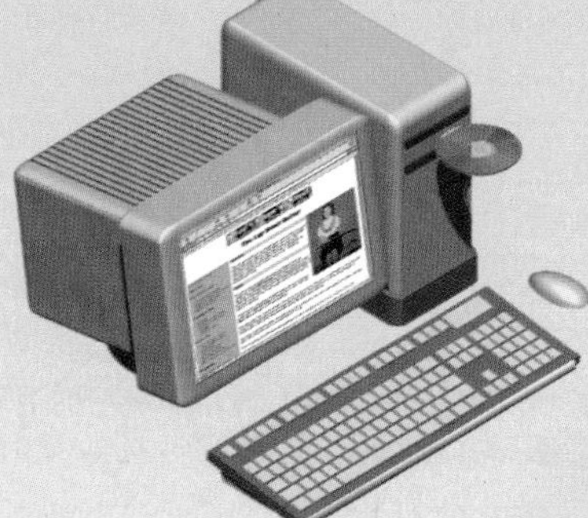

Hacker

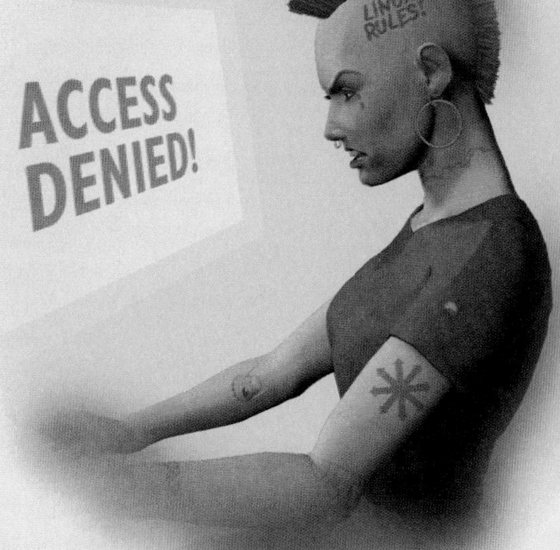
LINUX RULES!
ACCESS DENIED!

6 Uninvited traffic coming from the Internet is ignored. A hacker attempting to connect to a firewall-protected LAN can gain access to public servers only on the DMZ ports.

CHAPTER

21

How Metropolitan Area Networks Work

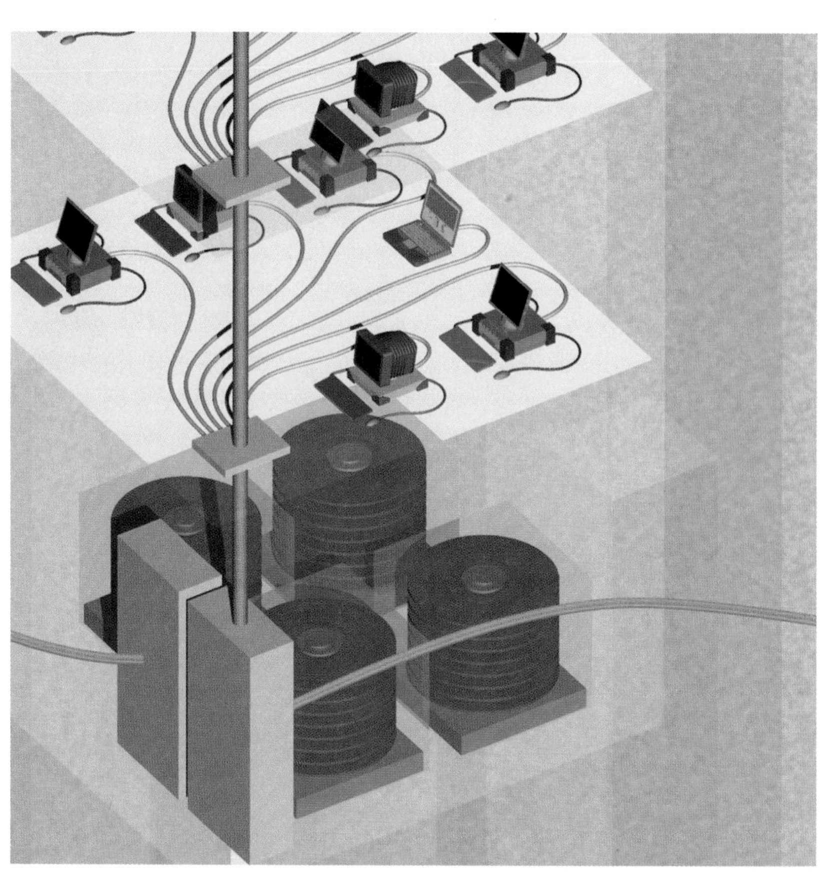

LANs, are, by definition, local—within 1,000 feet or so. But today, no business does business in just one place. A *Metropolitan Area Network (MAN)* is a service, provided by practically any kind of carrier that can link businesses within a city and provide gateways to national and international data traffic. A MAN might be a small or a large part of a complete private corporate network. The MAN can link different locations within one company or it can link companies doing business together into a business extranet.

MANs typically use fiber-optic cable and the carriers take advantage of any access they can get for their cables. In Chicago, they use old tunnels designed for coal carts and in some cities they link fiber-optic cables to massive power cables to use the existing power right-of-way. MAN systems often configure the fiber in dual rings using *the Fiber Distributed Data Interface (FDDI)* standard. The dual-ring configuration allows traffic to flow both ways, so if the fiber is broken in one place, the traffic can flow around the other way to maintain service. The 802.6 standard describes one type of metropolitan utility service.

You'll find a variety of carriers providing MAN services, such as the incumbent local exchange carrier (IXC), competitive local exchange carriers (CLECs), and cable television companies. The local exchange carriers are using digital subscriber line services for connections to the higher-speed MAN. Long distance carriers such as AT&T and WorldCom also typically offer metropolitan services.

Sometimes, it's impractical to get the right-of-way for a new fiber-optic cable installation to a building. In these cases, many carriers are offering various types of high-speed connectivity through what are called *fixed-point wireless* connections. Fixed-point wireless systems, also known as *digital microwave*, have been available for years, but we expect them to hit their stride in 2003–2004. There are a number of licensing problems to be solved in the United States, but the number of fixed-point wireless installations outside the United States will grow quickly. In some cases, the antennas for these systems are the size of a paperback book. In other cases, they require a small mast on the roof of a building. Typical wireless links can give connection speeds of up to 1.5 megabits per second (a *T1* service).

The most modern MAN services use IP packets over their facilities, so you can have direct connections to routers and switches. There are security issues with the widespread use of IP on always-on networks, so any IP MAN connection should be protected by a secure firewall.

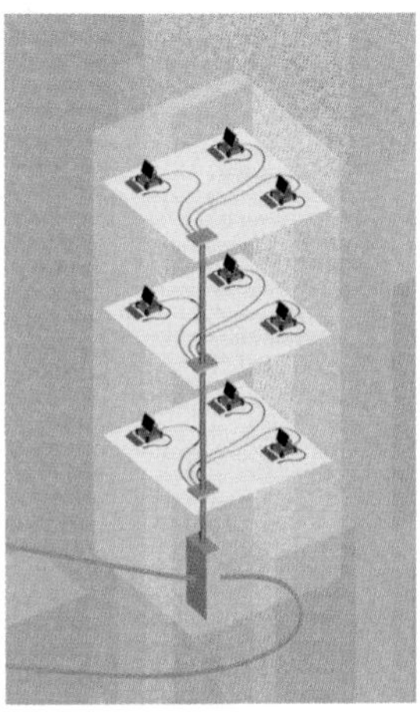

How Metropolitan Area Networks Work

1 Branch offices across the city have high-speed dedicated connections to the central office across a fiber-optic MAN. These connections allow applications to share centralized files and services such as security.

2 When branch offices or business partners aren't within the area served by a fiber-optic MAN, digital microwave systems can often do the job. Digital microwaves can provide fast connections without the need to have a physical right-of-way for cable access.

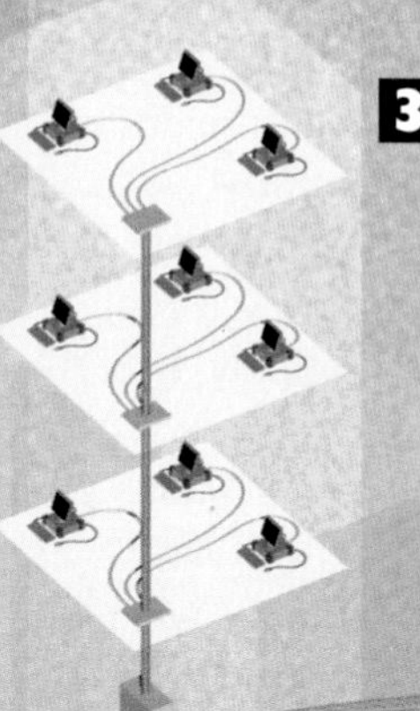

3 The network in the headquarters office provides a central point for data storage and backup, network management, and services such as security and Internet access. Centralized data storage is a major new application for MANs.

Fiber-optic loop

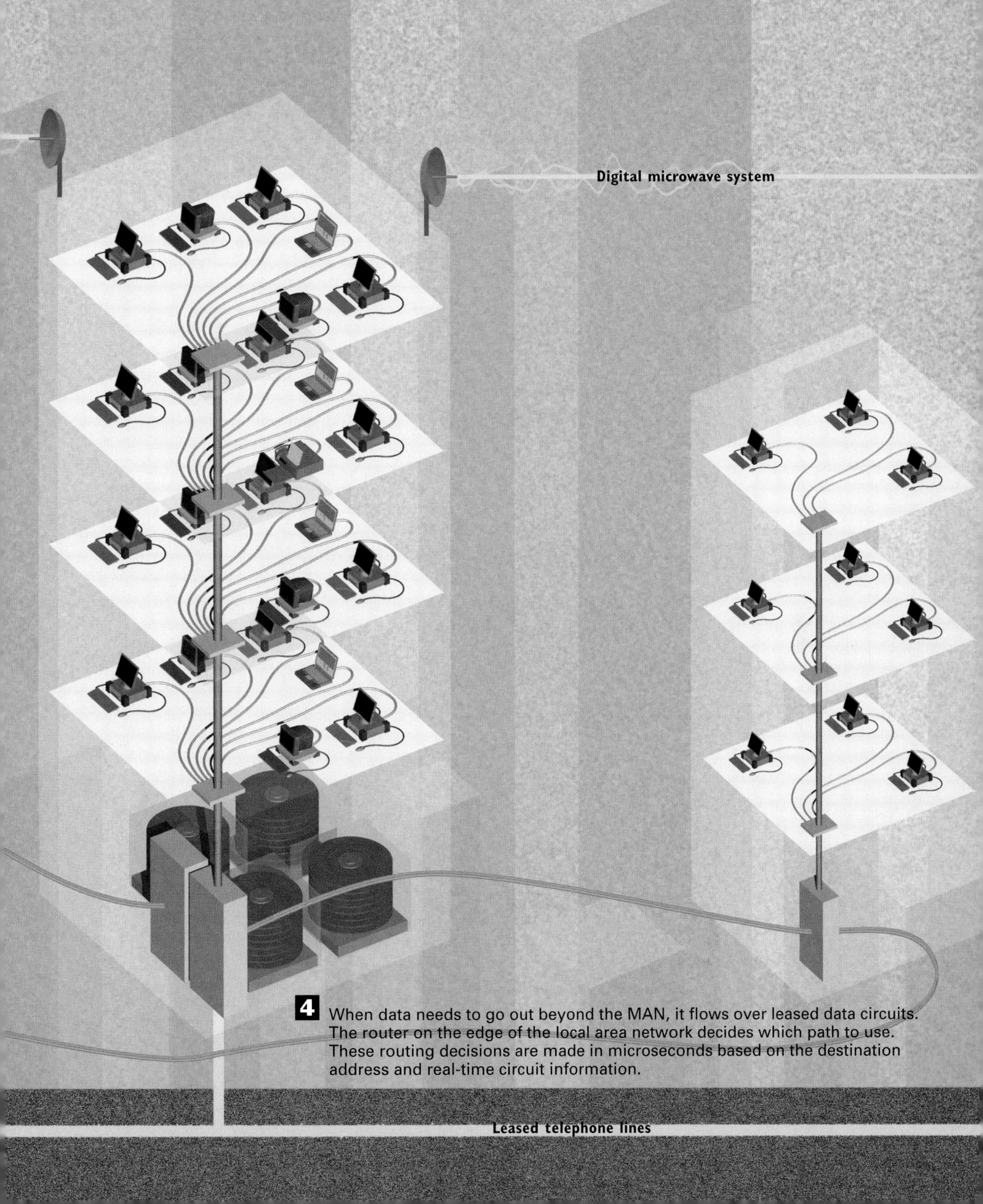

Digital microwave system

4 When data needs to go out beyond the MAN, it flows over leased data circuits. The router on the edge of the local area network decides which path to use. These routing decisions are made in microseconds based on the destination address and real-time circuit information.

Leased telephone lines

CHAPTER 22

How Circuit-Switched Digital Networks Work

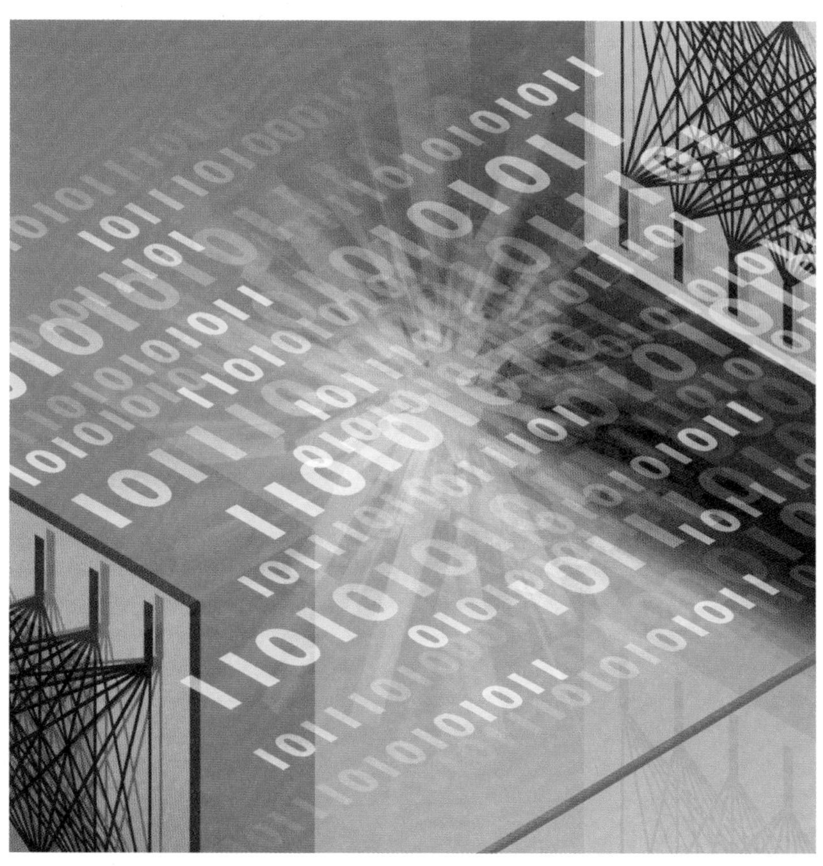

YOU can have several types of links in your private network. The network can combine dedicated full-time circuits called *leased lines*, *virtual circuits*, or *dial-up connections*. Full-period leased lines and virtual circuits have the benefit of being "always on." But, you pay for this always-on feature in monthly costs. Also, always-on connections make you always vulnerable to intrusion.

Instead of paying for LAN-to-LAN links on a full-time basis, you can dial up digital connections as you need them. Circuits that you dial up to make a connection are called *circuit-switched digital services*. Generally, a circuit-switched digital service is more economical than a leased-line service if you need connections for only three to eight hours a day or less. Circuit-switched digital services are perfect for linking electronic-mail servers on different LANs and for doing tasks such as updating inventory and order records from one network database to another at the end of each day. Additionally, when a dial-up connection is down, there is no way that an intruder can enter your network from outside.

The major portions of the public telephone systems are fully digital. They handle voice and data as a stream of 0s and 1s instead of analog tones. Only the last few miles of cable carry data in analog form. The only difference between the circuit-switched voice connection of phone calls and the circuit-switched data connections occurs in the cable between the telephone company's central office and the termination. Voice circuits use an older type of wiring system meant to eliminate distortion of the voice. Modems for voice circuits convert data to tones that traverse a few miles of cable until they become data again at the central office. When telephone companies install switched-digital services, new wiring systems carry the data in digital form all the way, and there is no need for modems.

Circuit-switched service vendors offer dial-up circuits capable of carrying maximum signaling rates of 56, 64, and 384 kilobits per second and 1.544 megabits per second. Switched-data circuits follow the same pricing scheme as switched-voice circuits. You pay for equipment and installation, a monthly service charge, and each call by the minute according to the distance. In some areas, switched-56 service costs no more than voice service.

The Integrated Services Digital Network (ISDN) is a circuit-switched digital service. ISDN marketing literature stresses combined voice and data applications, but companies such as Lucent and Cisco market practical ISDN routers for LAN-to-LAN services. These devices establish an ISDN circuit-switched digital connection between appropriate LANs when traffic appears, and then break down the connection when it is no longer needed.

The most popular ISDN service for linking LANs is basic rate interface, or BRI. This service delivers two data channels capable of carrying 64 kilobits per second each, *called bearer channels*, or *B channels*, and a separate 16-kilobit-per-second channel, called the *data channel*, or *D channel*. The D channel is used to signal the computers in the telephone switching system to generate calls, reset calls, and receive information about incoming calls, including the identity of the caller.

Circuit-switched digital services can provide handy and economical connections between LANs. They are a useful alternative to metropolitan and long-distance inter-LAN connections.

How Circuit-Switched Digital Networks Work

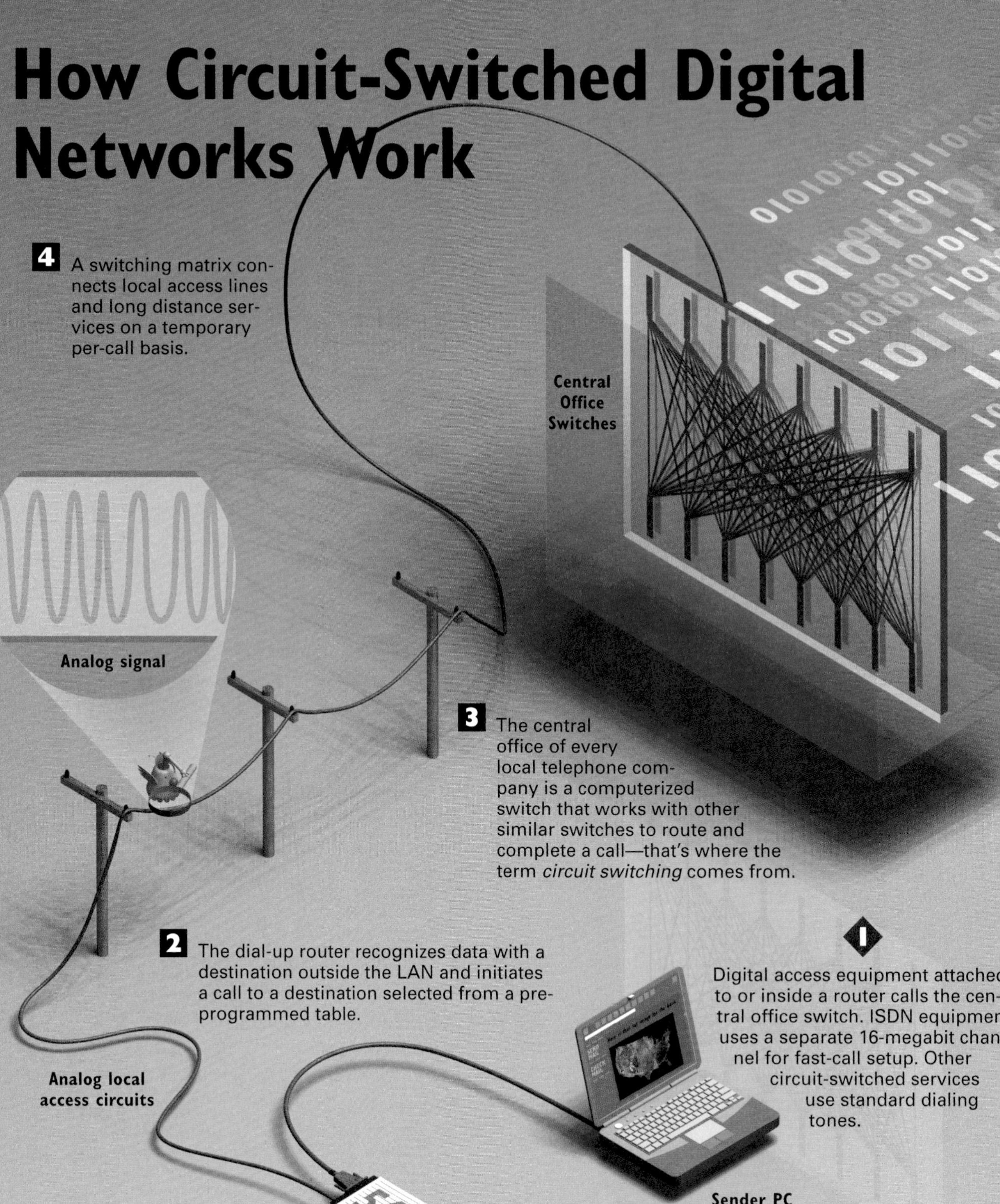

Central Office Switches
Analog signal
Analog local access circuits
Modem
56k
Sender PC

1 Digital access equipment attached to or inside a router calls the central office switch. ISDN equipment uses a separate 16-megabit channel for fast-call setup. Other circuit-switched services use standard dialing tones.

2 The dial-up router recognizes data with a destination outside the LAN and initiates a call to a destination selected from a preprogrammed table.

3 The central office of every local telephone company is a computerized switch that works with other similar switches to route and complete a call—that's where the term *circuit switching* comes from.

4 A switching matrix connects local access lines and long distance services on a temporary per-call basis.

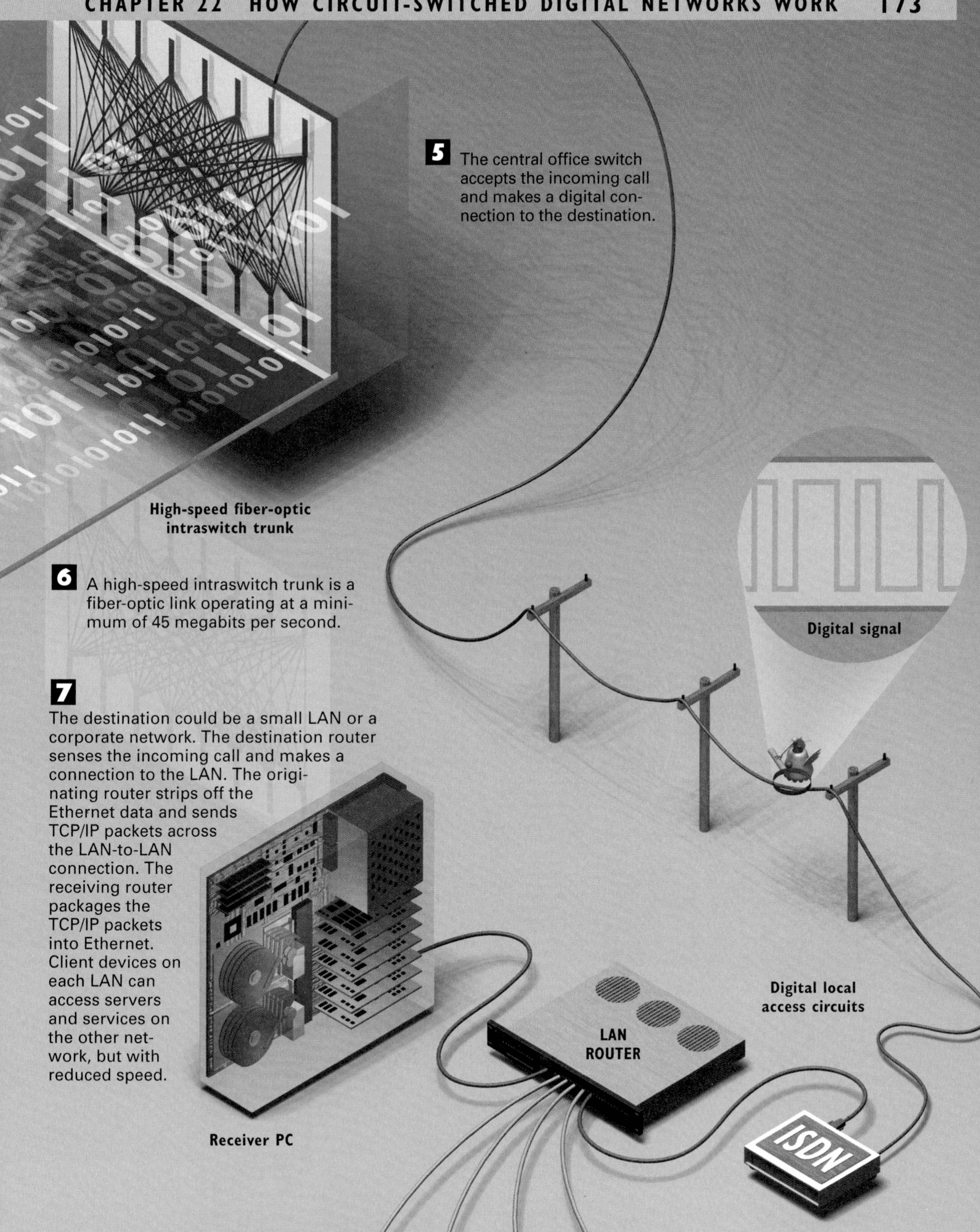
High-speed fiber-optic intraswitch trunk
Digital signal
LAN ROUTER
Digital local access circuits
ISDN
Receiver PC

5 The central office switch accepts the incoming call and makes a digital connection to the destination.

6 A high-speed intraswitch trunk is a fiber-optic link operating at a minimum of 45 megabits per second.

7 The destination could be a small LAN or a corporate network. The destination router senses the incoming call and makes a connection to the LAN. The originating router strips off the Ethernet data and sends TCP/IP packets across the LAN-to-LAN connection. The receiving router packages the TCP/IP packets into Ethernet. Client devices on each LAN can access servers and services on the other network, but with reduced speed.

How ISDN Works

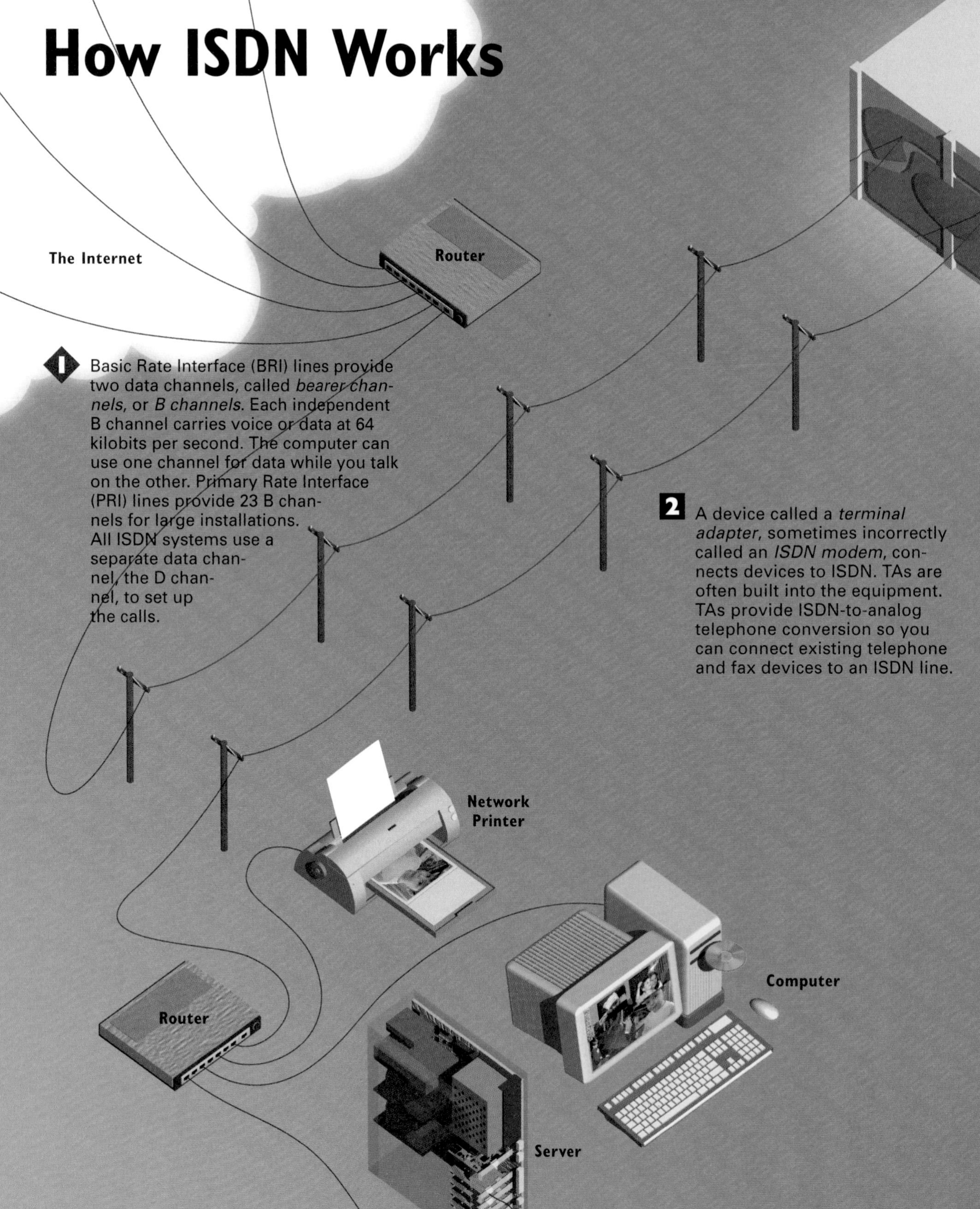
The Internet
Router
Network Printer
Computer
Router
Server

1 Basic Rate Interface (BRI) lines provide two data channels, called *bearer channels*, or *B channels*. Each independent B channel carries voice or data at 64 kilobits per second. The computer can use one channel for data while you talk on the other. Primary Rate Interface (PRI) lines provide 23 B channels for large installations. All ISDN systems use a separate data channel, the D channel, to set up the calls.

2 A device called a *terminal adapter*, sometimes incorrectly called an *ISDN modem*, connects devices to ISDN. TAs are often built into the equipment. TAs provide ISDN-to-analog telephone conversion so you can connect existing telephone and fax devices to an ISDN line.

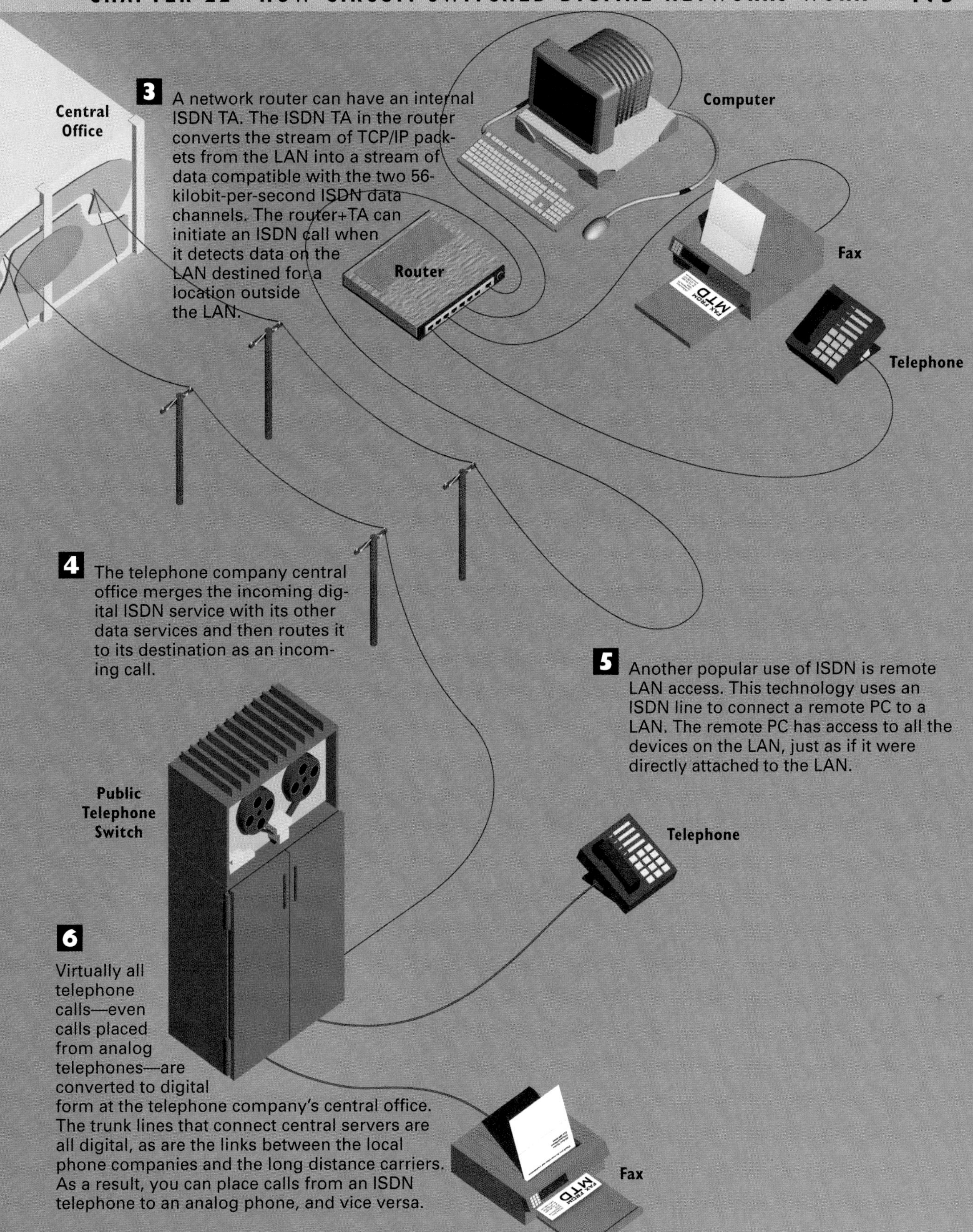
Central Office
Computer
Router
Fax
Telephone
Public Telephone Switch
Telephone
Fax

3 A network router can have an internal ISDN TA. The ISDN TA in the router converts the stream of TCP/IP packets from the LAN into a stream of data compatible with the two 56-kilobit-per-second ISDN data channels. The router+TA can initiate an ISDN call when it detects data on the LAN destined for a location outside the LAN.

4 The telephone company central office merges the incoming digital ISDN service with its other data services and then routes it to its destination as an incoming call.

5 Another popular use of ISDN is remote LAN access. This technology uses an ISDN line to connect a remote PC to a LAN. The remote PC has access to all the devices on the LAN, just as if it were directly attached to the LAN.

6 Virtually all telephone calls—even calls placed from analog telephones—are converted to digital form at the telephone company's central office. The trunk lines that connect central servers are all digital, as are the links between the local phone companies and the long distance carriers. As a result, you can place calls from an ISDN telephone to an analog phone, and vice versa.

CHAPTER

23

How Packet-Switched Networks Work

TODAY'S most popular alternative for a LAN-to-LAN connection is packet switching. Packet switching is a large category that includes services called *X.25*, *frame-relay*, and *cell-relay* technologies. Packet switching has been more popular in Europe and Asia than in North America because many North American organizations elected to stay with familiar leased-line services. However, aggressive pricing of frame relay has made it popular in North America.

The major appeal of packet-switching services comes from their flexible multipoint capabilities. LANs in many different locations can exchange data with one central location and with one another. The LAN portals can use different signaling rates and the packet-switched network buffers the data. Commercial packet-switching networks are also called *public-data networks (PDNs)*—or *value-added networks (VANs)*—because of the error control, buffering, and protocol conversion they can provide.

Although the other LAN-to-LAN alternatives typically involve flat monthly fees determined by distance and speed, packet-switching networks are, in a term of the trade, *usage sensitive*. That means you pay a basic monthly service charge and a fee based on the amount of data received by each of your ports on the network. Usage-sensitive billing can make packet-switching networks more attractive than full-period leased lines when your applications transfer data only a few times a day.

Full-period connections to the packet-switched network are available from your network portal device, and usually operate at rates of 56 kilobits through 1.544 megabits per second. The carrier you choose can make all the arrangements for the service and present the charges in one bill.

Until the mid-'90s, a protocol called *X.25* dominated packet-switched networks. This protocol uses a high-reliability belt-and-suspenders design to ensure the delivery and integrity of data shipped across the network. But networks using reliable digital circuits don't need all the accounting and checking provided by the X.25 protocol, so designers stripped off many X.25 functions, reduced the overhead, and developed a service called *frame relay*.

New developments in packet-switched systems focus on cell-switching technologies. Because the X.25 packet and the frame-relay frame are of variable length, the network must constantly adjust the flow and timing of messages. If the data bundles are all the same size, the network designers can tighten up the operation, gaining efficiency and reducing the complexity of the system. A technology generally called *cell relay* and an evolving cell-relay standard called *asynchronous transfer mode (ATM)* are designed for very heavy data loads. Operating at speeds of 1.544 megabits per second to 1.2 gigabits per second, ATM cells consist of 48 bytes of application information plus 5 bytes for the header. Network equipment can quickly route and move these uniformly sized bundles of data.

ATM is optimal for carrying digitized voice and video signals because the small cells offer little delay (a feature called *low latency*) as they transit the network. ATM is one of the core technologies of the global Internet.

Packet-switched systems offer reliability and flexibility for LAN-to-LAN connections. There is little up-front cost, and you can have service where you need it, when you need it, and for only as long as you need it.

How Packet-Switching Networks Work

1 Packet network interface devices, often embedded in routers, package the data from the LAN into packets appropriate to the specific kind of network. Each packet is labeled with the destination of the nearest packet switch that will move it in the direction of its destination.

2 Within the packet network "clouds," an interconnected series of switches continuously make decisions about the next destination of each packet. The goal is always to send the packet to the switch nearest its destination.

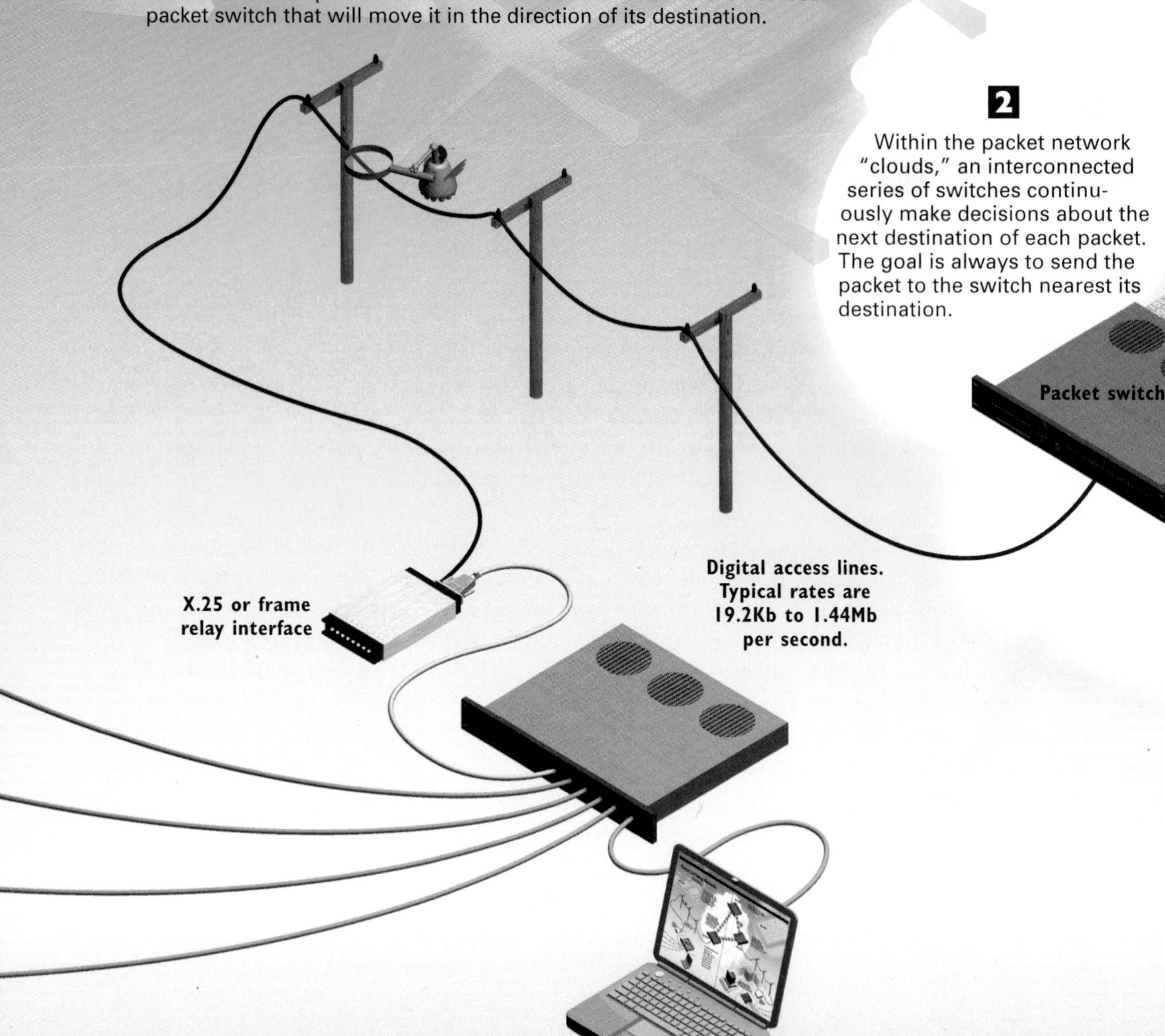
Packet switch
Digital access lines. Typical rates are 19.2Kb to 1.44Mb per second.
X.25 or frame relay interface

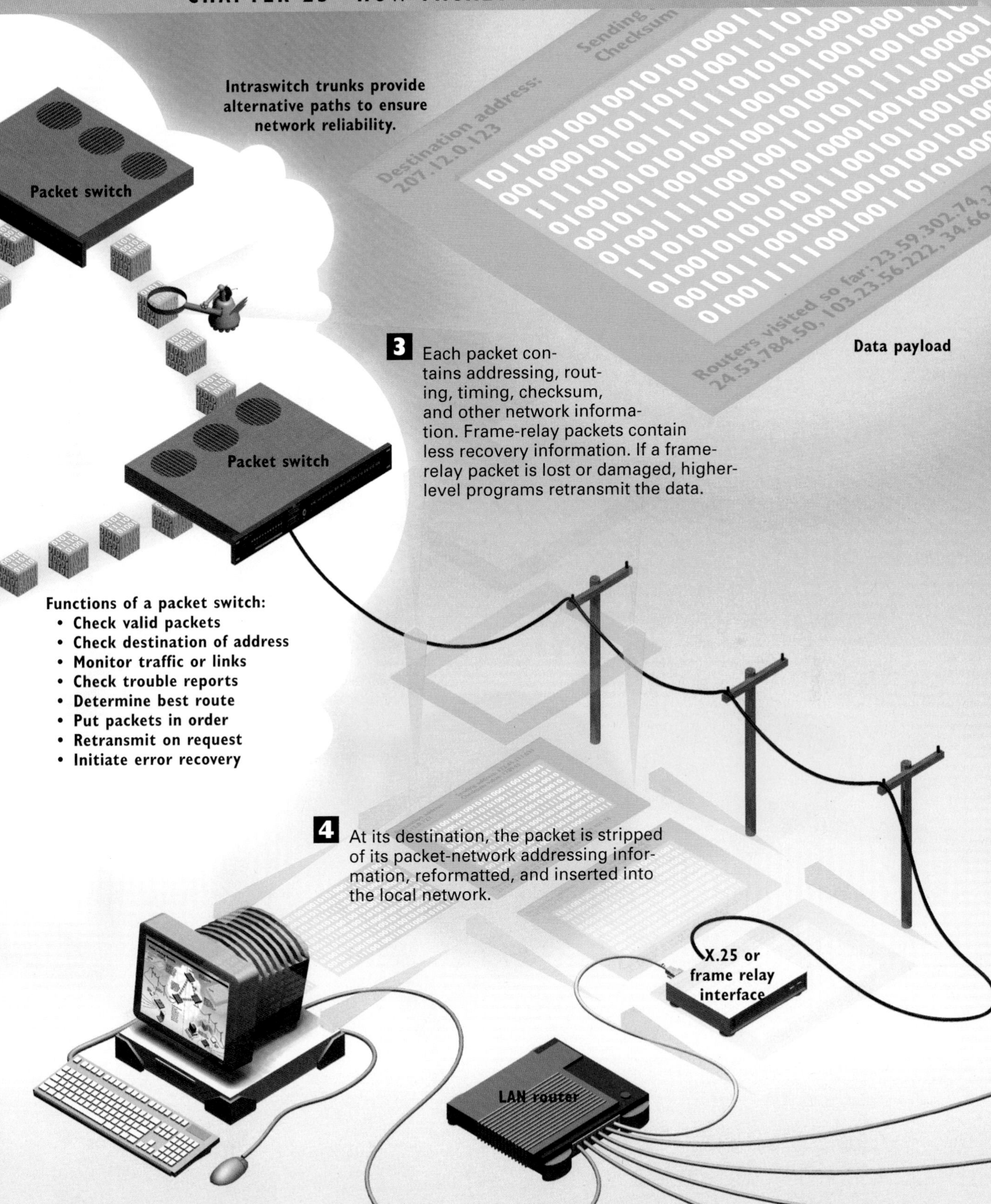
Intraswitch trunks provide alternative paths to ensure network reliability.
Packet switch
Packet switch
Destination address: 207.12.0.123
Sending
Checksum
Routers visited so far: 23.59.302.74, 23.5 24.53.784.50, 103.23.56.222, 34.66.75
Data payload
Functions of a packet switch:
• Check valid packets
• Check destination of address
• Monitor traffic or links
• Check trouble reports
• Determine best route
• Put packets in order
• Retransmit on request
• Initiate error recovery
X.25 or frame relay interface
LAN router

3 Each packet contains addressing, routing, timing, checksum, and other network information. Frame-relay packets contain less recovery information. If a frame-relay packet is lost or damaged, higher-level programs retransmit the data.

4 At its destination, the packet is stripped of its packet-network addressing information, reformatted, and inserted into the local network.

How an ATM Switch Works

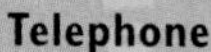
Telephone

Audio

Video and audio

Router
ATM-
equipped
computer

1 Digitized audio and video data enters into an ATM adapter through appropriate connections and is segmented into small cells following specific ATM application address-layer rules.

LAN frames

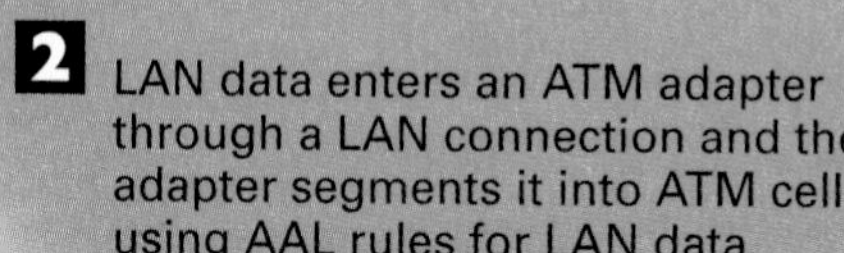

2 LAN data enters an ATM adapter through a LAN connection and the adapter segments it into ATM cells using AAL rules for LAN data.

ATM cells

3 The adapters inside ATM switches transfer the cells to and accept them from the switch's addressing functions.

How an ATM Switch Changes Packets into Cells

Service request—typically a maximum of 534 8-bit bytes
Error control
Length
Packet type
Service request

Data from an application is typically in a block of fewer than 1,000 bytes.

NetWare IPX packet—typically a maximum of 576 8-bit bytes

2 It is packaged with network information for handling by servers within a LAN. This might add another 600 bytes.

Error control
Length
Packet type
Destination network
Destination host
Destination socket
Source network
Source host
Source socket
Data field

Routing information—5 8-bit bytes
Each ATM call is always 53 8-bit bytes
Data payload—48 8-bit bytes
ATM segment and reassembly process
ATM cells
Bad cell
Bad cell
Bad cell

3 The ATM switch uses a complex formula to slice the network data into 8-bit cells. In concept, the loss of one or two cells will not destroy the intelligence of the data block.

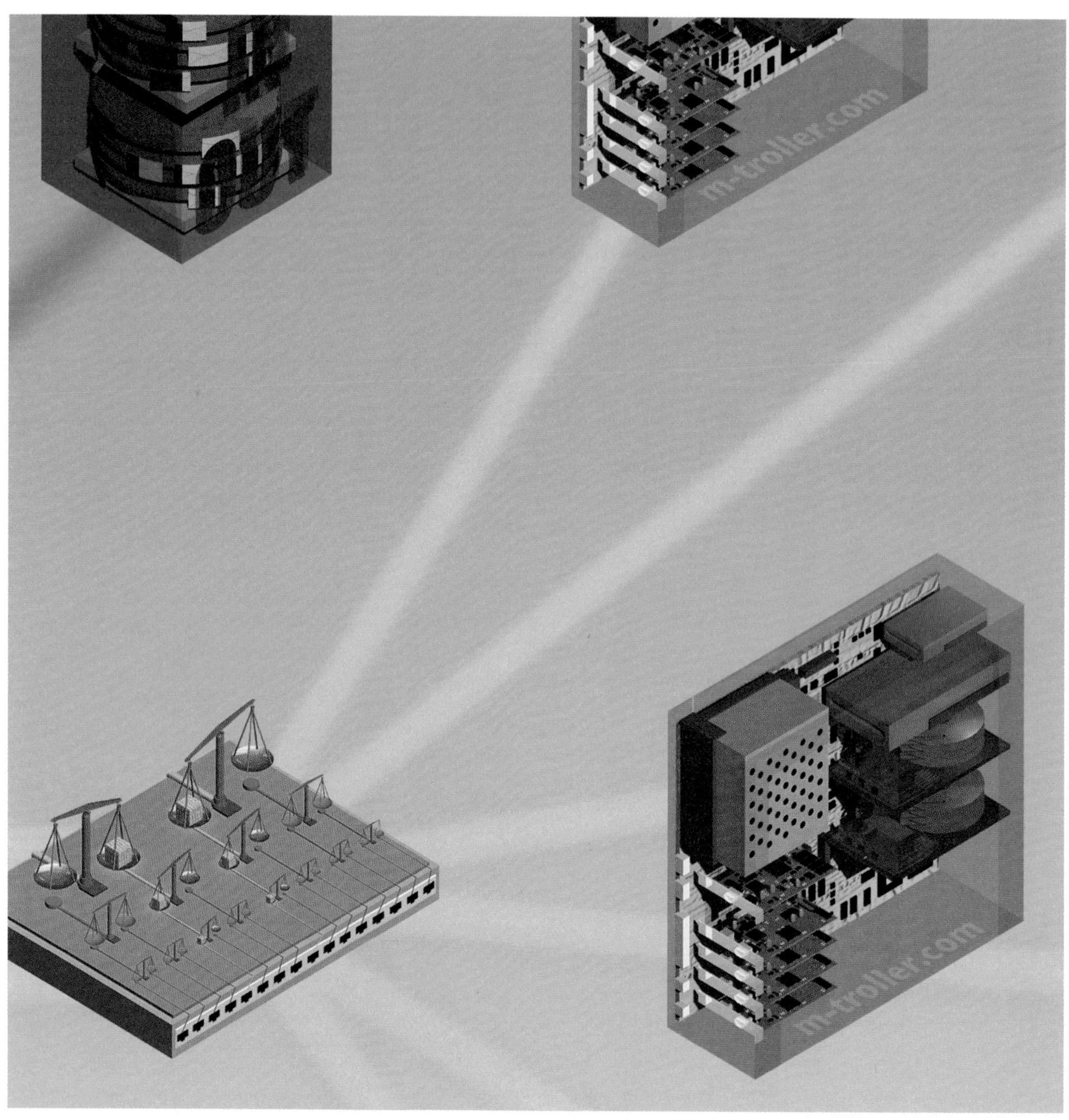
m-troller.com
m-troller.com

THE INTERNET

AS big as the Internet is, it is only the most visible manifestation of the worldwide adoption of a networking standard. And as free and as easy as it seems to be, the Internet came from an authoritarian background.

Today's Internet traces its roots directly to work sponsored by the U.S. Department of Defense (DoD). The DoD needed a communications architecture for its command and control systems that was self-healing, reliable, and universal. The requirement was for computers of different makes, models, and operating systems to communicate across a network with a wide range of delay, throughput, and packet loss. In the late 1960s, the Defense Advanced Research Projects Agency, working with industry and universities, started a network that was simultaneously a tool and a test. This network, the ARPAnet, was the development ground for the protocols and techniques used to communicate across today's Internet.

In the 1980s, the DoD's Defense Communications Agency acted as the guardian of the standards, but in the 1990s the roles of developer, engineer, and guardian for the emerging Internet passed to the Internet Society (ISOC), an independent organization. The ISOC has several subsidiary working groups, including the Internet Engineering Task Force (IETF) and the Internet Research Task Force (IRTF). If you follow the computer and communications news, you'll often hear about the ISOC and the IETF as they try to optimize the Internet for its role in modern business and culture.

The ISOC maintains a large library of documents online, and it would be impossible to write a book of this type without frequent reference to them. Fortunately, it's easy for you to read the same source materials. The ISOC uses Requests for Comments (RFCs) and Standards (STD) to describe concepts and standards. The RFCs often contain proposals from different commercial vendors, and a few are even intentionally humorous. The STDs contain the coordinated and accepted descriptions of how things should work—the protocols. Try pointing your browser at `http://www.isoc.org` for a full list of pages and links.

The RFCs and STDs go beyond basic connectivity and describe the network management, electronic mail, file transfer, and other functions used on the Internet and on other IP networks. The IAB has created and is expanding a complete computing environment based on layered and flexible protocols. In a computer communications system, software and firmware are designed to conform to specific protocols. There is an important point here that's worth stating another way: Software implements protocols, so protocols such as TCP/IP are not software. Programmers use protocols and standards to design software. Knowing the relationship between the protocols and the software can avoid confusion in many discussions.

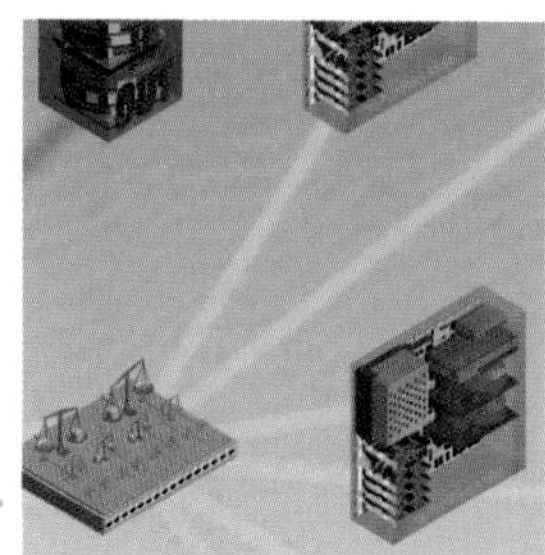

As you might expect, the software that implements a complex protocol such as TCP/IP is itself very complex. Protocol programmers typically design software in modular pieces, so that a change in one part of the software doesn't have an unwanted effect on some other part of the software. The functionality built into the software is designed in layers, based on the seven-layer OSI (Open Systems Interconnect) model.

The OSI model identifies and classifies seven distinct levels of functionality. The physical hardware connection—a twisted-pair cable, for example—is at the lowest layer of the model, and end-user application programs—Web browsers and email programs—are at the highest layer.

Data passes up and down through the layers, and each layer serves to provide a common interface to the layer above while performing tasks that are specific to some processor, operating system, or peripheral device. Driver software, residing on the bottom layer of an operating system such as Windows, passes data to and from devices such as LAN adapters, USB and serial ports, and communications adapters.

The lower layers of software follow the rules of the protocol by packaging the data coming from the application program into packets. You can think of each packet as a standardized envelope for data, complete with its own addressing and the equivalent of a postal code, street name, and house number. The packet envelope contains specific information such as the identification of the node originating the packet, the packet's size, and its destination address. Because your message is likely to be made up of many packets, and because they can easily get delivered out of order, they also are labeled as the first, second, third, and so on.

One of the main duties of the TCP protocol is to reorder the received packets in your computer before presenting them as a cohesive message to your application program. Both the format of the packet and its introductory information follow specific rules for that protocol.

Through the use of a common protocol, computers with completely different operating systems and processor hardware can exchange data that can be used by applications. That ubiquity is the magnetic appeal of the Internet and the World Wide Web. In the following pages, we show you how the complex elements of the Internet function to make it seem easy to gather information, exchange mail, and perform other complex functions.

CHAPTER

24 How Internet Connections Work

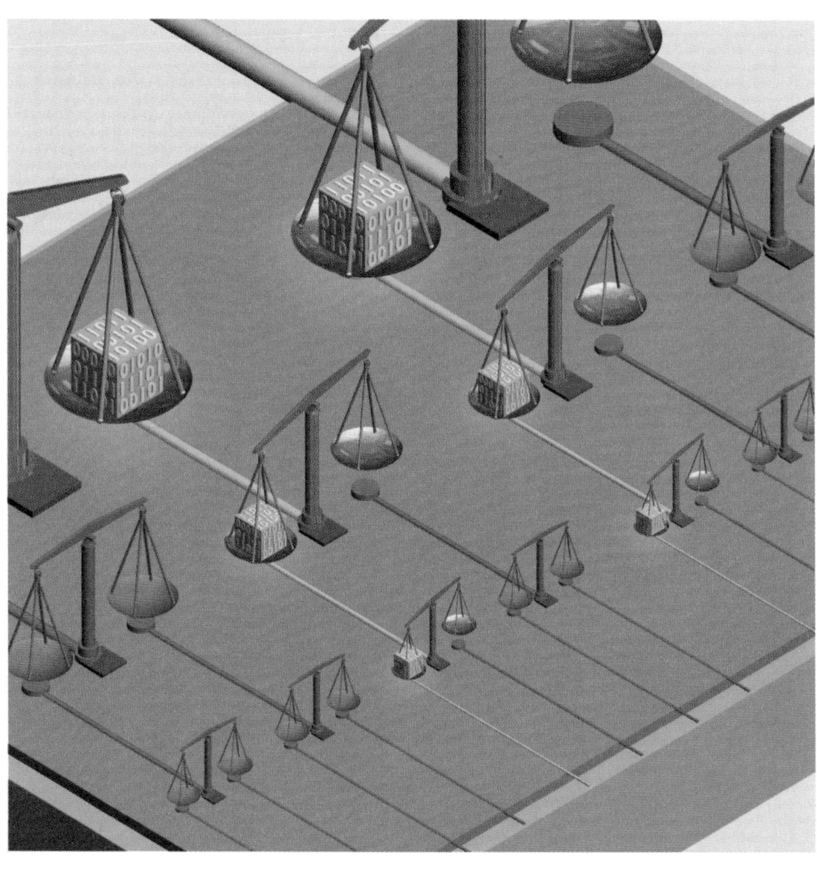

INTERNET is a compound word describing an immense number of agreements, arrangements, and connections. The Internet is literally a network of networks. In fact, it is typically a network of local area networks. A good analogy is between the Internet and a system of bridges linking millions of islands of various sizes. Each island has specific resources and capabilities, and each island has its own domain and a domain name to match. For shipping and delivery purposes, the domain names have affiliated addresses. Similarly, each Internet resource has a domain name and an IP address to match. In our island system, as in the Internet, many different companies built the bridges connecting the island domains, and some bridge systems are a little wider or sturdier than others, but together the entire system gives you a world to travel.

Some islands are private. You can establish an intranet for your organization that provides Internet-like services, but only for your employees or the members of your group. If you want to extend access to your close business partners, such as suppliers, retailers, or accountants, you can establish a limited-access extranet. An intranet or extranet might have only a small bridge to the Internet.

The services of the Internet make it appear as different things to different people. You might think of the World Wide Web portion of the Internet as a place to do research or order products. You're also probably familiar with the electronic-mail services of the Internet or your intranet. Dozens of other services work over the Internet to provide activities such as keyboard-to-keyboard chatting, real-time voice conversation, and the transfer, storage, and retrieval of files.

Technically, the Internet is an interconnected network based on the TCP/IP family of protocols. TCP (Transmission Control Protocol) and IP (Internet Protocol) are two protocols, or sets of rules, that govern how computers communicate with one another. A cluster of other affiliated protocols has grown around TCP/IP, and the entire family is regulated and maintained by the Internet Engineering Task Force (IETF).

Together, they determine how computers connect to one another and how they reliably exchange information. An important part of the IP protocol is the IP address. The IP addressing standard—four numbers between 1 and 256 separated by periods—defines a mechanism to provide a unique address for each computer on the Internet.

Additional protocols define activities that two connected computers can perform. For example, the Post Office Protocol (POP) controls electronic mail, and the Hypertext Transfer Protocol (HTTP) is the basis for the World Wide Web. Dozens of others exist, but all Internet protocols work over the TCP/IP protocols.

Today, anyone can subscribe to an Internet service provider, or ISP. An ISP typically leases a high-speed connection to the Internet backbone network and provides lower-speed access to many users. The ISP also provides a variety of value-added services such as email and Web pages with local content. You connect to the ISP using a modem, ISDN, or other service such as a cable modem, and the ISP routes your TCP/IP packets to and from the Internet.

The following pages visually describe the various elements of the large interconnected system called the *Internet*. We start with the Internet backbone and ISP connections and then show you how the most important protocols work.

How Traffic Moves over the Internet

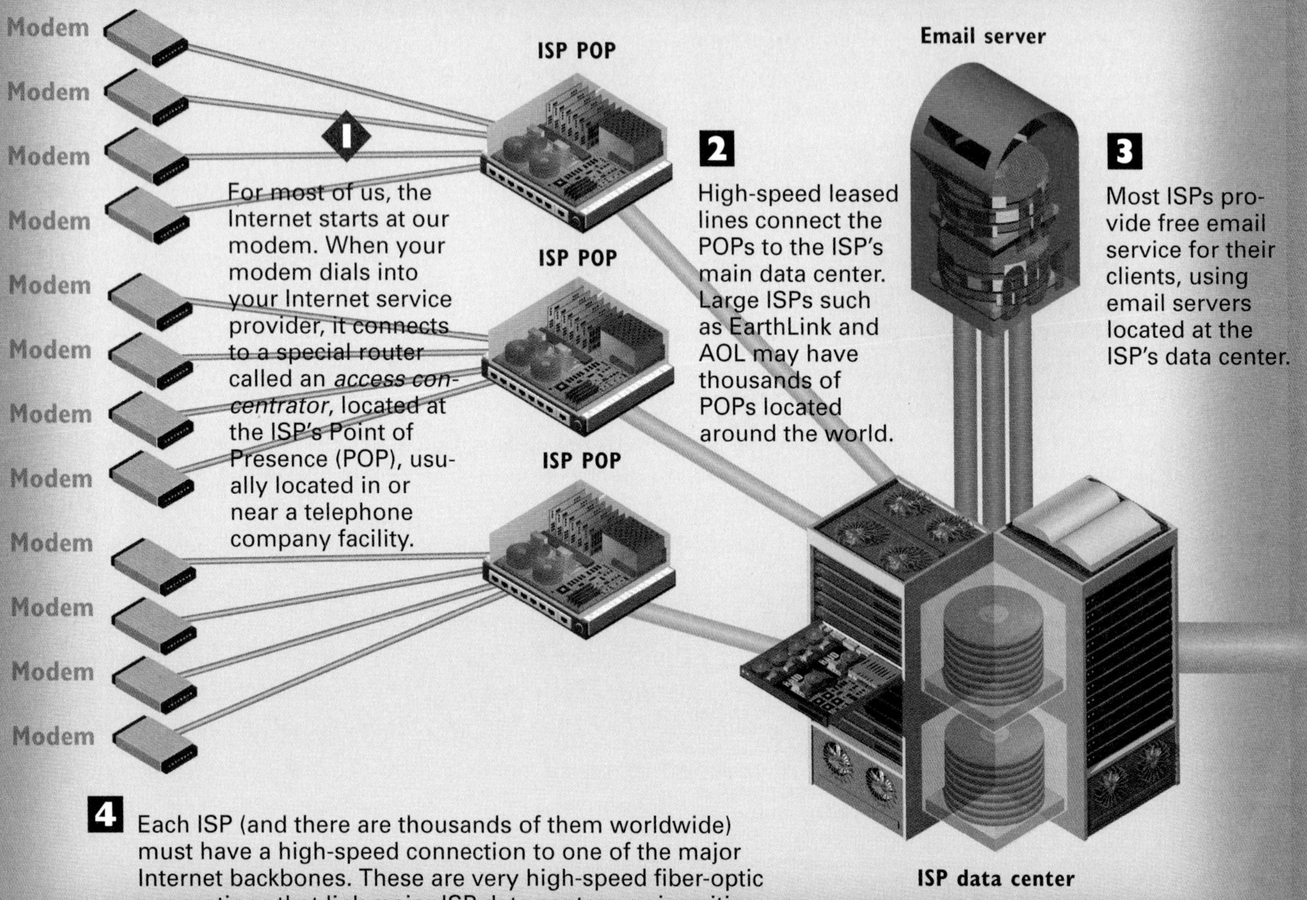

Modem

Modem

Modem

Modem

Modem

Modem

Modem

Modem

Modem

Modem

Modem

Modem

ISP POP

ISP POP

ISP POP

Email server

ISP data center

1 For most of us, the Internet starts at our modem. When your modem dials into your Internet service provider, it connects to a special router called an *access concentrator*, located at the ISP's Point of Presence (POP), usually located in or near a telephone company facility.

2 High-speed leased lines connect the POPs to the ISP's main data center. Large ISPs such as EarthLink and AOL may have thousands of POPs located around the world.

3 Most ISPs provide free email service for their clients, using email servers located at the ISP's data center.

4 Each ISP (and there are thousands of them worldwide) must have a high-speed connection to one of the major Internet backbones. These are very high-speed fiber-optic connections that link major ISP data centers, universities, and government agencies. All the major backbones are interconnected, so that if one fails, the others automatically pick up the traffic.

Server farm
Internet backbone
Router

8 The Internet wouldn't be very interesting without content, and most of that content comes from Web servers. ISPs often provide free hosting services for their users, and many business host their own Web sites. But organizations with heavy Web server traffic often outsource their Web services to a dedicated Web-hosting provider. These providers use heavy-duty server PCs connected to very high-speed data connections to provide a very high level of service and reliability.

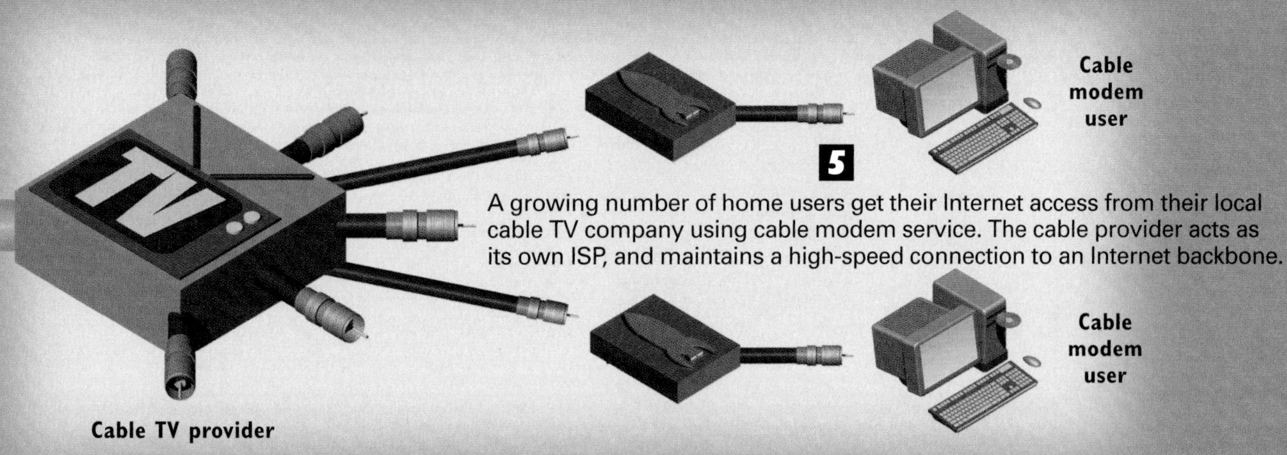
TV
Cable modem user
Cable modem user
Cable TV provider

5 A growing number of home users get their Internet access from their local cable TV company using cable modem service. The cable provider acts as its own ISP, and maintains a high-speed connection to an Internet backbone.

6 Many private businesses are connected to the Internet, often using business-class services from an ISP. These users are typically connected using a medium-speed data circuit leased from the local phone company.

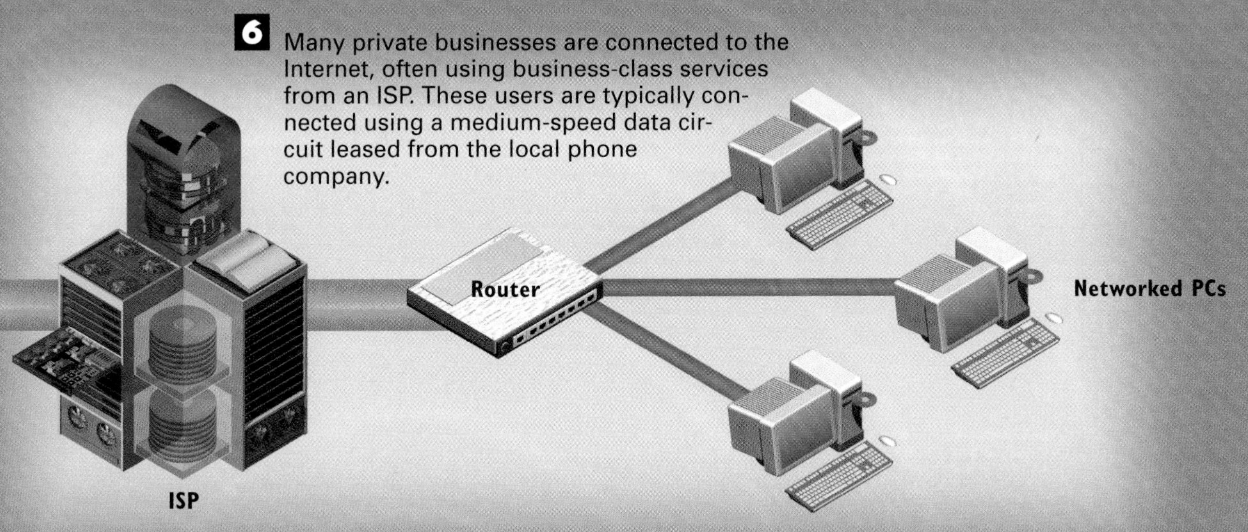
Router
Networked PCs
ISP

7 Some of us just can't live a plugged-in life anymore. Several wireless ISPs provide wireless Internet access using wireless PDA devices such as the Palm VII.

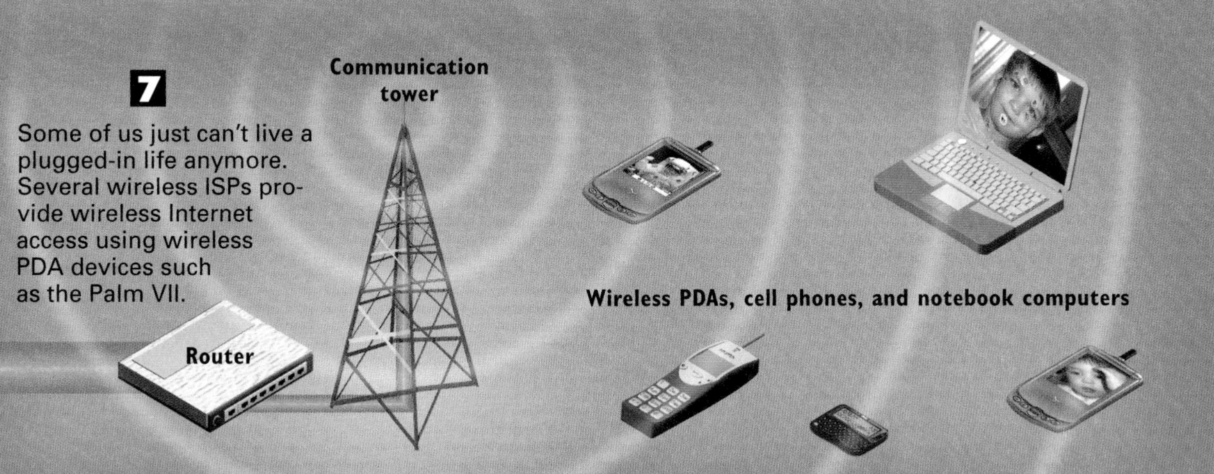
Communication tower
Router
Wireless PDAs, cell phones, and notebook computers

How Web Servers Work

Web
client

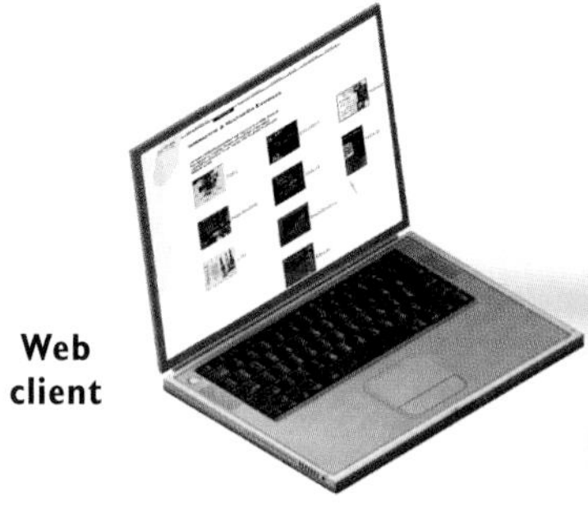
Web
client

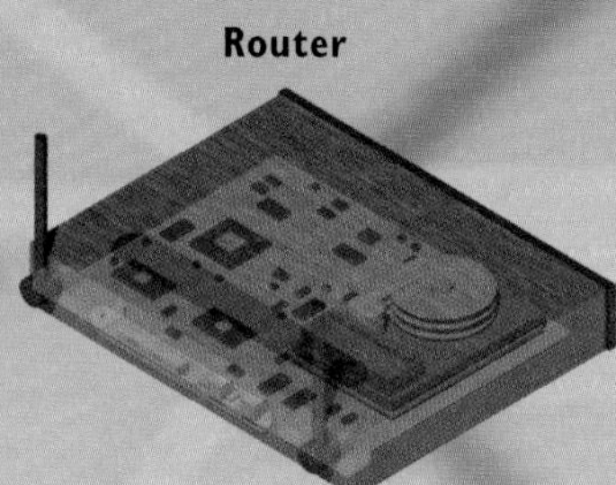
Router

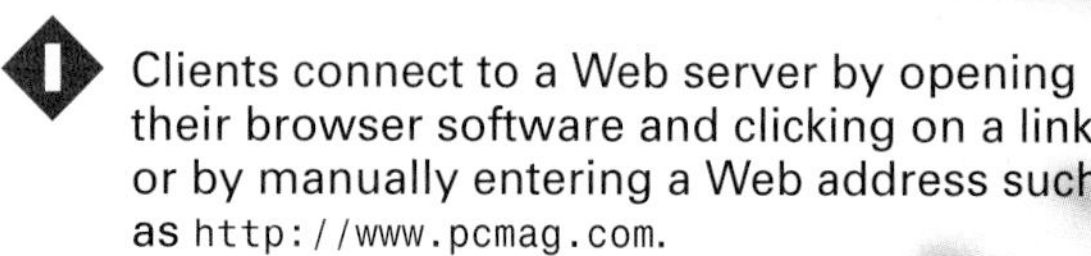

1. Clients connect to a Web server by opening their browser software and clicking on a link or by manually entering a Web address such as `http://www.pcmag.com`.

2. Commercial Web servers are typically connected to the Internet with a high-speed communications link connected to a router.

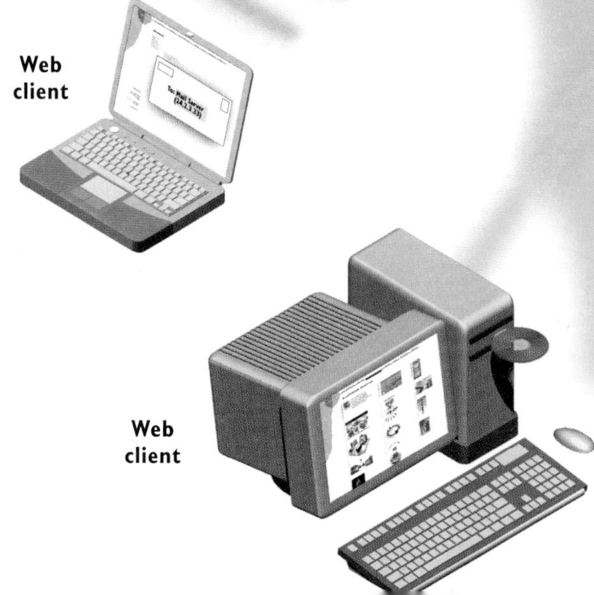
Web
client
Web
client

Mail
server

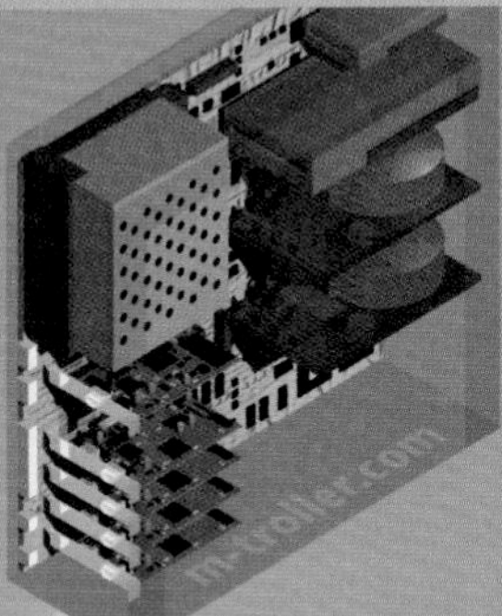

5 Web server software accepts requests from clients and delivers the appropriate content. Most Web pages are delivered using the Hypertext Markup Language (HTML), which allows page designers to freely mix text and graphics on the page. As clients request pages, the server retrieves the appropriate pages and sends them back to the requesting client. The browser software on the client computer formats the pages and displays them on the screen.

4 High-performance servers can deliver more traffic than a single Ethernet connection can handle. These servers often use multiple Ethernet connections to increase their data throughput.

Network Interface Cards

Load
balancer

3 High-traffic Web sites (such as yahoo.com and Amazon.com) use a load balancer to distribute traffic to a group of servers called a *server farm*. The load balancer makes sure that no single server becomes overloaded by allocating jobs according to server response time.

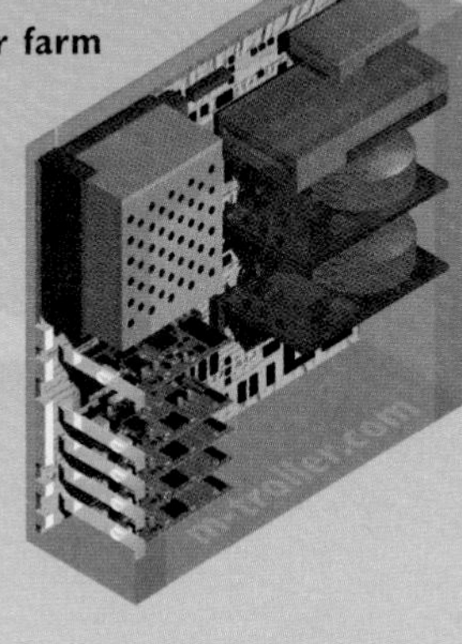
Server farm

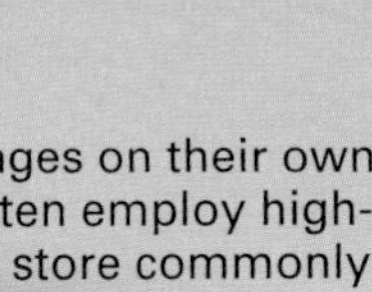
Web server

6 Many servers store Web pages on their own hard drive. Server farms often employ high-performance file servers to store commonly used pages.

High-speed disk storage

7 Private and pay Web sites often employ a separate authentication server to verify users' identities.

Authentication
server

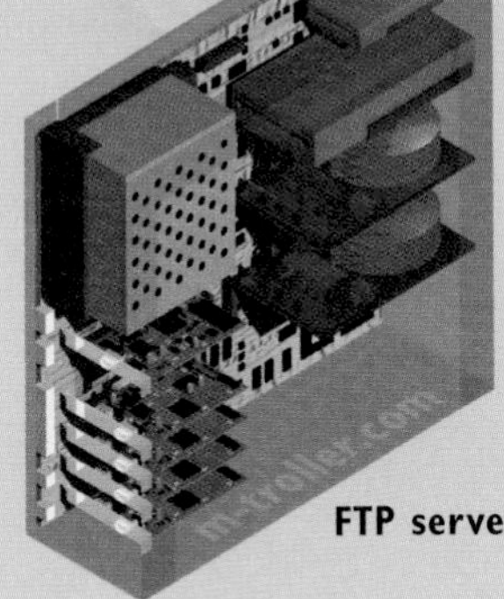
FTP server

How Email Works

2 The SMTP server accepts the message and temporarily stores it on the server's hard drive. At this point, the sending computer can disconnect from the server.

myISP.com
Originating mail server

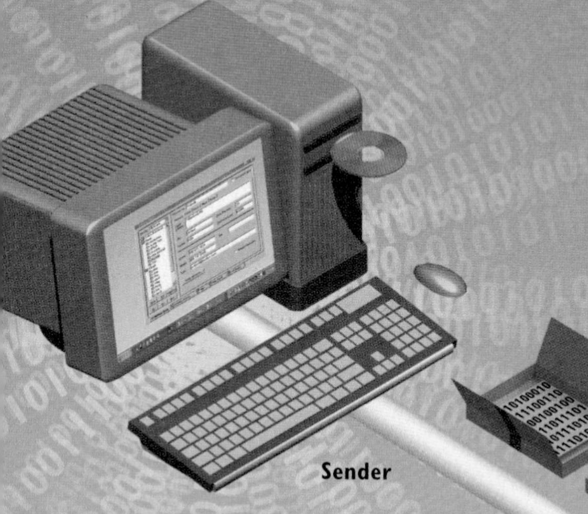
Sender

1 There are many different types of email-client software in use on the Internet, but most email systems use the Simple Mail Transfer Protocol (SMTP) protocol to send mail, and the Post Office Protocol (POP3) to receive mail. When a user composes a message and clicks Send, the computer contacts the user's mail server (typically located at an ISP) and delivers the message using the SMTP protocol. In addition to the message itself, the sending computer tells the server the email address of the message recipient.

SMTP protocol

SMTP protocol

The Internet

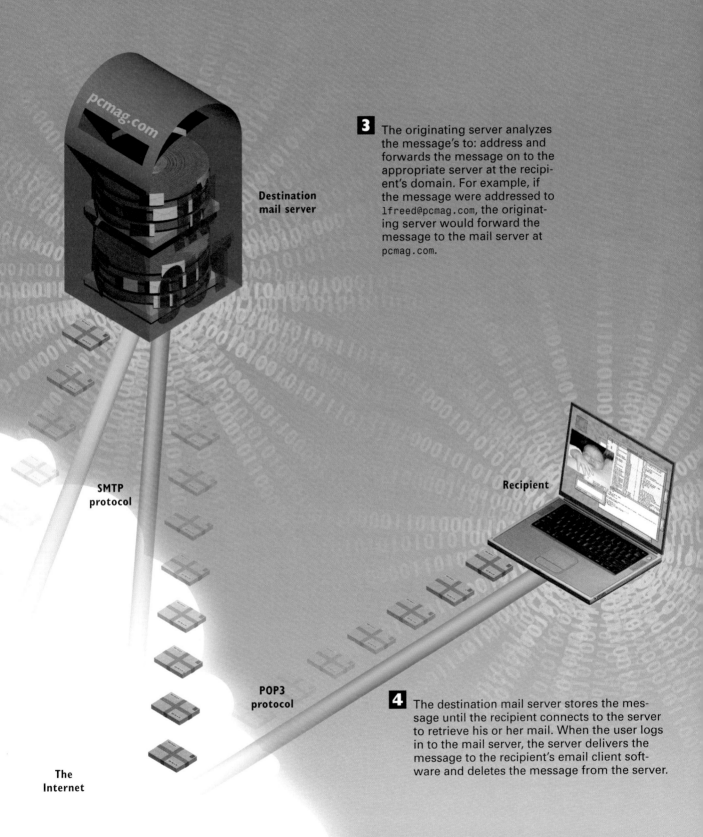

pcmag.com

Destination mail server

3 The originating server analyzes the message's to: address and forwards the message on to the appropriate server at the recipient's domain. For example, if the message were addressed to `lfreed@pcmag.com`, the originating server would forward the message to the mail server at `pcmag.com`.

SMTP protocol

Recipient

POP3 protocol

4 The destination mail server stores the message until the recipient connects to the server to retrieve his or her mail. When the user logs in to the mail server, the server delivers the message to the recipient's email client software and deletes the message from the server.

The Internet

How Home Networks Work

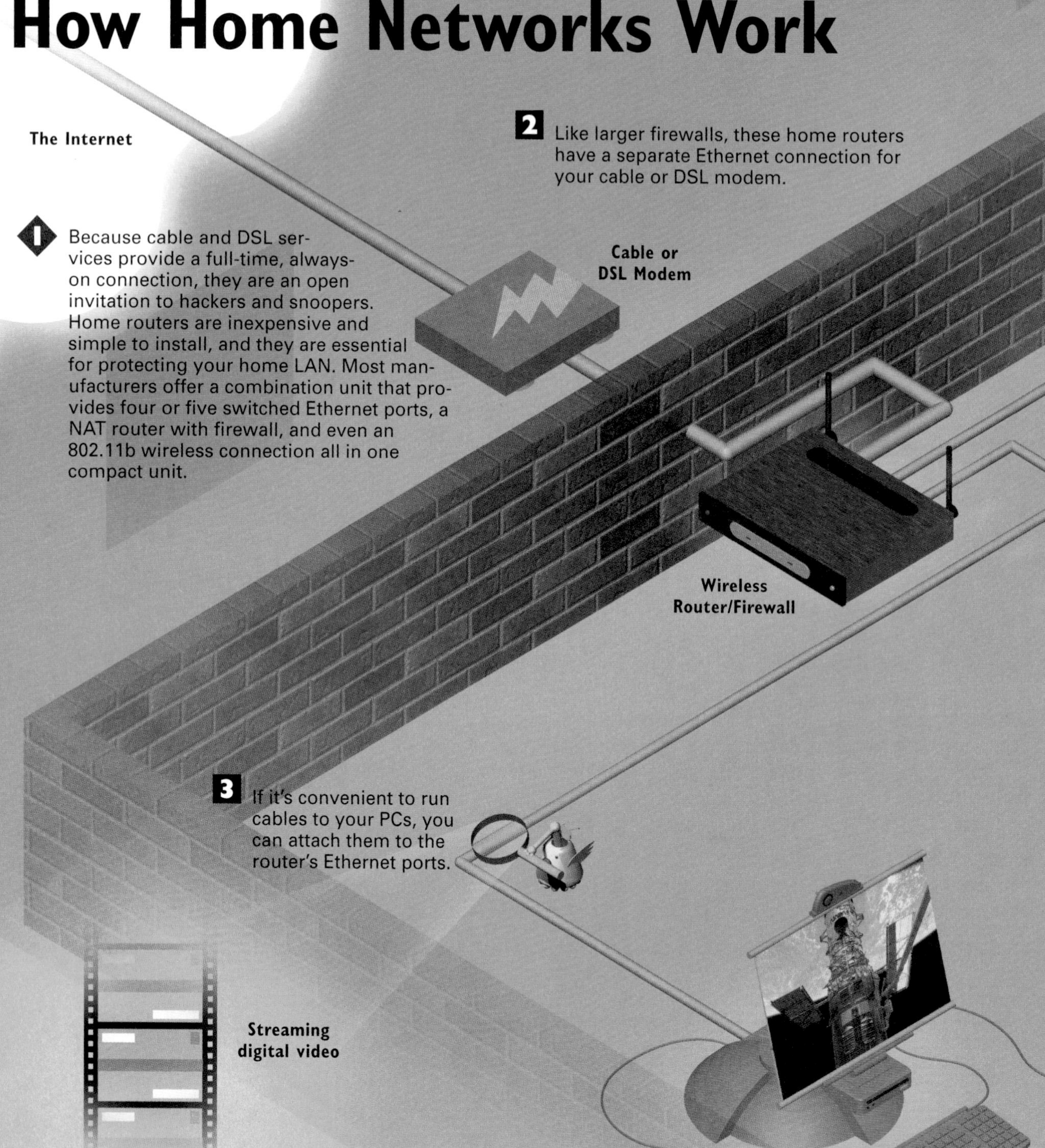
The Internet
Cable or
DSL Modem
Wireless
Router/Firewall
Streaming
digital video
Desktop
Computer

1. Because cable and DSL services provide a full-time, always-on connection, they are an open invitation to hackers and snoopers. Home routers are inexpensive and simple to install, and they are essential for protecting your home LAN. Most manufacturers offer a combination unit that provides four or five switched Ethernet ports, a NAT router with firewall, and even an 802.11b wireless connection all in one compact unit.

2. Like larger firewalls, these home routers have a separate Ethernet connection for your cable or DSL modem.

3. If it's convenient to run cables to your PCs, you can attach them to the router's Ethernet ports.

4 Some home routers offer special content filtering and time-of-day access limiting tools that let parents control their kids' Internet access.

WWW
WWW
Incoming Web pages

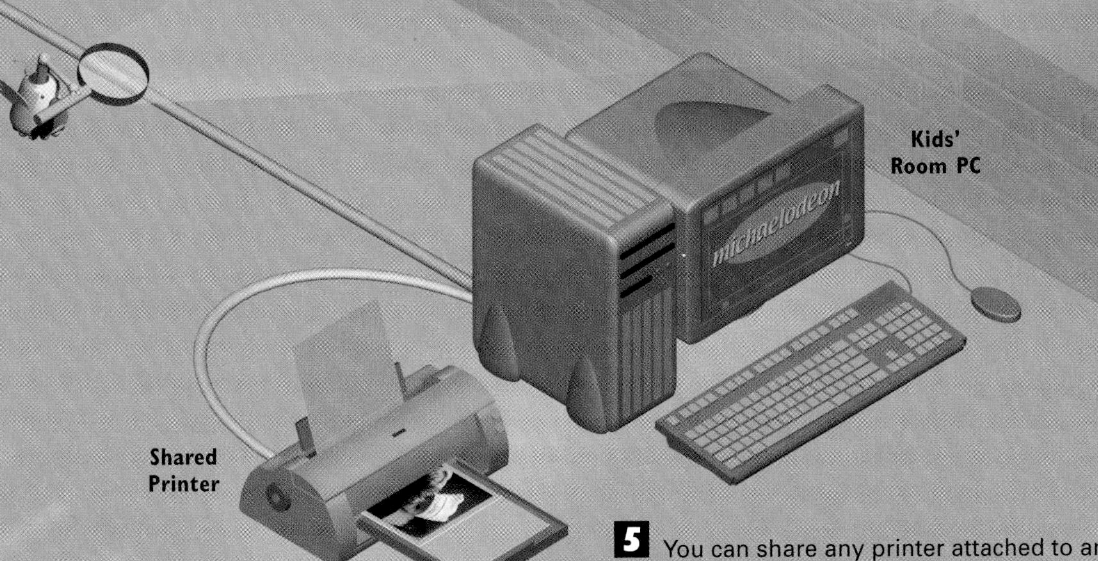
Kids' Room PC
michaelodeon
Shared Printer

5 You can share any printer attached to any PC on the LAN—as long as the PC is powered on.

6 WiFi Wireless access lets you surf the Net and read your email from anywhere in the house.

Laptop with WiFi card

CHAPTER 25 How Network Security Works

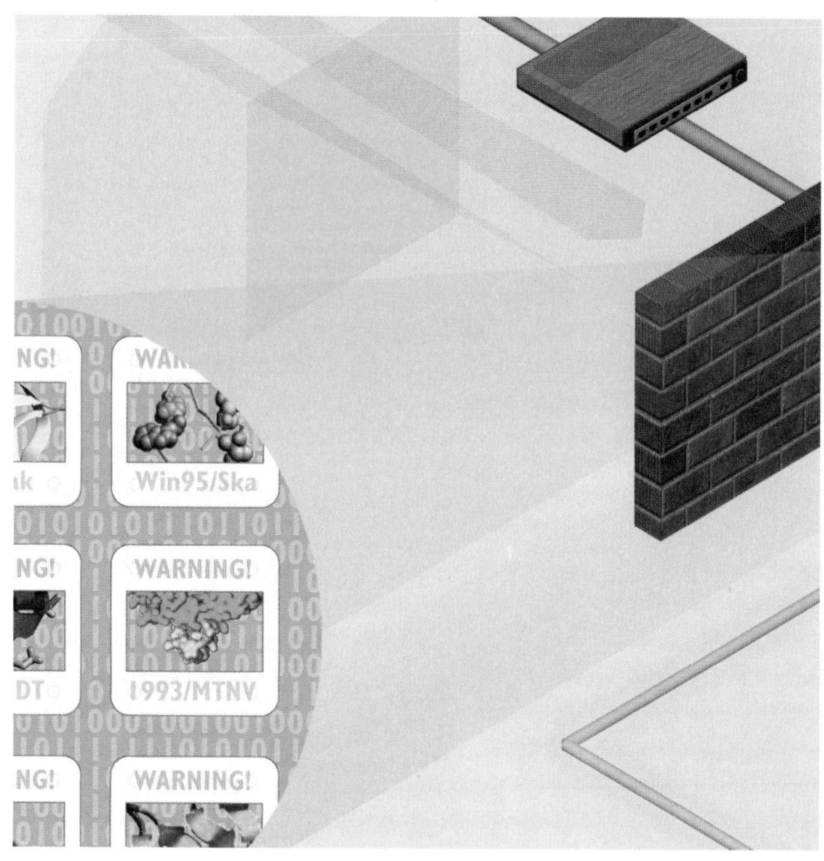
NG!
WARNING!
Win95/Ska
NG!
WARNING!
DT
1993/MTNV
NG!
WARNING!

MODERN security practices use layers of physical, administrative, electronic, and encrypted systems to protect valuable resources. Just as you can have too much insurance, you can have too much security. You should judge the threat and invest in secure systems designed to meet the threat.

You can roughly categorize the security threats as external and internal. The biggest internal threats are from a disgruntled employee or a snoop. External threats are particularly important if your company has a high public profile, but all companies and individuals with full-time external connections are vulnerable to intrusion or denial-of-service attacks.

All network security is based on administrative practices. The most powerful intrusion protection or encryption systems are meaningless if people don't protect passwords or keycards. Most security systems fail because of poor administrative security. Determined intruders will search your trash and try tricks or coercion to get the information they need to crack network security systems.

Physical security remains an important factor, but modern networks pierce the physical walls. Some hackers try to enter computer systems for profit or as a form of corporate or international espionage. Others break into computer systems purely for the challenge.

In wide area networks, particularly those with Internet connections, specialized routers called *firewalls* carefully inspect each incoming packet looking for authorized source addresses and rejecting any unknown addresses or even suspicious packets.

Encryption is the final layer of protection. Encryption systems obscure even the volume of information being transmitted and stored. Some operating systems and electronic mail systems encrypt files during storage, and all commercial-quality network operating systems offer encryption of passwords. Several companies offer encryption modules for routers and even network adapter cards so that all the data passing between networked devices is totally private.

The threat to data exists even in small companies. The larger the monetary stakes, the higher the threat. Good administrative security practices are a must for every organization. You can and should scale electronic protection schemes to match the value of the information and the threat.

How to Make Network Security Work

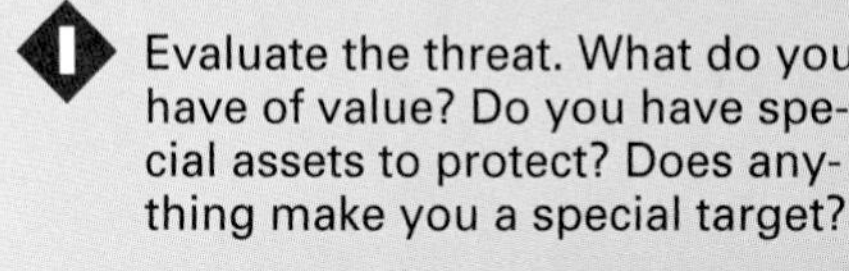

1. Evaluate the threat. What do you have of value? Do you have special assets to protect? Does anything make you a special target?

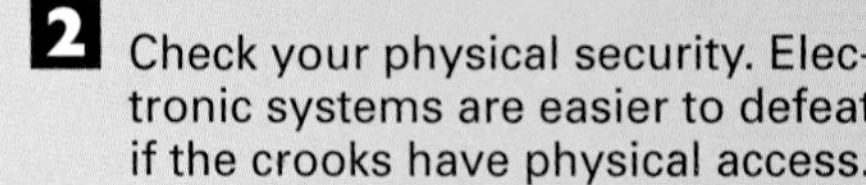

2. Check your physical security. Electronic systems are easier to defeat if the crooks have physical access.

ADMINISTRATIVE SECURITY
√ Passwords changed frequently
√ Protect passwords
√ Use authentication devices

3. Check your administrative security. Do you force frequent password changes? Do people properly protect passwords and authentication devices?

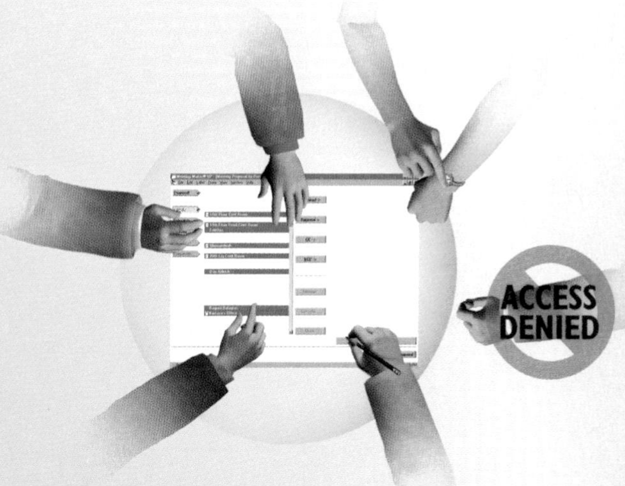
ACCESS
DENIED

4 Start to design your electronic protection with the threat, physical security, and administrative factors in mind. Start with strong authentication because other measures lose their value if you don't know who the people on the network really are!

5 Select firewall services appropriate for the volume of traffic and the threat.

begin 644 !WedMail.doc

6 Select encryption, intrusion detection, and specialized management services to meet your needs. Other related services include antivirus and URL filtering.

How Strong Authentication Works

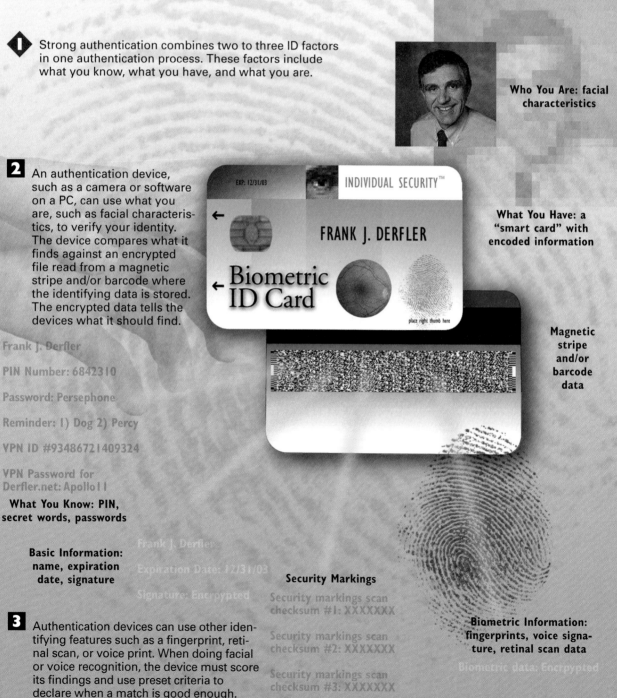

1. Strong authentication combines two to three ID factors in one authentication process. These factors include what you know, what you have, and what you are.

Who You Are: facial characteristics

2. An authentication device, such as a camera or software on a PC, can use what you are, such as facial characteristics, to verify your identity. The device compares what it finds against an encrypted file read from a magnetic stripe and/or barcode where the identifying data is stored. The encrypted data tells the devices what it should find.

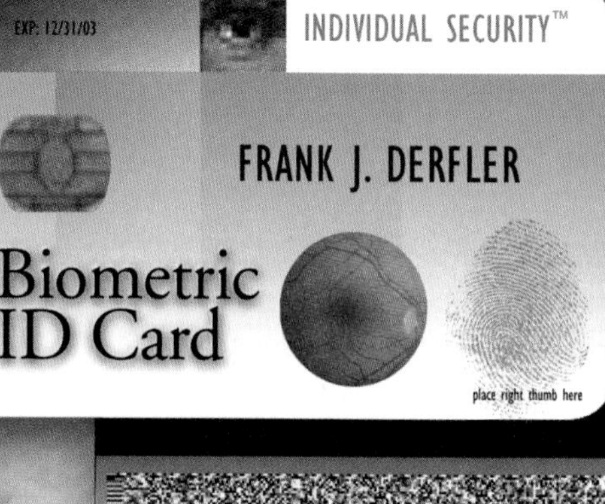
EXP: 12/31/03
INDIVIDUAL SECURITY™
FRANK J. DERFLER
Biometric ID Card
place right thumb here

What You Have: a "smart card" with encoded information

Magnetic stripe and/or barcode data

Frank J. Derfler
PIN Number: 6842310
Password: Persephone
Reminder: 1) Dog 2) Percy
VPN ID #93486721409324
VPN Password for Derfler.net: Apollo11

What You Know: PIN, secret words, passwords

Basic Information: name, expiration date, signature

Frank J. Derfler
Expiration Date: 12/31/03
Signature: Encrpypted

Security Markings

Security markings scan checksum #1: XXXXXXX
Security markings scan checksum #2: XXXXXXX
Security markings scan checksum #3: XXXXXXX

Biometric Information: fingerprints, voice signature, retinal scan data

Biometric data: Encrpypted

3. Authentication devices can use other identifying features such as a fingerprint, retinal scan, or voice print. When doing facial or voice recognition, the device must score its findings and use preset criteria to declare when a match is good enough.

How Encryption for Strong Security Works

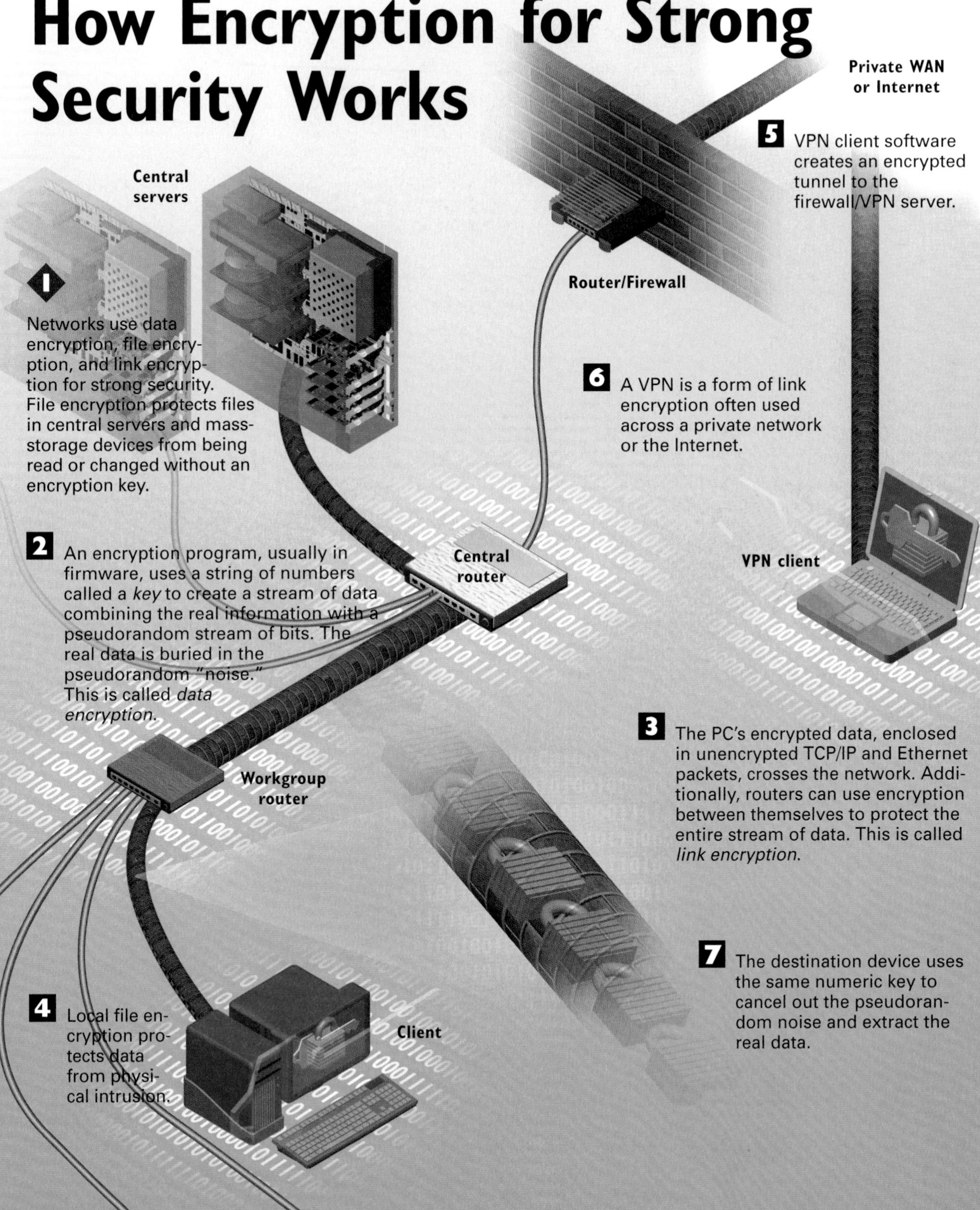
Private WAN
or Internet
Central
servers
Router/Firewall
Central
router
VPN client
Workgroup
router
Client

1 Networks use data encryption, file encryption, and link encryption for strong security. File encryption protects files in central servers and mass-storage devices from being read or changed without an encryption key.

2 An encryption program, usually in firmware, uses a string of numbers called a *key* to create a stream of data combining the real information with a pseudorandom stream of bits. The real data is buried in the pseudorandom "noise." This is called *data encryption*.

3 The PC's encrypted data, enclosed in unencrypted TCP/IP and Ethernet packets, crosses the network. Additionally, routers can use encryption between themselves to protect the entire stream of data. This is called *link encryption*.

4 Local file encryption protects data from physical intrusion.

5 VPN client software creates an encrypted tunnel to the firewall/VPN server.

6 A VPN is a form of link encryption often used across a private network or the Internet.

7 The destination device uses the same numeric key to cancel out the pseudorandom noise and extract the real data.

How Home Network Security Works

1 Internet service providers filter incoming data to remove some email virus and denial-of-service attacks.

2 A cable modem or DSL modem (either internal or external) provides the connection to the fast link. It filters data for inbound address, but this isn't much protection.

Data to and from the Internet

DSL or cable router

Updated virus profiles

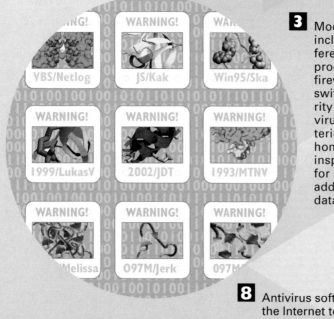

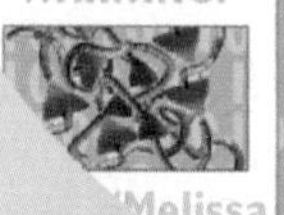

WARNING!
VBS/Netlog
WARNING!
JS/Kak
Win95/Ska
WARNING!
1999/LukasV
WARNING!
2002/JDT
WARNING!
1993/MTNV
WARNING!
Melissa
WARNING!
097M/Jerk
WARNING!

3 Modern gateways include several different functional products such as a firewall, router, and switch. Other security functions such as virus filtering and URL filtering might be part of the home gateway. They inspect and filter data for inappropriate addresses and data patterns.

Gateway router

8 Antivirus software contacts a central library through the Internet to update its virus-pattern files.

4 The firewall function inspects incoming data and blocks requests for inappropriate access or actions.

5 The router guides data to specifically addressed LAN devices while the switch makes the wired connection.

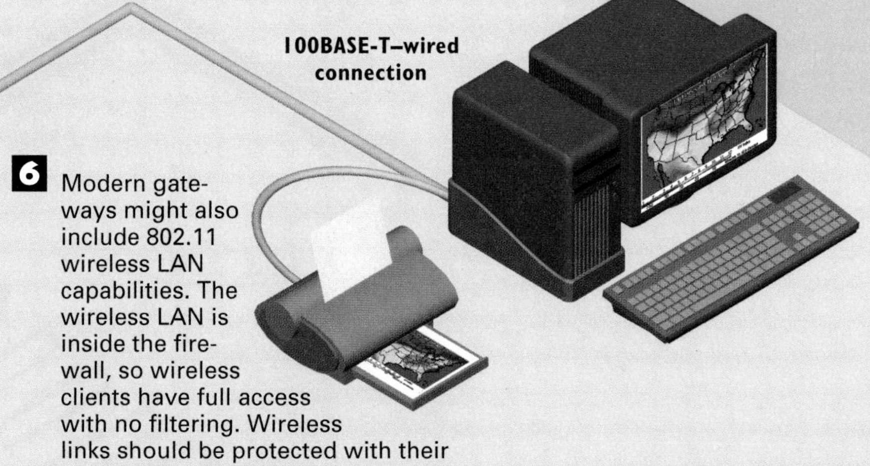
100BASE-T–wired connection

6 Modern gateways might also include 802.11 wireless LAN capabilities. The wireless LAN is inside the firewall, so wireless clients have full access with no filtering. Wireless links should be protected with their own passwords and encryption.

7 Antivirus software in each PC examines files, mail, and incoming data for specific patterns of data matching its library of known viruses and worms.

WiFi connection

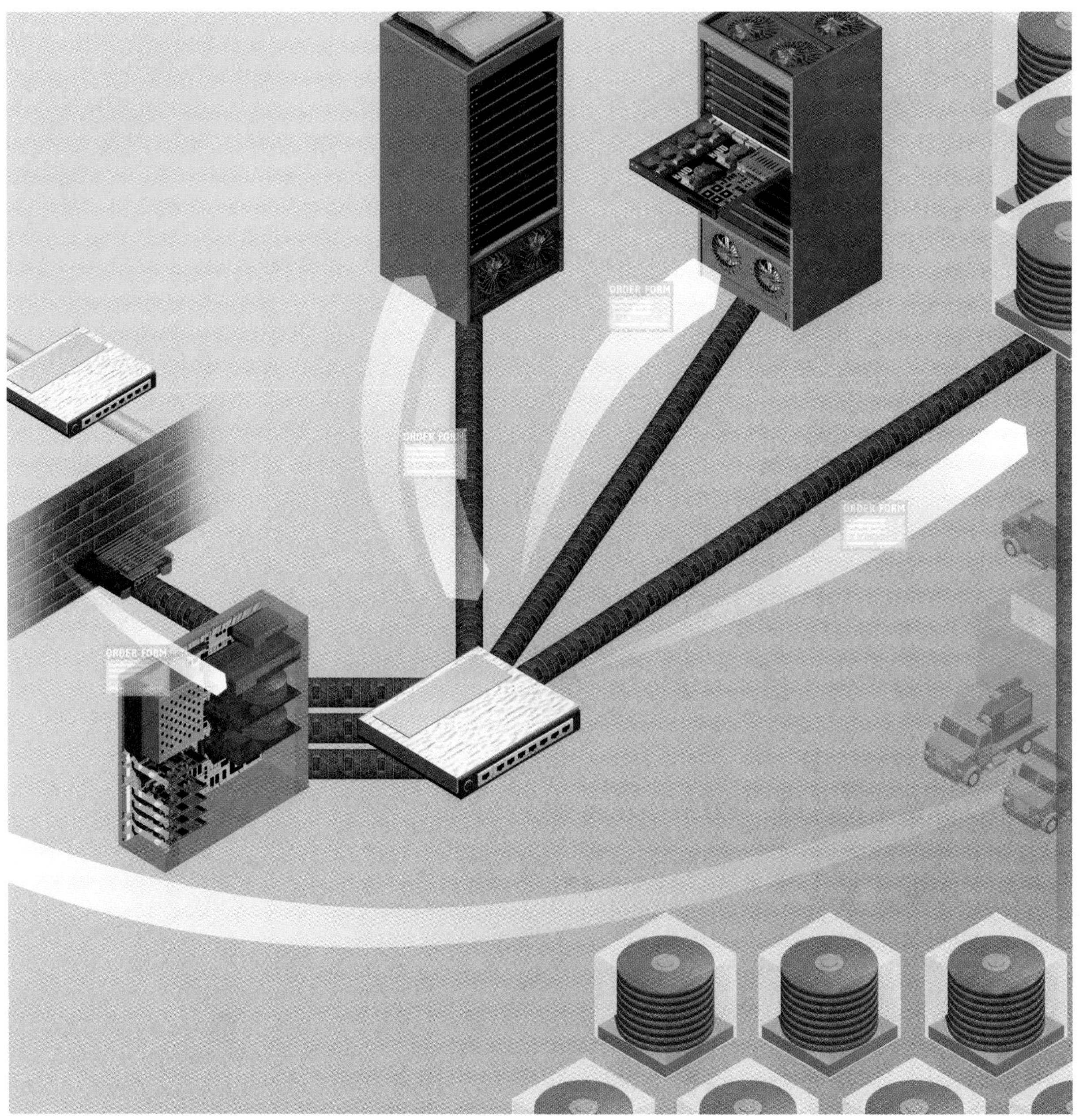
ORDER FORM
ORDER FORM
ORDER FORM
ORDER FORM

Networks for Online Business

EVEN the smallest businesses benefit from ordering and selling online. Online business activity can drive network design and justify network investment. Generally, the value of online business is in crushing costs and increasing revenue. Adding more dollars to the bottom line is the bottom line of online business and business-to-business (B2B) computing.

Whether you're dealing with marketing, customer contacts, purchasing, or any other part of your business, there is a way to squeeze out overhead costs using Internet and networking technology.

Online business includes concepts such as wholesale purchasing and retail customer relationship management (CRM) systems linked to internal enterprise resource management (ERM) applications. ERM systems include accounting, human resources, and manufacturing control. B2B is supposedly about the wholesale side of business, but the definitions are a matter of perspective. One company's finished goods are another company's raw materials. In online business, definitions fall to innovative management. Stand still for a moment in modern business and you're erased. If you get confused, remember that, from a business perspective, online business is always about cutting costs and increasing revenue.

Businesses of all kinds take material in, apply processes, and send it out for sale. The term *supply chain management* describes ways to improve the input side. Supply chain management systems establish communications with suppliers to reduce costs, improve planning and budgeting, and reduce handling.

Network connections for supply chain management must authenticate users and provide current information about inventories and costs. They typically blend lightweight database and Web server technologies. Networks for enterprise resource management grew from the call routing and computer telephony integration described in Part 2 of this book, and now integrate Web-based connections with client tracking and contact management functions.

The online purchasing portion of B2B is probably the greatest cost crusher. Online purchasing allows a business to centrally coordinate contracts, material quality, and costs while allowing employees anywhere to order supplies, parts, and services.

The U.S. Government Services Administration, with its well-known GSA Catalog, was established in 1949 to avoid "senseless duplication, excess cost, and confusion in handling supplies." It's the classic and modern epitome of supply chain management. But now, thanks to the Web, your company doesn't have to be the size of the federal government to benefit.

Even the smallest companies can leverage B2B and online purchasing. No magic formula can describe when it's worth organizing your suppliers into a supply chain, but the number of employees, locations, and suppliers are the primary variables. If your company has a few dozen employees and a dozen suppliers, you'll probably order through your suppliers' Web sites. You know you need better supply management if you find employees buying supplies outside of contracts negotiated for a discount.

Fast companies beat slow companies, so two major goals of modern supply chain management are to reduce wasted time and to pay for only what you need, only when you need it.

Today, a supply chain is a highly interactive process that can cover the entire cycle from product R&D, concept, and design through creation and delivery. The buzzword phrase "just-in-time delivery" describes supply chain management tied to a clock. If raw material arrives on your loading dock just in time to feed the manufacturing process, you reduce handling, storage, and cost. Knowing when all the parts will come together for manufacturing enables you to budget people, facilities, and even consumables such as electricity and gas while you beat the competition.

Within a company taking the first steps in supply chain management, the employees who are buyers in the company need access to online fax capabilities and unrestricted browsing. They will probably be issued digital certificates, and it's likely that their browsers will have to accept cookies. Larger companies can make suppliers come to them. A larger company can set up a specialized Web site for buyers within the company. Outside suppliers come to the Web site and upload catalogs, inventory data, and price lists. In most cases, this information is in a text file with commas separating the fields. In advanced systems, companies can take advantage of the Extensible Markup Language (XML) that provides ready-made language libraries for specific tasks such as inserting ads (adXML) and creating electronic catalogs (ecXML). The cXML 1.0 specification includes a full set of XML messages and documents for purchase order requests and acknowledgments, catalog definitions, a process for passing queries to other servers, supplier/catalog contents, and message queuing for batch processing through firewalls. The tools are all there to build your e-business application. See `www.xml.org` for more information.

The e-purchasing corporate Web site requires good security and protection from intrusion. High reliability is important but not critical to e-purchasing.

If B2B and supply chain management are about reducing costs then customer relationship management is about improving the bottom line by making more sales and building customer loyalty. CRM is much broader than the age-old principle that "the customer is always right." Instead, CRM says that each customer is different and will respond to specific kinds of care. CRM philosophy says that customers make buying decisions based on the overall experience of buying. Often, they'll even pay more to have a positive experience.

CRM systems range from online retail catalogs to applications that enable you to customize a product, such as a car or a PC, before it is shipped to you. They include call-center applications and contact-management applications. The principal characteristics of a network for CRM are reliability and fast response. Together, these characteristics take on the label *high availability*. High-availability networks combine the tortoise and the hare; they keep running and they're fast.

The following pages show how you get the flexibility and security you need for supply chain management and the high availability you need for customer relationship management.

CHAPTER 26

How an Online Business Infrastructure Works

ORDER FORM
ORDER FORM

AS businesses adopt and integrate the productivity of networking, the focus has moved from cables and connections to higher-level software and interactions. This chapter contains two illustrations. One shows the functions of online business, and the other shows the infrastructure you need to support those functions. You only need to understand the functions to have a discussion. You must understand the infrastructure to have a business.

You're probably familiar with customer relationship management (CRM) systems. They solicit and take orders and provide all kinds of personal support by telephone and online connections. Supply chain management is less well known, but just as important. Just-in-time ordering, accurate pricing, and tight inventory control are the major features of supply chain management.

In modern online business, your competition is only a click away. If your online site falters, stumbles, or even hesitates, fickle users will abandon their shopping carts and click someplace else. The term *high availability* describes the combination of speed and reliability you need in modern business.

Outsourcing is the first high-availability option. Outsourcing offers specialized equipment, connectivity, and expertise. However, outsourcing invariably raises questions of accountability, loss of control, and possible cost escalation. We generally support outsourcing, but if you want the operation under your thumb, the best thing to do is to run it yourself.

Redundancy is the key to high availability in business systems. Redundant network connections, CPUs, power supplies, and even clusters of servers keep things running despite component failures. Redundant sources of power, including UPS and generator systems designed for server rooms, are fundamental. Software glitches are more common than component failures, so having completely redundant instances of the application on separate servers is smart. Our advice is to use redundancy inside servers, particularly in hard disk drives, and in the design of server systems.

You get redundancy in Web servers and in database servers in different ways. Redundant Web servers work in parallel under the control of devices called *load balancers*. Database servers, which do more internal processing and don't communicate with the same intensity as Web servers, typically use a technique called *server clustering* to keep operations reliable. Typically, one server in a cluster takes over full operation from a server that falters. In contrast, load balancing takes place on an application-by-application basis.

Each major computer manufacturer has computers designed to act as servers with redundant pieces and parts. High-availability options include multiple CPUs, redundant power supplies, redundant disk arrays, and error-control memory modules.

A high-availability server system combines redundant servers with load balancers that control the workload going to each server. Normally, the load balancer distributes connection requests to specific servers based on the nature of the request and the availability and capability of the server. If one server fails, the load balancer cuts it out and shares the load among the survivors. The servers don't have to be identical or even run the same operating system. The load balancer accounts for performance differences.

Redundancy and careful planning are the keys to creating a high-availability network system for online business systems.

The Elements of Online Business

B2B markets and online purchasing
A modern company uses online purchasing for just-in-time delivery, controlled pricing, and managed inventory. Supply chain management functions interact with the financial and operations centers within the company.

Supply chain management

Accounts payable
Accounts receivable
General ledger

Supply Chain Management

Network connections give purchasing agents access to catalogs, inventory, and accounting records from suppliers. The efficiency of the network makes it possible to order economical quantities for timely delivery.

Fabrication
Creation
Manufacturing

e-Purchasing

Maintenance
Repair
Operations

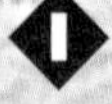
e-Business systems bring the raw materials, services, and consumables into the organization.

2 e-Business processes facilitate planning, budgeting, accounting, procurement, and fabrication within the organization.

Enterprise Resource Planning

Applications interconnected across the network report the status that is collected into a functional view of the enterprise.

Customer Relationship Management

The Customer Relationship Management (CRM) system dominates the client-facing side of online business. These functions interface with the company's marketing, sales, and support activities.

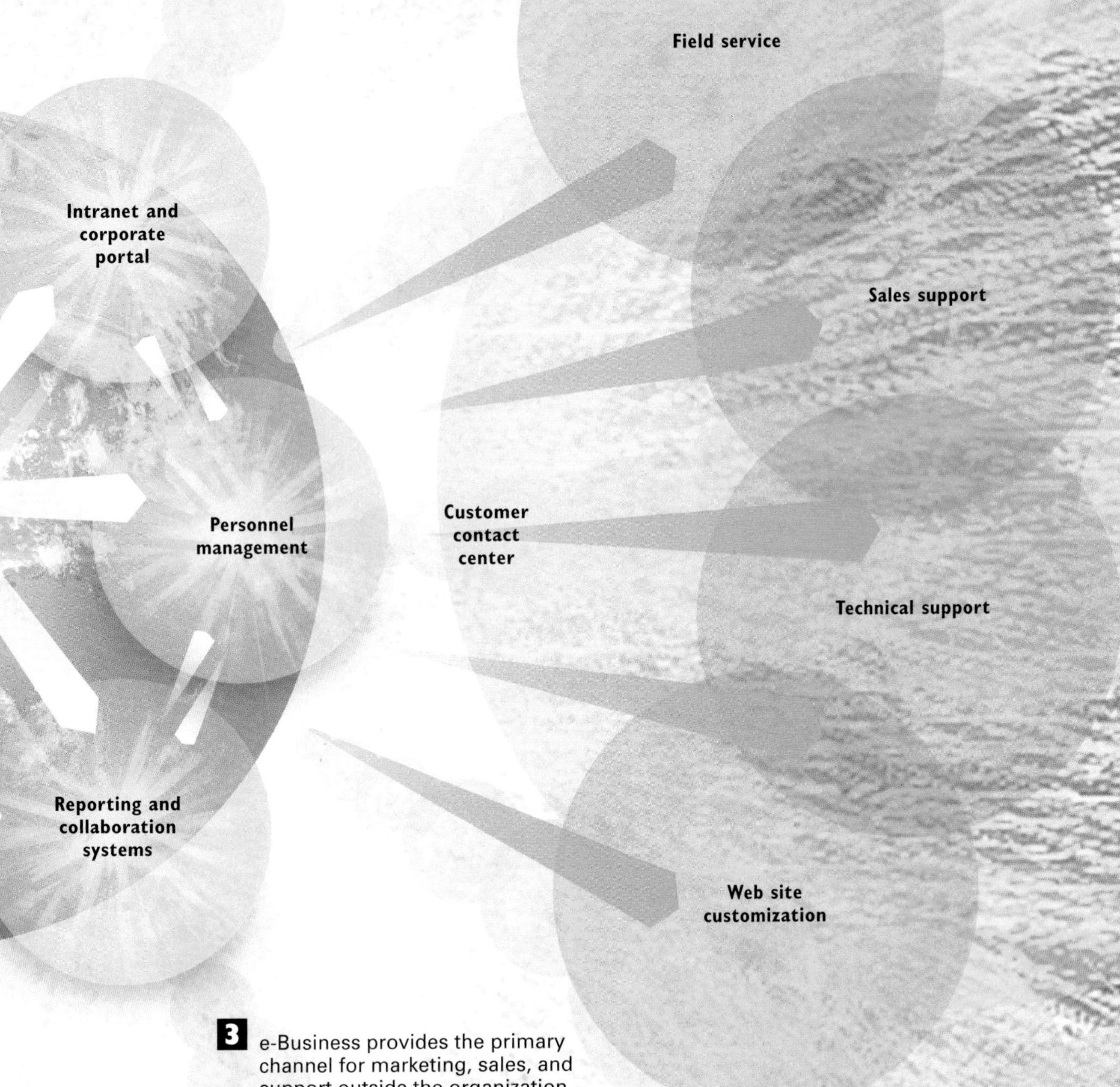
Field service
Intranet and corporate portal
Sales support
Personnel management
Customer contact center
Technical support
Reporting and collaboration systems
Web site customization

3 e-Business provides the primary channel for marketing, sales, and support outside the organization.

The Network Infrastructure for Online Business

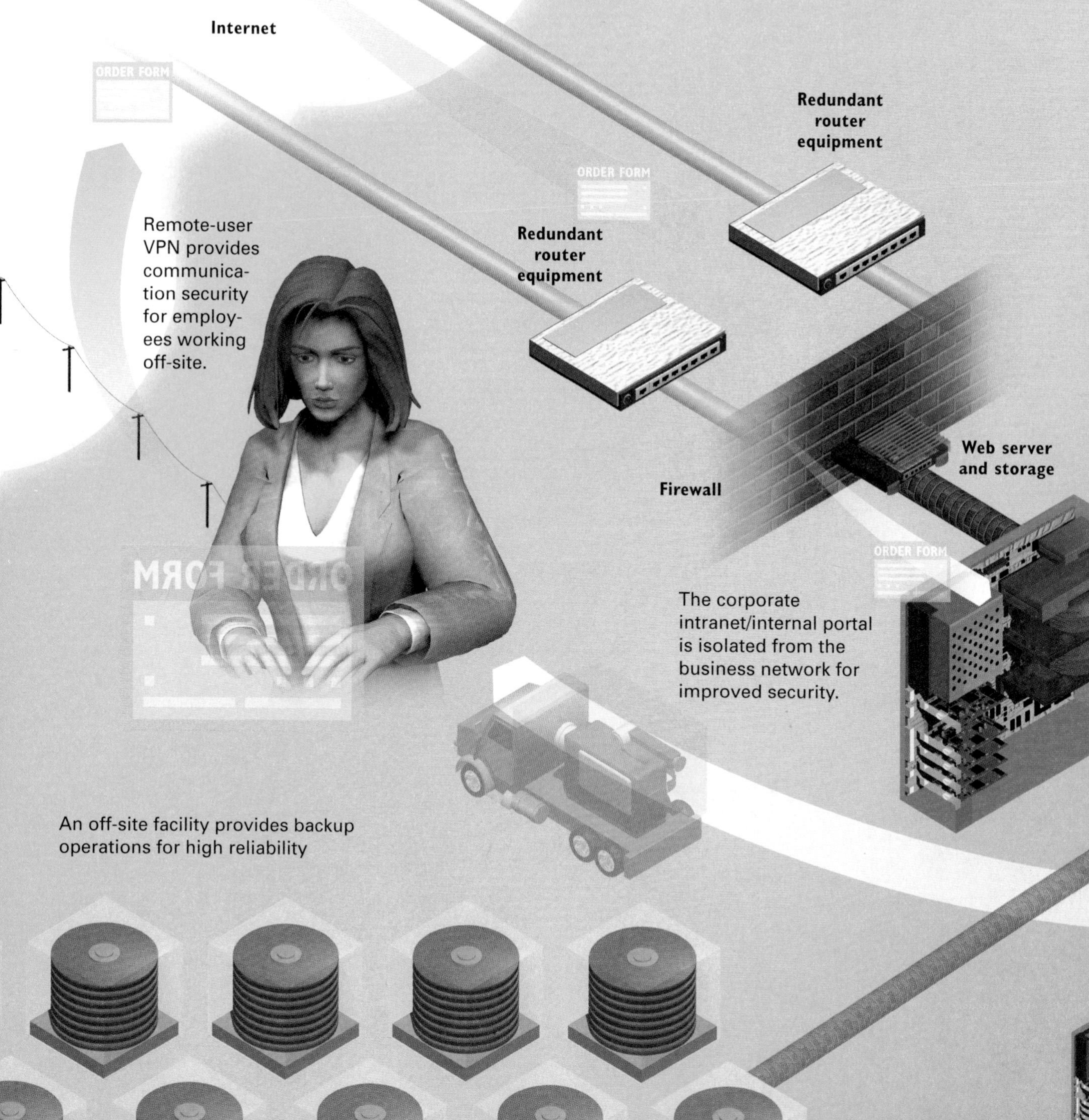
Internet
ORDER FORM
Redundant router equipment
ORDER FORM
Remote-user VPN provides communication security for employees working off-site.
Redundant router equipment
Web server and storage
Firewall
ORDER FORM
ORDER FORM
The corporate intranet/internal portal is isolated from the business network for improved security.
An off-site facility provides backup operations for high reliability

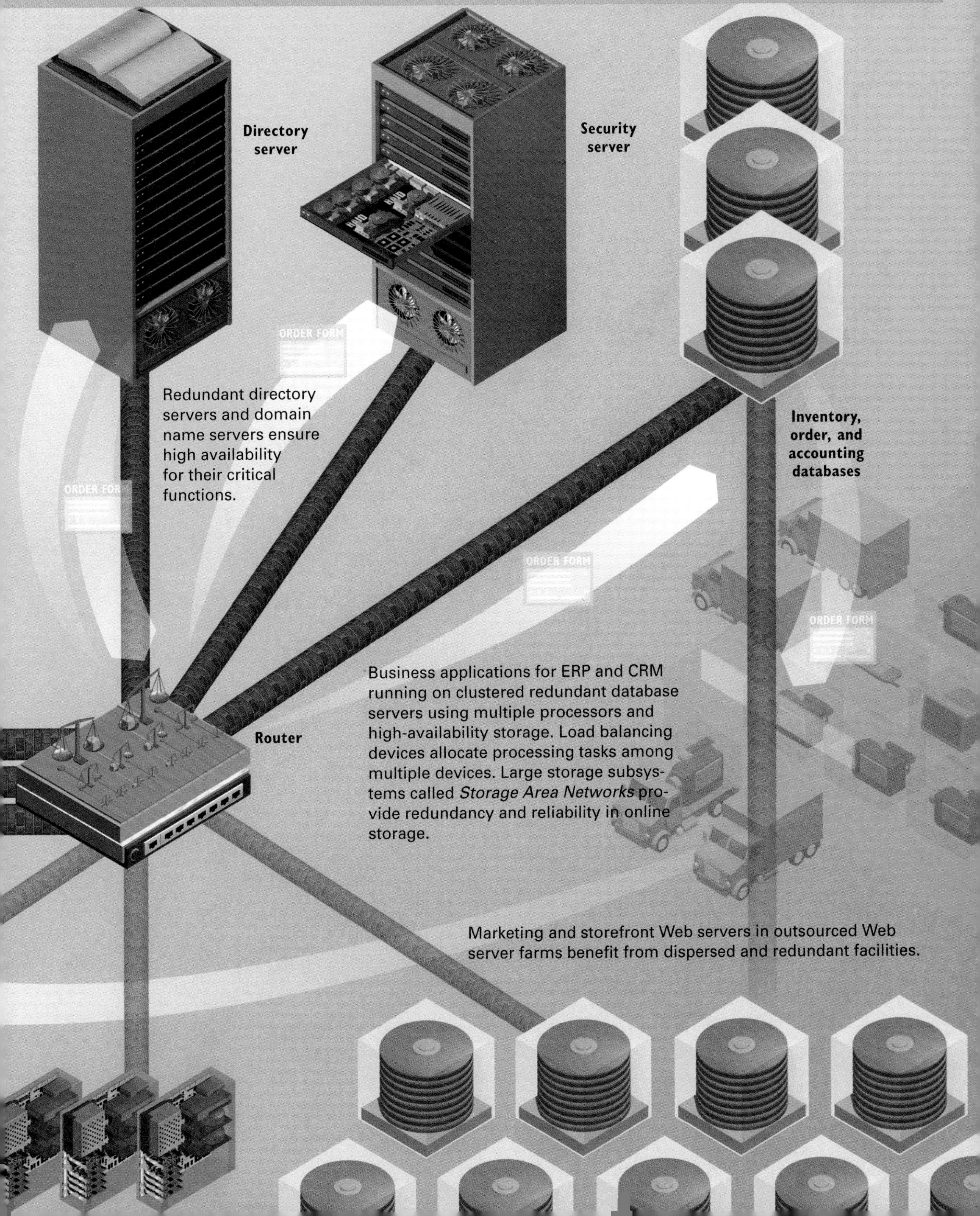

Directory server

Security server

Inventory, order, and accounting databases

Redundant directory servers and domain name servers ensure high availability for their critical functions.

Router

Business applications for ERP and CRM running on clustered redundant database servers using multiple processors and high-availability storage. Load balancing devices allocate processing tasks among multiple devices. Large storage subsystems called *Storage Area Networks* provide redundancy and reliability in online storage.

Marketing and storefront Web servers in outsourced Web server farms benefit from dispersed and redundant facilities.

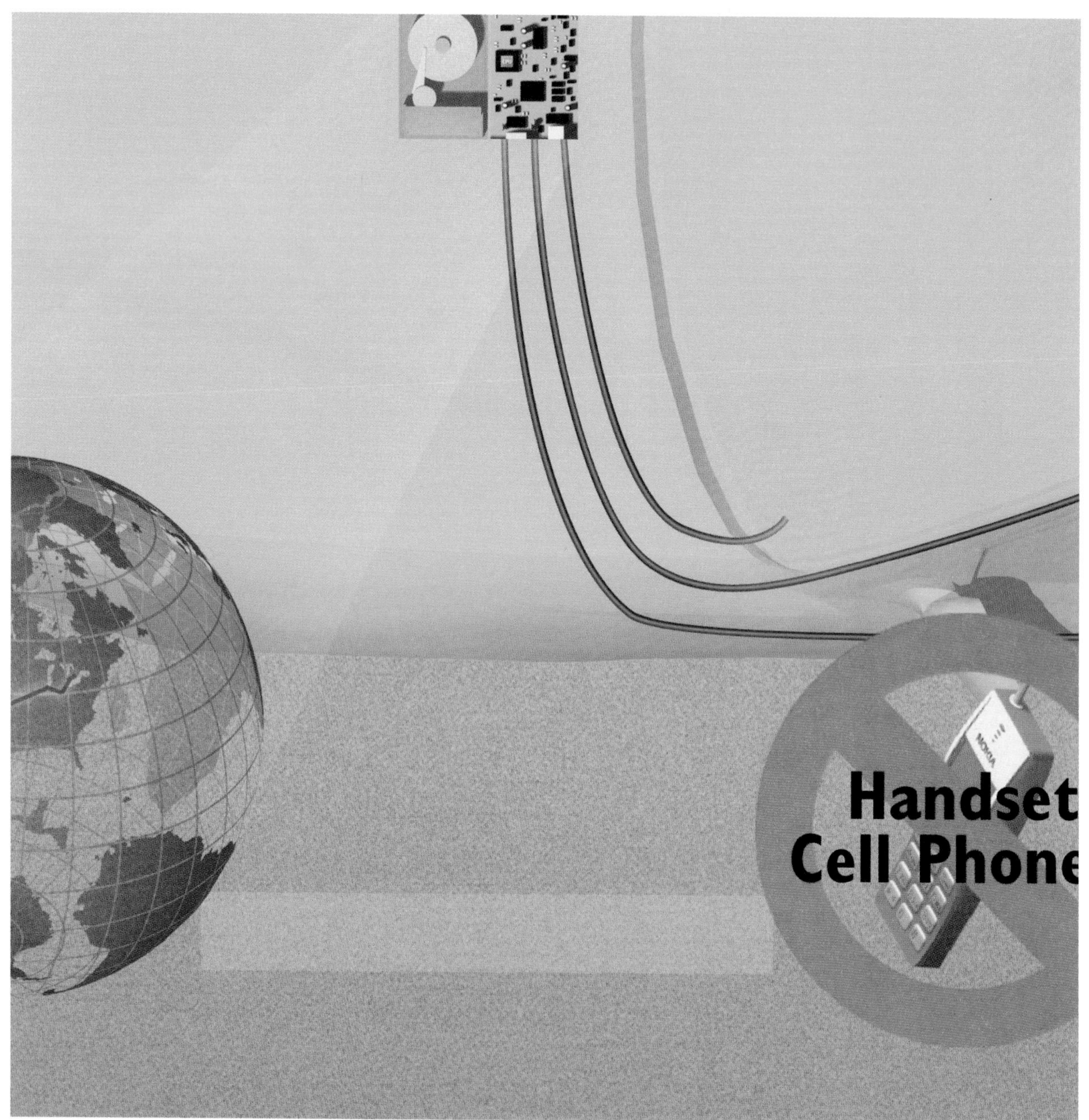
Handset
Cell Phone

INTERTAINMENT

Intertainment is a term that describes how we use the Internet to improve the entertainment and information experience at home, on the road, and in the office. Intertainment has several elements such as *Telematics* and *convergence*.

Telematics is the integration of the Internet and new modes of electronic entertainment into the automobile. Telematics combines technologies such as satellite transmission, wireless connectivity, voice recognition, location determination, and even radar to improve your ride. Networking, using the Internet protocols and technologies such as 802.11 wireless networking and Bluetooth, is an important part of Telematics. In effect, the car becomes its own LAN with dedicated and changing links to wide area networks. Inside this LAN-on-wheels, there are wired and wireless links to telephones, music players, sound reproducers, displays, and other networked devices.

Convergence is a general term that we use to describe the mergers of technologies at two levels: network convergence and media convergence. Network convergence is invisible to users, but fundamental to the capability. Media convergence delivers Intertainment to the customer.

On the network level, the term *convergence* describes how the use of the Internet protocols makes the transmission media unimportant to everyone except network managers and designers. Users won't know or care how the information or entertainment flows.

Today, each business and home has as many as five networks: Power, Telephone, Security, Computer data, Video/audio (television/stereo). Although these networks have some rudimentary interconnections today (for example, modems, cable boxes, and security systems use the telephone lines), they are reaching out toward one another in more meaningful ways. Today, we can economically use power lines to carry data and ask for entertainment information across the computer network, but much more is coming. Gateway devices at the network edge of each home or business will choose from among the available connections to connect and interconnect devices. Major appliances will send short simple messages such as "Running hot, need maintenance" across power lines. Video and audio systems will use wired and wireless LAN connections to control the selection of entertainment programs. The data on each type of network connection will converge into one or more devices and will have access to wide area network links for specific tasks.

The maturity of TCP/IP networking provides a proven common network transmission scheme. Network convergence allows content developers and service providers to create and deliver narrow-focus and broad-interest content quickly, economically, and with a high probability of being paid. Network convergence makes possible the other side of the convergence team: media convergence.

Media convergence results from the merger of many different audio and visual presentation systems. When television blends with the Internet, high-fidelity sound reproduction blends with television, photography blends with the Internet and television, and these things

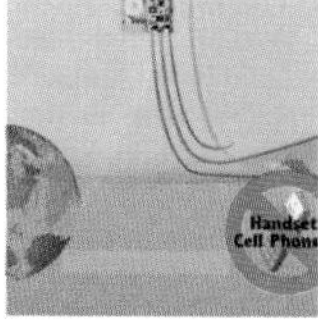

interact almost without regard to location, and then you see media convergence! The result is the ability to use many different devices to present sound and images from many different sources. The benefit to the user is the customization of the Intertainment experience.

Not too long ago, people were satisfied to receive information and entertainment as it was broadcast. The arrival of the videocassette recorder eroded the need for the viewer to synchronize with the broadcaster. The all-news and all-business cable television networks further weakened the link between broadcaster and viewer. The Internet stretched it to a thread and media convergence might break it completely.

Today, devices called *personal video recorders (PVRs)* can check current television listings, record programming based on the customized personal criteria of the viewer, and make it available for replay at any time. Some of these boxes can communicate with similar devices across the Internet. We expect PVRs to gain many more functions, such as the capability to seek out specific movies or music, and to grow into one of the multifunction centers for Intertainment in the home. Other linked centers will include home computers, stereo systems, wireless personal devices, and even the car parked in the driveway.

Because this is the age of instant customization, no two merged media networks have to look alike. Some people will focus on music and retain dedicated component audio systems able to play music from digital sources, such as MP3, and from other more traditional sources such as FM radio. Other people will focus on games or on television for sports or movies. Digital photography will link to personal publishing so that people can tell their own stories in many formats.

Media convergence uses network convergence to wrap back into Telematics. The home audio system and car audio system should be able to update each other with new content and new personal preferences. The car's navigation systems can use the home's Internet connection to get updates on road construction and to exchange schedule and calendar changes made from the car, home, or wireless personal device.

The convergence of networks and media in homes and automobiles will call for the services of people with strong technical knowledge to make it all work. Some services will come from the telephone and cable companies, but there will be major opportunities for entrepreneurs with the proper knowledge of how networks work and certification from specific organizations.

Network convergence is in place. Telematics is coming as a way to differentiate automotive products. Media convergence has to leap legal and regulatory hurdles placed by industries that want to protect their present sources of revenue. We're confident that innovators will find ways to leap over or go around the barriers to reach new sources of revenue by delivering customized entertainment and information.

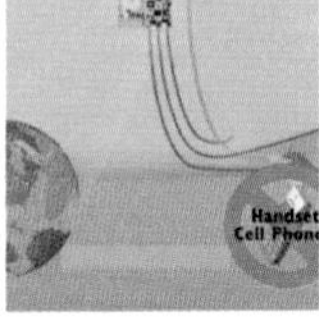

CHAPTER 27 How Convergence Works

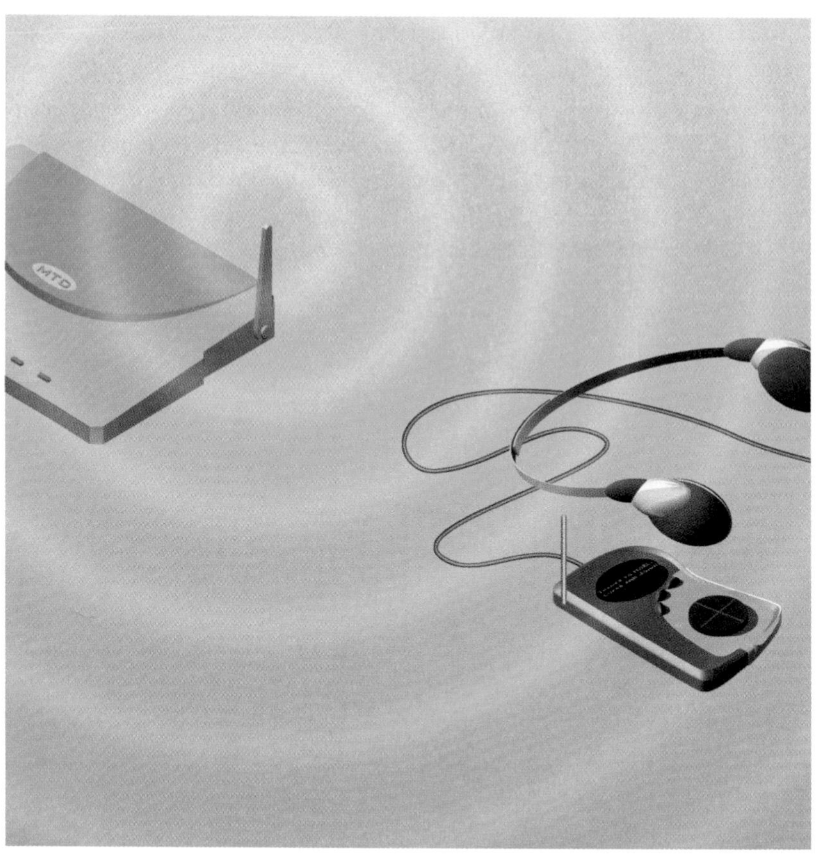
MTD

UNTIL this point, most of this book has been about network convergence. The cables, signaling, networking software, and routers we've described are now mature commodities that make it possible for devices of many kinds to interconnect. Network convergence is here and now—mainly because of the wide acceptance of the TCP/IP networking protocols and of connections such as Ethernet, wireless Ethernet, and mobile wireless systems.

Media convergence and Telematics are now emerging and we expect them to mature quickly. Media convergence links television, desktop computers, Internet connections, music sources, game devices, digital cameras, handheld personal devices, and various displays. These devices will use network links that include Bluetooth and 802.11 wireless, USB connections, and wired Ethernet. Telematics is the application of network convergence and media convergence inside a moving automobile.

Media convergence works through the capability of the devices on the converged network to process many different kinds of inputs. Display devices can accept video from television tuners, digital video from computers, and inputs from other sources. Personal video recorders will sort through many audio and video inputs to find material desired by their owner. Handheld devices will combine the features of digital cameras, PDAs, telephones, and Internet browsers. If individuals care to be identified by their handheld devices, their customized music selections can follow them through a house and into an automobile.

Although media convergence devices handle the various inputs, these devices will also exchange messages that tell them what to do with these inputs. Instructions will describe how to display, reproduce, store, or sort the inputs. The combined capability to handle multiple inputs and to respond to outside direction provides the customized experience we call *Intertainment*.

Similarly, Telematics blend the various sources of entertainment and information available within an automobile. Because automotive safety is a prime concern, Telematics will make more use of voice recognition and voice synthesis than you'll find in home systems. Automobile systems will exchange and route a variety of information that the user never sees and limit the audio and video presentations to what is appropriate for the environment at the time.

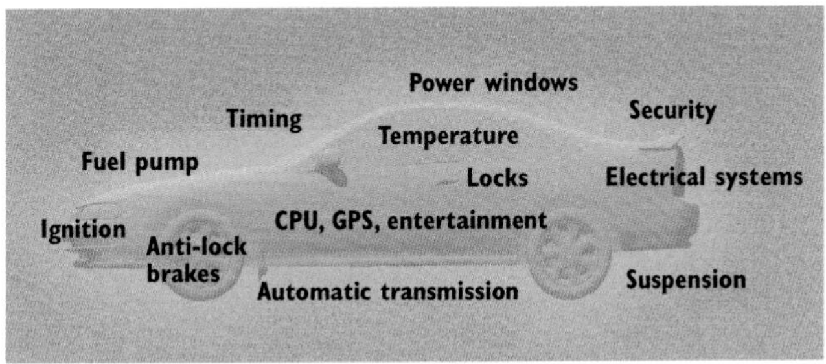
Power windows
Timing
Security
Temperature
Fuel pump
Locks
Electrical systems
Ignition
CPU, GPS, entertainment
Anti-lock
brakes
Automatic transmission
Suspension

How Media Convergence Works

1 Not long ago, we'd have labeled this diagram "The Home of the Future," but most of this technology is here today. The center of the Media Convergence universe is a broadband Internet connection connected to a wireless router. All the other devices in the converged home connect to the Internet through the router, using a wired (Ethernet) or wireless (WiFi) connection.

Router with 802.11 wireless connection (WiFi)

PC with DVD-ROM or DVD writer

2 PCs have become an important part of many home entertainment systems. Most home PCs now include a DVD player and high-quality audio hardware, making it possible to enjoy movies or music without any additional equipment. The PC also operates as the control center for many other devices. By embedding a tiny Web server in each device, manufacturers can build "headless" devices that have no knobs or switches; they are controlled using the Web browser on the home PC.

3 After a slow start, the Personal Video Recorder (PVR) is finally catching on. These devices store your favorite programs when they are broadcast so that you can watch them later. PVRs store programs on hard drives rather than magnetic tape, so playback is faster and easier, and you never have to rewind. PVRs obtain scheduling and program information from a master server on the Internet, and they display this information on your TV's screen so that you can pick the programs you want to record. Most current-generation PVRs use a dial-up connection to download programming information; next-generation devices will use the home's broadband connection.

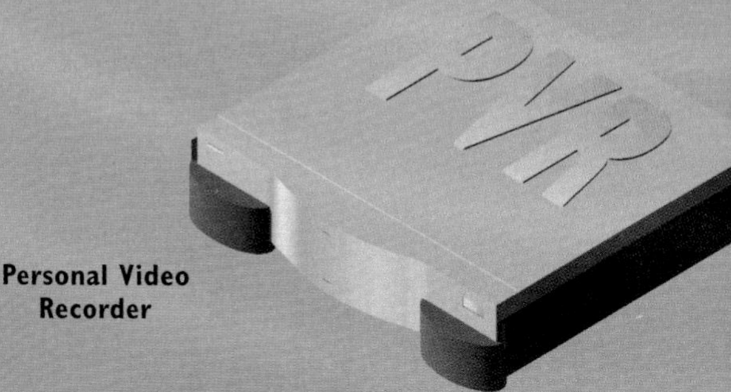
PVR

Personal Video Recorder

MP3 player with WiFi connection

4 Napster and the MP3 file revolutionized the music industry. Current-generation MP3 players require a USB connection to your PC to download music, but the next generation of players—including units that connect to your home entertainment system—will connect directly to the Internet, using your home's WiFi connection.

Car equipped with MP3 player and WiFi wireless connection

5 As long as you're collecting MP3 files, wouldn't it be nice to listen to them in the car? GM plans to add WiFi capabilities to many of their cars so that users can transfer MP3 files to their cars while they are parked in the garage.

How Telematics Work

1 The combination of inexpensive microprocessors, wireless digital telephone service, and the Global Positioning System allows drivers to enjoy convenience and safety features that were unimaginable just a few years ago.

4 Many cars come with a garage door opener as standard equipment. The newest generation of remote controls—called *HomeLink*—can also turn on your lights and deactivate your home security system when you pull into the garage. The HomeLink devices operate via a tiny two-way radio system built into the sun visor on many new cars. HomeLink uses a digitally coded security system to keep intruders out.

Computer, GPS system

Integrated garage door opener

2 GM's OnStar system uses a combination of GPS positioning information and wireless phone service to provide assistance to drivers nationwide.

Microphone for hands-free phone operation

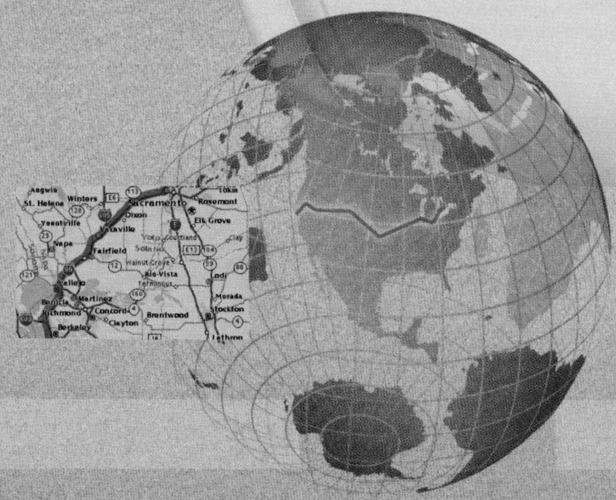

Handset Cell Phones!

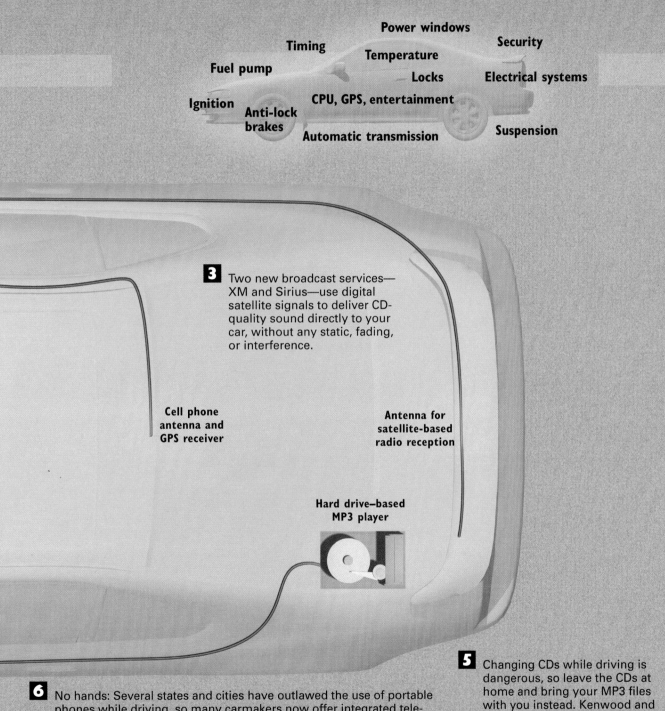

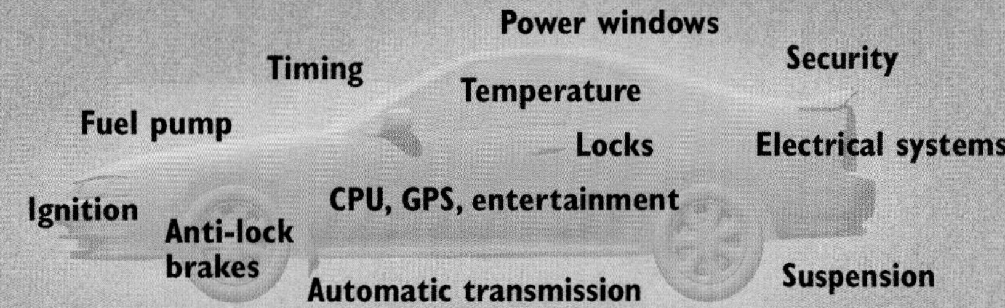
Power windows
Security
Timing
Temperature
Fuel pump
Locks
Electrical systems
Ignition
CPU, GPS, entertainment
Anti-lock brakes
Automatic transmission
Suspension

3 Two new broadcast services—XM and Sirius—use digital satellite signals to deliver CD-quality sound directly to your car, without any static, fading, or interference.

Cell phone antenna and GPS receiver

Antenna for satellite-based radio reception

Hard drive–based MP3 player

5 Changing CDs while driving is dangerous, so leave the CDs at home and bring your MP3 files with you instead. Kenwood and several other stereo makers now offer hard drive–based MP3 systems designed specifically for cars. These systems connect to your home PC, so you can move files back and forth between the PC and the car.

6 No hands: Several states and cities have outlawed the use of portable phones while driving, so many carmakers now offer integrated telephones that allow hands-free operation. These phones integrate with the car's stereo system, so they can turn down the music when you answer the phone. Some carmakers offer driving directions, concierge service, and emergency assistance using the car's built-in phone.

Index

Numbers

A

B

C

K-L

M

N

O

P-Q

R

S

NATIONAL
MORE THAN 2 MILLION COPIES SOLD
BESTSELLER

HOW IT WORKS

The How It Works series offers a unique, visual, four-color approach designed to educate curious readers. From machine code to hard-drive design to wireless communication, the How It Works series offers a clear and concise approach to understanding technology—a perfect source for those who prefer to learn visually. Check out other books in this best-selling series by Que:

How Computers Work
BY RON WHITE
SEVENTH EDITION

How Computers Work, Seventh Edition
ISBN: 0-7897-3033-2
US $29.99
CAN $44.95 UK £21.99

How Computers Work, Seventh Edition offers a unique and detailed look at the inner workings of your computer. From keyboards to virtual reality helmets, this book covers it all.

SEVENTH EDITION
How The Internet Works
by Preston Gralla

How the Internet Works, Seventh Edition
ISBN: 0-7897-2973-3
US $29.99
CAN $44.95 UK £21.99

How the Internet Works, Seventh Edition clearly explains how the Internet works and gives you behind-the-scenes information. Find out what actually happens when you send an email or purchase goods over the Web.

HOW NETWORKS WORK
Frank Derfler Jr.
Les Freed
SEVENTH EDITION

How Networks Work, Seventh Edition
ISBN: 0-7897-3232-7
US $29.99
CAN $44.95 UK £21.99

How Networks Work, Seventh Edition visually demonstrates how the components of a network function together, With this book, you will learn how an electric signal is transmitted, how firewalls block unwanted traffic, and how everything in between works.

HOW WIRELESS WORKS
by Preston Gralla

How Wireless Works
ISBN: 0-7897-2487-1
US $29.99
CAN $44.95 UK £21.99

How Wireless Works is your key to understanding current and emerging wireless technologies. This book shows you how wireless home networks communicate, how cell phones access the Internet, and much more.

que

www.quepublishing.com